The Routledge Concise History of Southeast Asian Writing in English

The Routledge Concise History of Southeast Asian Writing in English traces the development of literature in the region within its historical and cultural contexts. This volume explores creative writing in English across different genres and media, establishing connections from the colonial activity of the early modern period through to contemporary writing across Southeast Asia, focusing especially on the Philippines, Malaysia, Singapore and Hong Kong.

In this critical guide, Rajeev S. Patke and Philip Holden:

- interweave text and context through the history of creative writing in the region
- examine language use and variation, making use of illuminating examples from speech, poetry and fictional prose
- trace the impact of historical, political and cultural events
- engage with current debates on national consciousness, globalization, modernity and postmodernism
- provide useful features including a glossary, a further reading section and chapter summaries.

Direct and clearly written, this concise history guides readers through key topics while presenting a unique, original synthesis of history and practice in Southeast Asian writing in English. It is the ideal starting point for students and all those seeking a better understanding of Southeast Asian literatures and cultures.

Rajeev S. Patke and **Philip Holden** are Associate Professors in the Department of English Language and Literature at the National University of Singapore.

Routledge Concise Histories of Literature series

The Routledge Concise Histories series offers students and academics alike an interesting and accessible route into the literature of a specific period, genre, place or topic. The books situate the literature within its broader historical, cultural and political context, introducing the key events, movements and theories necessary for a fuller understanding of the writing. They engage readers in the debates of the period, genre or region adding a more exciting and challenging element to the reading.

Accessible and engaging, offering suggestions for further reading, explanatory text boxes, bullet pointed chapter summaries and a glossary of key terms, the Routledge Concise Histories are the ideal starting point for the study of literature.

Available:
The Routledge Concise History of Southeast Asian Writing in English
By Rajeev S. Patke and Philip Holden

Forthcoming:
The Routledge Concise History of Canadian Literature
By Richard J. Lane

The Routledge Concise History of Nineteenth-Century Literature
By Josephine Guy and Ian Small

The Routledge Concise History of Science Fiction
By Mark Bould & Sherryl Vint

The Routledge Concise History of Southeast Asian Writing in English

Rajeev S. Patke and Philip Holden

Routledge
Taylor & Francis Group

LONDON AND NEW YORK

First published 2010
by Routledge
2 Park Square, Milton Park, Abingdon, Oxon OX14 4RN

Simultaneously published in the USA and Canada
by Routledge
270 Madison Ave, New York, NY 10016

Routledge is an imprint of the Taylor & Francis Group, an informa business

Typeset in Sabon by Keyword Group Ltd.
Printed and bound in Great Britain by TJ International, Padstow,
Cornwall

British Library Cataloguing in Publication Data
A catalogue record for this book is available from the British Library

Library of Congress Cataloging in Publication Data
Patke, Rajeev S. (Rajeev Shridhar)
The Routledge concise history of Southeast Asian writing in English /
Rajeev S. Patke and Philip Holden.
    p. cm.
Includes bibliographical references and index.
1. Southeast Asian literature (English) – History and criticism.
I. Holden, Philip. II. Title.
PR9570.S644P38 2009
895.9–dc22   2009003457

ISBN 10: 0-415-43568-4 (hbk)
ISBN 10: 0-415-43569-2 (pbk)
ISBN 10: 0-203-87403-X (ebk)

ISBN 13: 978-0-415-43568-0 (hbk)
ISBN 13: 978-0-415-43569-7 (pbk)
ISBN 13: 978-0-203-87403-5 (ebk)

Contents

viii   *Contents*

Illustrations

Figures

Tables

Acknowledgements

This book would not have been possible without the help of several individuals and institutions: the publisher's experts, whose advice and comments proved invaluable; Polly Dodson and Emma Nugent, who saw the book through the press; the Faculty of Arts and Social Sciences at the National University of Singapore whose research grant (R-103-000-057-112) facilitated trips to overseas libraries during 2006–08; Robbie Goh and the administrative staff in the Department of English Language and Literature at NUS, especially Yau Geok Hwa, Lee Yoke Leng and Hasnah bte Abdul Hadior, who gave us their unfailing support; Teo Moi Ying and the acquisition staff at the Central Library of NUS, who made it possible for us to source materials for the library while working on the book; Mrs Lee Li Kheng from the Department of Geography at NUS who helped in preparing the maps; and the scholars who helped open up the field of comparative studies in English for Southeast Asia, especially Dudley De Souza, Shirley Geok-lin Lim, Lily Rose Tope, Bruce Bennett and Dennis Haskell; and the staff of the several libraries whose resources proved indispensable to our project, especially at the University of the Philippines at Diliman, the Ateneo de Manila University, the University of Hong Kong and the University of Malaya.

We take special pleasure in expressing our gratitude for the warmth, kindness and hospitality we received from Dick and Lily Rose Tope, and Isabela Banzon in the Philippines. Lily and Isabela were generous with making scarce materials available and in their comments on our work-in-progress. Vince Serrano was kind enough to share his knowledge of contemporary writing in the Philippines. Helpful insights were also given by Patricia May Jurilla, Neil Garcia, Jonathan Chua, Cristina Pantoja Hidalgo, Robbie Kwan Laurel, Charlson Ong and Butch Dalisay. In Singapore, Edwin Thumboo and Lionel Wee read and commented on chapters of the book, and Ismail Talib was as reliable as ever with checking facts. Huzir Sulaiman and Charlene Rajendran gave useful initial pointers to Malaysian drama in English, and David Smyth was generous in sharing bibliographical information concerning Southeast Asian authors. Our two research assistants were invaluable: Gabriela Lee helped us collect bibliographical information concerning the Philippines, and as a practising creative writer herself, introduced us to a new generation of Filipino writers, and Mark Lu compiled bibliographies on the other regional literatures. Andrea Grimshaw, working for Routledge, gave the entire manuscript the most thorough scrutiny, keeping us from many sins of commission and omission. Wherever errors remain, the fault is our own.

We are grateful to the following authors for permission to quote material from their publications: Luisa Igloria, Boey Kim Cheng, Fatima Lim-Wilson and Yong Shu Hoong. We are also grateful to Jenny Yap for permission to quote from the work of her brother, the late Arthur Yap.

1 Introduction

Overview

Southeast Asia encompasses a huge diversity of peoples, languages, societies, cultures and literary traditions. English came to the region fairly recently, as part of the growth of European and American imperialism, and stayed past the era of empires to become a key intermediary for the processes of modernity and globalization. The modes of literary expression it has inspired make for a compelling story. Our narrative is mindful that a more complete picture would need to relate literary expression in English to writing in other major languages of the region. Within that larger ideal – difficult to realize within the confines of a single book even for a group of regional scholars – the narrative of literary productions from and about Southeast Asia in English merits reading on its own. Our main aim is to bring together texts that experts in their respective fields tend to treat separately, and our enterprise has profited from the work of scholars who have helped bring the Anglophone writing from the various regions of Southeast Asia together in a comparative context. We hope that this book will serve as a useful introduction to the literatures of Southeast Asia in English.

The geographical dimension: English in Southeast Asia

English is a global language rich in regional variety. It flourishes in Asia amidst a plurality of cultures expressed in a variety of languages. Having outgrown colonial origins, it combines a contemporary role as a medium of higher education and international communication with a capacity to bridge disparate linguistic and cultural communities. English is also cultural capital, and indeed the use of it may at times indicate privilege. The number of writers using it as a creative medium has grown steadily wherever the appeal of its expressive resources has been accompanied by the sense of joining a larger community of writers and readers. Authors from Southeast Asia have given proof of this appeal for more than a century, and produced a body of work ample in range and variety.

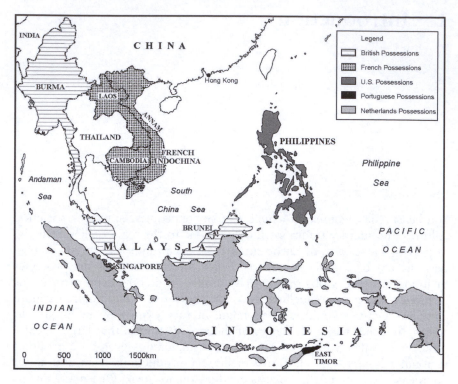

Figure 1 Map of Southeast Asia, 1939.

Within Southeast Asia, a tradition of using English as a creative medium narrows primary attention to three modern nation-states: Malaysia, Singapore and the Philippines, to which we have added a fourth territory, Hong Kong. Even though it is not linked to the three nation-states either by geographical proximity or by membership of a group such as ASEAN (Association of Southeast Asian Nations), Hong Kong's inclusion is important for three reasons. First, it has strong historical links to the region we now call Southeast Asia. A shared history of British colonialism meant that there were strong connections between Chinese and other communities in Hong Kong and the Straits Settlements. Hong Kong was also an important place of refuge for Filipino revolutionaries, and later, a place of recreation for the Filipino Anglophone elite. Second, Hong Kong was often popularly considered part of Southeast Asia during its separation from China at the height of the Cold War. During this period there were increased connections with the Philippines, Malaysia and Singapore; and indeed possibly the most influential Filipino novel of the twentieth century, Nick Joaquin's *The Woman Who Had Two Navels* (1961), is set in the territory. Third, contemporary Hong Kong shares with Singapore, Malaysia

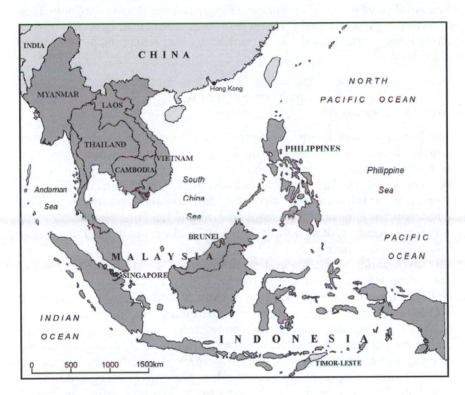

Figure 2 Map of Southeast Asia, 2009.

and the Philippines an experience of the role played by English within a context of multilingualism; this in turn has influenced the territory's literary production, complementing writing in Chinese with growing confidence in using English for creative purposes, even if only by a tiny minority of expatriates and English-educated writers born or settled in Hong Kong.

Our secondary interest in this literary history extends to the marginal role played by English in the cultures of the other nations of Southeast Asia, where literatures in the national or regional languages represent the dominant form of literary expression, but leave some space for writing in English. We omit reference to translations from and into English, not because they are not of great significance, but rather, because there is such a wealth of material translated into English that it needs a critical history of its own, especially since such work activates issues across languages that need a very different context from that provided by a literary history such as this. Once it is recognized that English is only one – and by no means necessarily the largest – piece in the linguistic jigsaw, we can have a better sense both of the scope and the limits of our current undertaking. In the societies that provide us with our primary materials, English is most extensively used in the Philippines and Singapore; and despite the dominance of Malay in Malaysia, and Cantonese (now supplemented by Mandarin) in Hong Kong, English has shown increasing signs of remaining indispensable in both areas.

The historical dimension: from colonial to contemporary history

The history of how English came to Asia is part of the larger history of how the European languages spread across the world in a gradual, uneven and often involuntary process that extended from the sixteenth to the nineteenth century. The expansion was the indirect but lasting consequence of the gradual European mutation of exploration and economic enterprise into territorial annexation, political control and religious evangelism – the global consequences of modern Western colonialism – in which Europe was followed, with variations, by the United States.

Decolonization was slow and asynchronous. The Americas fought for their independence before the rest of the colonized world. In Asia, colonialism came to an end after the Second World War. Decolonization proved a complex and problematic undertaking, and some argue that cultural decolonization remains an incomplete and ongoing project in many former colonies, despite decades of political autonomy. Colonialism altered colonizers and the colonized in ways that proved long-lasting. Ironically, one of the most enduring influences of colonialism survives – indeed thrives, especially through English – in the form of the literary cultures generated from the colonial experience by the peoples who assimilated the languages to their societies while assimilating themselves to the languages, developing through those interactions the potential for adaptability and new growth that provides us with the materials of our literary history.

The British brought their language to the Malaya peninsula in the early nineteenth century and to Hong Kong in the middle of the nineteenth century. Shortly thereafter, the Americans brought their version of the language to the Philippines, spreading it rapidly there from 1898. English was disseminated to the peoples living in the various colonial territories in circumstances that differed widely from one territory to another, and it was assimilated at speeds that depended on the educational policies implemented by the colonizers – policies that were not always explicit or internally consistent. In addition, English was frequently appropriated by groups whose interests diverged from those of colonial governments, and put to new uses.

The economic and demographic growth of Singapore and Hong Kong, and the colonial policies that shaped them, neither needed nor encouraged the widespread use of English. The majority of writers from the region came to the language rather late in the day, at the eve of Empire. In contrast, the Americans propagated their language in the Philippines swiftly and systematically, replacing the thin purchase of the earlier colonial language of Spanish. Filipino writing in English had thus gained a sizeable lead in quantity and sophistication by the time the notion that local writers might create a new literary culture had begun to take root in British Malaya. Indeed, in both areas, the call for the right to self-rule often initially found expression in the colonial language, and English continued to have a place as an intercommunal language in the period of decolonization.

During the colonial period, English coexisted in a relation of uneasy tension with national, regional and community languages. The Philippines achieved independence in 1946, the Federation of Malaya in 1957, Singapore separated from Malaysia in 1965, and Hong Kong exchanged the role of British colony for that of a Special Administrative Region of the People's Republic of China in 1997. After colonialism, English remained, and in the postcolonial era, despite an ambivalent relation to nationalism, English continues to play a prominent role in the life and culture of the Philippines and Singapore, a significant but more muted role in Malaysia and Hong Kong, and a marginal but often expanding one in the other nations of Southeast Asia. The manner in which it entered daily living, and the degree to which it attracted writers, were linked to the aspirations it engendered among ordinary people and the language policies of which it became part in the political projects of national unity, economic development and social modernity. The continued importance of English in the region is linked to the access it provides to global media and the systems of knowledge, trade and technology that remain goals for individuals and nations intent on their share of a rapidly and unevenly globalizing world.

The structural dimension: how this book works

In order to address the concerns and scope of inquiry we outline above, the volume commences with chapters giving two contexts: first, a brief history of Southeast Asia from the early modern period onwards, and second, an account of the challenges and possibilities opened up by the use of English in a multilingual context. Our next two chapters begin the work of literary history, and they do so by following two distinct historical strands. Each keeps the notion of 'writing' in peripheral vision, while maintaining that specific kind of writing which commonly aspires to be read as 'literature' (as distinguished, for example, from genres such as history, biography, autobiography, journalism, etc.) in central focus. Thus Chapter 4 covers the dissemination of English under British colonialism in Malaysia, Singapore and Hong Kong, and then explores literary writing in English during colonialism and during the process of decolonization. Chapter 5 does similar work concerning American colonialism in the Philippines; where the history of the dissemination of the language is necessarily shorter, but is balanced by a larger volume of literary production in English under colonialism, under the Commonwealth, and after independence from 1946 onwards.

We have chosen the terminal date for Chapters 4 and 5 as 1965. All historical periodization is, of course, arbitrary, resulting from the imposition of a taxonomic grid on the continuities of history, yet we feel this choice is justified for a number of reasons. In the case of Malaysia and Singapore, 1965 represents Singapore's separation from Malaysia, and thus the final chapter of the formation of contemporary nation-states from former British colonies in the region. In the Philippines, the year would not have seemed momentous at the time, yet in retrospect it is surely significant: the election of Ferdinand Marcos as president would radically change Philippine politics for two decades. Two other events in the region in 1965 were also of great importance. The failed coup against Sukarno in Indonesia resulted in a counter-coup that would bring Suharto to power; in South Vietnam, the first American combat troops arrived. Both events are markers in a transition from a period of decolonization to the more rigid divisions of the Cold War, and are representative of larger political movements in the region that influenced social policies to which writers and artists in turn responded.

The succeeding chapters are unified by genre rather than country or region in order to fulfil the possibilities suggested by the volume's regional approach. In writing these comparative chapters, we have made two strategic decisions. First, we have given slightly more length to poetry than to prose fiction or drama in order to facilitate quotations necessary for illustrating the manner in which poetic language works in a multilingual environment. Second, we have divided coverage into two distinct historical periods, pre- and post-1990. If 1990 contains less memorable historical events in the region than 1965, it does mark, at least approximately, a transition from the Cold War to a new, increasingly transnational world order in which neo-liberalism became dominant. This transition has had a profound effect on the region, caught as it is within capital and cultural flows. The tyranny of space requirements has resulted in a primary concentration on the traditional genres of poetry, drama and prose fiction, but we do conclude with a brief account of how new digital media are transforming literatures in English in the region.

The methodological dimension: a comparative approach

Literary histories based on the nation-state often find themselves drawn to narratives that claim a manifest or implied congruence between the development of literary traditions and the development of the nation. The comparative approach we adopt here is less prone to interpret all literary change as a function of national identity or culture. Instead, it provides a wider perspective from which to relate what authors write in a given time and place to the events, changes and continuities that constitute the life and culture of their communities. We have tried to remain alert to how literary writing invokes or alludes to 'society' and 'tradition', and to how such writing relates to ideas and values, whether personal or collective. We are also mindful of how literary writing affects ideas and beliefs pertaining to race, class, community, gender, sexual preference, religion and ethics.

> What is at stake is not to portray literary works in the context of their age, but to represent the age that perceives them – our age – in the age during which they arose. It is this that makes literature into an organon of history; and to achieve this, and not to reduce literature to the material of history, is the task of the literary historian.
> Walter Benjamin, 'Literary History and the Study of Literature' (1931)

Keeping these general considerations in mind, we have tried to present a balance between what could be described as the intrinsic and extrinsic dimensions of Southeast Asian writing in English. The idea of intrinsic dimensions refers to the internal relationships between themes and techniques, and the relation of formal features and expressive nuances to literary conventions (whether indigenous or foreign). The extrinsic dimension complements the intrinsic and refers to (a) the social and cultural contexts for the creative use of English; (b) the impact on literature of institutions of civil society and state policy; and of mentorship, patronage, publication and circulation; (c) the relation of literature to the histories of individuals, communities and nations; to ideology, beliefs and practices; to the discourses of colonialism, postcoloniality, modernism, postmodernism and feminism; to its audiences, at home and abroad; and to local and international critical canons.

Obviously, no single book of this size can hope to attempt all this except by being selective in its emphases. We have tried to harmonize the demands of central vision with what we believe must be retained in peripheral vision. Our primary focus is thus on cultural activity centred on the literary uses of English in Southeast Asia. We also make room, however briefly, for three kinds of lateral awareness. The first concerns the relation of English in Southeast Asia to other linguistic cultures within the region; the second concerns English as used in other parts of the world; and the third concerns expatriate writing, both by those migrating to and from the region, whenever such writing bears witness to some aspect of Southeast Asian cultures and histories.

We aim not for the chimera of 'objectivity' but for persuasion aimed at promoting historical and critical awareness. The overview provided by any literary history is necessarily subjective. Our book is written from a perspective based on many years of living in Singapore, where we have worked as university teachers, having lived previously in other parts of the world, and bringing to our interest in the cultures of the region a degree of awareness of other societies and literatures. We write for the interested general reader and for the student of literature, and we recognize that literary histories are a form of stock-taking whose need is renewed whenever assumptions and values change, and whenever new writing adds itself to the changing canon of texts and values. Our literary history will have accomplished its purpose if we succeed in persuading new readers that the authors and texts we introduce in brief compass will reward further acquaintance, or, equally, if we cause readers familiar with the works we discuss within the contexts of national canons to view them afresh in a comparative light.

Conclusion

- A literary history of writing in English from Southeast Asia works within two limiting conditions, one linguistic and the other regional.
- English came to the region at varying times and speeds of assimilation, as a result of Western imperialism.
- Its continued and flourishing use today testifies to the ways in which the status of English as an international language has moved across boundaries of culture and imperial as well as postcolonial history.
- If writers from Southeast Asia assimilated themselves to English, they also taught themselves to adapt and modify the language and its literary conventions to suit their own needs and circumstances.
- The achievements that have resulted from that process provide the basic justification for a narrative that focuses on the development of English literary writing in the context of a multilingual Southeast Asia rich in the diversity of its cultures.

2 Historical contexts

Overview

This chapter gives a context by exploring the history of the region, looking not only at the four countries or areas where the English language has been dominant, but also setting their experience within a wider perspective. It first considers geographical, cultural and political factors that influence such a history, as well as suggesting the inadequacy of terminology drawn from elsewhere to account for the region's unique experience. Attention then moves to the networks of trade that characterized the early modern period, and then increasing, although uneven, colonial presence from the sixteenth to the nineteenth century. In the twentieth century, after the rupture of the Second World War, former colonies gained independence as new nation-states, only to be caught up in the conflicts of the Cold War. In recent decades, Southeast Asia has faced the challenges of globalization, urbanization and uneven development. The chapter concludes with a brief discussion of Hong Kong's unique historical experience, and the relationship between China's special administrative region and Southeast Asia.

Geography, culture and politics

Visitors coming from outside the region to any of the major cities of Southeast Asia are often struck by the complexity of the urban environment. Postmodern buildings jostle with the modernist edifices of the early nationalist period, and are intermingled with colonial architecture – sometimes neglected, increasingly lovingly restored, often hybrid in appearance – and older monuments that appear to arise from indigenous architectural traditions. On the bus or train, a number of languages may be heard; when commuters return home, they may well communicate in a different language or dialect from that used in their workplaces. Southeast Asians follow a complex variety of religious or cultural practices, some with ancient origins, others more contemporary in nature. If casual clothing styles on the street are now frequently those made popular by global youth culture, dress on formal occasions will often make strategic use of traditional elements.

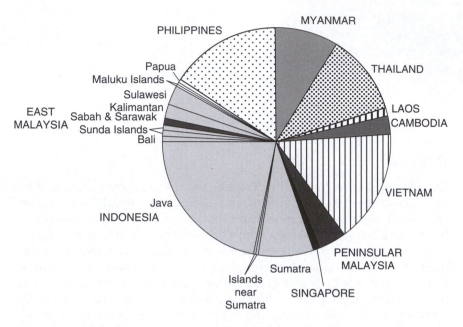

Figure 3 Population distribution in Southeast Asia.

While it is perhaps easy to read such cultural landscapes in both cities and rural hinterlands in terms of an opposition between local tradition and a modernity brought by globalization, the reality is much more complex. Southeast Asia has long been an area caught in the interstices of flows of both trade and cultures: in many senses it was globalized before globalization, postmodern before postmodernity. As the historian Tony Reid has noted, the region played a crucial role in world history from the fifteenth to the seventeenth centuries (1999: 3). As the source of the spices which would be instrumental in commodity trading it influenced the formation of modern European capital markets, and the setting up of the Dutch East India Company and its English equivalent. Recent historical work on the region, indeed, has moved beyond previous divisions of Southeast Asian history into a precolonial and colonial period to an account of a complex series of economic and political expansions and contractions of which formal colonization was only one.

Understanding literary texts in English in Southeast Asia thus necessitates a historical detour into the formation of Southeast Asian cultures and polities from the early modern period onwards. The first factor to consider is geography. The area is commonly divided into two sub-divisions.

Mainland Southeast Asia, consisting of present-day Myanmar, Thailand, Laos, Cambodia and Vietnam, is protected to the north by high mountain ranges. Mountains also separate the region from China to the west and the Indian subcontinent to the east (Dixon 1991: 36). South of the Asian mainland, an archipelago of islands of various sizes and population densities constitutes maritime Southeast Asia, comprising Indonesia, East Malaysia, Brunei, the Philippines and newly independent Timor-Leste. West Malaysia and the city-state of Singapore, while geographically occupying an intermediate position, belong in historical and cultural terms to the latter sub-region. The maritime region, like the mainland, was for a long time inaccessible to the outside world because of the long sea voyages necessary to reach it, and yet internal travel within the archipelago was relatively easy.

Southeast Asia's geography has influenced language, religion and social organization. The vast majority of inhabitants of maritime Southeast Asia speak Malayo-Polynesian languages which are either national languages (Malay, Indonesian and the Tagalog-based national language of the Philippines), or which have regional and cultural significance (such as Javanese, Batak or Cebuano). Malayo-Polynesian languages have largely vanished from mainland Southeast Asia, and the national languages of the present-day nation-states show a variety of origins (Bellwood 1992: 106–111): several, such as Thai and Vietnamese, are the results of southward migration of peoples from further north. In both mainland and maritime Southeast Asia these linguistic patterns have been overlaid by the languages of migrants and former colonizers. Chinese languages are widespread in the region. South Indian languages, in particular Tamil, are also found in areas of immigration in the nineteenth and twentieth centuries. The influence of the colonial languages Spanish, Portuguese, French and Dutch has waned, but English has spread: it has official status in Malaysia, Singapore and the Philippines, and it serves as a lingua franca at regional forums such as ASEAN (Association of Southeast Asian Nations).

ASEAN is an organization promoting regional cooperation among Southeast Asian nation-states. Founded in 1967 by five countries, the organization now has ten members – Brunei, Cambodia, Indonesia, Laos, Malaysia, Myanmar, the Philippines, Singapore, Thailand and Vietnam. Timor-Leste, having been admitted to the United Nations in 2002, is preparing for membership.

The division between mainland and maritime Southeast Asia influenced the formation of nation-states. States of the mainland either suffered colonization by European powers, or – in the case of Thailand – maintained strategic neutrality as buffer areas. Yet each of the current mainland nation-states claims a direct historical connection with a precolonial polity. In mainland Southeast Asia, colonialism accelerated a process of centralization that began in the sixteenth century, resulting in the gradual elimination of competing centres of power and the formation of a number of 'capital cultures' (Watson Andaya 1992: 454) to which peripheral cultural groups acceded.

The nation-states of maritime Southeast Asia are, in contrast, more recently imagined communities that have emerged from the territorial conquests of former colonial powers. While indigenous maritime 'thalassocracies' (Taylor 1992: 173), or maritime-based kingdoms, did exist in the region between the seventh and fourteenth centuries CE, and a succession of strategically situated port cities rose and fell in influence (Dixon 1991: 38), political organization was often less centralized. The predecessors of the Philippines, Indonesia and Timor-Leste are thus American/Spanish, Dutch and Portuguese colonial entities, while present-day Malaysia, Brunei and Singapore represent a partial redrawing of the internal boundaries of former British colonial territories.

Early modern Southeast Asia

In cultural terms, Southeast Asia shares a common heritage of Indic cultures brought by traders from 600 BCE onwards (Dixon 1991: 42), although in Vietnam this has been overlaid by Chinese influence. Many Southeast Asian languages are written in scripts that originate in the Indian subcontinent, and cultural forms such as shadow theatre and dance that are found throughout the region make reference to Indian epics such as the Ramayana and Mahabharata. Hindu religious practices merged with pre-existing beliefs concerning the connection between natural and supernatural worlds (Owen 2005: 38; de Casparis and Mabbett 1992: 286–291, 305–317). Hinduism now, however, only remains as a majoritarian religious practice on the Indonesian island of Bali. In mainland Southeast Asia, it has now largely been replaced by varieties of another religious practice from the Indian subcontinent: Theravada Buddhism.

Theravada Buddhism is the prominent school of Buddhism in mainland Southeast Asia, and the most ancient of surviving schools of Buddhism. It takes its inspiration from scripture in Pali, an ancient Indo-Aryan language. In contrast to other schools of Buddhism practised in Tibet, China, Japan and elsewhere in East Asia, Theravada Buddhism stresses the role of monastic communities and has no overarching hierarchical authority. Theravada Buddhists lay greater stress on the life of the historical Buddha, Gautama Sakyamuni, and less on other buddhas and bodhisattvas (beings on the path to enlightenment).

The cultures of maritime Southeast Asia have been influenced by the more recent arrival of two other major world religions. The first of these is Islam, now a majoritarian religion in Malaysia, Brunei, Indonesia and the Southern Philippines. Muslim merchants had travelled in the region from the seventh century onwards. Islam, in its Sunni form, became dominant in maritime Southeast Asia from the thirteenth century onwards, and by the early sixteenth century was established in many major population centres (Taylor 1992: 176). There is considerable evidence that the mystical elements of Sufism appealed to indigenous Southeast Asian beliefs, resulting in syncretic religious practices that persist to this day (Reid 1999: 17–22). The second major world religion, Christianity, arrived through Spanish presence in the Philippines from the early sixteenth century onwards. Miguel Lopez de Legazpi's expedition in 1564 was charged with both the occupation of the Philippine Islands and conversion of indigenous peoples (Andaya 1992: 356). Catholicism remains central to life in the Philippines today, although as with Islam in Indonesia, it has developed through a syncretic appropriation of indigenous cultural beliefs and practices; it is also a significant religion in both Timor-Leste and Vietnam.

The first literatures of the region were often bound up with religious practice. Early writings in Burmese, Thai, Khymer and Lao often explicate Buddhist texts. Poetry and other secular genres were often written by monks, and also at the royal court, where classical modes of drama and dance evolved. In addition, folk literature was transmitted orally. Literature in Javanese evolved in a similar manner, although without the Buddhist elements (Grijns 1989: 133–135). Vietnam is again the exception here: a Confucian bureaucracy resulted in scholarly and literary works which were not directly connected with religion. As Vietnamese literature developed, writers contested the Sinic inheritance by developing a hybrid script, or *nom*, and increasingly using local content (Nguyen 1989: 84–87). Writing was probably introduced into the Philippines between 1000 and 1200 CE: early Spanish visitors recorded widespread literacy (Mojares 1983: 26–27). By the fifteenth century, Arabic script had replaced the older Indian-derived scripts in Mindoro and Sulu (1983: 25), and Roman script had succeeded its predecessors in the north by the seventeenth century (1983: 29). Literature in Malay, which would constitute the national language of both Malaysia and Indonesia, was also originally written in a script of Indian origin; the spread of Islam, however, led to this being replaced by a writing system derived from Arabic, used in most surviving literary texts from before the twentieth century. As with many other Southeast Asian literatures, traditional Malay literature is religious and didactic in nature, but there are also shorter poetic forms, and longer narrative epics or romances in both verse and prose based on mythical or historical events (Jones 1989: 108–109). The changes in scripts reflect an ebb and flow of cultural influences that was transforming Southeast Asian societies, resulting in transformations that were uneven, yet laid the foundation for more thoroughgoing metamorphoses in society in the colonial and national periods, when the pace of technological change accelerated.

The first transformation concerns trade, as the region became more firmly enmeshed in a world economy. Commodity trade in spices and silks rapidly increased, and a gradual shift towards plantation cultivation of tobacco, sugar cane and coffee persisted even during a decline in the middle of the seventeenth century due to natural disasters and external trade difficulties (Reid 1992: 504). Crops were not all cultivated for the outside world, but also for trade within the region. If rice was not yet a true cash crop, still being grown primarily for local consumption, it was more extensively traded and transported further than formerly (1992: 472).

Shifts in trading patterns and modes of production directly impacted Southeast Asian societies. The early modern period saw the rapid rise of maritime cities that were very different from earlier urban centres supported by rice-growing hinterlands. An extreme might be Melaka before its conquest by the Portuguese in 1511, supporting a population of approximately 100,000 but surrounded by uncultivated jungle, and thus almost entirely dependent on imports to feed its population (Reid 1992: 474–475). The dominance of trade brought profound changes to local modes of production and consumption: Indian cotton goods increased their penetration to such an extent that by the seventeenth century much Javanese batik was made using imported yarn, or even with muslin bought in from India (Dixon 1991: 52). Increasingly, too, the largest urban centres were under European government. Cities such as Melaka, Batavia and Manila were controlled by a succession of different European powers; the number of European settlers, however, was small, and such cities were full of migrants from the region and beyond. They constituted a zone of cultural and economic contact in which hybrid cultures developed.

It is important not to exaggerate the reach of colonialism in early modern Southeast Asia; by the early nineteenth century, European powers still formally occupied only the Philippines, some areas of the Indonesian archipelago, and a series of strategic port cities. Military technology advanced rapidly, with improvements in firearms, faster ships and improved fortifications. Europeans did not introduce all these technologies (Reid 1999: 8–9), but they often made strategic use of them, as they did of economic changes. The Manila galleon from Acapulco in Spain's American colonies set up a triangular trade between Mexico, Manila and Macau in which silver was exchanged for silk, cotton and cloth (Andaya 1992: 357). By the late 1600s, the Dutch East India Company held monopolies over the trade in various spices and had taken over several commercial centres in the Indonesian archipelago. Indeed, one commentator has identified the seventeenth century as a time in which a shift in power relations occurred; by 1700, despite superficial continuities (Reid 1999: 12), the contours of European control had been established. Yet to a casual observer the most significant presence in the port cities would not have been European, but Chinese. The last of the great voyages to Southeast Asia and beyond by the Ming court had been in 1433, and subsequent regimes implemented a ban on overseas trade until 1567. But trade continued, and the connections between Java and the Philippines and southern Chinese provinces such as Fujian and Guangdong grew stronger. By 1750, Manila had a Chinese population of 40,000, despite attempts by colonial authorities to limit it, while in 1740 half of the free population of Batavia was Chinese (Andaya 1992: 349). The presence of substantial Chinese populations in trading centres foreshadowed the greater population movements within and into the region that have marked Southeast Asia in the last two centuries.

Late colonialism and nationalism in Southeast Asia

The nineteenth century saw a gradual and accelerating imposition of centralized – most often colonial – rule in the region. Dutch control was extended in Java and then to other islands in the Indonesian archipelago by both military expeditions and treaties; Burma, through a series of armed conflicts, was annexed to British India, while Vietnam was dismembered into three states and brought together with Cambodia – and later Laos – into the French Indochinese Union. Spanish rule in the Philippines was superseded, after the 1899 Treaty of Paris, by a more interventionist American colonialism. British rule in Malaya was less systematic and more indirect; Singapore, Malacca (Melaka) and Penang (Pinang) were united as the Crown Colony of the Straits Settlements, while the states of the Malayan peninsula and Brunei remained nominally independent but governed by a system of indirect rule. Siam (modern Thailand) retained independence, but its territories were eroded by the British from the south and the French from the east, and it only maintained autonomy by accepting a strong British influence.

As empires expanded the nature of colonial rule began to change, becoming more rationalized. Much of this only enabled greater exploitation: the Cultivation System instituted by the Dutch in Java, for example, forced peasants to grow export crops for European consumption, while the British sold off private monopolies in goods such as opium to Chinese businessmen (Elson 1992: 139). Yet in the late nineteenth century there was also a further change: a greater emphasis on the civilizing mission of Europe and America in their colonies. The colonized, in the terms of this discourse, would advance – albeit at a glacial pace – towards autonomy and self-rule. Thus the 'Ethical Policy' in the Dutch East Indies from 1901 stressed both educational and infrastructural improvements to benefit the indigenous population.

In the Philippines, the transition from Spanish to American colonialism resulted in more thoroughgoing initiatives; by 1902, there were over a thousand American schoolteachers in the new colony, following Rudyard Kipling's call to 'take up the white man's burden' hitherto exclusively shouldered by European imperialists.

Reforms in colonial practice, however, only amplified systemic contradictions. Colonial regimes might dismiss challenges to their authority, such as Dipanagara's 'rebellion' in 1825 against the Dutch, or the 'disturbances' in Pahang in the late nineteenth century, as religiously based and therefore representing a refusal of modernity, yet such arguments became increasingly hard to maintain. In order to occupy the Philippines, American forces had to overcome Asia's first republic, which had emerged from an alliance of Spanish-educated elite Filipinos with other social classes, and which drew on symbolism from the Enlightenment, Christianity and folk culture. Less directly confrontational, yet equally corrosive to colonial power, were the demands for rights by comprador classes who held key positions in colonial societies. In Singapore, the most Anglicized of the Straits Chinese demanded to be recognized as British subjects, their patriotic zeal paradoxically eroding the divisions of the plural society that colonial power sought to maintain. Indeed, the structures of colonialism were often appropriated and turned against it. Higher education institutions were set up with the hope of producing indigenous classes that might serve, in Thomas Babington Macaulay's words, as 'interpreters' between the rulers and the ruled. Yet they often served as places where members of emerging nationalist elites could meet, exchange ideas, and think of strategies for the eventual end of colonial rule.

The societies in which nationalism took root and spread had often changed beyond recognition in the colonial period. Population growth accelerated in the late nineteenth and early twentieth centuries. Urban centres grew rapidly, and new ones were founded. Kuala Lumpur mushroomed from a camp for tin miners in 1857 to become the capital of the Federated Malay States in 1896. Colonial policies also promoted internal migration: the resettlement by the Dutch authorities, for instance, of Javanese peasants to other, less densely populated islands in the Indonesian archipelago. Migrants arrived from outside the region: Chinese settlers came to Thailand, Indonesia, Indochina and Malaya, while Indian labour was brought into Malaya and to Burma. Urban centres were often dominated by immigrants, encouraging the development of lingua franca for communication between groups. The spectacle of this rapid social change affected nationalists in two contrasting ways. Cultural nationalists might acutely feel the sensation of becoming strangers in one's own land; such sentiments were important elements in Malay and at times Burmese nationalism. Other nationalists – for example, those in Indonesia – might find in the lingua franca and hybrid cultures of the contact zones the possibility of imagining new national communities, although even here there would be tensions regarding the status of immigrant groups versus the indigenous *pribumi* (native peoples).

The urban centres of Southeast Asia in the early twentieth century thus were the crucibles of modern political associations and movements. Events outside the region were also influential. While an independent republic had been suppressed in the Philippines, Japan and later – fitfully – China were seen as potential models of Asian societies that had undergone modernization. In Europe, the collapse of multi-ethnic empires such as those of the Hapsburgs and the Ottomans into nation-states after the First World War suggested a model for decolonization.

The demise of colonialism was hastened by two further events. The first was the Great Depression after 1929. Demand for Southeast Asia's primary products collapsed, and left economies based on plantation production severely exposed; in the year that the Wall Street Crash occurred, rubber comprised over 60 per cent of Malaya's exports (Owen 1992: 184). The privations of the early 1930s exposed the thinness of colonial development. The second, more catastrophic event was the coming of the Second World War, and in particular the occupation of the region by Japanese forces. The Japanese advance was stunningly swift: six short months from the beginning of the campaign in Malaya on 7–8 December 1941 to the fall of the last bastion on the island of Corregidor in the Philippines on 6 May 1942. Throughout Southeast Asia colonial regimes were swept away.

During the brief three and a half years of Japanese occupation, the structure of colonial states was destroyed and confidence in their regimes shattered. Some areas of the region suffered war damage on a massive scale: Manila, for example, experienced the greatest destruction of any Allied capital apart from the Polish capital Warsaw. More widespread, however, was social disruption and privation caused by economic interruptions (Stockwell 1992: 335–336). Nationalists made a range of responses to Japanese rule. Sukarno and Hatta benefited from carefully nuanced cooperation with occupying forces in Indonesia, while Ho Chi Minh in Vietnam engaged in outright resistance to a Japanese occupation that worked through the structures of a French colonial order now aligned with the Vichy regime. Yet if the War provided opportunities for nationalists, it also created problems: damaged infrastructure took a long time to restore after 1945, and inter-ethnic rivalry was exacerbated by the different treatment of ethnic communities under Japanese occupation regimes (Stockwell 1992: 334–341).

In most of Southeast Asia, the colonial powers only returned to prepare for their precipitate departure. The Philippines gained independence from the United States in 1946, reverting to a schedule laid out before the Japanese occupation. Burma followed soon after in 1948. In Indonesia, Sukarno had been pressured to declare *merdeka* (independence) in 1945: the Dutch, after a delay, returned. Prolonged indigenous resistance and international pressure forced the Dutch to cede sovereignty. By 1950, Indonesia was a unitary republic. After Vo Nguyen Giap's victory over French forces at Dien Bien Phu in 1954, the French colonial empire in Southeast Asia was in effect at an end, but Vietnamese independence was achieved at the cost of a divided nation. In Malaya, the British remained a little longer, but when the British colonies of Sabah, Sarawak and Singapore joined the Federation of Malaysia in 1963, the formal process of decolonization in Southeast Asia was essentially complete.

Decolonization, however, did not result in the withdrawal of strategic interests by international powers in the region: Southeast Asia was now caught in the Cold War. The effects of the conflict were felt both in the guerrilla warfare practised by the Malayan Communist Party after 1948, and in the growing influence of the PKI (Communist Party of Indonesia) in Sukarno's Indonesia, followed by violent anti-leftist reprisals after Sukarno's fall in 1965. Its most far-reaching effects, however, were in Indochina. Vietnam was divided and in a state of war for two decades until 1975, and Laos was also drawn into the conflict. The nation to suffer most was Cambodia: the 'autogenocide' (Owen 2005: 484) of the Khmer Rouge resulted in two million deaths before the Vietnamese invasion in late 1978. Civil war persisted until the United Nations sponsored elections in 1993. Not until 1999, when Cambodia became the last of the nation-states in the region to join ASEAN, were the geographical divisions drawn by the Cold War finally erased.

The variety of histories of Southeast Asian states after the Second World War was reflected in the varied experiences of the region's inhabitants. National autonomy was often realized through an increase in the role of the state. State planning and intervention was seen as necessary, and industrial expansion in particular was stressed so that Southeast Asia would not remain economically dependent on its former colonial powers or newer neocolonial ones. Countries such as Malaysia, Thailand, Indonesia and Vietnam moved towards manufacturing away from agriculture and the exploitation of natural resources, although at an uneven pace. Semi-skilled workforces expanded, as did urbanization. By 1980, one Southeast Asian in four lived in a city.

Such changes brought benefits: there were improvements in public health, for instance, and increases in agricultural production outstripped population growth. Southeast Asian societies experienced the melting of structures that commentators from Karl Marx onwards have noted as a characteristic of modernity; traditional social class in many – but not all – situations began to give way to economic position, and new possibilities opened up for many individuals to fashion life scripts very different from those of previous generations. Women's entry into the workforce as autonomous wage earners offered the possibility of transformations in gender regimes. Yet many of these possibilities were unrealized, and the fact that Southeast Asia was increasingly embedded in global capital flows brought new problems. Social inequalities often increased, as did the division between the country and the city: government policies to alleviate these changes were mired in attempts by elites to preserve their powers. At times conflicts might lead to protagonists taking up arms against national governments; at other times, more passive forms of resistance were followed. Given high levels of social inequality throughout much of the region, many countries saw political regimes that rotated between authoritarian populism, thinly embedded and fractious democracies and military intervention.

A second challenge arose from the multicultural nature of the nation-states themselves. Indonesia, Burma and others were confronted with regional secessionist movements determined to carve out their own nation-states. All states, however, negotiated between notions of indigeneity that sometimes granted precedence to one ethnic group and the presence of minority communities. Malaysia's New Economic Policy from the early 1970s onwards, for example, was explicitly designed to create a *bumiputera* – essentially Malay – middle class (Yong 1992: 430) and to actively rebalance an economic order that had its origin in colonialism and privileged other groups, especially the Chinese. And, as with projects to redistribute wealth, such initiatives frequently benefited only a privileged group, rather than enabling wider social transformations.

The 1997 Asian financial crisis, when a sudden withdrawal of foreign direct investment caused economic hardship and social turmoil, illustrated the paradoxical situation of Southeast Asia at the end of the twentieth century. Changes in societies in the previous fifty years had brought real benefits to some and the prospect of improvements to many more. Yet as the pace of change increased, so the region seemed to be entering a period of greater instability; in late modernity, many Southeast Asians seemed to be entering a risk society in which national governments had increasingly little power – for good or ill – to directly intervene.

Southeast Asia today

The rise of India and China in the last decade has given a greater impetus to the formation and consolidation of a Southeast Asian regional identity. On the political level, there is apparent regional unity, with all regional states bar Timor-Leste now members of ASEAN. Economic connections are seemingly ever closer, with commitments by ASEAN member states to reduce trade tariffs as part of a global turn towards neo-liberalism and free markets. Singaporean companies have invested in neighbouring states from Myanmar to Indonesia, Indonesian migrant labourers flock to Malaysia to find work, while Thailand has established itself as the regional automobile manufacturing hub. Most political leaders in Southeast Asia share a common commitment to developmental goals to be achieved through the production of manufactured goods and the provision of services in an increasingly globalized market. At the same time, popular rhetoric within national boundaries often focuses on the social inequality that

Table 1 Statistical information about selected Southeast Asian countries and Hong Kong

	Population (approx.)	Area	Main religions	Main ethnic group	GDP per capita	Literacy read, write at 15
Brunei	0.38 million	5,770 sq km	Muslim 67% Buddhist 13% Christian 10%	Malay 67% Chinese 15%	$51,000	92.7%
Hong Kong	7.02 million	1,092 sq km	local religions 90% Christian 10%	Chinese 94.9% Filipino 2.1%	$42,000	93.5%
Malaysia	25.3 million	329,750 sq km	Muslim 60.4% Buddhist 19.2% Christian 9.1% Hindu 6.3%	Malay 50.4% Chinese 23.7% indigenous 11% Indian 7.1%	$13,300	88.7%
Philippines	92.7 million	300,000 sq km	Roman Catholic 80.9% other Christian 9.6% Muslim 5%	Tagalog 28.1% Cebuano 13.1% Ilocano 9% Bisaya 7.6% Ilonggo 7.5% Bikol 6% Waray 3.4%	$3,400	92.6%
Singapore	4.6 million	692.7 sq km	Buddhist 42.5% Muslim 14.9% Taoist 8.5% Hindu 4% Catholic 4.8% other Christian 9.8%	Chinese 76.8% Malay 13.9% Indian 7.9% other 1.4%	$49,700	92.5%
Thailand	65.5 million	514,000 sq km	Buddhist 94.6% Muslim 4.6%	Thai 75% Chinese 14% other 11%	$7,900	92.6%

Source: Adapted from CIA – The World Factbook, as updated June 2008. Online: https://www.cia.gov/library/publications/the-world-factbook/ accessed 15 July 2008).

global modernity brings, and acknowledges – even if this is not accompanied by action – the need for intervention to ameliorate such inequalities.

A closer examination of the region, however, reveals the fragility of regional unity. The human development index of the United Nations Development Programme's 2003 figures place the most developed nation in the region, Singapore, in twenty-fifth place worldwide, with the least developed, the Lao PDR, trailing at number 133. Ideologies of 'development' can, of course, be questioned, but these indicators show the varied nature of societies in Southeast Asia, even without illustrating the uneven distribution of wealth within nation-states themselves. In Malaysia, the Philippines and in Thailand, despite a move away from agriculture towards industry and services, there is still tension, and indeed perhaps growing inequality, both between cities and rural areas, and within cities themselves. In the latter two countries, these tensions have led to the overthrow of elected governments whose populist programmes have alienated the urban middle classes. Singapore, Malaysia and Thailand are perhaps the three countries in the region that have the most integrated economies. Each has experienced rapid growth accompanied by growing social inequality: the GINI index in each nation in the early 2000s was over 40, in contrast to the scores of 20 achieved by some European nations.

In terms of political system, too, Southeast Asian nations exhibit wide diversity. Laos and Vietnam are dominated by party leaderships overseeing essentially one-party states. Brunei is close to an absolute monarchy, while Myanmar still suffers under military rule. In Cambodia, Singapore and Malaysia a single party or alliance of parties has achieved a dominance that is, in Antonio Gramsci's terms, hegemonic, so that party, government and state often merge in the public imagination, with the state taking over many of the functions of civil society. The Philippines, Thailand (despite periodic military intervention) and post-1997 Indonesia seem superficially more democratic, in that governments regularly change after elections, and their influence is checked by the presence of a more vibrant civil society and media. The reins of power, however, are often passed between members of wealthy, urban elites.

The fractured nature of politics and societies in Southeast Asia certainly has its costs. In the late 1980s and early 1990s it seemed as though Southeast Asian nation-states might provide a model for thinking about a modernity different from that of the West. This was the time of the popularization of Asian Values discourse by such figures as Malaysian prime minister Mahathir bin Mohamad and Singapore prime minister and later senior minister Lee Kuan Yew, a rewriting of Max Weber's Protestant ethic to suggest that not Calvinism, but rather the putative communitarianism of Asian societies would provide the motor for capitalist development. Yet in the ensuing decade, ASEAN and other regional bodies have struggled to provide a forum for collective policy making. The 'ASEAN way' of consensus and non-interference in the interests of member nation-states is, indeed, less cultural than pragmatic: huge social and political disparities mean that common interests are frequently aspirational rather than real. This lack of ability to act collectively is perhaps most sharply shown in the inability to reverse environmental degradation (Elliott 2004) in Sumatra, Kalimantan and the ecosystem centred on the Mekong River. A lack of unity also has economic effects; after an initial impetus, attempts to reduce tariffs across an ASEAN free trade area have run into structural impediments, with individual countries now negotiating bilateral pacts with partners outside the region. Aspirations for unity, however, still remain strong. It is possible that the Thirteenth ASEAN Summit in Singapore in 2007, which resulted in the drafting of a landmark ASEAN Charter, marks a significant intensification of regional integration and cooperation.

Fractures present across the region, however, might also be seen as a reassertion of a feature of Southeast Asian societies present from the very earliest times: their hybridity. Just as the region was pivotal to earlier waves of globalization, so it may be argued that it now provides a test case of the effects of cultural and economic flows on a global scale in a new global modernity after the end of the Cold War. Rather than being seen, as it was for much of the twentieth century, as playing catch-up in processes of development, modernization and industrialization that had already reached fruition elsewhere, Southeast Asia at the present, while still caught within these narratives, offers the possibility of a critical reading of the occlusions and assumptions that underlie such concepts.

The first of these occlusions is the place of religion in modern life. In European thought, modernization was inseparable from secularization. In Southeast Asia, religion provided a mark of difference from colonial rule and a means of expression of cultural authenticity to motivate a national narrative. In other ways, religion in the region had been central to the making of the modern world: Singapore was a centre not simply for trade, for example, but for gathering for pilgrimage to Mecca for Southeast Asian Muslims. While the state has acknowledged the place of religion – even in resolutely secular nation-states such as Vietnam and Singapore – it has also been troubled by the extent to which majoritarian religious practices should be endorsed in public life: recent tensions in Malaysia, for instance, have focused on whether citizens have the right to renounce Islam, and whether this decision should be made by Islamic or secular courts. Movements for local autonomy have frequently taken on religious associations: the percentage of Catholics in the Timor-Leste population grew markedly during the twenty-five years of Indonesian rule. If religious practice on a formal basis has now been increasingly rationalized, forms of unsystematized religious practice are still vibrant, even if they conflict with the teachings of temples, mosques and churches. As Aihwa Ong has noted in her study of women factory workers, such forms of folk belief may also have the capacity to enable individuals to tactically interrogate the structures of the modern economy and state (Ong 1987). Discussion in the twenty-first century of the renewed place of religion in global modernity still frequently opposes secular modernisms to fundamentalism. The complex manner in which religion, and especially Islam, is incorporated into the social imaginaries of Southeast Asian nation-states thus opens up the possibility of more nuanced analyses.

A second area in which Southeast Asia challenges comfortable assumptions is with respect to community and democracy. All states in the region, as we have noted, have some form of democratic deficit, and some are openly politically repressive. A careful look at Southeast Asian societies, however, may result in some reflection on the nature of democratic or representative governance itself. Much commentary on Southeast Asian societies, Ariel Heryanto and Sumit K. Mandal (2003) note, often views them as being in transition from authoritarianism to democracy, and then mourns the manner in which each society periodically deviates from the narrative of democratization. Rather, Heryanto and Mandal argue, we might note that authoritarian structures and regimes are often not forced on a general population by a small elite; in many cases significant proportions of Southeast Asian populations have consented to 'social relations and a political order that outsiders conveniently label as "authoritarian" in character' (2003: 2). The complex roles of various social actors in what Heryanto and Mandal call 'post-authoritarian' societies such as Malaysia and Indonesia (2003: 14) may have much to tell us about possibilities for agency worldwide, given the growing corporatization of politics in European and North American nation-states. Chaiwat Satha-Anand, indeed, has coined the term 'authoritarian democracy' to describe the situation in Thailand in which an elected government is illiberal in its mode of governance (2006: 186); the concept has resonance within the region, and is applicable elsewhere in the world.

A third area in which Southeast Asia seems important is in the effect on the region of globalization. As we have seen, such processes of transformation are not new to the region, and the rhetoric of new nation-states in the post-independence era seems to have been a brief interruption, rather than a radical transformation of, a narrative of cultural and economic traffic stretching back into the past. Southeast Asia is certainly caught up in the movement of peoples that has characterized this later phase of globalization worldwide. Unskilled labour moves into, within and outside the region: the Philippines and Indonesia are a source of foreign domestic workers for cities such as Kuala Lumpur and also for countries outside the region, while labourers from China work on construction projects in Singapore. Philippine nurses staff Bangkok hospitals whose target market is foreign health tourists; urban professionals fly from city to city in the region and beyond.

Such mobilities have introduced new tensions within nation-states, challenging what Joel S. Kahn has referred to as the 'rationalized nationalisms' of Sukarno and his post-independence contemporaries (1998: 25).

As regimes in Southeast Asia have turned to economic growth as a means of legitimization so, Kahn suggests, the field of culture has become contested, partly ceded to oppositional groups demanding recognition (1998: 21). These groups, however, are frequently not simply ethnic or cultural minorities in a traditional sense, but are now firmly connected to transnational diasporic communities. The plight of Indonesian Chinese scapegoated in riots during the fall of Suharto's regime in Indonesia in 1997, for example, was highlighted not through the cautious official media, but through independent media such as the website http://www.huaren.com, which brought together a community of people of Chinese ancestry. A more prosaic example might be the Eurasian community in Malacca's rediscovery of its 'Portugueseness' and self-reinvention for tourism (Sarkissian 2000). Such transformations provide new challenges for notions of citizenship: they are not unique to Southeast Asia, but the fragmented and hybrid nature of Southeast Asian societies perhaps makes the manner in which they are contested particularly acute.

Discussions of new identities inevitably lead to the new information and communication technologies. Southeast Asia demonstrates the unevenness of the reach of these technologies: while Singapore has a rate of usage of mobile phones that exceeds that of the United States, most citizens of Myanmar, even if they can afford internet access, confront one of the most extensive internet censorship regimes in the world. The internet has opened up new possibilities for community and identity-formation in the region, enabling pan-regional, pan-Asian, and indeed international communication and collaboration by environmental, women's or LGBT (lesbian-gay-bisexual-transsexual) groups. It has also permitted the formation of innovative news sources that escape some of the restrictions on print or broadcast media imposed by nation-states. Most recently, the spread of more interactive forms of communication on the internet (sometimes referred to as Web 2.0) have extended this effect; a proliferation of blogs (weblogs) and video-sharing sites have enabled the formation of new communities and information sharing across national boundaries. Yet new technologies have not simply eroded national boundaries; they have also been made strategic use of by nation-states for surveillance, and, more subtly, to interpellate citizens.

One of the most interesting effects of the rise of new technologies has been in multilingual environments, in many of which English is used. The English language has been used by regional elites for over a century, and has, from the early twentieth century onwards, increasingly become a means of communication in the region between speakers of different languages. Even in areas where English has been widely spoken, however, nation-states after independence have at best had an ambivalent attitude to it, perceiving it as a language with economic benefits, but as also carrying the dangers of deculturalization. As the use of English grows in Southeast Asia, however, hybrid forms have increasingly developed: notably Taglish, Singlish and

Manglish in the Philippines, Singapore and Malaysia respectively. The short messages on mobile phones, blogs or social networking sites often switch from language to language, offering the possibility of new cultural expressions outside the purview of the state. Literary production in the region has often reflected and explored a growing variety of Englishes, while at the same time remaining aware of transnational audiences whose members may belong to very different reading communities.

Discussion of Southeast Asia in the chapter above has made no reference to Hong Kong. In the precolonial period there was little connection between what is now the Chinese Special Administrative Region and Southeast Asia: Chinese voyages to the region for trade or exploration mostly departed from established ports in Fujian and Guangdong province.

The initial element that linked Hong Kong and Southeast Asia was colonial rule. The British took possession of Hong Kong Island in 1841, and continued imperial ambitions in the nineteenth century led to the cession of the Kowloon peninsula in 1860 and a hundred-year lease on the New Territories in 1897. The development of the city of Victoria as a port led to migration from surrounding Guangdong province and, to a lesser extent, from other regions of China. Hong Kong developed as a largely ethnically homogenous city, with a small population of Europeans resident in an ethnically exclusive area on the Peak. Communities other than the Chinese did exist. Eurasians, Portuguese nationals from the nearby enclave of Macao, and Parsees all performed the function of colonial compradors, but their numbers were less significant than in the Straits Settlements, and the communities less influential: Eurasians, indeed, often integrated into the Chinese community (Tsang 2004: 64). The only other significant non-Chinese group consisted of Indians who came in as soldiers or policemen: subordinated in class terms, they did not contribute to the emergence of an English-speaking public sphere.

Hong Kong developed as an intellectual centre for Chinese before the 1911 Revolution in China, with dissident intellectuals such as Kang Youwei and Sun Yatsen spending time in the colony protected from the Qing government (Tsai 1993). As a node in a network of ports, Hong Kong also played a role in Southeast Asian politics: Emilio Aguinaldo, the Philippine revolutionary, for instance, was exiled there in 1897. Despite the presence of elite English-medium schools and the founding of the Anglophone University of Hong Kong in 1911, however, most intellectual life was in Chinese.

Hong Kong's survival as a British colony for fifty years after the Second World War and Japanese occupation was a product of a series of omissions and coincidences. In the immediate aftermath of the War, the Chinese Nationalists were more focused on the conflict with the Communists: after the latter had triumphed, Britain's prompt recognition of the People's Republic of China and Hong Kong's role as a financial conduit between China and the outside world resulted in China claiming sovereignty, but delaying retrocession until, in Mao Zedong's words, 'the time is ripe' (quoted in Tsang 2004: 153). Hong Kong, indeed, served not only as a commercial, but also a cultural conduit between the Chinese in Southeast Asia and their ancestral land (e.g. Wickberg 2006: 20–31). Migration of industrialists from Chinese commercial centres such as Shanghai, and the diminution in Hong Kong's role as an entrepôt resulted in the territory becoming a manufacturing centre, and in rapid economic development. In the 1980s, as China began to open up through Deng Xiaoping's economic reforms, the territory's manufacturers set up factories in neighbouring areas of Guangdong province, and Hong Kong became a services and financial hub for China's growing economy. By the time of its return to China in 1997, Hong Kong had become a developed society, having achieved sustained economic growth to match that of Singapore over the previous three decades.

Hong Kong today faces several challenges. Democratization, begun rather hypocritically by the British after the 1984 declaration, has stalled after 1997, although it remains possible that in future Hong Kong people will be able to directly elect their chief executive. Questions of autonomy and a distinct Hong Kong identity are still much debated, and there is growing concern regarding environmental degradation. In anxieties surrounding the run-up to retrocession in 1997, many Hong Kong professionals gained citizenship in Canada, the United Kingdom, Singapore or the United States. Many have now returned to work or live again in Hong Kong. In addition, Hong Kong has long been a conduit for flights and other contacts between China and Taiwan. Such factors have given Hong Kong a pivotal role in what Tu Weiming has characterized as 'cultural China' (1991: 1), with Hong Kong movies and popular music in Cantonese and Mandarin achieving widespread popularity in Chinese communities worldwide. English-language culture has remained less central, although not invisible, in articulations of Hong Kong identity: if colonialism pulled Hong Kong into the periphery of Southeast Asia, retrocession has drawn the territory closer again to China and East Asia.

Conclusion

- Southeast Asia is an exceptionally diverse region in terms of geography, culture, politics and languages.
- Southeast Asia's experience of colonialism was diverse and uneven, resulting in a wide variety of imagined communities in postcolonial nation-states.
- English is the only language introduced to the region under colonialism to thrive, and it is now taking on a role in trade, regional political contacts, and – in some nation-states – cultural production.

- Studying Southeast Asia may make us question normative ideas regarding the role of political liberalization, religion and technology in development.
- Hong Kong's close contact with Southeast Asia was largely the result of colonialism, and it remains to be seen whether this will persist now that it is a Special Administrative Region of China.

3   Linguistic contexts

Overview

Any approach to the literary productions of Southeast Asia in English stands to profit from two types of recognition: that when an author living in a multilingual society chooses to write in English, the choice has political and cultural as well as linguistic significance. To choose English in contemporary Malaysia, for example, represents what sociolinguists might call a 'marked' political choice, since the nation-state enjoins, and the majority of the national readership expects, Malay from Malaysian writers, whereas a similar choice would be relatively 'unmarked' in Singapore today, where English has largely prevailed over the other local languages. A second type of recognition entails awareness that when English is chosen in a multilingual society, the linguistic resources accessed either consciously or involuntarily by an author can range across a very wide spectrum, from Standard English to localized variations of intonation, rhythm, colloquialism, phrase and vocabulary.

Bilingualism and multilingualism in Southeast Asia

Since the 1960s, the number of people who speak English, and the degree of fluency with which they speak it, has grown steadily in all the English-speaking parts of Southeast Asia. Nevertheless most authors, especially those who were born in the first half of the twentieth century, handle the language more as a skill learnt in school than as involuntary knowledge acquired through family and community. That is one way in which the context of writing in English differs between countries which are largely monolingual and those which are not. *The Oxford Companion to the English Language* notes that 'In the social context of languages like English, especially in England and the US, the traditional tendency has been to consider the possession of one language the norm' (McArthur 1992: 126). Arguably, even in the US or the UK, at least in some cities, English might be acquired amidst other languages (for example, Spanish in some parts of the United States and perhaps an Asian language in some parts of metropolitan Britain); and in such cases, ideologies of language-use might downplay or repress the significance of multilingual choice, since the societal norm in either country as a whole gravitates powerfully towards English.

In contrast, most Southeast Asians can understand and speak at least two (and often more than two) languages, independent of their level of literacy. English is acquired amidst a plurality of languages, and its acquisition generally retains some vestige of the influence of other languages. In the Philippines, English speech habits are influenced by Filipino, Tagalog, Ilocano, Cebuano and other regional languages; in Malaysia, by various forms of Malay, Hokkien, Cantonese, Tamil and other minority languages; in Singapore, by Malay, several Chinese 'dialects' and Tamil; and in Hong Kong, by Cantonese and, more recently, by standard Mandarin.

'Chinese' refers to a group of spoken languages which have settled for their written form on variations of a single and simplified system of transcription: 'The main varieties of "Chinese" (Cantonese, Hakka, Hsiang [Xiang], Kan [Gan], Mandarin, Min and Wu) are as distinct from one another as English from Danish or German. Cantonese, though traditionally described as a "dialect", is a major language spoken by millions in China, Hong Kong, Singapore and elsewhere in Southeast Asia. It is often contrasted with Mandarin (Chinese), the range of dialects spoken in and around Beijing and, in its educated form, the traditional governing language of the Chinese Empire' (McArthur 1992: 212). Most Chinese are not native speakers of Mandarin, but Mandarin occupies a unique position with reference to other 'dialects' because there is only really one form of written Chinese (which is based on ideograms rather than pronunciation): 'The Chinese writing system is at least 2,000 years old ... In the People's Republic, a form of Mandarin has been developed as *Putonghua* (common speech), a unifying national standard and medium of instruction in schools that is written and printed in a simplified system of traditional characters (some 2,000 in number) and also, for certain purposes, in a system of Romanization known as *Pinyin* ("phonetic spelling")' (McArthur 1992: 213).

The history of Southeast Asia shows that multilingualism is the consequence of social patterns in which people from different language-communities have lived in close proximity, interacting with one another as a routine aspect of daily life. When such interactions have continued over extended periods, from colonial to contemporary times, the barriers separating distinct language-communities have become more porous. Colonization and urbanization reinforced patterns of social communication developed through a long history of migrations and settlements. The familiarity acquired with the languages of other communities depends on need and context rather than education in school. Such familiarity does not imply an equal command of or interchangeable use between two or more languages. Actual practice follows a pattern described by sociolinguists as *diglossia*, which refers to 'the use of two or more varieties of language for different purposes in society' (McArthur 1992: 312), especially in situations where there is a fairly systematic association between a given variety and high social status, and other varieties and neutral or low social status. In speech as well as writing, context determines choice. Because English was associated with colonial education and the modernization of the nation,

Table 2 Languages of Southeast Asia

Country	Languages (primary languages in bold)
Brunei	**Malay** (official), English, Chinese
Cambodia	**Khmer** (official) 95%, French, English
Indonesia	**Bahasa Indonesia** (official, modified form of Malay), English, Dutch, local dialects (the most widely spoken of which is Javanese)
Laos	**Lao** (official), French, English, and various ethnic languages
Malaysia	**Bahasa Malaysia** (official), English, Chinese (Cantonese, Mandarin, Hokkien, Hakka, Hainan, Foochow), Tamil, Telugu, Malayalam, Panjabi, Thai , and several indigenous languages of East Malaysia, including Iban and Kadazan
Myanmar (Burma)	**Burmese**, and other minority ethnic group languages
Philippines	**Filipino** (official; based on Tagalog) and **English** (official); eight major dialects: Tagalog, Cebuano, Ilocano, Hiligaynon or Ilonggo, Bicol, Waray, Pampango, and Pangasinan
Singapore	**Mandarin** 35%, **English** 23%, **Malay** 14.1%, Hokkien 11.4%, Cantonese 5.7%, Teochew 4.9%, **Tamil** 3.2%, other Chinese dialects 1.8%, other 0.9% (2000 census)
Thailand	**Thai**, English (secondary language of the elite), ethnic and regional dialects
Timor-Leste (East Timor)	**Tetum** (official), Portuguese (official), Indonesian, English and at least 15 other indigenous languages
Vietnam	**Vietnamese** (official), English (increasingly favoured as a second language), some French, Chinese, and Khmer; mountain area languages (Mon-Khmer and Malayo-Polynesian)

Source: Adapted from CIA – The World Factbook. Online: https://www.cia.gov/library/publications/the-world-factbook/ (accessed 5 October 2008).

its use has tended to focus on the formal domains of technical education, business, law, international relations and the metropolitan work-space. In contrast, an indigenous language, acquired as a natural part of growing up in a community, is more likely to be used in informal situations associated with relaxation, intimacy, casualness and the spontaneous expression of emotions and feelings. In the Philippines, for instance, a survey carried out in 1982 indicated that being bilingual between Filipino and English was essential for any business or industry in the country, and in non-Tagalog areas, one needed to be trilingual 'in the local Vernacular, Filipino and in English' (A. Gonzalez 1988: 108). In speech as well as writing, the perception of how differences between varieties are linked to status or class can be consciously used as a form of 'accommodation', a process of adjustment and negotiation in which a user accommodates consciously to the register and style of a specific class of speaker in order to facilitate better relations across perceived differences in class and speech habits.

Spoken English in Southeast Asia

English as generally spoken in Malaysia and Singapore, Hong Kong and the Philippines shows internal differences as well as similarities. A very small minority in each country approximates closely to Standard English; a much larger majority occupies the continuum from elementary to intermediate levels of proficiency. Internal variations depend on four factors: context, educational proficiency, socio-economic background and the primary language whose influence precedes the acquisition of English. The most informal registers often coincide with speech habits based on a relatively basic education, and are accompanied by various kinds of simplifications concerning grammar and idiom, complemented by liberal mixing between rudimentary English and an indigenous language. Those with a more advanced level of education – which generally translates into greater proficiency in English – find themselves able, if so inclined, to move freely along the continuum from formal to informal registers.

Large countries like Malaysia and the Philippines reveal further differences between English as spoken in the metropolis and the provinces. Whenever speech habits depart from Standard English, the underlying reasons are often related to the patterns created by indigenous languages. Involuntary habits are hard to unlearn, and while education and exposure to international print media and the global entertainment industry show signs of reducing the gap between regional speech habits and Standard English, enough differences remain to suggest than one can venture a general description of Southeast Asian English, based on the belief articulated by Edgar Schneider that the historical development of various forms of postcolonial English are 'instantiations of the same underlying process' (2007: 5). Some of its distinctive features are reflected in writing when authors attempt a form of linguistic naturalism, but many features are not captured by literary writing, since most authors who write in English aspire to a homogenizing stylistic medium based on Standard English. While some features of spoken English are unique to specific parts of Southeast Asia, others are similar to the speech habits of other former British colonies in South Asia, Africa and the Caribbean.

Consider intonation and rhythm: many ex-colonials speak English in a monotonous or 'sing-song' rhythm. This effect is the accidental outcome of the tendency to give approximately equal time to pronouncing each syllable in an utterance, neglecting the stress-based rhythm of Standard English (Bautista and Gonzalez 2006; Hickey 2004; Schneider 2007: 72–78). English as spoken in Singapore, the Philippines, Papua New Guinea and Africa often blurs the distinction between long and short vowel sounds by tending towards a short vowel sound for both parts of such pairs as *bit/beat*, *rid/reed*, *sit/seat*, *this/these* (Platt *et al.* 1984: 33). A similar shortening of diphthongs is observed in words like *so, late, rate, take.* Other distinctions that get blurred include the difference between 'l' and 'r' sounds in pairs like these: *light/right, belly/berry.* Another tendency relates to the sound of the voiceless 'th' in words like *thick, throw, thud*, which gets uttered as a 't' sound, and the voiced 'th' in words like *this, the, that*, which often gets pronounced as a 'd' sound, so that the difference between *den/then* and *tick/thick* gets blurred (1984: 38). The absence of aspiration in uttering the sounds of 'p', 't', 'k' at the beginning of words tends to blur another kind of distinction observed by Standard English, between word-pairs such as *ten/den, pair/bear, pig/big.* Many Southeast Asians who lack proficiency in English, and speak Chinese as a primary language, tend to use glottal stops in place of final consonants such as 'p', 't' and 'k'. Thus a sentence like 'They pick me up at seven' is likely to sound like 'They pi' me u' a' seven' (1984: 41).

In Malaysia, spoken English varies depending on whether the speaker was educated in an English-medium or a Malay-medium school (Platt *et al.* 1983: 12). Peter Lowenberg notes that 'Among Malaysians, the term Malaysian English tends to refer to a more or less controversial variety that centres on the colloquialisms of those educated at the English-medium schools. Its essence is distilled in the cartoons of K. H. Boon in the *Malaysian Post*, 'Myself so thin don't eat, can die one, you know?' (McArthur 1992: 640). Since the 1960s, English is more widely used in Singapore than Malaysia, and average proficiency is higher. Distinctions between Singaporean and Malaysian English exist, and are discernible to local speakers, but the two varieties share a common history and several characteristics, such as a shifting of the stress to a later syllable in polysyllabic words (*educáted* instead of *éducated*), a tendency to reduce final and medial consonant clusters (*jus* instead of *just*), the pronunciation of 'h' as 'haitch', and other speech habits. The influence of indigenous languages on the syntax of spoken English in Malaysia and Singapore is seen in such constructions:

> This one can wear with many thing one (Chinese pattern)
> You wait here, I will go and come (Indian)
> Not good like that, afterwards people talk (Malay)
> > (Platt and Weber 1980: 20)

The tendency to duplicate words is common in colloquial speech:

> Take bus no good. Always stop stop stop.
> We buddy buddy. You don't play me out, OK?
> > (Low and Brown 2003: 59)

> Why the veggie got bitter-bitter taste?
> Make it smaller-smaller.
> Don't always stay in the house. Go outside walk-walk.
> Late for lecture already still stroll-stroll-stroll.
> > (Lim Choon Yeoh and Wee 2001)

Examples of spoken English from Malaysia and Singapore:

> Here got many nice houses.
> I work about four months already.
> Sometime, we use to speak Mandarin.
> Is very cheap.
> Is not very far from here.
> You check out now, is it?
> Q: You are going steady? A: Not actually la, but very closely.
> This is quite nice also.
> This coffee house got lot of customer.
> My father, he speaks the deep Hokkien.
> Last time is not so difficult.
> > Platt and Weber (1980: 61–86)

The Philippines has over 170 languages, of which a round dozen have more than a million speakers, with Tagalog and Cebuano each having more than 20 million speakers. Filipino, the national language, is a standardized version of Tagalog. The use of English in the Philippines is a result of the enthusiastic promotion of the language by the United States in a colony which it took over from the Spanish in 1898. The Philippines were granted

Commonwealth status in 1935 and independence in 1946. The concerted effort by the Americans to spread English to the masses contrasts sharply with the long preceding period of Spanish rule, during which the Spanish language was taught to a relatively small set of privileged locals and *mestizos*, although its influence spread to the many indigenous languages of the Philippines.

In a pattern common to most parts of Southeast Asia, English is more widely used in metropolitan than rural areas. As in Malaysia and Hong Kong, while English plays a crucial role in education, business and administration, and remains the preferred language for many formal contexts, indigenous languages dominate the media and popular usage, either Filipino, the language of the region (if the region happens to be other than Luzon), or Taglish. The last deserves special mention. The apparent similarity between the terms Singlish, Manglish and Taglish should not be allowed to obscure the fact that the nature of the hybrid is different in each case. The hybrid that results from the absorption of English into Tagalog is known as 'Taglish' ('mix-mix' or '*halo-halo*' in local parlance), while the adoption of Tagalog words into regional English gives us 'Englog' or 'Konyo English', of which *Wikipedia* cites the following as an example: 'Let's *tusok* the fishballs' (i.e. 'Let's skewer the fishballs'). A related phenomenon, seen from the perspective of English influenced by Malay, gives us 'Manglish'. The term 'Singlish' is somewhat different in that it does not refer to the import of English words into an indigenous language but the reverse: a form of colloquial Singapore English characterized by distinctive intonations, patterns, words and expressions borrowed, adapted or influenced by a combination of Chinese and Malay. Roger Thompson comments that 'Taglish is the creation of educated Filipinos ... Mixing Tagalog and English is so widespread in Metro Manila that it is hard to say what the home language is since Manilans learn English as a second language in the home. In essence, Taglish has become Filipino street English ... Taglish has become an auxiliary spoken language with no body of literature except in tabloids' (2003: 40–41).

As with the other varieties from Southeast Asia, the rhythms of spoken English in the Philippines are syllable timed, that is, syllable stress does not always follow the pattern of Standard English (e.g. *eligíble*, *establísh*, *cerémony*). The distinctions between long and short vowels common to Standard English are not always followed. The distinction between 's' and 'z' sounds is not followed, voiceless sibilants are used in words like *bees*, *cities*, and unvoiced 'th' sounds (as in *thin*) and voiced sounds (as in *then*) are rendered through 't' and 'd' sounds (e.g. this=dis, thin=tin) (Hickey 2004: 576–79).

Both English and Filipino are official languages in the Philippines, but Filipino has grown to be even more widely used than English. Taglish is very common in spoken situations as well as in the media. In grammatical terms, as in other new varieties, tense is not always marked, resulting in constructions such as:

He go to school.
She drink milk.
Some of them crying because teacher ask them to read stories
   in Filipino.
We have done it yesterday.

The present progressive is commonly used for habitual behaviour, instead of the simple present, as in 'We are doing this work all the time'. Transitive forms are treated quite flexibly, as are prepositions. Perfect tenses are used when not expected in Standard English ('I have seen him yesterday'), and the progressive is used when not needed in Standard English ('He is going to school regularly'). The definite article is used where it may not be expected ('the Rizal College') (Thompson 2003: 53).

In terms of vocabulary, extensive loan-words are used from indigenous languages and also from Spanish: *bienvenida* (welcome party), *despedida* (farewell party), *estafa* (fraud, scandal), *merienda* (afternoon tea), *querida* (mistress), etc. Loan-words from Tagalog include *barangay* (community), *boondock* (mountain), *carabao* (water buffalo), *kundiman* (love song), *tao* (the common man), etc. Local neologisms include *carnap* (steal a car), *cope up* (to keep up and cope with), *holder-upper* (someone who engages in armed hold-ups), *jeepney* (a jeep-like bus), etc. The vigorous popular development of Taglish and Filipino has begun to overshadow English in ordinary usage, although it retains its role in most formal domains. Creative writing is at least as vigorous in indigenous languages as in English, a situation that parallels the literary situation in Hong Kong and Malaysia (where writing in Cantonese and Malay respectively far exceeds writing in English in terms of number of authors, scale of publishing and size of readerships), and differs from that in Singapore, where writing in Mandarin, Malay and Tamil has been long overtaken by writing in English, both in scale and status.

The relatively narrow domains in which English is used in Hong Kong creates a wide gap between expatriates who use it as a first language, and local Chinese, whose average grasp of the language shows many influences from Cantonese and other Chinese 'dialects' (Hickey 2004: 573–574). By 1993, according to Kingsley Bolton, the number of people trilingual between Cantonese, English and Mandarin was 38.3 per cent (2003: 115), even if many of these may reveal no more than a basic level of proficiency in English. In their speech habits, long vowels of Standard English get shortened (e.g. *teks* for *takes*, both *port* and *pot* are pronounced like the latter; the vowel in *food* is shortened to sound like the vowel in *foot*), glottal stops take the place of terminal 'k' and 't' sounds, and sibilants are rendered voiceless. The plural and third-person marking of Standard English tends to disappear, producing constructions like 'He give all de picture to you'. The absence of tense markings produces utterances like 'Mandarin, I learn privately'. The use of the definite article lacks consistency (e.g. 'De farmer dey do de gardening ou[t] si[de] dere'). Relative clauses shed their verbs ('This is the student admitted last year'), and the distinction between active and passive voice is not always observed ('I am boring [bored] in lectures'). Colloquial usage allows phrases such as *discuss about*, *list out* and *return back*. The plural form is used rather loosely, permitting words such as *equipments*, *furnitures*, *staffs* (Bolton 2003: 213). Hong Kong English has contributed several words to the general lexicon of English, such as *mini-flat* and *batchmate* (Bolton counts 318 words, 2003: 211).

English has not been the primary of language of choice for creative writing in Hong Kong and Malaysia, but it thrives in Singapore. In the Philippines, it has produced the largest body of creative writing in a colonial language from Southeast Asia. The sheer density of the human population, the length of time for which English has been actively taught in the country, the vigour of the indigenous languages, all combine to suggest that the only comparison for English in the Philippines is outside Southeast Asia: with India.

English in Southeast Asia: code-mixing

The use of different languages for formal and informal contexts is not a rigid practice. While using one language, bilingual or multilingual speakers sometimes introduce elements of another language into their utterance. There are many reasons why this is done. The most frequent reason has to do with the fact that most indigenous languages lack technical words for terms in science and technology, which they import or adapt from a language such as English. Other reasons concern connotation rather than denotation: a speaker might introduce words and expressions from one language into another because they evoke associations for which there might be no equivalent in the first language. Or a speaker might feel more comfortable mixing the relative formality of one language with the informality evoked by another language. Sociolinguists refer to such practices as code-switching and code-mixing, in which a tag familiarly used in one language is attached to utterances in another language. Code-switching to language mixing forms a continuum: speakers have the option of deciding whether or not to juxtapose elements from different varieties. Further along the continuum, the element of choice begins to disappear, as speech habits stabilize to a point where the fusing of varieties becomes more like a constraint or rule rather than an element of free choice.

Here are some examples. First, a twenty-nine-year-old female traffic warden replying to a question on family planning: 'I willing to stop lah! No point to have more kids lah – because we think of working ah so we have not time with the kids lah' (Platt *et al.* 1983: 39). A brief literary example can be cited from Ee Tiang Hong's poem 'Heeren Street, Malacca-2': 'Jaga on charpoy fast asleep' (*jaga*: Baba Malay for 'watchman'; *charpoy*: Hindi for 'a light bed made of rope-webbing tied to a wooden frame') (Thumboo 1973: 15).

The most obvious type of code-mixing in Southeast Asia works in two ways, which sociolinguists describe as Englishization and nativization. The first refers to the assimilation of elements from English into a regional language; the latter to its reverse, the adoption of speech patterns, syntax, intonation or vocabulary from an indigenous language into how English is spoken (and written). Countless examples occur in daily life and the print media, in which Malay, Chinese, Tamil, Tagalog and all the other languages of Southeast Asia accommodate English words and expressions in their common usage. The international dominance of English augments a tendency that was initiated through colonial encounters.

The kind of English used in literary productions from Southeast Asia depends on how authors learnt the language, the kind of books they modelled themselves on, and the degree to which their work reflects the speech habits of their society. How far any piece of writing declares its models, and the degree to which it reflects the spoken idiom, tends to vary from author to author, and from genre to genre. Drama, fictional dialogue and poems that dramatize voices offer the greatest scope for refractions of local forms of spoken English. Narrative prose, non-fictional prose and lyric verse written in an authorial first person are the genres most likely to aspire to an individual style that blurs the distinction between standard and regional English.

The general point to recognize in reading English writing from Southeast Asia is that there are many ways in which spoken versions of English have become modified through their assimilation of elements from indigenous languages, and these might not always be reflected – or reflected accurately – in literary writing. At the simplest level the influence is felt when loanwords from regional languages get absorbed into Standard English. The most familiar borrowings into English from Malay include: amok, kampong (village), durian, godown, mango, mee goreng (fried noodles), orangutan, sago, sarong, etc. Borrowings from Chinese include: dim sung, fung shui, ginseng, kung fu, ketchup, kow-tow, lychee, sampan, tea, tycoon, typhoon, etc.

Southeast Asian writing in English is similar to writing from South Asia, Africa and the Caribbean in frequently accommodating words, phrases and idioms from indigenous languages into the author's English or into the language ascribed to fictional characters. Such code-mixing enables an author to build up a sense of local atmosphere, as when N. V. M. Gonzalez mixes Tagalog and Spanish expressions in *Children of the Ash-Covered Loam and Other Stories* (1954): 'He got his bolo from Nanay, slipped it into its sheath and hurried down the path to the *kaingin*. Tarang could see the tall dead trees of the clearing beyond the hinadong tree and the second growth' (Platt *et al.* 1984: 181).

The appreciation of such allusions needs shared languages between authors and readers. In speech such mixing might be an unconscious aspect of bilingualism; its use in writing signals the author's intention to evoke local associations and represent local speech habits in naturalist terms. Such mixing takes the risk of needing a gloss that might impede the flow of the reading experience. Missing the point of an allusion, or needing help (as with a joke), is likely to leave a reader discomfited or alienated. Moreover, not all attempts at mixing words from one language with a literary discourse in another language feel either comfortable or apt. Here is an experiment that does not quite come off, from a poem titled 'Ahmad' by Wang Gungwu, who published the first volume of poetry in English from Singapore, *Pulse*:

> Thoughts of Camford fading,   [portmanteau: *Cam*bridge/Ox*ford*]
> Contentment creeping in;
> Allah has been kind;
> Orang puteh has been kind.   [Malay: white man]
> Only yesterday his brother said,
> Can get lagi satu wife, lah!   [Malay: one more]
>
> (Wang 1950: 13)

Writers sometimes help readers by incorporating clues or translations into their code-mixing. 'What shall we do with Lily', a contemporary poem from the Philippines by Isabela Banzon illustrates the tact underlying this procedure:

> but what shall we do with Lily?
> X means kiss, secret is rahasia,
> entah, I don't know, mungkin, maybe
> and you on the ferry heading back to the office.
>
> (2009: 48)

The relation of spoken to written English

There is more to the impact of multilingualism on writing than code-mixing. Writers sensitive to how a language has evolved in a specific region and community can articulate their sense of the interface between language and sensibility by creating an entire discourse that is mimetic of the speech habits of speakers who are characteristic of a particular class and a specific level of literacy. In colonial societies, these transformations of English concern a frequently occurring phenomenon that becomes a process of linguistic contestation. It begins with what a conservative view might call 'liberties' and what a liberal view might call 'variations' in grammar, syntax, pronunciation, intonation or rhythm. What might start off as liberties or errors in imitating the speech habits of native speakers of English, when perpetuated and habilitated by entire communities, move upwards along the gradient from 'wrong' to 'non-standard' to 'legitimate' regional variants, regardless of how politicians legislate for or against them and irrespective of whether linguists delineate them descriptively or prescriptively.

When regional variants accumulate sufficient numbers and a certain degree of self-confidence, they seek acceptance as viable modes of self-expression and communication, regardless of their divergence from Standard English. Thus Australian or New Zealand or South African or Canadian or American or Jamaican English (to take just a few examples) have evolved in slightly different ways, subscribing to norms of competence that overlap only partially with Standard English as spoken in the United Kingdom. However, as the poems by Nissim Ezekiel, written in 'very Indian English' illustrate in the context of South Asia, certain speakers develop language variations which are unconvincing in terms of 'authenticity' or individuation, because their speech habits are often the result of a mixture of misconception and error concerning a norm of 'correct' English that they subscribe to either explicitly or implicitly, which they fail to execute convincingly in respect to 'correct' performance at the level of pronunciation, intonation, grammar or idiom.

Consider first an example which shows an author intent on capturing the exact nuances of an observed speech habit. Paul Theroux, in a novel set in 1960s Singapore, *Saint Jack* (1973), makes his narrator reflect on the difficulty of transcribing the exact inflections of a localized form of expression with a mixture of satire and realism:

> Big Hing was especially agitated and saying everything twice. 'Sit down, sit down', then, 'We got a problem, we got a problem'.
>   True Chinese speech is impossible to reproduce without distraction, and in this narrative I intend to avoid the conventional howlers. The 'flied lice' and 'No tickee, no shirtee' variety is really no closer to the real thing than the plain speech I have just put in Big Hing's mouth. Chinese do more than transpose *r* and *l*, and *v* and *b*, and *s* and *sh*. They swallow most of their consonants and they seldom give a word an ending: a glottal stop amputates every final syllable. So what Big Hing really said was, 'Shi' duh" and, 'We go' a pro'luh' ....
> (Theroux 1973: 11)

The habits of pronunciation satirized by Theroux are not an isolated phenomenon. The case of Singlish continues to be debated in contemporary Singapore. On the one hand, the government promotes a 'Speak Good English' campaign. On the other hand, some Singaporeans continue to endorse Singlish, simply by continuing to use it, or by enjoying its exaggerated use in television serials that permit audiences to laugh with and laugh at its many idiosyncrasies. At a more elevated level, readers of poetry can also point to the 'Singlish' poems of Arthur Yap, whose skilful ventriloquism captures with an equivocal mix of satire and sympathy precisely those speech habits that such campaigns would like to eradicate. '2 mothers in a h d b playground' has become a classic of the literary canon. Its initial stanzas will have to suffice here to suggest what is at stake in the debate over Singlish:

> ah beng is so smart,
> already he can watch tv and know the whole story.
> your kim cheong is also quite smart,
> what boy is he in the exam?
> this playground is not too bad, but i'm always
> so worried, car here, car there.

>   at exam time, it's worse.

> because you know why?

>   kim cheong eats so little.
> give him some complan. my ah beng was like that,
> now he's different. if you give him anything
> he's sure to finish it all up.
>
>   (Yap 2000: 101)

Yap's literary use of linguistic ventriloquism highlights the differences in norms that are activated when linguistic performance gives the slip to its idealizations. Some condemn Singlish speech habits as a form of incompetence; others sidestep the issue of whether Singlish is a form of performative incompetence promoted to the level of localism by insisting that if Singlish speech habits do take place, then they are a 'slice of life', and therefore 'legitimate' as a truth about the cultural anthropology of local speech habits which art can, and should, represent. The Singapore government regards representation of undesirable (because economically counterproductive) speech habits as a form of condoning that is tantamount to an oblique endorsement of the reprehensible. For the reader of literary texts, the critical issue is slightly different. What any critical reader might want to keep apart are acts of stylistic ventriloquism (of the kind exemplified by the Yap poem) and authorial styles whose individuality is based on failing to achieve, or managing to be ignorant of, collective and consensual norms about what constitutes competence for a given community of language users. What the Yap poem highlights is that while the People's Action Party (PAP) may have resolved to eliminate Singlish, many Singaporeans regard their version of the language with a more complicated ambivalence in which amused self-deprecation is mixed with the recognition that, for better and worse, Singlish serves as a unique marker of local identity.

For an example of sustained linguistic ventriloquism, we can turn briefly to another Singapore text, Stella Kon's play *Emily of Emerald Hill* (1984). Set in 1950, the one-character play is memorable for its linguistic representation of a specific combination of ethnicity, migrant history and linguistic hybridity: 'a modern Nonya', a descendant of Chinese migrants settled in Malaya for several generations, whose community has adopted and adapted several aspects of the Malay language and culture:

> Hello, Bee Choo? Emily here. Just want to remind you, don't forget dinner tomorrow night, Richard's birthday. Ya-lah, the boy so big now, grown-up already, going to England next month. I asked him whether he's happy to go, you know what he said? 'Mummy, to go to England happy also – but to leave my home very sad lah!' Yah, rascal-lah dia. All right, give my regards to your mother eh, hope she'll be better soon … I see you eh Bee Choo? Bye-bye.
>
> (Kon 1989: 2)

Yet another aspect of the linguistic reality of multilingual societies such as Singapore is refracted by the plays of Kuo Pao Kun (1939–2002), who developed the practice of putting together a multilingual play script based on active contributions by a large ensemble of contributing actors drawn from all the major language groups in Singapore. The published text of a play like *Mama Looking for Her Cat* (1988) provides a monochromatic and translated English transcript of what is performed on stage in several languages: Hokkien, Mandarin, Cantonese, Teochew, Tamil and English. Given this mix, any production, even in Singapore, must expect some part of the play script to be partially or completely opaque to substantial portions of the audience. The production accepts that likelihood, committed to the representation of exactly that kind of multilingualism in which not everyone engaged in conversation with someone else necessarily follows everything said by the other, or succeeds in communicating everything through whichever language is used. A selective and deliberately constructed 'fidelity' to the multilingual and not-always-mutually-comprehensible dimension of social reality thus becomes an explicit part of the intention subsidizing the play, independent of, or parallel to, whatever else is being conveyed through dialogue and plot. Here is a brief example from a scene 'between a Hokkien-speaking old woman and a Tamil-speaking old man anxiously trying to understand each other':

> MAMA: I have a cat.
> OLD MAN: I also have a cat.
> MAMA: My cat is this small.

MAMA: My cat is this small.
OLD MAN: Ah, we all have a cat.
OLD MAN: Your cat meow, meow. My cat miu, miu.

(Kuo 2000a: 129–30)

The stylized simplicity, repetition and contrast of *meow* and *miu* make a crucial point: the creative potential realized through the performance of multilingual predicaments involving linguistic parallelism is a sociological corollary to the kind of interaction that leads to code-switching and code-mixing. Their coexistence provides a fuller account of multilingual societies than either language on its own.

The willingness to attempt such representations, and the confidence that they might gain recognition as more than local curiosities, was slow in developing. Its development was based on the realization that such representations captured a unique aspect of local reality, which had no equivalence in Standard English, or in societies using other varieties of English. The significance of authors such as Arthur Yap, Stella Kon and Kuo Pao Kun is that they helped local audiences acquire a measure of linguistic self-recognition and self-respect which are neither accessed nor recuperated through mastery over Standard English, however admirable that accomplishment might be for other reasons.

Conclusion

- English is used throughout Southeast Asia in bilingual and multilingual contexts.
- The ways in which English is spoken in Southeast Asia differs from Standard English in small but distinctive ways that are more noticeable in spoken than in written English.
- The use of spoken English in Southeast Asia has a complex social dimension in relation to indigenous languages; the use of English for literary purposes creates new relations between indigenous and West-derived cultural traditions and practices.
- The use of English in Southeast Asia has led to the assimilation of elements of English into indigenous languages.
- The influence of indigenous languages has also led to varying degrees of change in terms of the speech patterns, syntax, intonation and vocabulary of each country and literary tradition using English in Southeast Asia.

4 Malaysian and Singaporean writing to 1965

Overview

Though the British presence in the Malayan peninsula dates back to the late eighteenth and early nineteenth centuries, indigenous writing in English began much later, and its first appearance in the late nineteenth century was confined to a specific minority. Major developments in creative writing in English had to wait until after the end of the Second World War. While the British prepared for decolonization and independence for the region in the 1950s, Malayan writers set about the task of defining or inventing a Malayan consciousness in English. Much of the early writing turned to the genre of poetry, which continues to be the elite genre preferred among writers. Fictional writing followed, much of it in the form of the short story, while drama remained the slowest genre to take root in the region, indicating the difficulty experienced by playwrights in reconciling the needs of plausible theatrical representation with local English speech rhythms and intonation.

The British in Malaya

The spread of British influence over the Malayan peninsula was gradual, just as the subsequent dissemination of the English language to the peoples of the region was selective. The obliqueness of both developments helps account for the fact that though the English landed in Malaya and Singapore in the late eighteenth and early twentieth century respectively, writing in English did not consolidate into a recognizable local tradition until after the Second World War.

Western schooling was brought to Malaya by missionaries. The first English-medium schools were set up soon after the establishment of the Straits Settlements. Stamford Raffles, who acquired the island of Singapore for the British East India Company, devised a plan for a 'Malay College' and a 'Singapore Institution', which would assemble knowledge about local cultures and societies while educating the sons of the local aristocracy in English and educating Company officials in local languages (Wong and Ee

1975: 39). Raffles died while his institution was little more than a dream, but his ideas on governance set the pattern for the colonial stereotype of the idyllic Malay: 'The Malay, living in a country where nature grants (almost without labour) all his wants, is so indolent, that when he has rice, nothing will induce him to work' (Alatas 1971: 28). This stereotype helps explain the reluctance with which the British brought their language to Malaya, a reluctance reinforced by the unforeseen consequences of English education in British India.

In *Indian Education: Minute of the 2nd of February, 1835*, Macaulay argued that since 'a single shelf of a good European library was worth the whole native literature of India and Arabia', the only consideration before the Company was the creation of Indian intermediaries who could be taught enough English to make them 'a class who may be interpreters between us and the millions whom we govern; a class of persons, Indian in blood and colour, but English in taste, in opinions, in morals, and in intellect' (1952: 729–30). His programme of cultural conditioning needed a secular curriculum, and the English literary canon was thus introduced into India well before it became part of the general educational system in Britain. What was meant to transform a few soon spread to the many, producing three types of individual not anticipated by the Anglicist lobby: malcontents, nationalists and writers.

British administrators feared similar results in Malaya. E. C. Hill, the Inspector of Schools in Malaya, suggested in 1884 that teaching English to Malays would render them 'unwilling to earn their livelihood by manual labour', thus creating 'a discontented class who might become a source of anxiety to the community' (Pennycook 1998: 98). Meanwhile, the British also faced the responsibility of catering to the educational needs of a population that had begun expanding as a direct consequence of two developments, one endorsed, and the other initiated, by them. The first was the rapid growth of the Malayan tin-mining industry (controlled by ethnic Chinese business interests, and leading to the large-scale import of fresh labour from mainland China). The second was the British investment in rubber plantations and in the expansion of rail and road networks (which created an intensive need for workers that was fulfilled by the recruitment of cheap labour from India).

The demographic changes produced by these two developments laid the foundations of long-term tensions between immigrant minorities and the indigenous Malay majority. These were exacerbated by the British decision to 'protect' the Malays (by keeping their education confined to Malay), while the immigrant minorities had the option of sending their children to schools using their respective native languages or to schools using English. By 1938, there were over 100 English schools, 788 Malay schools, 331 Chinese schools and several hundred Tamil schools in British Malay (Solomon 1988: 10–16). Three features of the selective dissemination of English in Malaya are worth noting: those conversant in English formed a relatively small class of elite colonials. The census of 1957 reported only 6 per cent of the population of approximately 400,000 using English on a daily basis. Second, the role of language in education got tied up with ethnic divisions between Malays and the immigrant races. Third, Malay nationalism grew to be resentful of English as a language it had been kept from, which it then sought to marginalize in its programme of national education.

Malayan writing in English 1800–1945

Before 1945, British and other visitors and residents produced extensive writing about the Malay peninsula. Non-Europeans commenced writing in English by the second half of the nineteenth century, in the school magazines of elite schools such as Raffles Institution in Singapore. Initial efforts were sporadic, tentative and imitative of European forms and subject-matter. By the 1890s an English-speaking elite had come into being in the Straits Settlements that had different interests from those of the colonial government. English-language periodicals such as the *Straits Eurasian Advocate* and the *Indo-Chinese Patriot*, commencing publication in 1888 and 1895 respectively, are testimony to the existence of non-European Anglophone communities. In literary terms, the most important publication was the quarterly *Straits Chinese Magazine* (1897–1907), founded by two Straits Chinese men who returned from study in the United Kingdom, Lim Boon Keng and Song Ong Siang.

Although the magazine's title affiliated it to a specific community, the Straits Chinese or King's Chinese (an acculturated community in the Straits Settlements who played Macaulay's envisioned role as an intermediary class between the colonizers and the colonized), from the outset the publication had wider ambitions. Modelled on contemporary British equivalents such as *Blackwood's* and *Cornhill*, the magazine featured a variety of articles, editorials, brief news items, poetry and short stories. The short fiction is, in retrospect, the most important, constituting the first body of indigenous creative writing in English from the region.

Many of the stories are didactic, urging young Straits Chinese men against the temptations of gambling and moral dissipation. Others argue, strategically, for recognition for the Straits Chinese in colonial society. Thus 'Lost and Found' by the pseudonymous Lew See Fah (i.e. Lucifer, possibly a pseudonym for Song Ong Siang) describes the detention of a young Straits Chinese man on a trumped-up charge, and his struggle to claim the right of a British subject to be tried under British law. In Wee Tong Poh's 'Is Revenge Sweet?', the perspicacity of a Straits Chinese doctor in finding out the truth behind a wrongful conviction is contrasted with the incompetent bumbling of the European Inspector Catspaw of the Gambling Suppression department.

Song and Lim, qualified as a lawyer and a doctor respectively, knew only too well the trials of having to work with colonial officials who occupied positions of authority and yet had no professional training. Further stories engage with the complexity of a colonial life world, and the formation of community identities in the interstices of colonialism. Chia Cheng Sit's 'From My Father's Diary', attempts, as would future generations of Malaysian and Singapore writers, to found contemporary identity by exploring a hybrid past located in Singapore itself. 'The Travels of Chang Ching Chong', in contrast, portrays the process of migration to China in a fantastic narrative reminiscent of Swift's *Gulliver's Travels*. It concludes with representations of contemporary Singapore through the palindrome 'Ganiserop', with the injustices of colonialism represented as an inverted gender order in which females oppress and buy and sell males.

The short stories and poems in the *Straits Chinese Magazine* at times protested against injustice within the colonial order of things, but they never envisioned the overthrowing of the order. Indeed, their disruptive power perhaps came from mimicry, from their repetition of an Englishness that was not quite English. Thus the poem 'The Bellicose Mongolians' pictures the Straits Chinese volunteer as a loyal subject of the British Crown faced with the derision of both the expatriate community and the 'scant sympathy' of the 'elders of his people' ('Straits Chinese Volunteer' 1901: 135–136). At times such mimicry seems no more than an accession to colonial values, as in some of the stories and in later writings by the Straits Chinese, such as the elaborate praise of British rule in Lim Boon Keng's novel *Tragedies of Eastern Life* (1927), or the promotion of thrift, hard work, discipline and subjection to the demands of capital in the narrative of Yap Pheng Geck's 'The Coolie' in the later *Straits Chinese Annual* (1930). At others, it provides sharp dislocations. The short story 'Traveller's Rest' by 'H. G. F.' depicts a Straits Chinese traveller crossing the wilds of Northumberland, in the very north of England, in order to rendezvous with an acquaintance from Malaya. In a strategic inversion of colonial discourse, it is England's present-day inhabitants who become savages, while the English landscape is as exotic as any Malayan jungle. A further development might be seen in the writings of Ruth Huang, born in Singapore but resident in China, who abandoned any attempt to describe a hybrid present and wrote a series of historical novels based on three of four legendary Chinese beauties, *Yang Kuei-fei* (1924), *Hsi Shih* (1931) and *Chao Chun: Beauty in Exile* (1934), using her Chinese name and her husband's surname to become Wu Shu-Chiung.

Outside the Straits Chinese community, English-language writing was sporadic. Gregory de Silva, a Eurasian writer from Malacca, published four novels on a wide range of topics that drew on various community histories. *Only a Taxi Dancer* (1939) concentrates on the Nanyang Chinese, following a refugee who leaves Shanghai for Singapore and then returns to China as a nurse in the war of resistance against Japan. *The Princess of Malacca* (1937) and *Lupe* (1939) are historical novels set in Portuguese Malacca. *Suleiman Goes to London* (1938) recalls Hugh Clifford's novels *Saleh* and *Sally: A Sequel* (1908) in depicting the reverse voyage of a colonial subject to the imperial metropolis and his attempted return to Malaya: however, the novel does not make strategic use of expatriation to practise any form of anti-colonial critique, and indeed resorts to stereotypical depictions of Malay indolence. Francis Ng's *F. M. S. R.* (1935) envisions Singapore in terms similar to the London of T. S. Eliot's *The Waste Land*, the poem's rhythms imitating a modern symbol of speed and the compression of time, the Federated Malay States Railway of the title.

By the 1940s, however, new concerns were beginning to penetrate what we might now call Malayan Literature in English. In exile in London in the years of the Second World War, law student Sinnathamby Rajaratnam (who would later rise to the position of an independent Singapore's first minister for culture) wrote discursive essays examining the situation in Malaya and the prospects for decolonization, and a series of short stories. Rajaratnam's prose grapples with the new forces of anti-colonial nationalism: in his essays, published in the American journal *Asia*, he looks ahead to the problematics of a new Malayan nationalism, and the competing claims of both the indigenous Malay community and the children of Chinese and Indian migrants for citizenship. His stories, however, sidestep the question of a multicultural polity by being set in monocultural communities: either in villages from the Ceylon of his childhood, or, in the case of the single story 'The Tiger', in a rural Malay *kampong* (village), presumably in a rural area of the peninsula. Most of Rajaratnam's stories are not concerned with opposition to colonialism, but rather with the possibility of action that might transform traditional societies presented to the reader as feudal: in many of the stories, the energy of youthful peasant farmers threatens the age-old privilege of landlords. Although written in London, Rajaratnam's fiction introduces a nationalist politics that would become a much more central concern of fiction and poetry written in Malaya in the immediate post-war period.

British Malaya: refers to the Malayan states that came under British control during the period from 1874 to 1957.

Malay: refers to the language indigenous to the Malayan peninsula, and also to the people born in the region.

Malaysian: refers to the citizens of modern Malaysia, which became independent in 1957.

The ethnic profile of the Malayan peninsula changed dramatically during the period of British control, and these changes laid the foundation of many subsequent political and cultural developments. In 1910, Malays were the dominant majority on the peninsula; by 1957, recent immigrants represented a much larger proportion of the total population: 36 per cent Chinese and 11 per cent Indians. The Independence Act of 1957 specified Malay as the national language (while English was retained as an 'alternate official language'). When the policy was reviewed in 1967, the Chinese lobby failed to secure recognition for Chinese as a national language. Racial riots between the Chinese and the Malays erupted after the elections of 1969. In 1976, 'English-medium primary schools were completely converted to National schools ... Thus ended approximately a century of English-medium primary schooling in the Malay states' (Solomon 1988: 46). The next twenty years saw English held at arm's length (except as a second language in schools) and the Malay language promoted in the context of a growing tendency towards Islamic fundamentalism.

The People's Action Party, or the PAP as it is commonly known in Singapore, has been the dominant political party in the island-state after its creation in the pre-independence Singapore of the mid-1950s, and its victory in the general elections of 1963. The PAP has ruled Singapore over the entire period of its status as an independent republic, from 1965 to 2009.

In Singapore, PAP policy since independence has designated Malay as the national language and nominated three other languages to the status of official languages: Chinese (Mandarin), English and Tamil. The nomination of English was meant to help neutralize ethnic loyalties, while making it easier for Singapore to join the global community of international English; that of Malay retained a link that respected history and geography; that of Tamil protected the rights of the Indian-origin minority; and that of Mandarin helped Singapore retain cultural links to mainland China, while also helping defuse clan and dialect loyalties based on the languages and cultures of the Chinese provinces from which the majority of Singapore's population had migrated. In 1969, the government implemented the policy of requiring a second language at the School Certificate Examination. The containment of dialects and ethnic languages continued with the introduction of a new national system in 1987, which made English the first language in all school education.

The effect of policy on society is evident from the fact that the predominant household language for the period from 1980 to 1990 showed a decline in the use of Chinese dialects, inversely linked to the growth of English (Gopinathan 1998: 20). On the positive side, the PAP managed to avoid the kind of fallout that ethnic tensions produced in many parts of Asia and elsewhere; on the negative side, the cost has been the cultural attrition suffered by the dialect cultures of Singapore, and the worry that the dominance of English might contribute to a cultural vacuum in a situation where the desire to pursue social and economic modernity has to be reconciled with the attempt to define and support alleged 'Asian values'.

Malayan poetry in English: after the Second World War

After the Second World War, the absence of a local university was increasingly noted in the Malayan peninsula. This lack was filled in 1949 through the merger of Raffles College and the King Edward VII College of Medicine into the University of Malaya. The creation of a campus for the university in Singapore was followed by the setting up of a second campus in Kuala Lumpur in 1959. The two entities became autonomous universities in 1962. School, college and university were the institutions through which a small minority of the Malayan population gained access to English, to the jobs and professions that were opened up by English, and to the Western literary canon that was rapidly disseminated through these institutions in the colonies. College and university life provided a catalyst for brief forays into the occasional essay, story or verse modelled on Western styles and genres. Very few among those who appeared in student publications during the 1930s and 1940s sustained their literary interest for long. The handful who did laid the modest foundations for a new literary tradition.

The cultural aspirations of typical student publications of the 1930s, as evident from the *Raffles College Magazine*, were derivative. Colonial education reproduced in the Malayan an admiration for the Western canon, which was transmitted with earnest enthusiasm by numerous British teachers. Colonial dependency fed on the illusion that there was little cultural distance between Britain and its colonies, while colonial diffidence fed on the opposite delusion, that to imbibe British culture diligently in the colonies was a sufficient end in itself. This double bind lasted until perceptions about Western imperialism changed during and after the Second World War. Once the British had been defeated ignominiously by the Japanese, their Empire lost its aura of invincibility. The realization that political autonomy was close at hand began to grow. Its impact on literary writing was oblique and gradual. It took the form of a determination to use the colonial language for creative writing but adapt it to the task of representing Malayan themes.

When the *Raffles College Magazine* resumed publication in 1946 as the *Raffles College Union Magazine*, the poems that appeared there were just as gauche as those of the previous decade. For example, E. H. Lim's attempt to represent Singapore at the time of the Japanese invasion in the poem 'On the Road to Arab Street' begins: 'From deep its bleeding heart / This broken city disgorged / A trail of suffering humanity' (Vol. 1: 28). One of the early university poets, Richard Ong, did better with his poem 'Rumba', which acquired a degree of contemporaneous fame for its articulation of the pluralities of a multicultural society. The literary material that appeared in *The Cauldron*, which started publication in 1947, and in *The Malayan Undergrad*, which started publication in 1948, remained insipid. Likewise, an anonymously written 'Ode to an Amoeba', from *The Cauldron* (1949), begins, 'Wriggle, wriggle, little cell / How I wonder what the hell / Makes you wriggle all the time / In an undulating rhyme' (Anon., 1949: 28). If the verse of the period is not always as naïve, it is often lugubrious or portentous, as in the case of 'Asian Peasant' by Richard Ong from Singapore, which asks with a quaint rhetoric that provides an inadvertent pastiche of eighteenth-century stylistic traits: 'What sweeper / Pale to the ears with eddied dust will scorn / His pariah's task? Or what frail earth-carrier, / Caught in the dread chores an ant, will face / His tomorrow but with pride for his place?' (Ong 1949: 22).

With the formation of a new university, a number of new magazines began publication: *Raffles College Bulletin* (1948), *Magazine of the University of Malaya Students Union* (1949–52, 1960), *The New Cauldron* (1950–60), *Chichak* (1954), *Write* (1957–58), and *Hujan Mas* (1959), followed in the 1960s by *Phoenix* (1960), *The Seed* (1960–62), *Lidra* (1961), *Monsoon* (1961), *Varsity* (1961–62), *Focus* (1961–62), *Tumasek* (1964), *Tenggara* (1967–90) and *Commentary* (1968–). Doggerel made room for recognition that writing needed a new frame of mind if it was to remain relevant to its time and place. The notion that a national or regional consciousness had to be invented – rather than simply being represented – had been voiced at least as early as in 1931–32 in a student essay published in *Raffles College Magazine*: 'What are the forces that will bind together the different racial elements into one Malayan or rather Malaysian type?' (Vol. 2.3: 7). This concern came to the fore in the late 1940s. In 1949, the author of an essay on 'A University for Malaya' urges recognition that 'Malaya does not live by tin and rubber alone. We must have a Malayan culture' (Vol. 3.3: 24). Another essay, on 'Malayan literature as seen through the eyes of J. J. [Puthucheary]', from *The New Cauldron*, laments that 'the stress on English literature has curbed the growth of our literary sense', and recommends that 'Malayan literature should present accurately this country and its people' (1950–51: 18, 19).

A radio talk of 1950 on 'Talking of Verses by Malayan Students' by Beda Lim diagnoses the problem thus: 'if a student in Malaya writes about flowers and trees and lakes, or things like that, he is doing no more than echoing the English poets he has learnt at school ... The great difficulty in a place like this is that we do not have a tradition of poetry [in English] to fall back upon' (1949–50: 60). The solution was to 'try and make something new out of the bits and pieces that you could point to and say: That is Malayan' (1949–50: 60). The kind of new writing that Lim spoke of began to appear gradually. The first volume of poetry in English published from the region was Wang Gungwu's *Pulse* (1950), a slim booklet comprising sixteen pages. It was followed by Lim Thean Soo's equally slim *Selected Verses* (1951), and *Poems (1951–1953)* (1953),

Edwin Thumboo's *Rib of Earth* (1956), Wong Phui Nam's *Toccata on Ochre Sheaves* (1958), and Ee Tiang Hong's *I of the Many Faces* (1960). These publications represent the first significant verse output in English from writers of the Malayan peninsula. Wang Gungwu, Lim Thean Soo and Goh Sin Tub stand out in historical significance for the lead they took in approaching the challenge and opportunity of injecting local elements into their verse; while Edwin Thumboo, Ee Tiang Hong and Wong Phui Nam were noteworthy for sustained commitment to their craft, although each published sparingly after the first decade, and took a while before coming out with a second and third volume. Wang and Goh wrote in English and Malay in their early years: Goh won a prize for a book in Malay in 1964. Wang was born in what later became Indonesia, educated in Malaysia, China, Singapore and England, and also published stories and poems under the pen-name Awang Kedua. He took up an academic career as a historian and became a distinguished academic administrator in Malaysia, Australia, Hong Kong and Singapore, but did not return to literary writing after the early 1960s. In subsequent years, Goh and Lim were drawn more towards fictional prose than poetry, and after busy careers which did not always leave time for writing, each achieved recognition largely for works in prose.

Wang Gungwu's verse made an impact on his contemporaries. It was written in a variety of styles and tones. A poem like 'Plus One' illustrates what he could accomplish when rhythmic propulsion was willing to remain close to conventional metre. More often, he preferred free verse characterized by precise imagery, much of it influenced by T. S. Eliot, and given to turning post-Romantic symbols inside out, thus fixing the reader's gaze steadily on the more disorienting aspects of contemporary realities. The first poem of *Pulse* (1950), 'To Tigerland', is typical of the verve with which allusions to local detail are made a staple of the verse: 'The lallangs leer at the breed of mosquitoes, / The parangs rust in their sheaths. / There the wood-smoke has turned to dust; / There the children make their wreaths' (1950: 1). The title poem shows a determination to make the allusion to local detail an insistent part of the reader's experience: 'Baju biru full of tailings, / And sams unhooked at the neck' (1950: 2). Taken a step further, the inclusion of Malay or Chinese words and phrases creates a polyglot effect, as in the final lines of the penultimate stanza of 'Ahmad': 'Orang puteh has been kind. / Only yesterday his brother said, / "Can get lagi satu wife lah!"' (1950: 13). Such experiments were called *Engmalchin*.

Engmalchin: A portmanteau term that came into currency during the early 1950s in British Malaya, and alluded to the way in which the English of a poem made room for Malay and Chinese words and phrases. Several young poets tried this strategy in the 1950s, and the use of occasional scraps of multilingual usage continues to occur in later verse writing from Malaysia and Singapore, which remains indebted to the mimeticism that subsidized *Engmalchin* for a while. The systematic use of *Engmalchin* in verse proved short-lived, since its localism risked alienating English-language readers unfamiliar with Malay or Chinese.

A more interesting alternative was tried out by Hedwig Aroozoo (later Hedwig Anuar). The few poems she published in periodicals during 1951–56 remain notable for their wit and their robust handling of contemporary political realities. In 1956, as tensions built up over whether Singapore would merge with Malaysia, the chief minister of Singapore, Mr Lim Yew Hock, spoke of the situation to the media in terms of a courtship: 'Well, gentlemen, the love-making has started. As you know yourselves, once you start making love, there are always chances of a marriage' (Anuar 1999: 16–17). Aroozoo's poem 'Love-Match?' takes up the analogy in neat burlesque:

> The lady says she's willing
> She declares the prospect thrilling,
> But the gentleman isn't quite so sure.
> He's not quite so romantic,
> He's driving her quite frantic –
> Can it be that she lacks enough allure?
> (1999: 16)

While the young men around her were busy getting the weary tones of T. S. Eliot into their verse and then busy keeping them out, her handling of a serio-comic mode in 'Rhyme in Time' (included in *Litmus One*) produces effects that are at once exuberant and serious.

In the case of her contemporaries, Lim Thean Soo and Goh Sin Tub, the sights, sounds and feel of Singapore are kept in focus, though sharply observed detail and a plain, unfussy approach to diction and rhythm cannot always avoid a sense of the prosaic. In contrast, Edwin Thumboo's *Rib of Earth* (1956) remains a fascinating first volume. Of mixed Tamil and Chinese parentage, Thumboo was educated in Singapore and worked in the civil service before joining academic life in 1966, and becoming a senior educational administrator and the most influential English language poet in Singapore. The twenty-two short poems of *Rib of Earth* establish a sense of style that is suggestive yet mysterious, with a knack for beginning poems on a note whose resonance evades paraphrase: 'Silence growing on a stem' (1956: 2); 'Mist squats on God's land. / We see the day's mood change' (1956: 4); 'Day loses its transparency, / The winds fold up and die' (1956: 19).

Not all the poems carry suggestiveness to a satisfying conclusion. Thumboo's predilection for a taut, muscular tone forces more compression than suits the subject-matter. In his long poem, 'The Cough of Albuquerque' (*Write* 1958), the choice of a lyric mode fails to secure a progression that needs more than brilliant images to sustain the burden of the poet's intent. Regardless, *Rib of Earth* is free of the desire to supply local colour as an oblique way of representing a Malayan consciousness. The most ambitious poem is also the most successful: 'For Peter Wee'. The influence of Eliot can be heard, but the echoes hover in a poetic space the poet makes his own. The first section reiterates a question: is there anything more than 'a lipless sleep' 'beyond the ash'? The tight quatrains of the second section name the pitfalls – illusions, lies, retreats – that make knowing difficult. The final meditative section harmonizes the thirst for knowledge with the cunning of the gods and concludes with the idea that to accept the breathing of the earth is to refrain from asking if the birds 'Make lamentation for the day's return'. *Rib of Earth* puts together a small body of writing confident of making English viable for poetry in the Malayan peninsula.

Thumboo's contemporary and friend Ee Tiang Hong was born in Malacca of Chinese parents whose ancestors had settled in the region for several generations. He worked as an educationist in Malaysia until growing unease about the racial tensions that followed the riots of 1969 estranged him from what he had regarded until then as his homeland, and he migrated to Australia. The poems in *I of the Many Faces* (1960) are dry in tone. Faith and hope about god or mankind are subdued in light of the evidence of human frailty. Ee's characteristic manner ranges from the ironic to the sardonic. He is at his best in a poem like 'I of the Three Monkeys', which dramatizes the voice of a government puppet who asks for mitigation of harsh judgement against him on the grounds that he has tried to resemble the proverbial three monkeys in not hearing complaints, in not seeing the mob's retreat from justice, and in not speaking for or against grievances or retribution. The poem's irony that this declaration should stand in for apology and atonement is tight-lipped but sharp in its moral outrage.

Ee's 'Song of a Young Malayan' offers an alternative to the aims of *Engmalchin*. The poet as ventriloquist takes the representation of local speech habits to a grey zone where the reader could be left undecided about whether the poet intended affection, amusement, derision or acceptance of the fate of the English language at the hands of a Malayan consciousness: 'Not say I don't appreciate poetry: / But you speak of poetry which have no rhyme' (1960: 13). Ee's edginess about English as the agent of acculturation goes deep. The final poem of the volume begins by wondering if the enterprise of writing poems in English in Malaya is a 'Dead End' (1960: 24). The idea feels like chasing 'frail butterflies'. He wonders if there is any point wasting all his time trying to sing in 'mimicry of foreign birds', but the final stanza retrieves a cautious manifesto. If the 'mining pools' and 'latex flowing' of Malaya have to find embodiment in rhythm and song, their power will have to provide sustenance for a new poetry in English.

Our third significant poet of this period, Wong Phui Nam, was born in Kuala Lumpur to a Malaccan father and a mother who had moved recently from China to Malaysia. He studied at the University of Malaya between 1955 and 1959, taking an active role in producing *The New Cauldron* and in co-editing the anthology *Litmus One* (1958). After getting a degree in economics he moved on to a career in finance which kept him away from poetry for some part of his adult life. His *Toccata on Ochre Sheaves* (1958) comprises two pages of notes and six pages of verse arranged in five irregular sections of free verse. It was followed by a set of poems from the early 1960s published in the anthology *Bunga Emas* (1964), and collected in *How the Hills Are Distant* (1968). A curious feature about the poetry and its articulation of a sense of cultural alienation within Malaysia is that the writing gives no indication that in 1968 Wong married a Malaysian Muslim, and took the name Mohammed Razali.

Wong's work is mythopoeic in orientation and burdened by a sense of isolation, and an abiding sense of dereliction and fragmentation. Its style could be described as fluently neo-Romantic, though he complains of feeling awkward in using English in a Malaysia that has made all non-Malays feel like second-class citizens after independence. His imagination draws freely on Chinese culture to which he is linked through his immigrant paternity and on Western culture to which he declares an elective affinity. His poems neither fear obscurity nor avoid it; they appear emotionally self-preoccupied. They reveal the sincerity of one who feels, broods and writes of the psychic self with whatever means are at hand, desperately resourceful.

Toccata reanimates the Osiris myth, mindful of necrophilia: the death, dismemberment and metamorphosis of the Egyptian hero provide the loosely symbolic scaffolding on which the poem stretches its allegory of poetic melancholia. Wong has a vivid imagination, capable of producing lines like 'Tessellated in the liquid siftings of the moon' (1958: 64). He also suffers from never knowing when to stop with a good effect: metaphors and images are piled one upon another, excess and surplus unworried about becoming self-defeating.

Wong's poems of the early 1960s, collected in *How the Hills Are Distant* (1968), are more accessible than *Toccata*. They lament that the poet cannot establish 'commerce with the ghosts of those who died', and 'the land yields no speech to us' (V; text changed in 2006: 9). If he could establish a connection with the past and its cultural presences, that would extend 'the habitations of a private landscape' (VI; text changed in 2006: 11). Without that extension, there is only 'the mild hysteria of lalang, green under road-lamps' (VI; 2006: 12). The self separated from its (Chinese) lineage – and living among a (Malay) people whose demons and 'legendary kings' are lost to them – is like 'This branch of cut lime / hung by my amah by the door' (VII; 2006: 14). The annals of the Malays are like 'flotsam' in contemporary Malaysia (VIII; changed to 'jetsam', 2006: 16). Without the larger context supplied by access to a historical heritage, contemporary life is 'manic' and dead as stone (IX; 2006: 18). The poem ends on a note of defeat: here there are no shrines, nor pilgrimages, only 'a time to endure' (XX; 2006: 33). The rest of the volume shows Wong working with the Chinese classics, shoring these fragments in translation against his sense of ruin in Malaysia.

In general, Malayan verse of the 1950s promises more than it delivers, and is rarely free from uncertainty in respect to rhythm, tone, idiom, form and style. If outlandish diction was an obvious vice, a more insidious problem surfaces when poets respond to the expectation that 'Malayan literature should present accurately this country and its people' (J. J. [Puthucheary] 1950–51: 19). Was this to happen spontaneously or as something program-matic? When the British writer D. J. Enright took up a post as the Johore Professor of English at the University of Malaya in 1960, his inaugural lecture urged Malayans not to think of culture as something created by fiat or committee. Meanwhile, the dual problem confronted by the search for a local consciousness became apparent: what were the features that might be said to constitute Malayan thought or culture, given the ethnic differences between Malay, Chinese, Tamil, Eurasian and Europeans? What was the kind of English apt for the articulation and representation of such diversity? Since not everybody who regarded Malaya as a home was an indigenous Malay (a distinction reiterated lucidly in an editorial note to the December 1958 issue of *Write*), who had the right to define or describe 'Malayan'?

Enright cautioned local writers that 'the implied dichotomy between "social function" and experience or "self-expression" is a false one', reiterating the familiar British alternative, that literature should remain free of agendas, thus better able to attend to the role of 'a report on experience' (Edmund Blunden's phrase) or 'a criticism of life' (Matthew Arnold's phrase) (1962: 20). But Malayans new to writing would have none of that, and some version of the dichotomy between self-expression and social relevance continues to haunt the literary landscape of Singapore and Malaysia to this day. In another essay of the period, Enright drew attention to a technical problem: writers not native to English were likely to work with an uncertain sense of natural rhythm: 'most English verse written here is not so much characterized by rhythmical perversity ... as by rhythmical nullity. Nothing is definably wrong, but little is definitely right' (1959–60: 15). This may sound patronizing and severe, but it was not unwarranted.

Imagery and allusions were easy to produce, but once British metrical conventions had been set aside, the inability to sustain a viable poetic rhythm remained a problem. Images, allusions and symbols were of little help when the idiom was sing-song or flat-footed. It did not help that the verse insisted on wearing its influences rather obviously on its sleeve, and strived to sound thought-compelling in ways that often produced obfuscation and portentousness. Regardless, the best of the early verse is true to the spirit of experiment. Its willingness to take risks also gives proof that writing, taken seriously, needs a local habitation. In Thumboo, Ee and Wong, it also shows the first presentiments of memorable writing.

Several anthologies were published in the period that separated independence for Malaysia from independence for Singapore. *Litmus One* (1958) and *30 Poems* (1958) were confined to poetry, while *The Compact* (1958) represented short fiction and *Bunga Emas* (1964) represented fiction and verse in English, Chinese and Tamil. *Litmus One* (1958) contains material from the preceding decade of university writing, and shows itself eager to periodize the achievement of a mere decade into three partially overlapping phases. The first phase, according to the Introduction (probably written by Wong Phui Nam), consisted of writing by the 'pioneers', namely Lim Thean Soo, Beda Lim and Goh Sin Tub, who are described as creating a 'new Malayan nationalistic spirit', while drawing on the mental landscapes of T. S. Eliot and the Auden generation, and pursuing experiments with hybrid diction. The second phase refers to only one poet, Wang Gungwu, who is given credit for precise imagery, the introduction of Malayan idioms and imagery into his English verse, and for his influence on other poets. The third phase refers to poets who rejected *Engmalchin* and the influence of Eliot and the metaphysical poets, and put themselves to tutelage with Dylan Thomas, Hart Crane and Wallace Stevens. In 1958, Lloyd Fernando rejected the periodization as premature, but by 1962, Arthur Yap was willing to treat it matter-of-factly as a reasonable account of literary origins.

The second anthology of the same year, *30 Poems* (1958), was compiled by Tan Han Hoe. Circumspect in claim and modest in achievement, it collects a mere ten new poems for 1957–58, and highlights the work of four among its eight contributors: Lian Hock Lian, Oliver Seet, Tan Han Hoe and Wong Phui Nam. Lian Hock Lian is minimalist and muted in idiom, and rarely breaks free of neo-Romantic trappings. Oliver Seet and Tan Han Hoe are even less convincing in their struggle to invent novelties of diction or imagery. Tan describes a woman stretching across a couch as cold 'Across her impersonal longitude' (Tan 1958: 26), and Seet speaks, in 'Carnage Acre', of 'the garner of your wholesomeness' as unable to 'Resist the famine of tomorrow's termites' (1958: 23). The one positive feature of the anthology is the vivid simplicity of the poems by Wong, as in 'The afternoon swam by / like a giant fish / with red translucent scales' (1958: 32).

The third anthology, *Bunga Emas* (1964), was edited by T. Wignesan and published from London and Malaysia. It sets the pattern for many regional anthologies of the future in its multilingual inclusiveness: the three main non-majority languages of Malaysia are represented (English, Chinese, Tamil) in short stories and verse. English verse is represented by Wong Phui Nam, Goh Poh Seng, Oliver Seet, Lee Geok Lan, Tan Han Hoe and Awang Kedua

(Wang Gungwu); the English short story by S. Rajaratnam, Lee Kok Liang, Awang Kedua, Ooi Boon Seng and Wignesan. Lee Geok Lan was the only woman included in the anthology. Her handling of short, unpunctuated verse lines shows a degree of skill in the management of verse syntax, but the emotional temperature produces effects of verbal overkill (for example, 'I hold my heart / in a fist of fear', 1964: 46) and odd or awkward phrases ('the sun seeps my eyes', 1964: 47). Women poets publishing at this time, but not included in the anthology, include Wong May and Daisy Chan Heng Chee.

Other Malayan anthologies of the period, such as Lloyd Fernando's *Malaysian Poetry in English* (1966), or a special issue of the Indian monthly *Poetry* (July 1966) guest-edited by Edwin Thumboo, or *Tumasek Poems* (1966), also edited by Thumboo, and David Ormerod's *A Private Landscape* (1967), all show that there were many more poets writing in Singapore and Malaysia by the mid-1960s. The most notable feature of the new writing is the increase in the number of women poets: Fadzilah Amin, Muh Lan, Daisy Chan, Theresa Ng, (the expatriate Cecile Parrish), Pretam Kaur, Mauren Ten, Wong May, Claire Tham and others, including Shirley Lim and Lee Tzu Pheng (see Chapter 7).

Early Malayan fiction and drama

The college and university magazines of the 1930s, 40s and 50s included short stories almost as regularly as verse. The modest scale of the genre continues to find a steady supply of part-time and full-time adherents from the Malayan peninsula, even if the poets continue to attract more critical attention than the storytellers. Commentators have suggested that regional literary ambitions in English are more drawn to verse than prose, either because poetry is perceived as high-brow, or simply because it makes fewer demands on the author's awareness of society, leaving individuals free to attend to the needs of self-expression. The early fictional prose does not fare badly in any comparison with verse. A routine preference for narrative realism seems to have kept authors away from the kind of stylistic self-consciousness that blights much of the early verse. A desire to evoke the recent past in plain prose is natural when a country and its peoples are as prone to continual metamorphosis as the Malayan peninsula, and this motive ties the stories of Goh Poh Seng and Lim Thean Soo, for example, to the task of supplying the immigrant nation with a store of local memories. Dialogue does present problems: what idiom and vocabulary is one to adopt in using English to represent people speaking various forms of colloquial Malay, Chinese, Tamil, Singlish or Manglish?

An early story by Lloyd Fernando, 'On the Night of the Wayang', was criticized for its implausible rendition of the speech habits of Chinese farmers in Singapore by Ngiam Tong Dow, although he conceded that the story deserved recognition as one of 'the first and few attempts to assimilate and describe the local scene' (1958: 2). Fernando did better with his next story in the same journal, 'The Labourer', where a Tamil speaker's Singlish is captured more convincingly: 'Arokiam, brother! Why you not come in? Why you stand there?' (1958: 7). Issues of linguistic fidelity continued to hamper several of the stories collected in the first local anthology of short fiction, *The Compact* (1959). Several poets appear there as short story writers, among them Ee Tiang Hong, Lloyd Fernando and Awang Kedua (Wang Gungwu). The last named is more convincingly purposive in his stories than his verse, especially in the unusual way in which he stages a clash of values and personalities between a father and son in 'A New Sensation'. Ee and Arthur Yap (especially the latter's 'Noon at Five O'Clock' and 'A Five-Year Plan', which appeared in successive issues of *Focus*, 1962) turn in fine performances in the genre of the very short short-story.

Some of the most interesting early narratives in prose are in the form of autobiographical writing by two women, Sybil Kathigasu and Janet Lim. Each suffered torture at the hands of the Japanese, showed courage under stress and received succour from her Christian faith. Kathigasu's narrative *No Dram of Mercy* (1954), left incomplete at her death, gives a moving account of how this wife of an Ipoh doctor was betrayed to the Japanese by the wounded anti-Japanese guerrillas to whom she was attending. Shortly after the war, the author succumbed in London to an injury received from the boot of a Japanese soldier during her incarceration. Shirley Lim notes that 'as a part-Irish Eurasian', Kathigasu 'was a privileged woman in a colonized society', whose narrative goes against nationalist ideology in pre-independence Malaya because of 'the protagonist's unswerving pro-British stance, her sympathetic view of the MPAJA (Malaya People's Anti-Japanese Party), and her Catholic faith' (1994: 166). Regardless of the 'ideological gulf' between Kathigasu and 'ordinary Malayan people' (1994: 167), her narrative has the immediacy of first-hand experience recounted without fuss or exaggeration.

Janet Lim's *Sold for Silver* (1958) recounts the story of her life from early childhood to the end of the war. Its style is direct and its attitude to everything that happens to her matter-of-fact. Lim survived the war and distinguished herself as a nursing administrator in post-war Singapore. Born in Hong Kong, she was abandoned by her mother, and sold into slavery in Singapore in 1932 at a very young age. Later, she freed herself, joined the church, studied with missionaries, worked as a nurse, and fled by boat during the Japanese air-raids over Singapore. First shipwrecked, then captured and tortured by the Japanese, she escaped and returned to Singapore. The language of the narrative is acknowledged as having received smoothing by an English mentor; nevertheless, what comes through is a resilient author, as straightforward in writing as she appears to have been in her life. Both Kathigasu and Lim write in a manner that could be said to avoid any kind of self-reflexivity about narrative technique.

For a highly developed grasp of technique deployed in the service of a wide range of motifs and disquieting subjects, we turn to the fictional prose of Lee Kok Liang. Born in a Chinese family which had settled in Penang for several generations, Lee was educated locally, and in Melbourne and London. After returning to Malaysia, and after a brief stint in politics, he settled to the practice of law. His first story was published in a university magazine from Melbourne in 1949. Later he published stories from London, Malaysia and Singapore. A selection appeared as *The Mutes in the Sun and Other Stories* (1964), another as *Death is a Ceremony and Other Stories* (1992). One novel was published in his lifetime, *Flowers in the Sky* (1981). Another, based on a journal he kept as a student during the period 1952–54, was published posthumously as *London Does Not Belong to Me* (2003).

This novel shows Lee's capacity for generating intensity through a style that is direct yet laden with a constant suggestion of powerful forces at work beneath the seemingly mundane surface of everyday incidents and encounters. London itself figures as cold and busy, unmindful of the marginal young characters gathered there for a brief period from all corners of the declining Empire. The novel is narrated in the first person, with evident awareness of Western novelistic techniques. The narrator studiously avoids giving himself a name, although we are allowed to gather that he is from Southeast Asia, and is perceived as ethnically distinct by the young Australian and English women and men he is associated with in their bohemian existence. Sexual energies, sometimes of the ambiguous kind, are everywhere evident in the narrator, and in most of his friends. There are suggestions that the narrator is found attractive by white women, and also by at least one of his male friends. Sexual liaisons are set up and broken off in a complex chain: everybody seems to be intently searching for some significance that seems to elude them, always just out of reach. Political and racial awareness of difference flickers into recognition time and again. The novel proffers the reverse image of London and its denizens from that found in the Norman Collins novel *London Belongs To Me* (1945), which was made into a movie in 1948. Lee's novel shows the other side: the recent capital of Empire, drawing to its centre young men and women each in search of a sense of meaningful relation which remains unfulfilled.

The dark cast of mind incipient in this early novel comes to the fore in the short stories. Loneliness, incompleteness, deprivation, lack and need are dominant motifs in the early stories. John Kwan-Terry's description of one of Lee's stories can be treated as applicable to much of the early work: 'dispossession, rendered with comic or compassionate detachment' (1984: 147). Likewise, Syd Harrex speaks for most readers when he describes the first collection of short stories as presenting 'alarming, powerful profiles of individuals brutalised, ostracised, alienated by authority figures or fellow victims' (1994: 834a). Bernard Wilson notes that while the first novel and the early stories differ in their locale – the former set in London, the latter in 'the north-western states of Malaya/Malaysia against the backdrop of the Chinese-Malaysian community', they share a common preoccupation 'with isolation, repression and the mutilation (psychological and physical) of self' (Lee 2003: 315).

Lee could access a quieter tonal register, as in 'Return to Malaya', first published in *Encounter* (1954). There, the unnamed first-person narrator offers an imagistic account of a Malayan returning home, noting with neutral fascination his renewed encounter with the sharply specific quality of everything mundane that characterizes his corner of Malaya – children playing in the streets, the sounds of Peranakan Chinese speaking Hokkien, a servant learning how to ride a bicycle, the assorted smells typical of a Malayan village, the cry of a street hawker, the prettiness of the second wives of the better-off bourgeoisie, the village shopkeeper who stocks 'everything' (Lee 1963: 196), the narrator's variously fascinating grand-aunties and grand-uncle, and finally, his mother, 'her arms hugging a huge earthen jar in the corner' (1963: 202). Each detail is observed with a surreal clarity that is a special feature of Lee's early style, making him the most compelling author to have used English from Malaya during the 1950s and 1960s.

Drama has long remained a distant and impoverished cousin to verse and fiction in the Malayan peninsula, as in many postcolonial countries, and the reasons are not hard to find. David Birch notes that 'a problem of language and register' troubled all Singapore English writers who 'felt their work needed to be literary drama' (1997: 28). Theatrical performances in English may date back in Singapore to as early as 1833, but writing and publishing had always been easier than putting together a viable production. Until the 1950s, such productions were imports from the West, performed by expatriates for expatriates, with Shakespeare as the staple. Colonial dominance over this part of the entertainment sector left room for little that was not borrowed from the Western repertory, transplanted uneasily into the colonies. Lloyd Fernando recollected bitterly in 1957 that the last time a British theatrical company visited Malaya was in 1945 (when John Gielgud played Hamlet), and locals were admitted to the performance only in select numbers, as ushers: 'We can't say we are not to blame for a good deal of the superciliousness with which we are regarded in these matters' (1957: 8). Local productions were confined to Western fare: a University Dramatic Society production of Chekhov, and Gilbert and Sullivan by The New Scene Shifters are examples of typical fare.

Local theatre took a long time to grow out of its humble origins in amateur theatre and student productions. Birch draws attention to Ron Chandran-Dudley's *The Birthday Party* (1954), a production by The Experimental Theatre Club, the first such body that called for local material and authorship (1997: 24). In 1958, Goh Kiat Seng contrasted the reception given to two recent student productions, Lloyd Fernando's 'Strangers at the Gates' and

Mohd. Ali bin Abdul Aziz's 'The Decision': positive for the first, because 'it was almost an extract from the life of the English-educated section of Malayan society'; lukewarm for the latter, since 'a Malay plot in a Malay stage tradition was presented in English dialogue' (Goh 1958: 11). Much the same can be said of another short play by Aziz, 'The Fugitive' (1959), or his radio play 'The Reward' (1959). A new beginning was initiated in 1961 when a small group of young theatre enthusiasts, led by the Cambridge-educated Lim Chor Pee (b.1936), founded The Experimental Theatre Club, with the aim of supporting the production of local plays. Lim's *Mimi Fan* was staged in 1962, and *A White Rose at Midnight* in 1964, the same year as his essay 'Is Drama Non-Existent in Singapore'. Both plays were well received, but Lim withdrew from the theatrical scene to pursue a career in law. The narrative of English-language drama from the region that follows these developments is continued in Chapter 8.

Conclusion

- The influx of immigrants from China and India into Malaya changed the ethnic proportions of the Malayan peninsula during the late nineteenth and early twentieth centuries, with major consequences for educational policy, language use and sectarian politics.
- Malayan writing in English had a belated beginning in the late nineteenth century, followed by a few sporadic examples of creative writing in the first half of the twentieth century.
- New traditions in English from Malaysia and Singapore gathered momentum swiftly after the foundation of a university in Singapore (and later in Kuala Lumpur).
- Early writing, especially in the genre of poetry, set itself the task of defining a Malayan identity that was to be articulated in English.
- The genre of the short story established itself from the 1950s, but drama took much longer to get established, and much of the more interesting literary writing was in the genre of poetry.

5   Filipino writing to 1965

Overview

Systematic English-medium education policies under American colonialism led to an explosion of English-language writing from the 1920s through to the beginning of the Second World War. The use of English always existed in tension with the desire to create a new national language, Filipino, and debates in the 1930s frequently focused on the social utility of literature. Short fiction was the dominant form before the war, pioneered by Paz Marquez-Benitez, and reaching prominence in the hands of writers such as Arturo Rotor and Manuel Arguilla. The immediate post-war period saw the publication of more novels, and the most important English-language play in Filipino literary history: the most influential figure here was Nick Joaquin. While male writers dominated, women played significant roles. Paz Marquez-Benitez pioneered the short story in English, and the long-neglected poems of Angela Manalang Gloria are now receiving critical attention, as are the feminist stories of Estrella D. Alfon. In the period after the Second World War, Filipino literature in English attracted greater scholarly attention, and became institutionalized through being taught at universities. Despite the influence of New Criticism, however, a concern with the politics and indeed emancipatory potential of literary publication in English persisted among Filipino scholars and writers.

Educational policies and the dissemination of English

English came much later to the Philippines than to British colonies in Southeast Asia. There is a puzzling reference to the language in Apolinario Mabini's draft of the Malolos Constitution of the Independent Philippine Republic of 1899, in which the official language of the republic is proclaimed to be Tagalog, but supplemented by a note that when 'the English language shall be sufficiently extended throughout the Philippine archipelago, it shall be declared the official language' (A. Gonzalez 1980: 18–19). This clause vanished from the final draft of the constitution; ironically, the American colonial regime that defeated the forces of the Republic enabled

Mabini's ideas to be carried out at a pace he had not envisioned. The so-called Thomasites, American teachers who arrived in Manila on board the converted cattle ship the *S. S. Thomas* in August 1901, fanned out throughout the archipelago, introducing an English-medium education system whose scope far exceeded that of British colonies, with the aim of making English the lingua franca of the archipelago. Members of the Spanish-speaking *ilustrado* elite had previously sent their children to the universities of Europe; in 1903 the first hundred young *pensionados*, or overseas scholars, departed for study in colleges in the United States. In 1908, the flagship English-medium American University of the Philippines was established in Manila with sixty-seven students; within two decades, this would grow to nearly eight thousand.

While individual testimonies frequently cast doubt on the efficacy of the English-medium education system, especially in its initial years, statistics do show a profound change in language use. In 1870, only 2.4 per cent of the population claimed the ability to speak the colonial language of Spanish (A. Gonzalez 1980: 3); in the 1939 census this proportion remained constant at 2.6 per cent, but English speakers now constituted 26.6 per cent, slightly exceeding Tagalog speakers at 25.4 per cent (A. Gonzalez 1980: 26). Tagalog speakers would, of course, still largely inhabit only specific regions of the archipelago. Publishing in Tagalog and other languages of the Philippines continued and remained vibrant, and there was considerable influence between literatures in different languages. Literacy among the young in Spanish declined swiftly: 80 per cent of civil service examinees elected to be examined in Spanish in 1905, but the proportion had dwindled to 1 per cent in 1925. Yet the decline in literature in Spanish took at least a generation to become pronounced, and indeed the period from 1900 to 1942 has been characterized as the 'Golden Age of Philippine Spanish Literature' (Marino 1989: xix). By the 1920s and 1930s, however, there was a large urban English-speaking population, and an English-language reading public which provided a ready market for locally produced literature.

Filipino literature before the Second World War

Filipino literature in English began, as literature in English in Singapore and Malaya would, on the university campus. The University of the Philippines emphasized the humanities, with a College of Liberal Arts one of the first colleges established. In October 1910, the campus literary magazine, *College Folio*, was first published, containing essays, poetry and short fiction (Santillan-Castrence 1967: 549). Most early poems and short stories were imitative of English and American themes and forms. As the audience for writing in Spanish declined, some Spanish-medium writers, such as the poet Fernando Ma. Guerrero, crossed over into the medium of English, achieving only limited success. The increasing size of an English-reading public, however, widened opportunities.

Many commentators see 1925 as marking a key turning point; the *Philippines Free Press*, which had first published short stories in 1924, issued an invitation to Filipino writers to contribute creative work, and two women writers who would later be significant contributors to Philippine literature in English published their first works. The early poems of undergraduate Angela Manalang Gloria might initially appear little different from those of her contemporaries, influenced by American models such as Sarah Teasdale and Emily Dickinson; she was, however, to become one of the most influential early poets in English, making use of both Spanish and precolonial influences in her verse (Banzon 2003). The 1925 short story 'Dead Stars', by Paz Marquez-Benitez, marked a more radically new departure in both technical sophistication and thematic concerns. Its protagonist, Alfredo Salazar, has to choose between two women: the 'uniformly acceptable' Esperanza to whom he is engaged and the romantic but dangerous possibilities offered by the vivacious Julia Salas (Marquez-Benitez 1975: 13). In giving up Julia, Alfredo chooses a modernity based on social conformity, work and self-denial over the possibilities of romance. In effect, he chooses the modernity of American colonization over nostalgia for a Spanish past, noting at one point that 'Americans are rather essential for my entertainment' (1975: 9), and yet he is consumed by regret for the possibilities he has abandoned. Marquez-Benitez would publish only one further story, but as a teacher at the University of the Philippines she would mentor a later generation of writers.

The short story quickly became the pre-eminent form of literary expression in English in the Philippines before the Second World War. Its growth as a genre can be plotted by the annual listings of best stories by the writer and critic Jose Garcia Villa. In his first listing in 1927, Villa acknowledged the 'absence of literary qualities in our short stories' (2002: 35), but by 1930 he condemned critics who disparaged Filipino short fiction as 'the victims of an imbecilic superiority complex': the Philippines had 'produced excellent short stories' that stood comparison with the best produced internationally (2002: 53). By the early 1930s, short stories were regularly published by magazines such as the *Philippine Magazine, Philippines Herald Magazine, Sunday Herald Magazine, Graphic* and the *Philippines Free Press*, and were also central texts in a critical debate about the nature of Filipino literature in English. Villa had hundreds of stories to choose from every year: he could now turn his attention to the 'ignorance and stupidity' of editors who rejected more 'progressive' or experimental fiction (2002: 285). Even at this early moment, Philippine literature in English was transnational: several Filipino writers published stories in the United States in major journals such as *Prairie Schooner* or *Story*.

Most critical accounts of the development of fiction in the Philippines use a developmental model, in which writers move from imitation of European and North American models to more authentically Filipino self-expression. This was certainly writers' own experience at the time: reading widely in contemporary American literature, they sought to appropriate movements in fiction in English to represent and intervene in the society in which they lived. Thus Arturo Rotor's 1937 summative essay reviewing the previous decade of short-story writing is mostly devoted to an attempt to escape an anxiety of influence from a non-native tradition featuring, successively, Maupassant and Poe, Sherwood Anderson, Ernest Hemingway and William Saroyan. Only in the last section of the essay does the writer move away from negative definitions to consider in positive terms what a Philippine short story in English might be (1937a). Yet in retrospect it is possible to give a more nuanced reading of such a developmental narrative, an account that sees the stories as expressive of persistent contradictions in the colonial and proto-national modernity experienced by metropolitan writers.

In this reading, short stories move progressively from romantic, frequently rural settings, to more metropolitan ones, yet they persist in their use of gender as an allegory of colonial and an incipient national modernity. In Rotor's own celebrated 'Zita' (1930) a young teacher, Reteche, returns to a rural setting, imbued with ideals of romanticism and Enlightenment thought. He is engaged by a local landlord to tutor his daughter, Zita, who will eventually be going to the capital and entering society there. While the dramatic tension of the story is the unarticulated desire between Reteche and Zita, Reteche's attempt to mould the young woman into the image of someone he has previously desired is powerfully suggestive of the disciplinary processes of modernization. Rotor's 'Flower Shop', published a few years later in 1934, is set in urban Manila; its journalist narrator helps out in the shop in order to get inspiration for a feature story. The characters he encounters illustrate hypocritical social relationships in middle-class society in the capital; since the gift of flowers by men to women often lubricates such relationships, Rotor's social critique is again gendered. Women writers were perhaps particularly acute in their use of personal relationships as social metaphors. Estrella D. Alfon's 'One Day and the Next' (1938) uses a gift of clothing to a young woman to represent the taking on of social roles; Paz Latorena's 'Desire' (1928) employs a woman's search for love with an American to explore the exoticism expressed in America's paternalist relationship to the Philippines.

The first Filipino short story collections in English were Zoilo Galang's *Tales of the Philippines* (1923), *The Box of Ashes and Other Stories* (1924) and Jose Villa Panganiban's *Stealer of Hearts* (1927); much more influential was Jose Garcia Villa's *Footnote to Youth*, published in New York in 1933. Villa's range is impressive, ranging from the realist title story to stories such as 'Malakas' that show the influence of folk tales. The trilogy of stories 'Wings and Blue Flame' describes the beginning of Garcia's protracted sojourn in America, and is formally innovative, consisting of short, numbered paragraphs that give them almost the appearance of a prose poem; they are also overtly homoerotic. Perhaps most intriguing are the stories towards the end of the collection in which Villa revisits the heroic narrative of revolution embodied by national hero and novelist Jose Rizal. Stories such as 'The Son of Rizal' and 'The Man Who Looked Like Rizal' describe, not without wry affection, attempts by marginalized figures to claim kinship with the revolutionary hero, and their futile attempts to mould their lives to accord with the narrative in which he is a central figure.

Rotor's *The Wound and the Scar* (1937) was also an influential collection, but perhaps the best exemplification of developments in the short-story form in the 1930s is given by Manuel Arguilla's *How My Brother Leon Brought Home a Wife* (1940). Arguilla's early stories such as 'Midsummer' feature lush, romanticized and sexualized rural landscapes inhabited by hypermasculine and conventionally feminine figures: they are perhaps the literary equivalents of the exotic canvases of the painter Fernando Amorsolo. In the middle of the 1930s, Arguilla moves to ironic accounts of the urban bourgeoisie: the consumptive compositor in 'Caps and Lower Case' who struggles to summon courage to ask for a raise, or the insipid narrator of 'The Maid, the Man, and the Wife', who attempts to evade the desires of his domestic servant. By the end of the 1930s, Arguilla is writing more socially engaged stories that, at their best, acutely dramatize the problematics of imagining the nation faced by an Anglophone elite. 'The Socialists' describes the visit of members of the Socialist Club of Manila to rural leftist rally. It is focalized through Comrade Lirios, a young man from Manila, 'immaculate in perfectly creased white wool trousers and glossy double-breasted alpaca coat', and carrying both a copy of *Das Kapital* and an 'expensive German-made camera in a brown leather case' (1940: 203). Lirios watches the proceedings with a mixture of scorn and regret, conscious of his distance from the rural masses with whose interests he has previously thought himself aligned. Arguilla, tragically, was to be killed during the Japanese occupation of the Philippines.

The novel in English developed more slowly, gathering momentum towards the end of the 1930s; Resil Mojares lists twenty-three novels written in English in the Philippines before 1941 (1983: 338). Zoilo M. Galang's *A Child of Sorrow* (1921) was the first. While it has been criticized for its sentimentalism, the novel does contain sharp social criticism of the corruption of government officials, and shows the influence of a romantic literary tradition from Galang's native language, Pampangan, in which he had also published widely. Galang's prefatory claim that he would try to blend 'the best that is *local* and the best that is *foreign*' was one that other writers would also follow (1921: i). Maximo Kalaw's *The Filipino Rebel* (1930) is set in the revolutionary period and celebrates heroic resistance to the Americans in a style reminiscent of Rizal. Through his protagonist Juanito Lecaroz's simultaneous political rise and moral decline Kalaw also addresses the passivity and self-interest of the Philippine political classes under compadre colonialism; in an introduction Kalaw, as would many a Filipino writer after him, explores difficulties attendant upon writing 'in a borrowed tongue' (1964: xvii).

Two novels written a decade later show the transformation that had taken place in Philippine writing in English in the 1930s. Juan Cabreros Laya's *His Native Soil* (1941) expresses, in a parallel manner to Arguilla's short stories, some of the conflicts faced by Filipinos in the social embedding of capitalist development under colonialism. Written while Laya was a student at the University of Indiana, the novel describes the return of its protagonist, Martin Venancio, to the Philippines after a period of study in the United States. He attempts to put his new expertise in business to use by encouraging his family members to sell their land and use the money to found a rice-trading business that will cut out profiteering middlemen. Yet the narrative is ambivalent regarding Martin's intervention: his insistence on running a business professionally destroys community ties, the business fails, and at the end of the narrative his father dies. And again a romantic plot parallels a socio-political one: while Martin is tempted by the rich and flighty Westernized Virginia Fe, he returns to the less demonstrative but more culturally authentic Soledad, and the last scene sees him leaving his hometown accompanied by her.

N. V. M. Gonzalez's prize-winning novel *The Winds of April* (1941) also follows the paradigms of much of the literature of the 1930s, its protagonist experiencing an itinerant childhood in Mindoro and finally moving as a young adult to the metropolis of Manila. Yet *The Winds of April* differs from its predecessors in its interweaving of rationally inexplicable events into an essentially realist narrative, foreshadowing the magical realism that would later be developed by South American writers in the 1960s, and indeed in later Philippine fiction. The novel's descriptions of the literary world of Manila are also elaborately self-reflexive. Manila of the late 1930s becomes a semiotic paradise, read by the young protagonist through a series of intertextual signs drawn from his experience in American and European literatures. And if the novel indulges in the fantasy of a self-fashioning individual in urban modernity, the protagonist's celebration of his independence is often cut short by the repeated contact with his father, whose career path has taken a very different course from that of his son and who serves as a reminder of a neglected but ineradicable cultural past.

Poetry in English also moved from simple imitation to a more complex series of appropriations of and negotiations with contemporary metropolitan literary movements. Villa was indisputably the central figure here. He was controversial from the start: the sexually explicit prose poem series 'Man-Songs', published in the *Philippines Herald Magazine* in 1929, resulted in the poet's conviction for obscenity and his suspension from the University of the Philippines. Villa departed for the United States, first to Arizona and then to New York, but he remained closely in touch with the literary scene in Manila. In his introduction to the formally innovative series of 'Poems for an Unhumble One', published in the *Philippines Free Press* in 1933, Villa outlined a theory of 'poetry as strict as sign language, even mathematics – meaningless to the uninitiate' (2002: 254). Under the influence of modernism, Villa developed a theory and practice of a radical vanguardist poetic language which escaped 'bourgeois ratiocination': the 'good poet', he noted, 'does not speak as one who orders ham and eggs' (2002: 255). His collection *Have Come, Am Here* (1942), continued earlier formal experimentation. The poems in the volume contain lush symbolism, often homoerotic and with strong Catholic elements, almost reminiscent of Pre-Raphaelite poets such as Dante Gabriel Rossetti. Their formal qualities, however, are modernist, Villa experimenting with punctuation, layout and a new rhyming method which he calls 'reversed consonance' (1993: 76), producing a 'subtler and stricter' effect than ordinary consonance or half-rhyme (1993: 76–77).

Other poets who produced substantial work include Manalang Gloria, who returned to writing poetry after a hiatus in the 1930s, and published the first collection by a female poet in the Philippines in 1940. Her best writing, exemplified in poems such as 'Tropic Heritage', engages with the contradictions between an American-inspired poetic practice and a Filipino environment. Manalang Gloria received little contemporary recognition, pleasing neither formalists such as Villa nor the demands of other writers for a 'proletarian literature', despite the fact that some of the best poems, such as 'Pier Seven' and 'The Outcast', do engage with social inequality. The poet occupies an important place in literary history: poems such as 'Filipina' parallel contemporary prose writers such as Estrella D. Alfon and foreshadow the more overtly feminist writing of half a century later. Aurelio S. Alvero's *Moon Shadows on Waters* (1934) is wide-ranging, with translations from Rizal and Balagtas jostling for space with poems set in other parts of East Asia and others, such as 'Hester Prynne', that are influenced by an American canon. Alvero is perhaps at his best when he is at his most contemporary: several poems explore speed as a function of the modern, and are set on board ships or in taxis, while 'Closing the Office' describes the end of the day in spare diction filled with foreboding.

Further individual collections were published by Luis G. Dato (*My Book of Verses* [1936]), and R. Zulueta da Costa (*First Leaves* [1937]). Zulueta da Costa's second collection, *Like the Molave* (1940), was much feted at the time. Its title poem, written in the declarative manner of the American poet Walt Whitman, draws on a speech by Philippine president Manuel Quezon, in which he expressed a desire for the Philippine people to be 'like the molave, strong and resilient, rising on the hillside, unafraid of the raging flood, the lightning or the storm, confident of its own strength'. The poem's effusive patriotism calls for Filipinos to 'Infuse the vibrant red / Into our thin, anaemic veins' (1940: 21), and leads to a disgust with cosmopolitan hybridity expressed in the formula 'The mathematical certainty endures: Philippines − (Spain + America) = MOLAVE' (1940: 46). Yet the title poem's project is undercut by companion poems in the volume. Many are lyrical in nature, and intensely private, some following conventional forms, such as sonnets, others using Catholic symbolism in a manner not so far from Villa. Poems such as 'A Symphony Concert' describe the hybridity of the Anglophone bourgeoisie in Manila in the 1930s in less condemnatory terms, working through contradictions in search of identity.

The two decades before the Pacific War commenced also saw several attempts to produce anthologies of poetry from the Philippines. *Filipino Poetry* (1924) by Rodolfo Dato was followed by the peculiar *English-German Anthology of Filipino Poets* (1934), edited by Pablo Laslo, and then by Carlos Bulosan's more comprehensive *Chorus for America* (1942). Yet the majority of poems written before the Pacific War were uncollected, and thus remain unread. As Gemino H. Abad was to note, the fact that newspapers were the most common avenue for publication meant that much poetry was populist, and thus not formally innovative; it was not until Abad's own scholarly work in the 1980s that much of this poetry became available to contemporary students of Philippine literature (1989: 13).

Drama in English, in contrast, remained undeveloped for much of the period. The 'seditious' nationalist plays performed in Tagalog and other Filipino languages immediately after the American occupation found a ready audience, recycling old love stories but now giving the characters names that had coded nationalist significance, or having figures on stage wearing differently coloured costumes that would temporarily coalesce into the shape of the proscribed Philippine national flag (Fernandez 1996: 102). English language plays had no such community base, and tended to be performed at the university or elsewhere in Manila. Jesusa Araullo and Lino Castillejo's *A Modern Filipina* (1915), staged at the Philippine Normal College, has the distinction of being the first Filipino play in English, and Carlos P. Romulo and Vidal Tan wrote and staged plays in the late 1920s and early 1930s, with little critical recognition or success.

The most prolific pre-war playwright in English was, despite his relative late arrival on the scene, Wilfrido Ma. Guerrero. Like his predecessors and contemporaries in other genres, Guerrero was a product of the Ateneo de Manila University and the University of the Philippines, supplemented by a brief period of study at Columbia University in the United States. His pre-war plays include the one-act dramas 'Half an Hour in a Convent' (broadcast on the radio in 1937 and first performed on stage in 1938), 'Wanted: A Chaperon' (1940) and 'Forever' (1941), as well as the more substantial three-act play 'The Forsaken House' (1940). Set in an upper-middle-class urban milieu, the plays dramatize generational differences between the English-educated young and their more traditional parents and guardians. At times this is an occasion for humour. 'Wanted: A Chaperon' sees the paterfamilias Don Francisco besieged on all sides: his servants refuse to grant him traditional respect, his dissolute son demands an allowance on top of his salary to finance 'expenses', and his daughter Nena goes to parties unchaperoned, dismissing her father's objections by informing him that 'there's nothing wrong' since she is 'an educated girl' (1976: 24).

Yet Guerrero also documents the darker side of the changes in the life world of metropolitan middle classes. In 'Half an Hour in a Convent' the 'bad girl' Yolanda commits suicide after being expelled from a convent: among her crimes are talking to male servants and reading salacious contemporary American jazz age novelist Vina Delmar in tandem with books on psychology (1976: 6). Guerrero, indeed, is sympathetic to the manner in which women's lives become sites of struggle over modernity. 'Forever' is an empathetic examination of the refusal of a wife to take back a repentant husband who has previously left her for another woman, despite social and emotional pressure to do so. 'The Forsaken House' brings the playwright's central concerns together. Set in the confines of a Manila house, the play shows the patriarch Ramon's fruitless attempts to control the lives of his grown-up children by keeping them away from 'the temptations of the outside world' (1976: 186). One by one they leave him: a son goes to America, a daughter elopes and another son moves out of the house to rent his own lodgings. After a series of family tragedies, Ramon learns that he needs not simply to discipline but also to provide 'peace and tenderness' for his children: the play ends with his reconciliation with his son Gonzalo, whose dissolute lifestyle has resulted in him contracting an unspecified sexually transmitted disease. Yet if the play, through the person of Ramon's wife, Encarna, critiques traditional gender roles – an early stage direction describes her as 'typical of the Filipino wife educated before the arrival of the Americans in the Philippines[,] ... brought up to obey the husband and be under his complete domination' (1976: 184) – it also seems unable to place women in the new, modern society. Of Ramon's three daughters one dies, another enters a convent and the third finds the reconciliation with Ramon enjoyed by her brother deferred indefinitely into the future.

As the Philippines achieved Commonwealth status in 1935, with the promise of independence a decade later, literary criticism moved from a concern with skill and aesthetics to engagement with the social function of art. The central debate was between Villa and Salvador P. Lopez. Influenced by Marxist literary criticism, Lopez dismissed literature that resorted to 'sniffing odorous flowers of emotion', calling for 'a red-blooded literature' produced by 'virile people winning victories towards freedom' (1940: xx). The formal experiments of Villa's modernism were thus dismissed as 'the amorphous compositions of a literary nihilist who recognizes no demands save only those arising from his narcissistic preoccupation with himself' (1940: 148).

From 1935 to 1946 the Philippines was formally known as the Commonwealth of the Philippines in a planned ten-year transition to full independence. The state was internally self-governing, with a popularly elected president and vice-president, but responsibility for foreign policy and control of the military remained in American hands.

Villa's reply to Lopez was more temperate: although he had leftist sympathies he was disinclined to 'mix ... politics and economics with art' (2002: 178). The presence of social criticism in literary texts, Villa noted, was *merely incidental ... and not the primary object* of art (2002: 178). The Lopez–Villa debate was magnified on a larger scale at the First Filipino Writers Conference on Modern Literary Objectives held by the Philippine Writers' League in Manila in 1940, where some participants protested against the 'literary dictatorship' of Lopez and the organizers. Yet this debate was supplemented by a further, more pressing question. A speech by Manuel Quezon at the conference rationalizing the choice of Tagalog as the national language provoked anxieties regarding the elite status and indeed the possible future of writing in English. Many university graduates in the 1930s sought to write proletarian literature and return to the masses, yet their social situation and linguistic competences made this almost impossible. Paradoxically, the most truly proletarian literature produced by a Filipino was being written not in the Philippines but in the United States by the former itinerant labourer, autodidact and labour activist Carlos Bulosan. His work was influenced by progressive writers such as Richard Wright and William Saroyan. Bulosan would find himself catapulted to prominence by an event that would radically transform the situation of all writers in the Philippines: the coming Pacific War.

In everyday discussion, Filipinos may often refer to the National Language, Filipino and Tagalog: the three words refer to overlapping but not quite identical concepts. The Filipino language is a standardized version of Tagalog, the language spoken in Metro Manila and adjacent areas of Luzon. While various initiatives to devise a national language from the Commonwealth period onwards stressed the need to devise a new language drawing not just on Tagalog but also on regional languages, pragmatic and historical reasons have resulted in Filipino (or Pilipino, as it is sometimes called) developing as essentially a formalized version of Tagalog.

After the war: 1945–65

The years of the Japanese occupation of the Philippines resulted in a slowing down and then a hiatus in local writing in English that lasted beyond the end of the war in 1945. The Philippines suffered greatly during fighting to evict Japanese forces at the end of the Pacific War. Manila's business district and old city were completely destroyed, as was the whole of Cebu City in the Visayas, the country's second metropolis. Independence from the United States came immediately after the election of Manuel Roxas in 1946, but many of the problems that would plague the country over the next half century were already starkly visible. Despite universal suffrage, a political elite continued to occupy most of the elected seats in national, provincial and municipal governments: attempts by the left to broaden democratic participation quickly became caught up in the politics of the Cold War. The 1946 Bell Trade Act required the rewriting of elements of the 1935 Constitution to establish neocolonial trade dependency on the United States, while the US–Philippine Military Bases Agreement of 1947 gave the United States access to facilities for the next century. The huge Subic Bay Naval Base and Clark Air Base developed into the two biggest American bases overseas, and remained potent symbols of the inability of Filipinos to control their own national destiny. The presidential elections of 1949 were marred by widespread fraud, and the 1950s and early 1960s saw a series of false starts and thwarted hopes for social transformation. Despite increased industrialization and urbanization, the Philippines remained a predominantly rural and agricultural economy.

Quezon had proclaimed Tagalog as the basis for a national language in 1937, and during the Japanese occupation and the short-lived Second Republic under Japanese rule, Tagalog was further encouraged. However, in the two decades after the War, less attention was given to language issues and English made something of a return, at least in public life. Roxas and his successors Demetrio A. Quirino, Ramon Magsayasay and Carlos P. Garcia all used English in public speeches, and the Philippine national anthem continued to be sung in English until Diosdado Macapagal signed an executive order mandating the use of Tagalog/Pilipino in 1963 (A. Gonzalez 1980: 99).

Literature in English thrived in what retrospectively seems to have been a somewhat insulated environment, resuming after post-war reconstruction. Magazines such as the *Literary Apprentice* recommenced publication, and new ones such as *Signatures*, focusing on poetry, and *Comment, Philippine Writing* and the *Diliman Review* started up. Book-length publication in the Philippines was encouraged through institutions such as the Barangay Writers Project. After the success of Bulosan's autobiographical *America is in the Heart* (1946), Filipino writers were widely read in America: novels such as Stevan Javellana's *Without Seeing the Dawn* (1947), Emigdio Alvarez Enriquez's *The Devil Flower* (1959) and Celso Al. Carunungan's *Like a Big Brave Man* (1960) were first published in the United States, and collections of Filipino essays and short stories were specifically produced for the US market. Many of the major writers in English spent time in the United States on fellowship schemes, and came into contact with contemporary American novelists and poets. In the Philippines itself, literary awards proliferated, as did writers' conferences: the founding of a Philippines chapter of PEN, the international organisation promoting cooperation among writers, resulted in a national conference in Baguio in 1958, which was followed by an Asian writers conference in Manila in 1962. The post-war period also saw the beginnings of the formal academic study of writing in English from the Philippines. In 1946, a course on Philippine contemporary literature was offered at the National Teachers College, and by 1960 over fifty masters and doctoral theses had been written on Philippine literature in English at universities in Manila and elsewhere. This in turn resulted in the publication of critical essays on contemporary writing in journals such as *Philippine Studies*, as well as the first book-length studies of literature in English from the Philippines.

Prose fiction still dominated as a literary genre. Some of the major pre-war short-story writers fell silent: Manuel Arguilla had been killed by the Japanese, while Arturo Rotor stopped writing. Others, however, continued. Estrella D. Alfon developed feminist fiction that challenged social norms. A description of a sexual encounter in the short story 'Fairy Tale for the City' (1955), indeed, resulted in her being prosecuted for obscenity. Undeterred, she sold mimeographed versions of the story to people attending the court hearings. Alfon's short stories were collected in *Magnificence* (1960); the title story is one of the most powerful, gradually unfolding a mother's discovery that the man who has volunteered to tutor her children is in fact a predatory sexual abuser. Another writer who had achieved prominence before the war, Juan Cabreros Laya, published a second novel, *This Barangay* (1950), set during the Japanese period, and the struggles of the Filipino people during the Pacific War became a theme of much fiction written in the immediate post-war period. Javellana's *Without Seeing the Dawn* and Edilberto Tiempo's *Watch in the Night* (1953) are both realist novels set during in the war years, Javellana's narrative reworking a Rizalian story of heroic nationalist resistance to fit its new historical setting; three of the five stories in Aida Rivera's *Now and at the Hour* (1957) also take place in the Philippines during the war.

A number of the writers who came to prominence after the 1950s wrote short fiction. Alejandrino Roces's humorous collection of stories on cockfighting, *Of Cocks and Kites* (1959), was well-received, although Arturo G. Roseburg's claim that 'Roces has done for gamecocks what Melville did for whales' (1959: [v]) was surely hubristic. D. Paulo Dizon is also often thought of as a humorist, but stories in his 1962 collection *Twilight of a Poet* reveal further facets to his writing. Stories such as 'The Man with Trembling Hands' and 'Girl on a Voyage' focus on protagonists who are alienated from their environment: a man employed as a factory security guard to spy on his fellow workers, and a young woman victimized because of her relationship with an American. A similar humour is found in Carlos Bulosan's stories of childhood and adolescence in rural Pangasinan in *The Laughter of My Father* (1944). 'The Capitalism of My Father', for instance, shows the whole system of tobacco harvesting and buying to be riddled with corruption, while 'My Father Goes to Court' pitches a robustly healthy poor family against a physically debilitated rich family in a court battle, with the former emerging victorious.

The most formally experimental short-fiction writer was Francisco Arcellana. Arcellana had published extensively in the 1930s and early 1940s, but his post-war short stories 'The Yellow Shawl' and 'Divide by Two' are his most original. 'The Yellow Shawl' has three distinct sections, each differentiated by time, narrator and point of view, and connected only by a single object: the yellow shawl that belongs to the mother of the nameless woman who is a protagonist of the story, and is passed on to her as a child after her mother is tortured by the Japanese. More formally conventional, but thematically innovative, were the short stories of the young writer Gregorio Brillantes, collected in *The Distance to Andromeda* (1960), in which fiction inspired by the author's experience of growing up in Tarlac repeatedly emphasizes the hybrid nature of Philippine modernity. In the title story, a young boy is fascinated by a film in which a group of space colonists leave an earth destroyed by atomic warfare for life in a new galaxy; this fascination is intercut with domestic scenes of family life. In 'The Rice Fields', a young soldier who has had his arm amputated contemplates returning home to his family, and working again in the rice fields; the last section of the story returns analeptically to the battle where he loses his limb, and, badly injured, seeks refuge in the rice fields of the country in which he is fighting (presumably Korea), wondering why they have not been planted. Such epiphanic denouements are common in Brillantes' stories: in contrast to much of the pastoral writing of the 1930s, there is here a consciousness that an uncontaminated tradition is an illusion to which the protagonists can never return.

The major prose writers in the post-war period wrote both short stories and, increasingly, novels. N. V. M. Gonzalez produced four short story collections, *Seven Hills Away* (1947), *Children of the Ash-Covered Loam and Other Stories* (1954), *Look, Stranger, on This Island Now* (1963), and *Selected Stories* (1964), and two novels, *A Season of Grace* (1956) and *The Bamboo Dancers* (1957). Like many of his contemporaries, Gonzalez spent time in the United States. However, he differed from many other English-language writers in two crucial respects. First, he published creative work in Tagalog, and second, he was interested in the Asian writing that was emerging with the coming of independence in the region, meeting figures such as the Malayan poet Wang Gungwu and Indian novelist Raja Rao. These concerns are reflected in his novels. *A Season of Grace* is set in Mindoro and describes the marginal lives of *kaingin* (slash and burn) cultivators, and mixes concrete accounts of poverty with a sensuous description of supernatural events which foreshadows magical realism. The life world of *kaingin* is explicitly contrasted with the actions of government officials whose behaviour extends colonialism. Gonzalez's strategic reversal of focalization at the end of the novel to reveal the poverty of official developmentalist perspectives on indigenous cultures predicts a similar tactic in Nigerian novelist Chinua Achebe's *Things Fall Apart* (1959). *The Bamboo Dancers* is more international in scope, following the path of expatriate Filipino sculptor Ernesto (Ernie) Rama from New York to Japan, then Taipei, and finally his return to his hometown near Dias in Siplog. Ernie is pulled this way and that by fate, and wanders in and out of other life stories that are more interesting than his own. The 'bamboo dancers' of the novel's title refers to the *tinikling* dance using bamboo sticks, which everyone Ernie meets in his travels mentions as a marker of Filipino identity, and which he finds both reassuringly familiar and conspicuously inauthentic.

Almost as prolific as Gonzalez in the period was Bienvenido N. Santos, who spent the war years in the United States reading English at the University of Illinois: he would maintain a close relationship with the United States, finally becoming an American citizen in 1976. Santos's first collection of short stories, *You Lovely People* (1955), describes Filipino expatriates in the United States. The stories of his second collection, *Brother, My Brother* (1960), are set in the Philippines, many in 'Sulucan', a fictionalized name for Tondo in Manila, where the author grew up. Many explore the impossibility of return from exile. Santos's two novels, *Villa Magdalena* (1965, but written five years earlier) and *The Volcano* (1965) further explore the problematics of cultural memory in a changed world. The first of these novels commences with the departure of a middle-aged Fred Medallada from Manila airport for the United States, after a final interview with the dying Don Magno Medallada, the paterfamilias who presides over the Villa Magdalena, the decayed mansion with which his life has been intertwined. Most of the rest of the novel is presented as an analeptic recollection of Fred's entry into the house as a young man, and his subsequent entanglement in the Medalladas' business and family affairs. Only at the end of the novel, after Don Magon's death, can Fred have all the windows in the villa opened up, so that he can 'breathe freely again' (1986a: 286). In *The Volcano*, Gonzalez uses a similar narrative strategy with different subject-matter: the Protestant missionaries Dr Paul Hunter and his wife Sarah prepare to leave the mission hospital at Abay in the Bikol region where they have lived and worked for thirty years. The Hunters are driven out by their growing irrelevance and the hostility of a more assertive Philippine nationalism; the narrative is an elegaic recollection of lives caught up in a larger narrative determined by forces its characters cannot control, just like the eruptions of Mount Mayon that periodically punctuate the story.

Although he wrote less than Gonzalez or Santos in terms of quantity, Nick Joaquin is perhaps the most important of the fiction writers in the two decades after the Second World War. Like Gonzalez, Joaquin was an active writer in the early 1940s, and in the immediate post-war period he published a number of short stories in *Prose and Poems* (1952). Many of

Joaquin's stories draw on the Spanish past in the Philippines, which he was anxious should not be deliberately forgotten under a nationalism that had made accommodation with American influence. Joaquin spent time studying in a seminary in Hong Kong, and many of his stories set in the Spanish period make use of Catholic symbolism: the power of Catholic rituals in his fiction, however, seems to arise primarily from their ability to transform and appropriate pre-Christian cultural forces. 'The Summer Solstice', for instance, is set in the 1850s, and features a husband and wife of the elite *principalia* class who are contemptuous of their servants' fascination for the Tadtarin, a festival with pre-Christian elements held at the same time of the feast of St John. Yet the Tadtarin, which celebrates women's power, attracts the wife to participate in it against her husband's wishes, and she uses her new-found confidence to challenge the patriarchal norms that govern her marriage. Joaquin's writing shows unmatched versatility, ranging from fables such as 'The Legend of the Virgin's Jewel' that are set in the Spanish colonial period, to 'It Was Later Than We Thought' a bricolage of fictionalized letters and extracts from diaries and essays written by members of an extended family in Manila just before the outbreak of the Pacific War.

One short story was extended by Joaquin into the novel *The Woman Who Had Two Navels* (1961), a complex modernist narrative set primarily in the expatriate Filipino community in post-war Hong Kong, but sending tentacles back into the past in the Philippines over the previous half century. Joaquin's novel is centred on two women characters, Conchita Vidal and her daughter Connie Escobar, who represent the cultural and political unconscious of Filipino nationalism. The elder of the two women has lived through the Filipino revolution and the subsequent American occupation, marrying first the fiery nationalist and poet Esteban Borromeo, and then switching allegiance to Manolo Vidal, a member of the comprador elite, 'too ripe, too florid, vaguely greasy although immaculate and pregnant with power' (1972: 121). Connie, in contrast, has fled to Hong Kong to escape her husband, Macho Escobar, having discovered that he is her mother's lover. Joaquin's narrative strategies are complex, and subplots often start only to be undermined as imagined or false. Narrative tension focuses on the two navels that Connie claims to possess, with readers never sure whether they really exist or are rather a figment of her imagination. The navels lend themselves to various allegorical readings which Joaquin raises but never fully clarifies. On one level they symbolize the divided cultural heritage of the Philippines. Yet they are traces of violence as much as traces of birth; they are compared to stigmata in Catholic iconography, and are mirrored in the two gunshot wounds made in the belly of the Chinese 'carnival god' Connie hides in the orchard behind her house in the Japanese occupation (1972: 166). The two women's sojourn in Hong Kong involves them with male characters who again symbolize elements of Filipino culture – veterinarian Pepe Monson, his priest brother Tony and their father, an officer in Aguinaldo's army who refused to swear allegiance to the Americans and has waited for forty years to be able to return to an independent Philippines. At the end of the novel Connie elopes with band leader Paco Texeira, who has indigenized American jazz in the Philippines, 'building the Harlem gods a bamboo habitation this side of the Pacific' (1972: 24): his identity as a 'guileless cosmopolitan' contrasts with the elder Monson's disappointed patriotism (1972: 24).

A concern with the retrieval of the past and its uses in the present occurs, indeed, in many works written in the early 1960s. Linda Ty Casper's *The Peninsulars* (1964) deals with the Spanish-speaking elite in Manila during the 1750s, but the world of violence and political intrigue she describes also critiques the Philippines of the 1960s. Kerima Polotan's *The Hand of the Enemy* (1962) and F. Sionil Jose's *The Pretenders* (1962) develop this theme more explicitly: in both cases the protagonist of their novels makes a personal connection back to erased histories of political resistance, even if knowledge of this past still cannot teach them how to act in a contemporary world. Jose's politically committed realism marked a partial return to the proletarian concerns of Lopez in the 1930s: in the ensuing decades, he would become one of the most internationally prominent figures writing in English in the Philippines.

While more plays in English were written and staged in the period from 1945 to 1965, they were still mostly produced by groups associated with the universities, although attempts were now made to reach a wider audience. Wilfrido Guerrero continued his prolific career as both playwright and director with the University of the Philippines Dramatic Club, and his plays also later toured the country through the group's mobile theatre. Guererro's post-war plays do have something of a production-line feel to them. This is not entirely coincidental, since several were sponsored by the USIS (United States Information Service); plays such as 'In Unity' (first produced in 1953) feature *barrio* inhabitants demanding democratic representation and pooling resources to make developmental improvements such as irrigation systems, and were clearly written with a didactic purpose in mind. Alberto Florentino's plays were staged either by the Ateneo Dramatic Guild or at the Philippine Normal College, and were more socially engaged, exploring issues such as the impossibility of the urban poor staying out of crime, or the eviction of squatters by the municipal authorities. Florentino experimented by having at least one of his plays staged in Tagalog, and he won the first of the Palanca Memorial Awards given specifically for drama in 1954 for *The World is An Apple*. Such awards, however, tended to encourage the writing of 'filing cabinet drama' (Fernandez 1996: 22), play scripts that were never performed. The plays of Alejandrino G. Hufana, for example, were collected as *Curtain-Raisers: First Five Plays* in 1964, but at the time of their publication had not been staged.

In these circumstances, the emergence of Nick Joaquin's *A Portrait of the Artist as Filipino*, the most important English-language work in Philippine theatre history, is all the more surprising. Joaquin probably wrote the play immediately after the war, but did not publish it until 1952. It is set in the old Spanish city of Manila, Intramuros, just before the beginning of the Pacific War, in a decaying mansion inhabited by the impecunious revolutionary artist Don Lorenzo Marasigan and his two daughters. Don Lorenzo has retired to his bedroom after an accident, leaving his daughters the gift of the painting that gives the play its title: a picture of the Greek hero Aeneas carrying his father Anchises from the burning city of Troy. As the other characters are quick to note, the painting is a double portrait: Aeneas in the picture is Don Lorenzo as a young man, and Anchises a portrait of him as he is today. In a stroke of theatrical genius, Joaquin never shows his audience the painting, which hangs on the fourth wall that separates them from the stage. The portrait thus becomes open to interpretation: for different characters it is a means of preserving the values of a dying past, a means of making money, an expression of patriotism, or an acknowledgement of the artist's futility and irrelevance in modern society. Yet the very illegibility of the portrait turns the play into a profound meditation on modern Filipino identity. In an age of nationalist desire for cultural purity, Joaquin foregrounds the hybridity of Filipino culture, and in particular urges the necessity of acknowledging the power of elements rooted in the Spanish colonial past. Joaquin's published version of the play was substantially cut for stage production by Daisy Hontiveros Avellana of the semi-professional Barangay Theatre Guild.

In poetry, as in prose fiction and drama, much post-war literary production explored questions of identity, attempting, in Gemino H. Abad's words, to 're-invent' the English language within a Philippine context, so that 'English in Filipino hands, under the pressure of ... circumstances and choices, becomes not English but Filipino' (1993: 12). Villa was less influential, and stopped writing poetry in the early 1950s. Several writers more widely known for their prose also wrote poetry. Carlos Bulosan's *The Voice of Bataan* (1943) commemorates nationalist resistance to the Japanese in the defence of Corregidor, but also acknowledges, in its conclusion, the uncertainty of values in a world in which such exemplary heroism is expressed. Bienvendio Santos's *The Wounded Stag* (1956) features poems set in the Tondo of his childhood, the America where he spent years in exile, and the devastated city of Manila to which he returned. Written over a decade, Santos's poems are richly intertextual, making frequent allusions to classical mythology and the Western canon and making Santos's own experience typical of a larger sensation of exile within the modern world. Nick Joaquin's poetry, as might be expected, draws on Hispanic and pre-Hispanic pasts; like Santos he also writes of exile and the dislocation of identity through sojourn abroad, in particular in the 'Stubbs Road Cantos', written when he was in Hong Kong (1952).

Such explorations of identity and belonging led to longer and more ambitious poetic work. Alejandrino Hufana's *Poro Point* (1961) is a collection based on the conceit of a poet, Geron Munar, returning to his birthplace from Manila in a reverse migration. The poems, written in blank verse, describe the inhabitants of the birthplace and then his family members, and the sequence concludes with the persona meeting the figure of Dalmas, a bandit who has a connection to a primeval or pre-Christian life-force. Ricaredo Demetillo's *La Via* (1959) describes a spiritual journey away from the sterility of modern life through an engagement with Christianity outside of the institutions of the Church; it shows clear influence of early modernists such as T. S. Eliot and W. B. Yeats. Demetillo's *Barter in Panay* (1961) is a more conscious attempt to write a national verse epic, narrating the Bornean settlement of the Visayas in iambic eight-line stanzas. Andres Cristobal Cruz's *Estero Poems* (1960) is more loosely structured, including both descriptive writing of Manila and the more politically pointed 'Clarius Poems', addressing the manner in which intellectuals become caught up with the interests of a political elite.

Critical and educational institutions

Gemino Abad has identified one trend as characteristic of poetry after the war – a movement from romanticism to a 'New Critical' approach. Demetillo, and his fellow poet Dominador I. Ilio (*The Diplomat and Other Poems* [1955]) studied poetry in the United States at the University of Iowa and were perhaps most instrumental in bringing about changes in poetic practice. They were supported by a growing critical tradition informed by New Criticism. Miguel A. Bernad's critical study of Philippine literature in English, *Bamboo and the Greenwood Tree* (1961), might be characterized as Jesuit Leavisism. Bernad, like F. R. Leavis before him, sees 'great authors' as providing a necessary counterweight to a 'worthless' American popular culture symptomized by Hollywood and rock music (1961: 4). Stylistically, Bernad praises restraint and lack of narrational comment, preferring the simplicity of Santos or Gonzalez to the 'too rhetorical' (1961: 54) prose of Joaquin. Leonard Casper's *The Wounded Diamond* (1964) is also New Critical in its approach, praising the stories of Arguilla as avoiding 'propaganda' by 'leaving the most important narrative matters unmentioned but not ... untold' (1964: 21), and criticizing Jose's *The Pretenders* in a discomfort with the politics, not the stylistic qualities, of the text. Historicism did not vanish from criticism, however: Lucila V. Hosilos, *Philippine-American Literary Relations, 1898–1941*, published in 1969 but based on earlier research, was the first book-length study to historicize Philippine literature in English as an emergent national literature whose rise paralleled that of other 'Afro-Asian Literatures' (1976: ix).

Many of the conflicts, tensions, and possibilities raised in two decades of writing were debated in the Symposium on the Relation of Literature to Social Change, held in Manila in March 1964, and attended by most of the major writers and critics of Philippine literature in English. Discussion returned to the issues raised by Lopez a quarter of a century before: the need to balance the social relevance of literature with the autonomy necessary for the production of art. As several commentators noted, Philippine literature in English was part of a literary context which moved beyond the nation: for better for worse, it had an inheritance that was both colonial and yet also international. Various solutions were proposed to this dilemma: a greater use of the national language of Pilipino – as it was then called – or other languages of the Philippines, the indigenization of English, or the embracing of a more radical tradition of English creative writing that might move beyond New Criticism. Other papers, however, noted how these issues were bound up with the mechanics of production and reception: the audience for English-language texts of all genres in the Philippines was small, and young writers, after producing one or two promising works, frequently fell silent. A panel dedicated to looking ahead at the prospects for the coming decade expressed at best cautious optimism; its members could not, of course, foresee the political upheavals of the next two decades, which would make the social role of the literary artist and her use of language ever more pressing.

Conclusion

- Education reforms introduced by the Americans created a sizeable English-speaking elite by the 1920s.
- Short fiction became the dominant literary form in the 1920s and 1930s, although Jose Garcia Villa's poetry also achieved prominence.
- Villa's disagreement with Salvador Lopez about the social utility of art established a paradigm for literary criticism in the Philippines.
- A post-war revival in the use of English resulted in greater scholarly and institutional attention to Filipino literature in English.
- Fiction dominated the post-war period, but the two decades were also marked by the production of the most important Filipino play in English, Nick Joaquin's *A Portrait of the Artist as Filipino*.

6   Narrative fiction 1965–1990

Overview

In the period after 1965, Singapore and Hong Kong experienced rapid economic growth, becoming developed economies in all but name by 1990. Malaysia's economic take-off was delayed, but by the 1980s the country had become one of the 'tiger' economies of Southeast Asia, having negotiated a political crisis after the civil riots that followed opposition election gains in 1969. In the Philippines, progress was less linear, with initial hopes placed in Ferdinand Marcos fading, and the frustration of new aspirations for social change after the 1986 EDSA People Power movement brought Cory Aquino to power. Economic transformations were paralleled with political realignments. Singapore and Malaysia grew gradually more distant after their separation in 1965, but this was counterbalanced by a growing sense of regional identity through ASEAN. The development of English-language fiction in each individual country or territory was influenced by diverse and often unique factors: educational and cultural policies that placed a stress on languages, as well as political or aesthetic sentiments of writers. Yet there were signs of growing shared regional identities in English language writing, of which the most prominent was Heinemann's Writing in Asia series, edited by Leon Comber from Hong Kong, which brought together writers in English and – through translation – other languages – largely from China, Hong Kong and Southeast Asia.

In the Philippines, Malaysia and Singapore, the novel became more dominant as a genre. Although writers before 1965 in Malaysia and Singapore had shared national aspirations and (briefly) nationality, by the late 1980s the difference in prose fiction between the two countries was growing more marked. While English-language fiction in Hong Kong during the period remained largely the province of visitors or expatriates, several texts that were more firmly embedded in the local emerged.

The Philippines

Any account of English-language fiction in the Philippines from 1965 to 1990 cannot ignore its political context, and in this the name of a single man, Ferdinand Marcos, looms large. Elected president in 1965, Marcos initially seemed to promise social transformation, yet he maintained power through vote-rigging, corruption and increasing violence. In response, a generation of Filipinos became radicalized: faced by student demonstrations and an intensification of the armed struggle by the New People's Army (NPA), Marcos declared martial law in 1972. Extrajudicial torture and killing marked much of the 1970s and early 1980s, until the Marcos regime, faced with crumbling international support, collapsed under the weight of demonstrations in Manila in 1986. Yet while people power temporarily united the Philippine nation, its longer-term efficacy remained uncertain: the new president, Corazon Aquino, widow of an assassinated political rival of Marcos, was herself a member of the elite. Aquino's election promised much, but did not bring about the democratization of Philippine society that many hoped for: what did result, however, was renewed debate concerning the political utility of literature that revived and extended the 1930s correspondence between Jose Garcia Villa and Salvador Lopez.

In the middle of the 1960s, Philippine literature in English seemed to be flourishing: well-crafted short stories were published, as in the 1930s, in vehicles such as the *Philippines Free Press* and the *Graphic*, with many writers, such as Nick Joaquin, F. Sionil Jose, Kerima Polotan and Gregorio Brillantes also working in journalism. Within the universities, there were a growing number of courses in Philippine Literature and creative writing programmes. The deteriorating political situation in the later part of the decade, however, made a New Critical focus on craft untenable: radicalized young writers were reading Mao Zedong's stress on the social utility of literature in 'Talks at the Yan'an Forum', Jean-Paul Sartre's socially engaged *On Literature*, or Frantz Fanon's account of the responsibilities of the postcolonial intellectual in *The Wretched of the Earth*. It is perhaps something less than a coincidence that Jose Maria Sison, later one of the chief theorists and chairman of the Communist Party of the Philippines, was originally an English major.

Established writers responded to the political climate, and the closing down of many literary publications and publishing houses after 1972, in a variety of ways. Some chose cooperation with the new regime: Polotan and her husband Juan Tuvera were close to Marcos, and edited *Focus Philippines* throughout the martial law period, publishing short fiction. Polotan's compromised status, further confirmed by her publication of a hagiographic biography of Imelda Marcos in 1970, however, led many progressive writers to boycott the journal. Others chose exile: Bienvenido Santos, for instance, was preparing to return to the Philippines in 1972 after finishing a stint teaching at the University of Iowa. His novel *The Praying Man* was serialized in Jose's *Solidarity* from 1971 and 1972. Its central figure is Cris Magat, who has risen to preside over a business 'empire built on fake drugs, bribery and corruption' (1982: 29) in which his only dilemma is how he should balance the peddling of political interests with his own desire to maximize profit. Cris's decline is counterpoised with the experiences of two other characters who maintain the integrity he has lost: his childhood friend Kosca, now in Chicago, is a sculptor, while his brother Ulo is a subaltern figure hunted by the police after leading an assault on the presidential Malacañang Palace in Manila. The novel could not be published after the imposition of martial law, and Santos decided to remain in the United States, becoming a US citizen in 1976 (Casper 1995: 23–24). *The Praying Man* was finally published in the Philippines in 1982, and much of Santos's later fiction is peopled by Filipino characters living in reluctant exile in the United States.

Several other writers chose to publish abroad. Edith Tiempo's *A Blade of Fern* (1978) and Linda Ty Casper's *Dread Empire* (1980), for example, were both published by Heinemann's Writing in Asia series from Hong Kong. Tiempo's novel, set in a 1936 mining community in Mindanao is less overtly political, enacting a gender politics in its opposition between the former teacher Bernardo, who has escaped from the moral confusion of Manila, and the adolescent Angela, who runs wild in the forest, collecting and pressing ferns: the novel continually hints at, but never quite expresses, a larger national allegory. Ty Casper's text represents a much more overt political intervention, its narrative commencing with the proclamation of martial law on 21 September 1972. The protagonist, Don Paco, an aging Marcos crony, is initially delighted to hear the news, but soon finds the certainties that founded his world are crumbling. His loss of favour with the President and the increasing disintegration of a Philippine body politic are paralleled by a physical disintegration, his body subject to seizures of increasing severity, rebelling against him even as he imposes his will on the world.

Among established writers who continued to publish in the Philippines, Nick Joaquin was protected by his pre-eminence. As always, he wrote in different genres, most notably journalism under the pseudonym Quijano de Manila, and accepted the award of National Artist for Literature in 1976 only on the condition that Jose Lacaba, the imprisoned editor of the *Graphic*, was released from jail. Joaquin's biographical *The Aquinos of Tarlac* (1983) represented a direct political intervention towards the end of Marcos's period of power, yet his solitary novel of this period, *Cave and Shadows* (1983), is concerned with a wider sweep of history. Its protagonist, Jack Henson, returns to Manila from Davao to investigate the mysterious death of a young woman, Nenita Coogan, whose naked body has been found in a sacred cave. While Joaquin's novel is plotted as a detective story, its real object of inquiry is not simply Nenita's death, but rather an extended exploration of the nature of Philippine culture as a palimpsest in which American elements are written over Spanish, which in turn express precolonial patterns of thought. At the same time, *Cave and Shadows* continually undermines itself: apparent narrative certainties are revealed to be fraudulent, while stories apparently retrieved from an oral Philippine past bear more than a passing resemblance to literary texts from the Western canon, such as Shakespeare's plays. Written at a time when either realism or allegory was a predominant mode, Joaquin's wide-ranging modernist narrative, with its complex intersection of chronotopes, predicted changes in Philippine fiction from the late 1980s onwards.

The most substantial body of fiction during the period of Marcos's rule and afterwards by an established writer, however, was realist in nature, and was produced by F. Sionil 'Frankie' Jose. Jose was a journalist and activist, founding and editing the journal *Solidarity*, which engaged with literature and culture both in the Philippines and in the Southeast Asian region from 1966 onwards, and opening the Solidaridad bookstore in Manila in 1967. While he is a prolific short-story writer, Jose is best known for the Rosales quintology of historical novels, collectively constituting a 'national epic' (Shirley Lim 1993: 25) and paralleling similar developments elsewhere in Southeast Asia, for example the Indonesian novelist Pramoedya Ananta Toer's Buru quartet. Although he was affected by the Marcos years – *Solidarity* was closed for a period and the publication of several of the volumes in the Rosales quintology in book form was delayed – Jose's unique contribution at the time was perhaps to be able to place the experience of the Marcos years within a history of social inequality stretching back to Spanish colonialism in the nineteenth century: in his quintology, national history is not so much a progressive narrative as a series of haunting repetitions.

An account of Jose's novel cycle is complicated by the fact that the order of publication of the texts does not follow the order of the historical events they narrate. The first novel in terms of historical setting, *Po-on* (1984, re-titled *Dusk* when published in the United States in 1993), was the last to be published. As several commentators have noted, the quintology plots a history of conflict in Philippine modernity, from internal migration to escape a feudal Spanish order and revolutionary insurrection (*Po-on*), through resistance to the hacienda system and explorations of the contradictory nature of metropolitan modernity in Manila before and after the Pacific War (*The Pretenders* [1962], *Tree* [1978, although serialized much earlier], *My Brother, My Executioner* [1979]), to the slums of Manila and radical opposition to the Marcos regime (*Mass* [1979]). In plotting this history through a series of fictional narratives, Jose adopts a primarily social realist mode, exploring what Georg Lukács referred to as a realization of the 'concrete potentialities' of individual characters in their engagement with society. The most influential reading of Jose's works, indeed, has argued that they mature from simple bourgeois psychological realism to become a national epic 'united by an ideological sensibility' in which all levels of society are represented: in the last two novels, *Mass* and *Po-on*, protagonists make an existential choice to sacrifice themselves for the nation (Shirley Lim 1993: 62).

A closer examination of Jose's novels, however, reveals a series of contradictions that are never finally resolved. Each novel repeats a similar plot: a young male protagonist rebels against an oppressive social structure, yet his rebellion results not in emancipation but in a further series of dilemmas. Social conflicts are repeatedly allegorized through gender: in several of the novels, the protagonist is asked to choose between two women, one representative of bourgeois metropolitan capitalism, the other either of a rural feudal order or a primal subaltern energy. In each novel, the male protagonist must also negotiate filial and fraternal relationships, often rediscovering family histories effaced or distorted in their public performance. Jose's novels, indeed, are perhaps most interesting when the demands of gendered allegory and realism conflict.

My Brother, My Executioner, for example, narrates the story of Luis Asperri, who leaves his father's hacienda to work as the editor of a liberal newspaper in post-war Manila. As he negotiates the limits of liberalism, Luis carries on two romantic relationships simultaneously, with his cousin Trining, representative of a feudal landowning family, and Ester, daughter of Eduardo Dantes, the proprietor of the newspaper he works for. Luis's dilemmas are further expressed through familial relationships with his father, the feudal *hacendero* Don Vicente, his mother, a peasant seduced as a servant girl by Don Vicente and now living in a nearby village, and his half-brother Vic, a leader of the *hukbalahap* insurgency that targets rural landlords in its quest for land redistribution. While the pedagogy of Jose's narrative is clear – Luis is eventually unable to break free from his class roots, and ends the novel awaiting death at the hands of the Huks – the text's literariness undermines its overt narrative strategy. The most self-consciously literary sections of the novel are four letters that Luis writes to his mother, to Ester, to his father and finally to his brother, which Jose presents to us as italicized interpolations into the third-person narration of the text. The letters read more like personal meditations than communicative acts, and are written in circumstances that makes their delivery impossible or unlikely: Luis's letter to Ester is written after her suicide, and his letter to his father is immediately followed in the narrative by news of Don Vicente's death. The letters are thus paradoxical: at one level they enact a fantasy of realism, of pure communication with their addressees unmediated by linguistic or contextual interference; yet at another they clearly have no communicative function at all, and are simply exercises in Luis's own subjectification. Jose's novels' concern with the limits of realism may, indeed, reflect his own position as an Ilokano writer reclaiming a cultural heritage and past through the English language, with the accompanying realization that he 'cannot go home again' (1999: 416).

Many writers, caught up in the resurgent nationalism and concern for social change in the 1960s and 1970s did attempt to go home, or at least to imagine a new home. Younger writers in English such as Ninotchka Rosca wrote short fiction to raise the consciousness of the middle classes concerning the hypocrisies of a highly stratified society: she was imprisoned, and later fled to exile in the United States. Other writers such as Andres Cristobal Cruz moved from English to Filipino in order to reach a wider audience. After 1972, opportunities for publication of the new, politically committed protest literature were fewer: writers might either resort to allegory or to underground publishing. Organizations such as the *Galian ng Arte at Tula* (GAT) attempted to bring a new social consciousness to metropolitan writing in Filipino. After the assassination of Benigno Aquino in 1983, a swelling of popular sentiment against Marcos meant that much protest literature was published as writers in both English and Tagalog came out in support of the opposition.

An example of such literature is Jose Dalisay's 'Sarcophagus', published in the 1985 special issue of *Philippine Studies* featuring new writing that was emerging as the Marcos era drew to its close. Its protagonist, a university lecturer, eats breakfast and then drives to work, mentally preparing for a lecture on ancient Egypt. As he reviews the lecture material, his mind wanders off at tangents to a history of human suffering and random violence that is only occasionally punctuated by observations concerning the contemporary Philippines: the presence of an army helicopter overhead, or newspaper headlines that another oligarch has fled to the United States. When he arrives at the parking lot, Dalisay's nameless protagonist is undisturbed by the student protestors waiting there. Like the body of the boy king Tutankhamen which he will commence his lecture with, Dalisay's protagonist is also 'serene in his sarcophagus', insulated by the privilege of academic contemplation from the political struggles of history that now manifest themselves in the present (1985: 294).

The period following the end of martial law, and especially after the fall of Marcos in 1986, was a fertile one for the Philippine novel in English. Many works written in the late 1980s review the experiences of martial law yet also return to other historical events, especially the revolutionary struggle against Spain and then America in the late nineteenth and early twentieth centuries. Leaving the realism of their predecessors behind, these novels are frequently influenced by postmodernism, consisting of fragmentary or interwoven and elaborately self-referential narratives, and drawing on traditions of metafiction and magical realism that have often been associated with South American writers such as Gabriel García Márquez, but which in fact also have roots within a Filipino literary heritage. An early example is Alfrredo Navarro Salanga's novella *The Birthing of Hannibal Valdez* (1984), set just after the end of the Pacific War. Salanga's key characters, the American commander Major Weepingwillow, or Hannibal's ex-revolutionary grandfather turned feudal *hacendero*, are presented as cartoon-like actors unaware of the irony of their own actions. Much of the novella consists of the grandfather's recollections told to

Weepingwillow in an attempt to compensate for his being 'left out of history' (1984: 29), and these recollections continually break the bounds of realist conventions, unsettling the frame narrative itself.

Three significant novels published in the period 1986–1990 illustrate the new directions that Philippine writers were exploring. The first in terms of publication is Ninotchka Rosca's *State Of War* (1988). In the first and third sections of the novel, in a Philippines apparently still under martial law, three companions, rich man's son Adrian Banyaga, activist Anna Villaverde and modern-day courtesan Eliza Hansen, celebrate a festival on the island of 'K__'. In a carnivalesque atmosphere where traditional hierarchies dissolve, the three friends confront their nemesis, Colonel Urbano Amor, who has tortured Anna while she was detained by the military. The narrative of the first and third section of the book centres on an ultimately unsuccessful plot by NPA guerrillas to assassinate Amor and his superior, the nameless Commander, who is clearly Ferdinand Marcos. The second section of the novel interpolates a much longer history of a Filipino family that a reader only belatedly realizes is Anna's. Rosca's narrative strategy and style recall Márquez in the marshalling of a cast of eccentric characters, the generational sweep, and the touches of magical realism that colour the narrative. History as a public narrative is one of patrilineal descent, but in its retelling it is held together by the lives of women who are brought into the family. A concern with women as enablers of history continues in the third section of the novel. The bomb placed by the insurgents blows up prematurely, leaving Adrian wheelchair bound, now fixed 'forever in a maze of words' (2005: 376). Anna, in contrast, escapes the island: she is pregnant with Adrian's child, and committed to joining armed resistance to the regime. The ending of *State Of War* indicates a feature of many novels written immediately after the fall of Marcos: belief in the possibility of radical, even revolutionary, social change is not yet subsumed by textual irony.

Initially published in the United States by Norton, Rosca's novel also raises the question of the growing distinction between Philippine literature and Philippine American literature. In some ways this was not a new question. Rosca's status as an expatriate Filipino writer paralleled the early experiences of Jose Garcia Villa, Carlos Bulosan, N. V. M. Gonzalez and Bienvenido Santos: issues that are also discussed in Chapter 9. Yet there were now two new factors: growth in interest in Asian-American writing in the United States, and a body of works by writers of Filipino heritage who had been born in the United States, or migrated to the country as children. A novel that exemplifies these issues written by such a writer is *Dogeaters* (1990) by Filipino-American Jessica Hagedorn, which achieved immense popularity internationally.

Dogeaters is a multilayered postmodern narrative exploring the intertwined lives of characters from various sections of society in Manila from the 1950s onwards, but focusing most closely on the Marcos years and Rio Gonzaga, who grows up in an upper-middle-class environment saturated in American culture. The novel plays with historical referentiality: most of the characters are fictional, but 'Rainer', the German lover of the gay DJ Joey Sands, who arrives in Manila for the International Film Festival, is clearly the German director Rainer Werner Fassbinder, while the assassinated opposition leader Senator Domingo Avila bears more than a passing resemblance to Benigno Aquino. Hagedorn's novel is assembled from a variety of textual fragments: brief excerpts from colonial accounts of the Philippines, newspaper reports, and sections of narrative recounted by a variety of third-person and first-person narrators. The juxtaposition of these texts is often calculatedly discordant: the brutal torture and rape of Avila's daughter, Daisy, for instance, is intercut with the script of the popular soap opera *Love Letters*. Stylistically, *Dogeaters* is also notable for its orchestration of different voices, including an exuberant use of Tagalog phrases and representation of the rhythms of Philippine Englishes. The narrative gathers pace as the novel comes to its end, and concludes with Rio, who has migrated to the United States, returning to Manila and acknowledging her distance from the events the novel has recounted. Yet Hagedorn has not finished with her reader yet: the penultimate section of the text is narrated by Rio's friend Pucha Gonzaga, casting doubt on her version of the events with which the novel has opened, and the final chapter, entitled 'Kundiman', substitutes a parody of the Ave Maria for the love song its title suggests.

Postmodern pastiche and parody, however, were not simply products of the Filipino-American experience. Such formal and stylistic innovations were also features of Alfred 'Krip' Yuson's *The Great Philippine Jungle Energy Café* (1988). In a move reminiscent of Joaquin – to whom the novel, indeed, makes many intertextual references – Yuson's narrative commences under Spanish colonialism in the nineteenth century. Through the interplay between two figures, the researcher and writer Roberto Aguinaldo in the present and the historical revolutionary Pantaleón Villegas or León Kilat, Yuson questions narratives of heroic masculinity from the novels of Rizal to those of Jose and beyond, connecting them to similar narrativizations of political and popular lives in the Philippines. Aguinaldo – who is clearly a self-portrait of the author – originally thinks of writing a film script, and several sections of the novel are written in this form, while others range from excerpts from scholarly histories to bawdy parodies of elements of the folk tale, epic or Bildungsroman. As León joins the Katipunan and moves towards betrayal and death, his narrative merges with that of Robert, now caught up in the violence of the Marcos regime. In the final scene of the novel, recounted in unpunctuated free indirect speech, León steps out of the confines of his story and enters a marquee in the jungle fronted by a sign indicating it is the 'Great Philippine Jungle Energy Café': he finds it inhabited by figures from Philippine history, as well as Yuson's own friends and acquaintances. Yuson's novel has been criticized for its apolitical stance compared with others written after the end of the Marcos years, but its subversive use of humour and exaggerated tale-telling reflects the experience of life during the early 1980s, when ridicule and satire constituted powerful forms of resistance.

Malaysia

Singapore and Malaysia began 1965 much less auspiciously than did the Philippines. On 9 August, a tearful prime minister of Singapore, Lee Kuan Yew, announced the separation of the city-state from Malaysia. Singapore's incorporation into a larger Malayan political union had been the goal of nationalists since the 1920s, yet its tenure as part of an independent Malaysia lasted less than two years: economic and cultural differences, the political ambitions of various parties, and incompatible visions of the manner in which a multicultural society might be structured drove the two countries apart. From 1965 onwards, the two nation-states followed increasingly divergent paths of development.

In Malaysia, the hegemony of the ruling Alliance was never as firmly established as that of the People's Action Party would be in Singapore, and was challenged from the right by the Islamic Party of Malaysia (PAS) from its strongholds on the east coast of the peninsula and from the left by the People's Action Party's Malaysian successor, the Democratic Action Party. In 1969 social riots erupted in Kuala Lumpur after the defeat of Alliance candidates by the independent non-communal Gerakan Rakyat Malaysia; Chinese homes were targeted and over a hundred people killed. A state of emergency was declared, and parliament suspended until 1971. Future governments would be much more socially interventionist: the New Economic Policy from 1971 onwards attempted to give the Malay community a greater role in the economy at the expense of the hitherto dominant Chinese, and criticism of the special status of the *bumiputera* (literally 'son of the soil', in practice largely referring to persons of Malay ethnicity) or the status of Malay as a national language was made illegal. Malaysia's economic take-off in the 1970s and 1980s as one of Southeast Asia's 'tiger' economies thus came later than Singapore's, and under conditions that alienated many middle-class non-Malay Malaysians, the very section of society that had produced the bulk of Malaysian writing in English. Education policies also resulted in the replacement of English by Malay as the primary language of instruction in most state schools.

The decline of English and the stress on Malay as a national language meant that prose writers in Malay, such as Shannon Ahmad and Keris Mas, overshadowed their Anglophone contemporaries, at least as far as ideas of a national literature went. Writing in English, as Lloyd Fernando noted, was now a 'sectional literature', and could only become part of the Malaysian environment by avoiding 'cocktail-party internationalism' and submitting to new national realities (1986: 143).

The effect of political and education policy changes on writing, however, was only gradually felt. Writing in English in Malaysia, and indeed on both sides of the causeway, initially showed continuity with the Malay(si)an fiction of the 1950s. Lee Kok Liang supplemented his earlier short stories with a novel, *Flowers in the Sky* (1981). Its protagonist, Mr K., a Malaysian–Indian surgeon, operates on a Buddhist monk; the novel tells the monk's story in a series of analeptic episodes, interleaved with a developing plot in which a statue of the Indian deity Ganesh is found washed up from the sea at the bottom of Mr K.'s garden. In both plots religion haunts a developmental modernity, yet such hauntings lack the intensity of similar events in Lee's earlier modernist short stories. The novel obeys realist conventions, and its comic subplot resorts to racial stereotyping. The failure of *Flowers in the Sky* illustrates a problem faced by many Malaysian and Singaporean writers of Lee's generation: the difficulty of writing a multicultural novel that moved beyond ethnic autobiography when a writer's experiences were largely bound within the confines of a single cultural community.

Despite the gradual decline of literary production in English-language writing in Malaysia after 1965, two very significant novels were both written in the period. The first of these was Lloyd Fernando's *Scorpion Orchid* (1976), published while its author was head of the Department of English at the University of Malaya at Kuala Lumpur. Fernando had graduated from the University of Malaya in Singapore in the 1950s, part of a generation of young Malayan writers of the time. He later studied for his doctorate at the University of Leeds when it was a key centre in the development of Commonwealth Literature: he was the only representative from Southeast Asia at the inaugural Conference on Commonwealth Literature at the university in 1964. *Scorpion Orchid* is a text which emerges out of contacts made with other writers at a time of decolonization, and it is set in the 1950s. The novel narrates the experience of four male university friends, each of a different 'race', thus miming both the divisions of colonial plural society and the government-sponsored multiracialism practised in both Malaysia and Singapore after independence. The narrative is haunted by violence, and as violence increases, the men are drawn apart and forced to confront the reality of powerful social tensions born of the effects of colonialism and inequality. Yet the novel counterpoises its four protagonists with two figures who are racially undecidable: the sex worker Sally/Salmah with whom each has assignations, and the holy man Tok Said, a shadowy figure living in peninsular Malaysia. Sally speaks both Malay and Cantonese fluently, resisting attempts by the protagonists to affiliate to her via race. Tok Said is variously described as Indian or Malay, and he eludes attempts by the colonial state to track him down.

Scorpion Orchid is remarkable not only for its content, but for its formal qualities. A third-person narrative with a variety of focalizers is intercut with other documents from the precolonial period or periods of other colonialisms: myths from the *Sejarah Melayu* (*Malay Annals*) jostle for attention with extracts from the first modern Malay autobiography, the *Hikayat Abdullah*, and extracts from a Japanese officer's account of Singapore in the Second World War. At other times the text plays historiographic games with the reader: an apparently genuine British colonial account of first contact is revealed to be a satirical fiction composed by one of the students. In both formal elements and historical context, then, *Scorpion Orchid* is a representative postcolonial text, and indeed appears to be a forerunner of the postcolonial genre that Linda Hutcheon would later call 'historiographical metafiction', embodied most famously in Salman Rushdie's *Midnight's Children* (1981). Yet it also has a specific historical context, its focus on violence embodying not only a memory of the 1950s but surely also a more recent event: the 1969 riots in Kuala Lumpur, and the state's subsequent growing intervention in matters of community and 'race'.

The second significant novel to emerge from Malaysia during the period was K. S. Maniam's *The Return* (1981). In contrast to *Scorpion Orchid*, Maniam's text is a linear narrative that resembles the Bildungsroman employed by earlier writers in Malaya and elsewhere to describe a process of emerging from colonialism: parallels might be drawn between the text and the work of African writers such as Mongo Beti, or with Chinua Achebe's second novel *No Longer at Ease* (1960). Using autobiographical elements, Maniam's novel follows the growth of a young Indian boy whose family operates a laundry in Betong, Malaysia, and his entry into English school. Ravi's growing contact with English-language culture results in an ambivalent mixture of empowerment and deculturation. As the narrative progresses, its focus changes. Ravi's sojourn in England at a teacher training college is no longer a narrative climax, but is skipped over in a few pages. Attention now centres on his father, who exiles himself to the margins of society and builds a house on state land near the river, sinking into insanity and eventual death. In contrast to *Scorpion Orchid*, political events are marginal: the Japanese occupation, the Emergency and the independence of Malaya are described only in terms of how they impact the inhabitants of the small town. Yet the trajectory of the narrative raises a central question that would haunt Maniam and many writers of his generation: the necessity for and yet the impossibility of a return to cultural roots from which one was distanced by a colonial education, and the ambivalent possibilities of making new affiliations and inventing new cultural forms.

A counterpoint to the novels of Maniam and Fernando were the short stories of Shirley Lim, published in the years after separation, and collected as *Another Country* (1982). Having studied at the University of Malaya, Lim went to the United States to study, and then settled there, maintaining a contact with Malaysia and Singapore through extended visits and sabbaticals. Many of the earlier stories in the collection are set in Malaysia, and have women protagonists who struggle to find space in a patriarchal society. The best known of these is perhaps 'Mr Tang's Girls', in which a Chinese-Malaysian patriarch becomes unnerved when confronted with the growing power of the sexuality of his teenage eldest daughter. Kim Li, the eldest of three sisters, breaks proprieties despite her father's attempts to discipline her, and the story concludes with an assault on the patriarch by his daughter. While Fernando and Maniam have always written within a national or community context, Lim's fiction is resolutely transnational. Some of the stories are set in the United States, and they frequently bridge different cultural spaces. In 'Two Dreams', for example, a transnational protagonist uses New York and Malaysia as contrasting 'dreams', each illuminating what the other space lacks, and yet finds it impossible to make an absolute affiliation with either. In this respect, Lim's writing lays the ground for an explosion of transnational writing about Singapore and Malaysia in the 1990s and early 2000s.

Singapore

The economic take-off that marked the late 1980s for Malaysia came earlier to its southern neighbour. Singapore transformed itself from a colonial entrepôt to a manufacturing centre for transnational corporations. The year 1965 to 1990 saw the building of new towns, ports and industrial areas, and an astonishing transformation of the built environment. Politically, the People's Action Party maintained hegemony, winning all parliamentary seats in the period 1965 to 1981, and facing only one or two opposition Members of Parliament for the rest of the 1980s. The period 1965–1990 was also the time at which the Singapore that still exists in a global popular imagination was made, marked by authoritarian rule and the development of an efficient, modern metropolis. The reality is perhaps more complex: Singapore's greatest transformations were perhaps as much cultural as political and economic. Government discourse moved from a stress on a culturally neutral modernity in the 1960s to anxiety about deculturation in the 1980s. Parallel to this came the rise of Asian Values discourse, in which a strategic reworking of Max Weber's Protestant ethic now saw Confucianism as embodying the spirit of capitalism.

Asian Values was a concept promulgated in the 1980s and 1990s by politicians such as Malaysia's Mahathir bin Mohamad and Singapore's Lee Kuan Yew. Asian Values discourse held that Asian societies were naturally communitarian rather than individualistic, and that Asian cultures attached greater value to authority, family, economic growth and social harmony rather than to individual rights or abstract notions of democracy. Proponents of Asian Values, buoyed by the development of the East and Southeast Asian economies in the 1970s and 1980s, argued that Asian societies might choose a culturally appropriate path of modernization. Critics pointed to a history of democratization in Asia and dismissed Asian Values as providing a rationale for authoritarian rule. The discourse declined after the 1997 Asian crisis threw into doubt the developmental model pursued by many Asian economies.

The 1980s thus saw Asian cultures in Singapore pruned and trimmed to fit to this model. Malay, while still the national language, now had only ceremonial importance: Singaporeans were now encouraged to make affiliation to racialized pasts from China, the Malay Archipelago or the Indian subcontinent. English, conceived as a language of technology and development, became the medium of instruction for all educational institutions: Mandarin Chinese, Malay and Tamil, were given 'mother tongue' status, providing cultural ballast against the Westernizing storms of modernity. The use of other Chinese languages – tellingly called 'dialects' – was discouraged, and Singaporeans encouraged to identify with racial communities through mechanisms such as ethnic self-help groups. Yet these changes also had an unlooked-for consequence. English moved from being a minority elite language to becoming the lingua franca of a new generation of Singaporeans; it became localized and from the 1980s onwards, a widening area of cultural production.

As in Malaysia, writers of a previous generation who had dreamed of a Malayan literature before separation were still active. Lim Thean Soo moved from poetry to fiction. In his most significant novel, *Ricky Star* (1978), Lim portrays Singapore society in the process of development. His alienated protagonist rises and then falls against a background of increased production: multinational corporations, the local garment industry and the soon-to-vanish lighter trade on the Singapore River. The pleasures of consumption also tempt: Ricky inhabits new air-conditioned coffee houses, with 'modern décor, dimmed lighting, soft music, pretty waitresses' (1978: 214). And social change beckons: Lim's novel features a male protagonist displaced from normatively masculine social roles, and also contains caricatures of assertive women who campaign for gender equality.

One of the earliest new voices in the period was that of Goh Poh Seng: poet, doctor, novelist, playwright and social entrepreneur. Born in Kuala Lumpur and educated in Dublin, Goh settled in Singapore in the 1960s and chose Singapore citizenship after 1965. Goh's novel *If We Dream Too Long* (1972) is set in a newly independent Singapore on the cusp of great change: its protagonist, Kwang Meng, attempts without success to escape the growing bureaucratization and surveillance that modernity thrusts upon him. Goh's second novel, *The Immolation* (1977), is set in an unspecified Southeast Asian country that is clearly Vietnam, and he is unique among his contemporaries in his concern for larger political changes in Southeast Asia. After his migration to Canada in the 1980s Goh would remain an important alternative voice as both a poet and a novelist, completing his third novel in the 1990s. Goh's concern with a wider Southeast Asian environment was mirrored by the writings of Ho Minfong, whose first novel, *Sing to the Dawn* (1984) is set in Thailand; his use of the Bildungsroman form was imitated, with less self-conscious irony, in Michael Soh's short novel *Son of a Mother* (1973).

The most prolific writer in English in Singapore from the late 1970s onwards, however, was Catherine Lim. Lim, a school teacher who migrated to Singapore, began with the two short story collections *Little Ironies* (1978) and *Or Else, The Lightning God* (1980), and published a first novel, *The Serpent's Tooth* in 1982, commencing a career of regular publication which, three decades later, shows no sign of abatement. Lim's early writing dramatizes intergenerational conflict in Singaporean-Chinese families caught up in an ambivalent process of modernization, and frequently centres on middle-aged women characters who experience these pressures acutely.

While the critical reception of Lim's works has been mixed – she has been criticized for stereotypical characterization, the middlebrow nature of her writing and the fact that there is little development or formal experimentation over her long career – her contribution to English-language literature in Singapore should not be underestimated. The author's texts were among the earliest Singapore literature in English taught widely in schools, and she also demonstrated that, despite Singapore's small market for fiction, it was possible to make a living as a writer. When she commenced publication in the late 1970s, much of Lim's work was genuinely innovative. The short story 'The Taximan's Story' from her first collection, for instance, is a monologue spoken entirely in Singlish by a taxi driver to a woman passenger. As in many of Lim's stories, the narrative unfolds an irony of which the narrator or protagonist is unaware. The driver, we learn, has physically abused his teenage daughter when he found her wearing makeup and hanging out at coffee shops. He now keeps her a virtual prisoner at home, and yet continues to make money by ferrying other teenage girls to romantic assignations. While other writers of fiction before Lim had experimented with the use of different varieties of English to represent a Singapore environment which is heteroglossic in Bahktinian terms in the use of different languages and registers within a language, few had consciously moved beyond the comic representation of non-standard English in dialogue. At a time when Catherine Lim seems to represent all that is canonical in Singapore writing, it is instructive to remember that in an essay first published in 1990 Shirley Lim would explicitly include her as part of a 'counter-tradition' of Singaporean writers who were deeply concerned with the social place of their works, in contrast to a prevailing concern with aesthetics; it is possible that critical foci may change again and that future literary histories will give her a more substantial place (Shirley Lim 1994: 119).

In the late 1980s, an expanding English-language reading public in Singapore resulted in increasing publication of fiction in English. Some works, in retrospect, seem transitional: Robert Yeo's *The Adventures of Holden Heng* (1986) reworks the alienated male protagonist of *If We Dream Too Long* and *Ricky Star* in a Peranakan setting for comic effect, while the fiction of Goh Sin Tub re-narrates ghost stories and urban myths. Others reflect the possibilities of generic specialization provided by an expanding market. Ovidia Yu's *Miss Moorthy Investigates* (1989) transposes the genre of the female detective story to a thoroughly modern city: the female protagonist lives with a woman companion, another professional, is quietly feminist in her actions if not in her words, and pursues the twists of a murder case reported by the English-language mass media. Colin Cheong's *The Stolen Child* (1989) gives an episodic account of a boy's childhood and adolescence. The narrative concludes with the central character as a young adult, in the liminal space of Changi, smoking a Camel cigarette lit with a Zippo lighter, waiting for a coming storm, watching a Boeing 747 take off from the new airport in an 'escape I can no longer be part of' (1989: 345): even as he mourns his imprisonment, he is surrounded by overdetermined symbols of globalization. Popular texts like Adrian Tan's *The Teenage Textbook* (1988) carved out new markets, in this case for young adult fiction.

In the expansion of English-language writing in the late 1980s two significant new voices emerged. The first, Suchen Christine Lim, provided a bridge between two generations. Born in 1948 in Malaysia, she was old enough to remember a past before Singapore's independence in 1965, yet the work of historical remembrance in her novels is, like that of a younger generation of writers, directed towards a critique of the present that is not simply nostalgic. Lim's first novel, *Rice Bowl* (1984), explores social and political activism in the late 1960s, and the manner in which different communities – religious and socialist, English-educated and Chinese-educated Chinese – attempted, and often failed, to work together; it also implicitly critiques the political quietism of Singaporeans at the time it was published. Her second novel, *Gift from the Gods* (1990), reaches much further back in time. While set in the post-war period in Malaya, it contains analeptic recollections by its characters of their migration from China to Nanyang (the 'South Seas', i.e. Southeast Asia) before the Second World War. In the novel, Lim explicitly makes connections between the past and the present through the device of a frame narrative. Yenti, a young woman who grew up in Malaysia and is now married to a pragmatic Singaporean husband, is presented to the readers as writing a journal, and as also reconstructing a written narrative of her mother's life across the barriers of culture, experience and language that separate them. The act of writing, Yenti notes at the conclusion of the narrative, is 'an act of remembrance as well as a severance of the ties that bound me to what I was' (1990: 213): knowing the past here does not museumize cultural affiliation, but rather encourages the formation of new identities in the present.

The second significant new voice to emerge at the end of the 1980s was Philip Jeyaretnam, one of a new generation of Singaporeans with no personal memory of the connection with Malaysia. His first collection of short stories, *First Loves,* was published in 1987, and achieved bestseller status. *First Loves* is a series of linked narratives, many of which centre on the developing perspectives of Ah Leong, a young man who lives in the HDB (Housing Development Board) heartland and who resembles the protagonists of Goh's and Lim Thean Soo's earlier novels. In contrast to his fictional predecessors, however, Ah Leong's alienation from society is less acute, and indeed much narrative energy is invested in his love affairs, as well as those of his friends and family. The city-state in which Jeyaretnam's protagonist grows up is already modern, and is marked by a politics of self-expression and personal autonomy, which often results in transgressions of societal boundaries. Many of the affairs are interracial, and relationships such as that between a young Singaporean-Chinese man and a Filipina maid highlight the changed dynamics of power in the region caused by Singapore's economic development and its importation of foreign domestic labour. In his first novel, *Raffles Place Ragtime* (1988), Jeyaretnam explores, again through the medium of personal relationships, the lives of young urban professionals in the city-state, and the persistence of class divides based on wealth and language. Its resolution, in which the protagonist Vincent Lim rejects the shopaholic yuppie Connie for his non-graduate secretary Veronica, is an implausible but well-intentioned effort to overcome these social contradictions. The son of a veteran opposition politician, educated largely outside the state education system in Singapore, and populating his fiction with majority Chinese characters, Jeyaretnam writes as a cultural insider who is also an outsider. He thus sidesteps the culturalism that marks much earlier Singapore fiction and implicitly rebukes the growing cultural essentialism of the political and social discourse of the late 1980s. Written at a time when educational and other social policies in Singapore were moving towards greater racialization, Jeyaretnam's fiction shows ethnicity as simply one element of identity that also includes wealth, class, gender and other components, and he also explores how social power is expressed in identity politics. His stories were hugely popular with an expanded English-language reading public, tracing through their characters the social fault lines in a city-state that had passed through almost a quarter-century of modernization since independence.

Hong Kong

Hong Kong fiction in English in the period 1965 to 1990 did not show the autonomous development found in Singapore, Malaysia or the Philippines.

The territory's continued status as a British colony on the edge of China made it an ideal setting for espionage thrillers such as John Gordon Davis's *The Years of the Hungry Tiger* (1974), John le Carré's *The Honourable Schoolboy* (1977) or Christopher New's *Goodbye Chairman Mao* (1979), and oriental – and in Edward Said's terms, Orientalist – historical family dramas such as Robert Elegant's *Dynasty* (1977) or James Clavell's *Tai-pan* (1966) and *Noble House* (1981). If no coherent tradition emerged, however, a number of interesting individual publications engaged with Hong Kong society and made greater use of the territory than simply as an exotic backdrop.

Alexander Cordell's *The Sinews of Love* (1965), for instance, depicts a failed interracial romance from the perspective of a young woman of Tanka ethnicity: Lily Chan's *Struggle of a Hong Kong Girl* (1986) follows the fortunes of an immigrant from China through a long-lasting but doomed love affair set against the disruption of the Japanese occupation and the immediate post-war years. Lin Yu-tang's novel *The Flight of the Innocents* (1965) ends in Hong Kong, after the escape of a group of Chinese to the territory during the Great Leap Forward; American resident C. Y. Lee's *The Virgin Market* (1964) explores the lives of a fisherman's family in the harbour of Aberdeen on Hong Kong Island. Han Suyin was to return to the subject-matter of her earlier *A Many-Splendoured Thing* in the fourth volume of her autobiography, *My House Has Two Doors* (1980), describing her affair with Ian Morrison with the veil of fictionalization now removed. Lin Tai-yi's *Kampoon Street* (1964), in contrast, addresses a more modern Hong Kong. The novel depicts the life of a family struggling to support a son through his education in a free-market economy where casual jobs vanish as often as they are created. Through the relationship of the daughter of the family, Riri, with the exploitative playboy Sunny Tung, Lin also illustrates the vast disparities in wealth in a Hong Kong in which the economy is just beginning to take off. With the exception of Lin Yu-tang's novel, however, all the others were published outside of Hong Kong.

Of all the fiction published before 1990, Lee Ding Fai's *Running Dog* (1980) is perhaps the most original and indeed the clearest example of Hong Kong literature in English. Published in Hong Kong in Comber's Writing in Asia series, Ding's novel enacts what we might call a territorial allegory. A young penniless migrant from China in the 1960s, Yau Man, rises to business success, riding waves of strikes and stock market crises. He marries Audrey Chen, the American-educated daughter of his benefactor, when Audrey finally rejects the glamour of romance with an American college friend. One of Audrey's brothers also prospers in business, while the other, fired by political idealism, goes to China. The novel ends in 1977, twenty years before the looming retrocession of the New Territories to Chinese rule, with the characters expressing patriotic fervour for a future in which China will be a world power, even as they are anxious how that future will affect Hong Kong.

The figure most readily identifiable as a Hong Kong writer who emerged on the international scene during this period was Timothy Mo. Born in Hong Kong to a Chinese father and English mother, Mo moved to the United Kingdom at the age of ten. His first novel, *The Monkey King* (1978), has a Macanese Portuguese protagonist, Wallace Nolasco, who engages in complex negotiations as a middle-man between colonial officials and the wealthy Chinese family into which he marries. The novel ends with Wallace finally assuming the mantle of Chinese paterfamilias, yet remaining haunted by the possibility that the role has consumed him. In a final dream he pictures not the effervescent Monkey King Sun Wu Gong of the Chinese classics, but rather a monkey 'immobilized with manacles' on a dining table, waiting for its brains to be devoured by expectant guests (1978: 215). Mo's second novel, *Sour Sweet* (1982), is set entirely in a Cantonese immigrant community in England: in both texts, Mo gleefully traffics in stereotypes, yet complex layerings of voice make the reader uncertain whether they are challenged or endorsed. Mo's most ambitious novel of Hong Kong to date is the monumental *An Insular Possession* (1986), a novel following the fate of Gideon Chase and Walter Eastman, two young employees of the Meiridian trading house at Canton who are swept up in events leading to the founding of Hong Kong. Mo's characters have close resemblance to real historical figures, and the novel intercuts articles from the newspaper the young men found and its rival publication with extracts from letters, diaries and court documents, as well as a more conventional third-person narrative. If the perspective on history given is largely European, Mo at times reverses the gaze so that the reader sees the 'rude Western barbarian' (1986: 23) from the outside, and the text ultimately becomes a series of complex layers of pastiche in which the possibility of intercultural communication is explored, if imperfectly realized. Mo himself has indicated that he is uncomfortable with the label 'Hong Kong writer', and his use of stereotypes and unsettling ironies has also made him a controversial figure. Much of his recent work, indeed, has been set outside Hong Kong, often in Southeast Asia. Mo's problematic and yet potentially fertile position as a global writer in terms of subject-matter, location and audience, is one that has become increasingly common in Southeast Asian writing in English in the period after 1990. If the period from 1965 to 1990 saw the differentiation of national traditions in Singapore and Malaysia, it also saw writers increasingly occupying transnational positions, calling into question the very national contexts in which they were embedded.

Conclusion

- English-language fiction in the period 1965–1990 was written during a time of political uncertainty and rapid, if uneven, economic growth.

- In the Philippines, the rise and fall of Ferdinand Marcos resulted in a renewed discussion of the politics of the literary text.
- Singaporean and Malaysian societies, reading publics and concerns articulated in prose fiction texts gradually diverged after 1965.
- Hong Kong fiction in English in the period, despite several interesting fictional texts, does not constitute a coherent autonomous tradition.
- Many major Southeast Asian writers became resident in the United States, Britain or Australia; a new generation who had grown up in diaspora began writing, complicating the definition of a Southeast Asian literary text.

7 Poetry 1965–1990

Overview

By the 1960s, the writers of Anglophone Southeast Asia had begun giving steady proof that poetry in English had come to stay. In the Philippines, the consolidation of literary trends already established before the Second World War was followed by the rapid assimilation of American tutelage in the craft of writing, and this in turn was followed by the consolidation of the canon-formation that had begun in the preceding decades. In Malaysia and Singapore, local traditions came to their first maturity after 1965 in the shadow of two very different kinds of public discourse about the formation of new nationhood and the role of English in its development, while in Hong Kong a small body of expatriate poetry made itself heard in a period which brought rapid economic and demographic growth to the colony. The circumstances of poetic writing differed from one region to another: in the Philippines, poets had taken in earnest to English half a century earlier than their counterparts in Malaysia and Singapore, while in Hong Kong, poetry in English would not be attempted by writers born in Hong Kong till the end of the twentieth century.

The comparative dimension

The writing scene in the Philippines differed from its counterparts in Anglophone Southeast Asia in several other respects: writers had access to, and often utilized, a range of multilingual creative options; English was assimilated fairly quickly by a relatively large proportion of the population; writers in English were able to access systematic opportunities for instruction in creative writing, at home and overseas, as part of their literary education; and the literary productivity in English from the Philippines is on a scale unmatched elsewhere in Southeast Asia, not only for sheer quantity, but also for variety, range and overall fluency.

Two additional factors are significant: many Filipinos are writers first and poets second, in the sense that neither the genre nor the language they write in is necessarily singular: most write poems and fiction, many write in more than one language, some are also active in writing for television and cinema. Filipino writers approach creativity almost in an abstract sense, as if the choice of language and genre were matters of secondary significance. Remarks attributed to N. V. M. Gonzalez ('I write in Tagalog using English words') and Santos (that he wrote 'in *Capampangan* using English words') indicate the flexible synergies at work in Filipino writing (Cruz: online). Although writers from other parts of Anglophone Southeast Asia have also tackled more than one literary genre, it would be fair to say that a facility with several languages and genres remains typical of Filipino culture, and bilingual creativity is rare in Malaysia and Singapore, but not in the Philippines.

There is also a cost to reckon with, and the worlds opened up by English have entailed a closing down of other linguistic options. The dominance of English over local languages has not always been accepted as a matter of course. Ricardo M. de Ungria, for instance, wonders if he must seek 'revenge' against the English language, 'Because it taught me, among other things, to think poorly of my native language ...? ... Because it has opened me up to a fascinating world where I am condemned forever to live as a stranger?' (Licad 2006: online). The same question is raised by Marne Kilates in the poem 'Allow me travel the space of words', where he acknowledges the responsibility of having to 'contend in the tongues of strangers' (1988: 3). Gémino H. Abad's 'English' is succinct in digesting the implications of choosing a foreign language: 'Their roots run deep / where we have never lived' (2004: 51), and Fidelito C. Cortes's 'English as a Second Language' images the language as a wall of 'impregnable verbs and impossible idioms', worth scaling because the poet can find 'Caught on its barbed war / of nuance, truth' (Abad 1999: 381).

Philippine poets have been going to American institutions of higher learning to learn creative writing for more than half a century. One of the earliest such programmes, started in the University of Iowa in 1936 and run by Paul Engle from 1941 to 1966, was attended by Edilberto Tiempo in 1946 and by his wife Edith in 1947. On their return from the United States in 1962, the Tiempos set up the Silliman National Writers Workshop in their home town of Dumaguete. A similar workshop was set up from 1965 in the University of the Philippines. Others followed. These workshops established a rite of initiation that a sizeable majority of Filipino writers have undergone over successive generations. In other parts of Anglophone Southeast Asia, where a British model of education prevailed, mentorship schemes of brief duration remained marginal to the academic curriculum, which has only recently begun to make provisions for training in creative writing.

Despite such differences, cultural productivity in English throughout Southeast Asia shares the importance given to English as a language endowed with cultural prestige and the power to confer global access to education, trade and the media, by what Han Suyin describes as 'its extravagant splendour, its monstrous capacity of growth, acquisition and incorporation of new words and phrases and concepts' (1991: 18). Contrariwise, as noted by N. V. M. Gonzalez, whenever writers have chosen to use English in multilingual and ex-colonial societies, 'they have set down on paper in a borrowed tongue; so that, while they have written of the people, they have not quite written for them' (1953: 326). An ambivalent regard for English is generally accompanied by a sidelong recognition of how colonial histories dispossessed the colonized from their own past, as remarked by Alfrredo Navarro Salanga in 'A Philippine History Lesson': 'We've been bitten off, excised / From the rind of things' (Francia and Gamalinda 1996: 250).

In this situation, all literary differences between Anglophone Southeast Asian cultures are bound together by the almost obligatory force with which poets using 'a borrowed tongue' have had to adapt its modes and habits to their own times and places, modulating the language to the expression of new idioms and identities. Another shared factor is the material circumstance of print publication for poetry. Given the need to make a livelihood outside the vocation, many young writers of the 1960s found that they could return to poetry only after establishing themselves in a profession that provided a regular livelihood, and some never came back. Local audiences for poetry continue to remain small and elitist. Literary reputations remain a matter of reviews and critical debate within their respective regions. In such circumstances, a good deal of the credit for keeping poetry in English alive goes to those who run periodicals and small printing presses, and promote anthologies. Among large publishers, Heinemann was responsible for bringing a range of Southeast Asian authors into print during the period from 1966 to the late 1980s.

Heinemann's Asian representative, Leon Comber, notes that sales of five to six thousand were considered good for a novel (1991: 83). Distribution remains a problematic feature of the book trade in Southeast Asia. In the Philippines, a sizeable number of literary titles have been published over the years, but readers of writing in English outside Philippine and Filipino-American quarters still remain poorly informed about this activity.

> The total number of books published in 2001 [in the Philippines] was at 5663. But print runs in the trade sector remain small, typically at 1000 to 1500 copies, while new literary titles have even less at 500 to 1000 copies. The numbers are hardly sufficient for a nation with a population of around 80 million and with a literacy rate of around 94 per cent.
>
> May Jurilla (2008: 55)

In terms of literary history, each region shows literary derivativeness making room for the development of recognizably individual voices. Poets moved away from self-conscious literariness to idioms closer to contemporary speech habits, whether local or loosely international. Once free verse became the norm during the 1960s and 1970s, poets returned to traditional forms rarely. Much of what is striking in poetry after the 1960s depends more on a poet's talent for imagery and metaphor than rhythm or form. When contemporary poets return to strict forms (as with sestinas by Fatima Lim-Wilson, Gémino H. Abad and Neil C. Garcia, or villanelles such as 'DH Sunday, Hong Kong' by Isabela Banzon) it is with a full sense that what is being attempted is a revisionary tour de force.

The accumulation of sizeable poetic canons in each Anglophone country has been followed by the bibliographical work of scholars: Gémino H. Abad and Edna Zapanta-Manlapaz (1988) for English poetry from the Philippines, Gene Tan (1994) and Koh Tai Ann (2008) for English writing from Singapore, and M. Quayum (2007) for English writing from Malaysia. Abad and his team also deserve special mention for having produced a set of three anthologies (1989–99) that have proved influential in defining a corpus for Filipino poetry in English. A similar role has been served, without the annotations of their Philippine counterparts, by the ASEAN-sponsored anthologies edited by Edwin Thumboo, and more recent compilations from Hong Kong edited by Mike Ingham and Xu Xi.

Philippines poetry in English 1965–1990

The 1960s were prolific for poetry in English from the Philippines. The first half of the decade saw the publication of first volumes from Oscar de Zuñiga, Alfredo O. Cuenca, Jr., Jose Ma. Sison, Carlos A. Angeles, Cirilo Bautista, Federico Licsi Espino, and E. San Juan, Jr. These were followed, in the latter half of the 1960s, by first volumes from Manuel E. Viray, Ernesto D. Manalo, Emmanuel Torres, Tita Lacambra Ayala, Marra PL. Lanot, Artemio M. Tadena, Elsa Martinez Coscolluela, and Rene Estella Amper. Bienvenido Lumbera and Myrna Peña-Reyes published interesting poems during this period, but did not collect them in a published volume until much later.

The newcomers of the 1970s included, among others, Hilario S. Francia, Jr., Ophelia Alcantara Dimalanta, Gémino H. Abad and Eric T. Gamalinda. The 1980s introduced several new poets, including Alfred A. Yuson, Simeon Dumdum, Jr., Edel E. Garcellano, Edgardo B. Maranan, Merlie M. Alunan, Clovis L. Nazareno, Alfrredo Navarro Salanga, Anthony L. Tan, Clovis L. Nazareno, Ricardo M. de Ungria, Emmanuel Lacaba, Isabela Banzon, Marjorie M. Evasco, Lina Sagaral Reyes, Marne L. Kilates, Jose E. Ayala, Luis Cabalquinto, Fidelito C. Cortes and Ramon C. Sunico. Any such list can only hint at the variety of Filipino poetry, and we shall be obliged to confine our attention here to a few representative examples.

Public recognition for poetic activity in the Philippines was consolidated through the setting up of a number of awards that continue to carry considerable prestige among peers and readers: the Philippine Free Press

Literary Award (from 1949), the Carlos Palanca Memorial awards (from 1950), and the annual Manila Critics Circle awards (from 1982). During the years of martial law (1972–81), book publication came under the control of a board of censors, and the National Artist awards were instituted. Ironically, they remain a small part of the Marcos legacy that survives, honourably, to this day. During the decade of martial law, state control over culture had the effect on writers of pushing those who were inclined to rebellion one way while it induced many others to move to safer subjects and styles.

In terms of the principal poetic accomplishments of the early part of the period under review here, we begin with Nick Joaquin, who is perhaps better known for his fiction, plays and prose, but also wrote poetry of great distinction. The work collected in *Prose and Poems* (1952) and *Collected Verse* (1987) consists of two kinds of poems. Both kinds share with his prose the polyphonic lyricism of 'someone who writes in English but really has a Spanish sensibility in terms of the ornateness of his language', as remarked by Resil Mojares (Dumdum *et al.* 2004: 192). The longer poems rely on a verse line resembling blank verse that combines meditative, descriptive and dramatic elements into narratives that are allusive and evocative. The shorter poems use rhyme and traditional metrical forms to express with melancholic zest themes whose savour is never too far from the morbid, articulated with an energetic gloom overlaid with Christian anxiety and retrospective guilt, as for example in 'Pascua Flamenca'. The most striking shorter poems, characterized by energetic rhythms and a brisk kind of melancholy, appeared in *The Philippines Free Press* during 1966–69: 'Villanelle Attempting Cold Comfort', 'Nope, Kilroy Was Not Yea But Mene Tekel & Sic Transit', 'From the Chinese Trip', and 'Stanzas in memory of General Emilio Aguinaldo'. Most were later retitled.

In its longer version, the last-named poem was retitled 'El Camino Real'. It illustrates the best that Joaquin managed with the dramatic poem based on historical materials interpreted in hindsight along lines typical of his attitude to history and heroism, in which, as the essays comprising *A Question of Heroes* declare repeatedly, 'The martyr as hero by accident is a recurring irony in our history' (1977: 1). The fictive time of the poem corresponds to the events of March 1901. Aguinaldo, the Filipino general who had withdrawn temporarily to the small town of Palanan in order to recuperate the Republic and sustain the Revolutions of 1896 and 1898, had hardly begun celebrating his thirty-second birthday when he was tricked and placed in captivity by Macabebe scouts led by five American officers and a Spanish soldier named Captain Lazaro Segovia, who had abandoned the Revolution in 1900 to accept employment with the Americans.

Jose Rizal (1861–96): Philippine national hero; author of two key novels in Spanish, *Noli me Tangere* (1887) and *El Filibusterismo* (1891);

proponent of peaceful reform in Spanish rule over the Philippines; his execution in 1896 acted as one of the significant catalysts for the Philippine revolution of 1896–8.

Andrés Bonifacio (1863–97): the son of a Tagalog father and a *mestiza* mother (of Spanish and Filipino parentage), Bonifacio was influenced by European revolutionary writing and Rizal, wrote a number of nationalistic pieces, joined a movement founded by Rizal with the aim of persuading the Spanish to liberalize their rule in the Philippines; then, after Rizal's arrest in 1892, founded the more aggressive underground resistance movement known as the Katipunan; after the execution of Rizal in 1896, declared independence for the Philippines from Spanish rule, fought the Spanish; was challenged in his leadership of the Katipunan by Aguinaldo, who had him arrested and executed on the charge of sedition and treason.

Emilio Aguinaldo (1869–1964): Born into a Chinese *mestizo* [mixed race] family, Aguinaldo entered politics at an early age, joined the secret Katipunan in 1895; rose rapidly to the rank of general; led an attack on the Spanish in 1896; wrested leadership of the Katipunan from Bonifacio in 1897; was exiled to Hong Kong later that year as the price for a treaty with the Spanish; returned in 1898 when the Americans attacked the Spanish; led the war for independence against US forces; was arrested in 1901, after which he pledged allegiance to the United States.

As the poem begins, the General and his captor are in conversation. The General meditates on his multiple failures. The poetic licence of retrospection permits the poet to make those failures explicit in a manner that conforms to his own reading of those fateful years. As Joaquin writes in *A Question of Heroes*, 'Aguinaldo had been given three chances. One was the chance to take Manila by storm before the Americans could land an army … Another was the chance to stick to his lines … so that they would be forced to *follow* the Filipinos into Manila' (1977: 148), and preceding these was the chance he had to make an alliance with the Spaniards well before they worked out a similar alliance against him with the Americans. Joaquin takes up the position that Aguinaldo – like Rizal, who 'died for what he did *not* believe in' (1977: 1), and like Bonifacio, who failed the Revolution he could have led to unity and victory – did not live up to the supreme need of the moment when his destiny called him to a choice that would determine the future of Filipinos. 'A single act of Aguinaldo could have startled us into a nation,' laments Joaquin (1977: 144). Tragedy is not truly tragic without the irony of belated self-knowledge, and so Joaquin must have his failed hero recognize where and why and how he failed. But tragedy must also be found at once both poetic and patriotic: therefore it must have amelioration, and hence a poem in which the protagonist admits his defeat does not end in failure; the poet insists that the spirit of the Revolution lives on, in the people, and in a futurity beyond Aguinaldo and his fate:

> the air now trills
> with music: the anthem of the Republic
> and the Revolution. [...]
> 'The people have spoken.' 'And the people are right,'
> Agrees the captain, 'their Camino Real
> Does not end here ...'

(1987: 74)

El Camino Real commemorates the strip of road which separated Manila from its Filipino liberators and Aguinaldo from a destiny that he should have grasped and delivered to his people with both hands. The poem makes it symbolic of a road not taken by the Filipino nation; a consummation devoutly wished for that still awaits realization, real as any hope, distant as any dream. Similar sentiments are given voice in Rafael Zulueta da Costa's poem 'Like the Molave', which won the Commonwealth Award (with Villa) in 1940, and begins with the line: 'Not yet, Rizal, not yet' (Abad 1989: 143).

An infatuation with national history is characteristic of the Filipino poetic imagination. It led several poets to epic ambitions in the 1960s and 1970s, with results that are modest but intriguing. As we have seen in Chapter 5, Ricaredo Demetillo was the first Filipino to attempt the long poem in English, *Barter in Panay* (1961). The poem gives contemporary voice to legendary historical material from the ancient *Maragtas*, which speaks of ten chieftains (*datu*) from Borneo migrating to the island of Panay where they established a community (in the thirteenth century) from which the present population of the Visayas is believed to be descended.

An equally ambitious but stylistically more adventurous attempt on the historical epic in verse was made a decade later by Cirilo F. Bautista in *The Archipelago* (1970). Like Demetillo, Bautista seeks an alliance between poetic nationalism and nationalist historiography while assuming an audience conversant with the history that he interprets. The material of *The Archipelago* ranges from the arrival of Magellan and Legaspi in the Philippines to the role of Rizal in the formation of the nation. As noted by Leonard Casper, despite its implied nationalism Bautista's poem remains 'Hispanic-oriented', whereas Demetillo foregrounds 'the visible Filipino and his artifacts' (Casper 1991: 81). Bautista uses an assortment of verse forms, and his style is capable of inventive conceptions such as 'a dream afraid to be / possessed by particulars' (1970: 37), but when self-indulgence prevails, ugliness results, as in lines like 'contumelious prehensile evening' (1970: 38). Bautista's second book-length long poem, *Telex Moon* (1981), is based on a single stanza form which is not able to avert the risk of monotony despite its air of experimentalism. In 1999, Bautista completed the set with the more varied and also more inventive volume, *Sunlight on Broken Stones*, which won the national centennial prize for the epic in 1998: underlining the ironic fact that the Philippines is the only nation in the Anglophone world to continue believing in the possibility of an epic poem, at least in terms of state-sponsored awards. If we turn to a more recent attempt at the long poem, 'Cantata of the Warrior Woman Daragang Magayon' by Merlinda Bobis, the difficulty of transforming mythic materials into contemporary poetry while trying to sustain a combination of narrative and drama on the basis of a short verse line is again underlined.

Regardless of genre, the evocation of historical events as the instigation for poetry remains a characteristic compulsion among Filipino poets. Federico Licsi Espino's robustly critical 'Abbadon's Monologue' plays on the Hebrew etymology of the protagonist's name (which signifies 'place of destruction') and presents a sardonic recognition on the part of a seventeenth-century Spanish clergyman of how, over the next three hundred years, his kind would reduce their distant colony in Asia to an abode of lost souls:

> Give me ample time and miching mallecho shall overtake
> This archipelago and my quick-sprouting tares shall
> Thrive, watered by the yellow benediction of my piss.
>
> (1976: 27)

The refractive index may vary from poet to poet, but Filipino writers show themselves drawn time and again to linking decisive moments from an invoked past to an urgent sense of present crisis, from Francia's 'Rizal: To a Friend Visiting the Summer Capital during Lent' (1970), to Bautista's 1997 poems, 'Bonifacio in a Prospect of Bones' and 'What Rizal Told Me'. The Rizal dramatized by Bautista makes us feel for him when he begins, 'I have learned the subtle virtue of regret, / how it can ride a mad horse and not fall off', and we understand what Bonifacio might have meant in saying 'I had neither treasury nor art / to subvert the stealers of my heart' (2006: 21, 17).

Poets who evolved distinct poetic styles pushed expressivity in new directions, as in the case of Carlos A. Angeles, whose volume *a stun of jewels* (1963), along with Edith Tiempo's *The Tracks of Babylon and Other Poems* (1966), are probably the most considerable volumes of poetry in English to be published from the Philippines in the 1960s. The two differ in style; each is 'complex' in a way that represents an opposite extreme from the studied 'simplicity' achieved by a poet like Bienvenido N. Santos, though Santos and Angeles are similar in the sense that their poetic activity fell into two distinct periods. Santos's first volume, *The Wounded Stag* (1956), was followed after a long gap by *Distances: In Time* (1983); Angeles virtually stopped writing poems for twenty years, from 1958 to 1978 (largely due to the pressures of his responsibilities as public relations manager of PanAm Airways), took up American citizenship, and came back to poetry only after retirement, in 'Balance of Our Days', the final section of *A Bruise of Ashes* (1993).

The apparent 'simplicity' of Santos can be deceptive because it never precludes depth. 'To Her Who Thinks Me Young', for example, works out an ingenious analogy between making poetry and making money (by stealth, by right and by rite). The first of the 'Minipo'ms' speaks with a candour that might remind readers of a similar effect in the American poet William Carlos Williams. This kind of 'simplicity' is particularly amenable to drollery, as when the poet urges his poems to go out in the sun, only to report wryly that they 'sit silent shaking their heads / staring at their shoelaces' (Santos 1983: 23). Other poems, like 'Dry Run' (1983: 33), adopt plain means towards enigmatic ends, and a late poem like 'Paper Boat Poems IV, glass mountains' (1983: 66) combines passionate sincerity with fluid syntax. Santos at his best shows how lightness of touch can be used to promote a form of ironic wisdom.

Angeles's early style was based on accommodating a fondness for rhyme and uneven line lengths to a habit of oblique syntax, with crucial words often placed in contexts where their occurrence creates surprise. Consider the key verb in the opening sentence of 'Gabu': 'The battering restlessness of the sea / Insists a tidal fury upon the beach'; also note how the verb and the punning adjective come unexpectedly in the final line of the same poem: 'It is the sea pursues a habit of shores' (Angeles 1993: 36). Consider one of the figures of speech in 'Badoc', where the poetic voice is shocked 'To find the belfry's burst brick belly / Wears moss, like sad defiance, to define a gash of green' (1993: 38).

Unexpected images metamorphose into novel metaphors; syntax and diction place themselves at the service of metaphorical energy; the style abjures a colloquial idiom. The special gains of this approach can be illustrated from his predilection for heliotropism: 'The copper sun that scalds the april boughs / Of summer, from the noon's burst cauldron' (Angeles 1993: 33); 'The darkening hoard of the sun's warmth / Drowns in the ruined lake' (1993: 34); 'the night-drenched sun against his eyes' (34); 'the sun, / Relic of unskilled fish, swims out of reach' (35); 'the core of the sun's intensity ... / The dazzling furnace of the sun's bright soul' (59); 'This sun that bowers pure beneficence' (Carbó 1995: 13). The uniqueness of his gift for metaphor is closely allied to unexpectedness of diction and syntax. This habit never quite leaves Angeles. For example here is a poem from the 1940s: 'It is a sign / Vaticinal of things not yet come' (Angeles 1993: 7), and here are two lines from 1993: 'In minor hands these words construct assemblage / from inferior earth amphoras' (Carbó 1995: 12). However, the later style does show itself capable of unforced naturalness, as in 'Jacaranda Tree', which begins: 'Cool mornings. Skies the color of bruised plums. / May and its promise of rain' (Angeles 1993: 73).

Edith Tiempo's career as a poet developed at a measured pace, from *Tracks of Babylon* (1966) and *The Charmer's Box* (1993) to *Extensions, Beyond* (1993) and *Marginal annotations and other poems* (2001). It is marked by swift assimilation of New Critical doctrines and poetic models, followed by the development of an independent style that mediates between lyric, anecdote and fable. During her first year in the United States, Cleanth Brooks's *Modern Poetry and the Tradition* (1939) exerted a formative influence on her attitude to form and convention. Brooks wrote: 'There is obviously no value in adhering to lifeless conventions. But a healthy tradition is capable of continual modification' (1939: 69). The density and intellectualism we encounter in Tiempo is similar to that celebrated by Brooks in the American modernist poets, in whose work 'the play of the intellect is not necessarily hostile to depth of emotion' (1939: 13). Her poems produce interactions between thought and feeling that correspond to the features Brooks praised in the metaphysical poets: 'The ability to be tender and, at the same time, alert and aware intellectually is a complex attitude, a mature attitude ... Moreover, the tenderness is achieved, not in spite of the wit, but through it' (1939: 23).

Tiempo's remarkable 1950 sonnet 'Lament for the Littlest Fellow' (1999: 186) is dominated through the tightly antithetical structure of octave and sestet by the image of a face behind bars: the marmoset's face in the octave, that of the 'sleeping you' to whom the poem is addressed in the sestet. What holds the quizzical meaning of the poem together is the question of resemblance: does the image of the cage establish and sustain a meaningful (though enigmatic) analogy between animal and human; specifically, between the old man in the monkey's eyes and the truant monkey latent in the sleeping human face? While capable of turning a sonnet with skill, Tiempo generally preferred free verse which organizes itself in stanzas or arrives at the conjunctions of rhyme only when the theme calls for them, as in the final stanzas of 'The Rhythm of Violets' (1977).

Her formalism is less a matter of writing to a template than a matter of reflecting on the idea of form as primal to nature: form is also regarded as central to the cognitive acts that constitute the primary perceptions which correspond to the forms of nature. A late poem, 'The Mirror' (1999: 224–225) declares, 'Word-glitter is never cracked'. The truth of poetry is in the intuitive grasp with which the poet can capture an aspect of the forms of nature in language, even when those forms metamorphose. This idea provides the unifying motif in the poems of the 1970s collected in *The Charmer's Box* (1993). Tiempo shares in the universe of discourse where a poet like Wallace Stevens could speak of 'The maker's rage to order words' as a 'Blessed rage for order'. Poetry gives voice to the recognition that the effort of setting energy in motion finds fulfilment in what Stevens called 'the act of the mind', which Tiempo describes as learning 'to brief / Divinity to mind' in 'The twig's tap / The bee's hum' (1993a: 13). What is blessed or divine is the mind being taught that its acts of apprehension correspond in their inwardness to the outer forms with which nature fuses wind, mist and light in tremors of stalk and leaf. Tiempo's poetry is 'complex' in two senses: the language is made to bear the impression of a very distinctive personality; and her poems require a certain amount of conceptual machinery before they can work their effect on readers.

Given the impact of a decade of martial law, the 1980s in the Philippines was a period of meagre publication outlets. Poets were forced to resort to slim chapbooks and privately printed volumes. The situation was to change for the better with the setting up of the Philippines Literary Arts Council (PLAC), which published the journal *Caracoa*, which was practically the only viable place to publish poetry in the early 1980s. Things improved when local publishers again took up poetry, and new ones like Anvil came on the scene; however, poetry still remains commercially unprofitable, and small print-runs soon become scarce, leaving a large part of the circulation of poetry to the ubiquitous and unabashed resource of the cheap photocopy.

From the 1950s to the 1980s, Filipino poetry modernized itself in stages from metrical to free verse and from formalist to experimental writing, without losing its grip on the need for a poet to establish a style that would individuate the writing. As poetic stylists, Angeles, Tiempo, Alejandrino Hufana, Virginia Moreno, Federico Espino and others represent the more self-conscious and crafted end of the spectrum: each wrote in an idiom that was highly textured. At the other end of the spectrum, we have an assortment of styles sharing a preference for a relatively straightforward syntax and diction, with rhythms close to colloquial speech. This mode is no less sophisticated than the other, but its values can be described as broadly cultural rather than narrowly literary; and its expressive preference is premised on clarity of thought which aspires to elegance or unfussy neatness of phrasing. These are the qualities that link the otherwise very different talents of Emmanuel Torres, Dominador Ilio, Manuel Viray and Eric T. Gamalinda.

The poems of Gémino H. Abad could be said to represent the full gamut from the literarily articulate to the minimalist ideal of direct simplicity. A style built on a wide academic knowledge of metrical forms and stylistic resources has gone through a progressive clarification of the relation between means and ends. A neat summation of this progress is illustrated by the poem 'I Teach My Child': 'The simple words first / And last. / They are hardest to learn' (2004: 33). From *Fugitive Emphasis* (1973) and the poems from *In Another Light* (1976) to the most recent poems from *In Ordinary Time* (2004), Abad's career reveals a gradual shift from the polysyllabic precision of his early work to the more direct, less wordy manner of his later poems, which are mindful of how hard it is to speak simply. The same ideal is explicit in the work of another poet who began publishing in the 1970s, Jaime An Lim, but did not collect his poems until *Trios* (1998). At his best, Lim's poems are exactly what they aspire to be: 'simple, lucid, compassionate, and honest' (Abad 1999: 655). In 'The Sorrow of Distances', a father asks his daughter if, as time passes, she will be there for him or have grown beyond his reach:

> Standing
> in the doorway.
> demure
> as a lady,
> solemn
> as a caryatid
> bearing
> the burden
> of a new world,
> your wrists
> weighed
> down
> By the bracelet of the years?
> (An Lim 1998: 13)

The felicity of the image is based on simplicity. Not only is the idea of distance transposed from time to space, but the years are realized in a concrete image, gracing and chaining her wrist.

'Simple' and 'complex', like 'literary' and 'colloquial', or 'textured' and 'elegant', are markers of temperament on a wide spectrum. The recognitions they provide always need supplementing from the many other factors which contribute to the distinctive quality of a poet's writing. Ilio, for example, is cosmopolitan in taste, sympathies and the range of his allusions and settings. Urbanity creates affinities between the styles of Ilio, Viray, Francia and Torres. Likewise, the poems of Moreno, Francia, Torres and Viray are informed by a personalized delight in painting (an art form in which each had some expertise), and an intuitive grasp of how the aesthetics of the visual medium might transpose to issues of poetic cognition. In contrast, Ophelia Alcantara Dimalanta – from *The Time Factor and Other Poems* (1983) and *Flowing On* (1988) to *The Ophelia Alcantara Dimalanta Reader, Vol. 1: Selected Poetry* (2004) – has remained consistent in her preference for a literary voice marked by a diction and syntax that does not apply itself (as many others do) to effacing the difference between poetic writing and the ordinariness of colloquial speech.

A different interaction between temperament and circumstance creates what we might call the 'urgent' style of poetry, written in direct response to the oppressive years of the Marcos regime. It shapes the work of Emmanuel Lacaba, Jose Ma. Sison and Mila D. Aguilar. Each was motivated by an ideological drive, the desire to move an implied audience to a specific attitude and mode of action. Their work blurs the distinction between poetry and propaganda; correspondingly, their idioms are exhortatory. Lacaba died the violent death of a political activist; Aguilar and Sison suffered political imprisonment (as did Emmanuel's brother Jose, also a writer). Lacaba's bilingual *Salvaged Poems* (1986), Sison's *Prison and Beyond: Selected Poems 1958–83* (1984) and Aguilar's *A Comrade is as Precious as a Rice Seedling* (1984) and *Why Cage Pigeons* (1985) illustrate what happens at the interface where commitment to writing meets commitment to action in a time of national crisis. As Aguilar's 'The Song of Revolution' affirms unironically, 'The firmness of her handshake / makes men's vacillations crumble' (Abad 1999: 223).

The assassination of Senator Aquino in 1983 led to the publication of a collective pamphlet, *In Memoriam*, authored by Cirilio Bautista, Alfrredo Navarro Salanga, Alfred Yuson and Ricardo de Ungria. A poem by Bautista from this pamphlet registers 'A Philippine History Lesson' as one that 'moves us away/from what we are' (1983: 14). Such poetry, written with a sense of topical urgency, was one of the lasting outcomes of poetic resistance to the Marcos years at their worst, as in the patterned use of syntactic repetition in Salanga's 'Seven Ways to Read an Elegy': five unrhymed verse lines are repeated and rearranged to give cumulative resonance to the grief whose arousal and allaying restores to poetry the function traditionally served by language in solemnizing the fullness as well as the emptiness of loss: 'O his hammer has lost its head / all else lie shattered in its stead' (1998: 37). Another sustained effort at making poetry out of resistance to the Marcos years is exemplified in the ironic dramatic monologues of Marne Kilates's 'Last Portraits' from *Versus* (1986). Likewise, *Waiting for the Exterminator* (1989) by Fidelito C. Cortes shows what a dry manner allied to a subtle but seemingly plain style can accomplish by way of social commentary.

When poets create a sense of artistic distance between the many provocations that give rise to anger, grief or exhortation and the artwork, the results fare better, as in the poems of Simeon Dumdum, Jr. He studied to become a clergyman in Ireland, then took up law, and has since worked as a judge in Cebu. He uses irony as a flexible tool whose capacity for critique does not forego pleasures of the mordant kind, as in 'Third World Opera'. The poem narrates tongue-in-cheek how when the governor is kicked in the groin by the actor who remembers him as the lackey of the dictator, the audience applauds and even the governor feels honoured 'At how much theater had progressed' (Dumdum 1999: 49). The approach to seriousness through subversive and sceptical modes adds a new element to the expressive scope of Filipino poetry in the 1980s, most notably in Alfred A. Yuson's *Sea Serpent* (1980) and *Dream of Knives* (1986), Dumdum's *The Gift of Sleep* (1982), *Third World Opera* (1987) and *Poems: Selected and New (1982–1997)* (1999), and in the deftly prodigal gifts of Eric T. Gamalinda's *Lyrics from a Dead Language* (1991) and *Zero Gravity* (1999). The title poem of the latter volume uses the phrase 'a breathless abeyance' (Gamalinda 1999: 47), which is apt to describe the effects produced by his wry and surreal poems.

The work of Yuson, Dumdum, Jr. and Gamalinda constitutes the first proof of the cumulative (and belated) assimilation of modernist and postmodern ideas about artistic practice into Filipino poetry. The effect of that assimilation is dramatic in Yuson's fiction, *The Great Philippine Jungle Energy Café* (1988), and we can see early signs of impatience with conventional modes of writing in his first two volumes of poetry, which are characterized by an inventiveness that does not lack for charm, as in the casual play of 'Ethnic Story': 'At the Japanese / tea garden sunlight falls on its knees. / A carp dream rises among the reeds' (1980: 26), or the quirky analogy between going on the boil and breaking the thin shells of boiled eggs in 'Pro and Con' (1980: 36). The qualities Yuson identifies as cherishable in the modernist poets of the West are revealing: 'calculated whimsy, tangentiality, offhandedness' (de Ungria 1995: 166). Yuson's by-now-canonical 'Andy Warhol Speaks To His Two Filipino Maids' manages to make a cheery meal of Pop aesthetics without glozing over any of the benign patronizing his Filipinas have to put up with as they serve soup and salad to the New York cognoscenti, invited routinely to the Pop artist's apartment chatting amiably about the 'coup / in your islands' (Abad 1999: 105). The energy such writing brings to a global conspectus in which art and rumour, maids and masters coexist without blinking is neither casual nor anarchic. Nor is it like the melancholic boisterousness of Joaquin's metered poems of earlier decades. Whereas that art held itself tightly against despair, this art hopes, like the breadfruit tree in Yuson's 'Dumaguete Desperadoes' (Abad 1999: 104), that humour can 'grow' as well as 'blow'. Such writing links energy to responsibility in a fresh take on a Yeatsian theme, as when Yuson asks himself in 'Dream of Knives': 'why do I bleed so / from such sharp points of dreams?' (Abad 1999: 103).

The new element that enters Filipino poetry in the 1980s can be described as a mode of letting poetry repair a leaking roof, with awareness that to have any sort of roof – and especially one which protects and shelters – comes at a price. Dumdum concludes in the half-punning 'Camping Out': 'He who has a roof / has a star for an enemy' (1999: 9). The poem 'America' builds up an 'Aw-gee!' response to the half-hyperbolical supposition nursed by many a Filipino pining to live in the United States, that 'everything there is big / and cheap', only to deflate the naivety with the final interjection, 'the moon was rising / and it was bigger than in / America' (1999: 48). The ability to approach large meanings obliquely and lightly becomes a noticeable feature in several other poets who began publishing in the 1980s, and leads to effects that can be charming, without any compromise in seriousness. Ramon Sunico's 'The Sad Art of Making Paper' from *Bruise/ A 2-Tongue Job* (1995) is one such example, elegant and powerful in its empathy for the Japanese cultural context in which making paper, writing poetry and loving beauty become united in an unexpected way. Another example can be found in Isabela Banzon's 'Icarus', in which the simple writing of – or waiting for – letters, allows a play on an aerogram as a modern missive that takes wing on thin sheets of paper. This associative fancy allows for a cautionary nuance to the pleasures and apprehensions that attend on writing poems and writing letters (acts on which much that is significant in life depends):

> But the sky's paper thin,
> The signature blurred
>
> To be meaning!
> I soar to a word.
> (1987: 13)

Philippine poetry: writing 'woman'

Women's poetry in the Philippines shows a strong continuity of concerns. Unsentimental motifs first articulated with painful clarity in the poems of Manalang Gloria find their successors in the poets of the 1960s. Lacambra-Ayala speaks feelingly in her second volume, *Ordinary Poems* (1963), of what it means to be harnessed to the routines of life in a patriarchal society, in which the only momentous events are mundane, so that 'history happens' merely and only 'when / a glass breaks' (Zapanta-Manlapaz 1994: 206). Her style combines apparent simplicity of manner with a tone sensitive to irony. In 'Dragon', when the blue dragon of her desires asks if she would go with him where there would be no work and only gulls and starfish for company, she engages with the whimsy, delicately turning it down at the end of the poem because there would be no one to spoon the soup for 'Baby'. There is no escape except in the recognition of a need that dissolves in fantasy, a recognition expressed in the most studied form of understatement.

By the 1980s, as we see in the poems of Marra Lanot, the questioning of traditional roles had become more insistent. The protagonist of 'Tribeswoman' ends on a repeated question, 'Could it be possible / It is wrong / To stand and wait / Like this', tied to 'The dream of my father / Sweat of my husband / Hope of my children'? Another poem, 'Wife', pictures the protagonist as someone floating in 'fishbowl silence', whose only choice is to float back into her room where she can 'Burst behind close doors' (Zapanta-Manlapaz 1994: 196–198; 201–202). By the end of the decade the articulation of resistance is complete, though it is still trapped in secretiveness. The justly celebrated poem, 'The Secret Language', by Luisa B. Aguilar-Cariño (who has since preferred to use the name Luisa A. Igloria), shows the protagonist leading a double life, in the daytime submitting to what is expected of her, but at night 'Composing my lost beads', reciting her true and secret name to herself, in a desperately solitary way of sustaining a self not colonized by others (1995: 43).

In contrast, Marjorie M. Evasco's *Dreamweavers* (1987) accomplishes a bending of the poetic impulse away from the rhetoric of alienation. It builds the foundations of a poetics sympathetic to feminist drives, but oriented less towards protest and resistance than towards a magical sense of community, in which womanhood draws sustenance from a complex web of affiliations that includes nature, a sense of community that grows in concentric circles centred on an expansive idea of the extended family, and the spiritual-mystical function of the female shaman (the *babaylane*). Evasco explains the notion of the 'dreamweavers' in terms used by one of the four maternal aunts who used to weave *tikog* and *romblon* mats for a meagre livelihood, and told her as a child about what the weaving signified in larger terms: 'in a world where our lives are circumscribed, when our tongues are tied or cut and we cannot translate our visions and dreams unto the larger world, our hands transform the materials we work with into testaments of how we dream, how we turn our useful arts into covert legacies which will one day reveal to the discerning eye how we made every workday bearable by transforming our ways of living with our ways of creating' (1987: 10). Evasco lives up to the responsibility by making of poetry a similar form of dream-weaving: 'the wisecraft / of the ancient loom' (1987: 68). Her book is organized in a progression, from 'Birth' through 'Daughters' and 'Women Voices' to 'Wise Women' and 'Pintadas' (paintings, as of masks or on rocks). It is in her work, and that of Luisa Igloria, that women's writing from the Philippines achieves its most promising contemporary embodiment, along with the gentle gifts of Merlie M. Alunan, who gives to that tradition a tone that is temperate and balanced, so that even frustrations in love or marriage can be articulated with assonance:

> We hammer the doors of silence,
> bruising with words we could not speak.
> How did we ever think
> We had no need of keys?
>
> (2004: 33)

Poetry from Malaysia and Singapore 1965–1990

The path taken by state language policy in Malaysia after independence in 1957, and especially from the 1970s, led to a diminishment of publishing outlets and readers for English poetry in the country. In Singapore, independence brought the opposite outcome: a quick consolidation of the role of English for the nation. Poetry flourished slowly but steadily, partly through individual volumes and partly through anthologies which served a dual function – retrospective and prospective – that enabled a very small local readership to keep alive a sense of poetic beginnings, while providing authors who were not yet ready for individual volumes the chance to keep themselves in print, as in Malaysian compilations edited by Lloyd Fernando (1966), David Ormerod (1967), K. S. Maniam and M. Shanmughalingam (1988); and Singaporean anthologies edited by Edwin Thumboo (1970, 1973, 1976), and Kirpal Singh (1972). As noted in the sympathetic account of

Malaysian women's writing by Nor Faridah Abdul Manaf and Mohammad Quayum, it was the example and leadership of university teachers of English literature like Fernando and Ormerod in Kuala Lumpur and Thumboo in Singapore that motivated several generations of young students to take up poetry. While many published sporadically in anthologies and periodicals, a handful stayed the distance.

The only individual volumes of poetry to appear in Malaysia-Singapore during the latter half of the 1960s were Wong Phui Nam's *How the Hills are Distant* (1968), and Hilary Tham's *No Gods Today* (1969). Wong May's *A Bad Girl's Book of Animals* was published in 1969 from the United States, as were her next two books. As far as contributions from overseas-based Malaysians were concerned, T. Wignesan's *Tracks of a Tramp* (1961) and Cecil Rajendra's *Embryo* (1968) can be counted among the earliest (followed, in Rajendra's case, by many more titles, generally published from overseas). Each displayed a willed commitment to poetry that led to much that sounds rhetorical and experimental rather than poetical today.

A more lasting contribution came from Wong Phui Nam. His poetic world was shaped in the 1950s and 1960s, and this might be the most appropriate place to provide an overview of his career (to complement the account of his early work in Chapter 4). Wong has consistently given voice to a sense of mixed feelings about writing from a Malaysia whose ethnic politics isolated and alienated the immigrant races. Unlike Shirley Lim, who migrated to the United States, and Ee, who migrated to Australia, Wong chose to stay on. Poetry in English from Malaysia reveals itself as a two-sided coin: one, indigenous Malay; the other, immigrant Chinese. Wong and Ee exemplify two aspects of the latter predicament. While a Malay poet such as Muhammad Haji Salleh celebrates community, the ethnic Chinese poets struggle to recuperate a sense of community in a condition of isolation aggravated by the politics of ethnicity. While the Malay poet affirms a bond between the Malay people and the continuities conferred upon their history by tradition, Wong and Ee speak bitterly of dereliction, suffocation and repression. Ee's work focuses on the damage done to his sense of community by the state-sponsored essentialist nationalism which promoted the ethnic Malay as the only true *Bumiputera* ('son of the soil'): 'there have been many and different orders of tradition in Malaysia, each with its own distinctive roots, and the several roots have tangled and intertwined for generations. It was a political decision which determined which root should be nurtured, and which pulled out' (Ee 1987: 15).

Wong Phui Nam's poems bespeak the effects of a similar dejection. Even his limpid translations from Chinese poetry are attended by the pathos of someone evoking a culture he is nostalgic for but recognizes he can only see through a glass darkly. In a personal statement made at a conference in 1984, Wong lamented a sense of triple alienation: from the Chinese tradition (by virtue of being a descendant of migrants) as well as the Malay tradition (by virtue of being Chinese); from an urban, materialist culture which was the product of colonial exploitation and devoid of spiritual freedom; and from the English language whose traditions he could neither access properly nor do without (1987: 215–217). His productivity after *How the Hills Are Distant* (1968) was interrupted by long periods of self-imposed silence, broken finally by *Remembering Grandma and Other Rumours* (1989), *Ways of Exile* (1993), *Against the Wilderness* (2000) and *An Acre of Day's Glass* (2006). The latest volume collects, revises and rearranges the cumulative work of over five decades. It provides a poignant sense of an *oeuvre* unified around the problem of having to draw upon cultural affinities from traditions the poet cannot quite call his own, while living in a place that he can neither leave nor quite affirm as home.

The 1970s brought an increase in book publications: over three dozen volumes of poetry, of which a handful display a reasonable degree of self-confidence. Two veterans from the 1950s published interesting new material in the 1960s: Lim Thean Soo and Goh Poh Seng. The other significant volumes from this period are Arthur Yap's *Only Lines* (1971), Robert Yeo's *Coming Home Baby* (1971), Chandran Nair's *Once the Horsemen and Other Poems* (1972) and *After the Hard Hours, This Rain* (1975), Ee Tiang Hong's *Myths for a Wilderness* (1976), Muhammad Haji Salleh's *Time and Its People* (1978) and Edwin Thumboo's *Ulysses by the Merlion* (1979). Muhammad Haji Salleh's single volume in English, like the many he has written subsequently in Malay and translated into English in *Beyond the Archipelago* (1995), speaks for the conditions of poetry from the perspective of someone sympathetic to the nationalist impulse in modern Malaysia, even though the poet frequently declares a dual loyalty to Malay and English. It is worth noting how two Peranakan-born poets react to the Malay world implied by Muhammad's poetry. Ee Tiang Hong describes it as 'a social structure set in a rural community, based on tradition, homogeneous in its values and beliefs, cohesive and involving face-to-face contacts' (Ee 1982: 44). Chin Woon Ping elaborates a more sharp recognition of what the Malay element in Muhammad Haji Salleh entails for the ethnic minorities in Malaysia: 'The preoccupation with ancestral roots and with cultural purity stems from Muhammad's overriding concern with the preservation of traditional Malay customs ... he equates the traditional society exclusively with the Malay one' (Chin 1983: 30–31).

The Indian-born, Singapore-raised Nair moved to work with UNESCO in Paris during the 1980s and has published no volumes of poetry after 1975, though he continues to write (and paint). His poems reveal a unique mixture of sincerity and urbanity, combining the expression of personal emotions with reflections that are thoughtful and passionate, often intent on placing the resolution of human dilemmas in the context of the natural environment in a language that is direct yet sensuous. The second volume is more personal than the first, and preoccupied with the retrieval of value, as in the injunction, 'Find strength, all is yet to be lost'. If Nair exemplifies the talent left hostage by the Muse with contingency, Robert Yeo illustrates the talent amenable to all contingencies. He has tried his hand ably at all the genres, from fiction and drama to poetry: in each case, his writing shows itself alert to the issues of the times, able to situate the specific concerns of Singapore and its rapidly mutating society within the broader perspectives of Southeast Asian history and geography with humour and a sane dose of the prosaically commonsensical.

The most significant poetic work for the 1970s came from Ee Tiang Hong, Edwin Thumboo and Arthur Yap. Yap was the most private of poets, to the degree that his highly distinctive idiom seems to court incomprehension, though his output was steady: *Only Lines* (1971), *Commonplace* (1977), *Down the Line* (1980), *Man Snake Apple & Other Poems* (1986) and *the space of city trees* (2000). Yap developed what is perhaps the most original style among all the poets writing in English from the region: elliptical, dense, oblique, ironic, allusive and altogether outside the long shadow of the British poetic tradition, extrapolating the principled use of lower case letters (and some of the attendant romanticism of the lyric poet's resistance to social norms) from the American poet E.E. Cummings. The cost of the effort was frequent strain, obscurity and an impression of the hermetic or of a very arch private joke, eccentric and involved. The gain was homogeneity within variety and a strong, recognizable manner which combines depth with genuine wit (a quality all too rare in poetry, especially from Singapore). Yap was also a painter who exhibited his graphic work in several countries in Asia, and his professional work as a structural linguist interacted with the action of several of his poems. His deliberate habit of seeming to go against the stream in the genteel and well-heeled conformism and docility of contemporary Singapore makes him something of an iconic figure for contemporary young poets who see a value in his resistance, which their own work arrives at much more cautiously.

Yap's poems are anti-confessional and non-lyrical (although occasional poems do articulate moments of lyric perception and an awareness of nature). His main strength is the dramatic mode applied to the short poem, either meditative or dramatic. The first kind vocalizes the poet thinking aloud in print; the second presents assorted Singaporeans, drawn from every social, economic and demographic register, whose accurately mimicked speech habits reveal more than the fictional characters might realize about the poet's oblique intentions. The meditative poems generally use a style that ranges from the prosaic to the pedantic. At its extreme, it is either inadvertently or deliberately self-parodic. Its vocabulary and syntax are drawn from books; its rhythms are remote from ordinary speech or song. It becomes distinctive largely through quirkiness of tone, and the laconic habit of playing with words, phrases and ideas. The poet rarely articulates his views in person, except through the involved implications of irony and satire. Yap's writing can appear self-preoccupied, oblique and compressed. Modernist attitudes drive the tone and syntax. Irony becomes the principal cognitive instrument, humour the chief antidote to boredom, passivity and despair. Here, for example, is the short poem 'statement':

> of course your work comes first.
> after that, you may go for a walk,
> visit friends but, all the same,
> it is always correct to ask
> before you do anything else.
> so if you say: please may I jump
> off the ledge? And go on to add
> this work is really killing,
> you will be told: start jumping.
>   (2000: 29)

Yap's irony cuts two ways: by never taking an obvious or clear position on an issue, he pluralizes the possible reactions one could give to the predicaments he dramatizes, leaving the reader both free and uncertain about the attitude the author would like to elicit from the reader. An ethics is at once implied yet elided in Yap's world of relativity. The compression or elimination of connectives, the telescoping of syntax and thought processes, the obsessive interest in jokes, mimicry, parody and subversion are some of the other features that constitute Yap's postmodernism.

Edwin Thumboo has been the most prominent presence on the Singapore literary scene, though his poetic output is not large: the first slim volume *Rib of Earth* (1956) was followed two decades later by *Gods Can Die* (1977) and *Ulysses by the Merlion* (1979), and then, after a long gap, *The Third Map* (1993) and *Still Travelling* (2008). What his fellow-practitioners Shirley Lim and Ee Tiang Hong had to say about his work remains instructive. Lim found that Thumboo's 'urbane poetics' acquires 'greater public presence' after his first volume, but at the cost of 'spontaneity, naturalness, simplicity, and private emotions' (1989a: 42). She noted that he created a public self by revising positions, so that claims on behalf of the universality of Western symbols, or for the importance of the British literary canon to the Asian poet, were tempered by the value found in a correspondence between the self and the nation. Lim also noted Thumboo's affiliations to a relatively traditional idiom and diction, and the expository manner he developed on the basis of a stylized grammar: 'The poem grows by extension of a main idea; for example, phrases are placed in apposition to the main idea. Conflict is controlled or diminished when the syntax itself avoids subordination and assertion of causal relations' (1993: 113).

In contrast, Ee Tiang Hong gives credit to the concrete and down-to-earth quality of Thumboo's later poetry, its 'accommodation and commitment to nation', and to Thumboo's use of his mixed Indian and Chinese ancestry to circumvent racial pride, keeping the spirit of nationalism 'muted, or sublimated, redirected' in the service of nation (1997: 71). Thumboo's career has been characterized by a faith in the viability of a poetic tradition in English for Singapore. His optimism represents the opposite view from that expressed in 1991 by his academic colleague, John Kwan-Terry, who worried that Singapore poetry in English reflected a 'sense of a dichotomized world, split between meaning and medium, utterance and message', and concluded that 'The poetry in English ... characterizes a literature not of arrival but of retreat, not of achieved meaning but of questioning, and not of certainty, but of doubt, even despite itself' (1991: 118–127).

In resisting such misgivings, Thumboo identified the task of the poet for Singapore as the need to encompass in poetry 'the impact of modernisation ... the loss of traditional values ... conflict between tradition and modernity ... the problems of urban life and the gap between generations' (Thumboo 1990: 27). He worried that since the 'aesthetic side of most Singaporeans has yet to develop', the literature produced in such circumstances might lack 'amplitude, complexity and subtlety' (1988: 135, 147). The only way to prevent that, he believed, was by valorizing a communal role for the writer: 'the poet's problems and celebrations are those of his society' (1985: 12). Most other poets remained uncomfortable with such a position, but Thumboo's own career shows the steadiness of his convictions, even as his poetry made increasing room for the celebration of human relations, as in friendship, recognizing in this commitment an essential corollary to the task of building hybrid communities.

The advantages of writing in English from Singapore rather than Malaysia are illustrated in the contrast between the careers of Edwin Thumboo and Ee Tiang Hong. Ee's fate demonstrates how newly independent Malaysia provided writers from its ethnic minorities with sufficient reason for voluntary self-exile. Shirley Lim wrote: 'After the disillusionment of the May 13 riots [1969] ... I had no nationalist idealism to imagine. The cultural parochialism that took shape in the aftermath of the riots in Malaysia, which includes race-based quotas, communalist politics, and separatist race-essentialized cultures, was absolute anathema to me' (1996: 279). Ee suffered even greater disenchantment and disenfranchisement. A poetic register based on linguistic economy and understatement was deflected, after *I of the Many Faces* (1960), into brooding on the consequences of an ethnic essentialism that served the cause of a very narrow kind of nationalism. The tragedy of exile fills with disaffection as well as poignancy all the poetry in the three volumes of the middle period (*Lines written in Hawaii* [1973]; *Myths for a Wilderness* [1976]; and *Tranquerah* [1985]). Lament is the only response possible to the metamorphoses being forced around him: 'An impending triumph' pushes him out of 'the vacant temples of our past' (Ee 1976: 48). Since he could not 'accept the new order' and 'Stomach the reversal of our lot' (1976: 53), the only choice left to him was self-exile – in his case, to Perth: 'And so, incredulous, I left, / With heavy heart' (1985: 36). Afterwards, there was nothing to do but philosophize the gains in loss: 'To each his own nostalgia, / the truth desire, / the pain that snaps' (1985: 57). The poems of his final volume rehearse a painful catechism of new beginnings, in which 'You have to learn, slowly, / all over again', and what the poet has to learn is how to live in self-imposed exile, 'listen, laugh, put up, / do as the Australians do' (1994: 37).

The poets who came to writing a decade or more after Arthur Yap included many women, among them the Chinese-born Wong May and the Malaysian-born Hilary Tham, who were the first women from the region to publish volumes of poetry in English. Each left her homeland in her twenties. May's *A Bad Girl's Book of Animals* (1969) was published in the United States and she obtained an MFA (Master of Fine Arts degree) from Iowa shortly thereafter. Edwin Thumboo, who anthologized Wong's early poems, described them as characterized by 'introspective self-sufficiency' (1973: xix). A poem like 'Marriage' also shows a rare capacity for quirky humour applied to the sorrows of Mr Pine at having given up his freedom to marry Miss Wisteria, and thereafter unable 'to escape from the nagging of his tetchy wife' (1973: 112).

Tham married an American Peace Corps worker, converted to Judaism and settled in the United States from 1971. The poems she published from Malaysia show more promise than accomplishment. Her *Selected Poems (1967–1969)* is a slim typescript published from the Department of English of the University of Malaya in Kuala Lumpur. The poems are a curious mixture of gaucherie and directness. 'Mist – a poet's creed' declares: 'I sing chromium-coated songs of dawn, /Dusted with talcum off a moth' (1969: n.p.). 'Be still my soul' speaks of 'cloudy roses blooming in dung', and another self-reflexive poem explains that 'My dishwater days I pour away, / Carefully saving the ore I sometimes find'. The distinctive ore mined by Tham is on display in a poem like 'Hate is not black', which declares that it is 'The orange of flaunting lallang; / The baked brown of burnt laterite' (1969: n.p.).

Shirley Geok-lin Lim and Siew-Yue Killingley began their literary careers as students of English in Malaysia. Killingley left for England in 1968, Lim for the United States in 1969. Killingley, in her many subsequent volumes of poetry, does not return to Malaysian themes as Lim and Tham do (and we turn to their later writing in Chapter 9). Several other women born in Malaysia-Singapore, such as Lee Geok Lan, Pretam Kaur, Susie J. Puthucheary, Theresa Ng, Daisy Chan Heng Chee, Muh Lan, Maureen Ten and Fadzillah Amin, published a scattering of poems in the periodicals and anthologies of the late 1960s and early 1970s. Faridah and Quayum (2001) provide a detailed account of their work, though it might be said that the fact that they wrote poems in English in a Malaysia soon to marginalize the role of English in society is more significant than the question of whether what they wrote can be regarded today as memorable poetry. This small and neglected body of writing has the virtues of sincerity and directness, but is often rather plain and flat in tone and style.

Geraldine Heng's *Whitedreams* (1976) was the first book of poetry in English by a woman to be published from Singapore (although Hedwig Aroozoo had written brilliantly during the 1950s, her poems appeared in obscure periodicals and had to wait until 1999 to be collected into a volume). Heng fails to deliver on what her persona's attempted lyricism requires for its plausible sustenance, and she gave up poetry thereafter to pursue an academic career first in Singapore and then in the United States as a medievalist. Other women who made an interesting contribution to poetry in English during the 1970s include Nalla Tan and Rosaly Puthucheary. Each published fairly copiously, and evolved a certain fluency in a personal idiom which remains readable without being strikingly original.

Poets with established reputations who published new volumes of poetry during the 1980s included from Malaysia, Wong Phui Nam; from overseas, Ee Tiang Hong, Goh Poh Seng and Cecil Rajendra; and from Singapore, Robert Yeo, Arthur Yap and Kirpal Singh. Singh's slim Calcutta-published *Twenty Poems* (1978) was followed by the more robust scepticism of *Palm Readings* (1986) and *Cat Walking and the Games We Play* (1998), which combine energetic and shrewd observations on human affairs with satire that is motivated by a kind of romantic idealism about social and personal relations. 'Types I have Known', for example, is sarcastic about 'the blessed' people who 'suggest trust, revel in treachery' (1986: 16). Singh's older friend Yeo measures with steady consistency Singapore's hard-won peace and prosperity against the turbulence of violent change all over Southeast Asia. Poem after poem in *Leaving Home, Mother* (1999) testifies to his ability to keep his mother-country and the region in which it works out its balances in stereoscopic vision. 'Proximities to Vietnam', for example, distinguishes geographical from moral proximity, so that the poet can confront his readers with the need to assess a difficult question, how it might be possible 'For stability / To support the expression of a policy / That negotiates and bombs at the same time' (1999: 135), and recognize the limits of consciences which gesture helplessly in the direction of 'further exercises in futility' (1999: 137).

The most significant new poet to enter the scene of writing in the 1980s (apart from Shirley Lim) was the Singaporean-born Lee Tzu Pheng, whose *Prospect of a Drowning* (1980) was followed by *Against the Next Wave* (1988) and *The Brink of an Amen* (1991). Other volumes of the decade from Singapore included Simon Tay's *Prism* (1980), Ho Poh Fun's *Moving Pictures* (1985) and a promising first volume by Boey Kim Cheng, *Somewhere-bound* (1989). The Malaysian poets who published first volumes in the 1980s were the lively, iconoclastic and satirically inclined Salleh Ben Joned (*Sajak Sajak Salleh: Poems Sacred and Profane* [1987]) and the sincere but somewhat drab Kuan Guat Choo (*Feelings* [1989]). Other poets to make an appearance in book form during the 1980s include the Brunei-born, England-educated Zariani Abdul Rahman, whose *Dance of Death* (1989) is a mixture of the devoutly Islamic and the exuberantly literary, which applies itself through a medley of allusive verse and prose to local legends, modern awareness of the environment and an urgent sense of imminent death, both of the spiritual and the literal kind, a fate brought upon the contemporary world, the poet alleges, by bad choices.

Lee Tzu Pheng can be described without exaggeration as the most consistently sensitive poet to have written in English from Singapore. Her poems speak with a voice of steady thoughtfulness. She can dwell on feelings without risking exhibitionism or sentimentality. Her first volume contains three quite remarkable poems. The Blakean 'Left Hand, Right Hand' presents with economy and precision a strange nexus between care and hatred such that while we would plant our hearts 'in the dark of our neighbour's ground', hoping that 'he may discover we cared', we would plant our hate 'in the dark of our enemy's ground', to show him that 'we dared' (1980: 8). This type of verse shows an unerring instinct for phrasing. In contrast, the meditative 'Bukit Timah, Singapore' and 'My Country, My People' reveal a gift for social commentary. The tone in each is quietly conversational. Understatement belies the seriousness of the critique applied by the poet to the modern drive for urbanization. The drive responds and corresponds to the compelling myth of modern progress. The poem does not evoke the spirit of sentimental nostalgia. It wonders aloud if society might have lost control over the compulsions that drive nations towards chimeras of development while transforming topographies, souls and the values that keep us human, weakening the capacity to resist the mutation of 'home' into a 'megapolitan appetite' (1980: 50).

Lee's second volume, *Against the Wave* (1988), adds further dimensions to her capability: religious themes come to the fore, as do engagements with the universal human appeal of fairy stories and music. Her third volume, *The Brink of an Amen* (1991), maintains a high level of meditative integrity. The range of subjects the poet handles has grown deeper and broader: the caprice of memory and love, the appeal of painting and literature, the struggle for women's freedom, the human element in events large and small, public and private. The title poem demonstrates the certitude of a negative capability wary of the false comfort of hope. The poem is careful to sidestep the solace words might proffer, preferring instead to wait on the threshold, just short of zeal or affirmation, 'On the brink of an amen', a luminous and liminal space that is 'simply a silence, / absolute, waiting' (1991: 27). Lee's next volume, *Lambada by Galilee and Other Surprises* (1997) develops in two directions: towards a firmer affirmation of religious faith and a new-found ability to engage serious issues lightly, spirited without becoming lightheaded or facetious; sensible, but with a wit that can scratch.

Conclusion

- Poetry in English came into its own in the Philippines well before the 1960s and has continued to do well in a variety of styles and modes.

- Poetry in English took slightly different paths in Malaysia and Singapore depending on the support given to English in state policies on education: it dwindled into relative neglect in the former, but flourished in the latter.
- The Philippine tradition shows a consistent preoccupation with national history and an aspiration towards an idealized nationhood that still remains thwarted.
- The Singapore tradition engages with the issue of nation formation and the role of poetry in this collective enterprise.
- Women's writing of great perceptiveness and power was produced in the Philippines and in Malaysia and Singapore throughout the latter half of the twentieth century.

8　Drama 1965–1990

Overview

In the post-1965 period, English-language drama in the Philippines, Singapore, Malaysia and Hong Kong developed in radically different directions, and yet these developments were driven by two common factors which influenced drama more deeply than fiction or poetry. The first of these was language policies, which influenced the extent to which English-language texts could claim to represent a national or local culture, and indeed the composition of any prospective audience. The second, not unconnected to the first, was politics: most of the major theatre practitioners of the period felt that theatre offered a powerful means to critique both the social inequalities inherited from the colonial era and new modes of governance introduced by postcolonial nation-states. Both these factors perhaps illustrate how drama is in many ways less portable and more closely bound to its immediate context than fiction and poetry. Drama may be performed abroad – as was the case with Kee Thuan Chye's play *The Big Purge*, written and performed while he was at the University of East Anglia in the United Kingdom – but it needs a local audience if it is to grow, and it has a more immediate relationship with that audience than do the other genres.

While discussion of drama in Hong Kong, the Philippines, Singapore and Malaysia will here proceed in discrete sections to reflect each country's different experiences, we should remember that there were a number of regional connections. Malaysian cultural worker and critic Krishen Jit, for example, travelled around Southeast Asia in order to collect information regarding both traditional and modern theatres, and as director and dramaturge incorporated his findings into his dramatic practice. Stella Kon's *Emily of Emily Hill*, one of the most important Singapore plays of the period, was first staged in Malaysia, and the close connection between the English-language theatre worlds of Kuala Lumpur and Singapore continues to this day. Finally, the Third Stage, perhaps Singapore's most politically radical theatre group of the period before members were arrested in the 1987 'Marxist conspiracy', had connections to the equally radical but more regionally influential Philippine Educational Theater Association (PETA).

Finally, we should be aware that surveying English-language drama in Southeast Asia over a period of twenty-five years necessitates compromises. The texts of many important plays remain to be published, and the meanings of canonical plays have been transformed in the hands of different directors. This chapter, and the later chapter on developments in drama after 1990, will thus stress the analysis of published dramatic texts over history of theatre or performance, while acknowledging that no consideration of dramatic texts can ignore the circumstances of their production and consumption.

The Philippines

In the Philippines, English-language theatre followed a trajectory of decline that has persisted to this day. Guerrero, Florentino and Joaquin continued to write in English for the stage, but opportunities for theatrical production in English became increasingly limited outside the university campuses. The decline of English-language theatre in the Philippines was no doubt in some ways due to the limitations of the medium itself. As Bienvenido Lumbera noted, Philippine drama in English ran into representational difficulties in the type of language it used. If it employed international standard English, speeches rang 'false when spoken by a Filipino character' (1984: 173). Attempts to use a 'bent' or more heavily Filipino English, however, resulted in performances that were either 'floridly sophomoric or woefully inarticulate' (1984: 173). Yet one might counterpose to Lumbera's strictures the examples of writers in Malaysia and Singapore in the 1980s who made use of distinctively Malaysian or Singaporean Englishes that provided greater rather than reduced articulacy. The withering of English-language drama from the 1960s onwards in the Philippines was thus perhaps less a result of internal failings than of powerful external factors.

The first of these was a cultural nationalism expressed in artists' conscious use of the national language, Filipino, or Pilipino as it was for some time called. From the 1960s onwards, writers such as Alberto Florentino moved from English to Filipino. More crucially, dramatists such as Rolando S. Tinio translated Western stage classics such as *Waiting for Godot*, *Death of a Salesman* and *Miss Julie* into the national language, expanding the stage repertoire. The Philippine Educational Theater Association (PETA), established in 1967, continued this process, performing not only Filipino translations of Brecht and Ionesco, but also of Nick Joaquin's *A Portrait of the Artist as Filipino*: increasingly, PETA and other theatre companies began to produce original works in Filipino. These were sometimes reworkings of older forms, such as Isagani Cruz's *Halimaw*, which revived the *sarswela* musical drama popular in a number of regional languages in the late nineteenth and early twentieth centuries. More frequently, however, dramatists experimented with a realist and Brechtian drama in a new theatre in Filipino and regional languages that aimed to promote social change, and which moved out of the theatre to the factory, marketplace and street. After martial law was declared in 1972, scripts had to be vetted before performance, and realism gave way to historical allegory to circumvent censorship, before the theatre of direct protest returned as the Marcos regime disintegrated.

Such developments, especially the demand for political relevance and a concomitant desire to reach a non-traditional audience, left English-language theatre increasingly isolated. Scripts were written and occasionally performed: Tinio wrote a comedy in English entitled *A Life in the Slums* (1975), while Ricaredo Demetillo produced a verse drama. Nick Joaquin was again the period's outstanding English-language playwright, writing three full-length plays. Yet even these show a waning of energy: two are essentially stage adaptations of short stories that had made the author's reputation over a quarter of a century earlier. The most successful is *Tatarin* (included in Joaquin 1979), which reworks Joaquin's story 'The Summer Solstice', changing its setting from the 1850s to a family mansion in Manila of the 1920s, and expanding the cast of characters. Joaquin's revisions certainly give the play a wider range of cultural reference than the original short story. The changed setting enables the author, much as he does in *A Portrait of the Artist as Filipino*, to dramatize the tensions not simply between Spanish and precolonial cultures, but also between both of these elements of Filipino culture and the legacy of American colonial modernity. Newly developed characters such as the son of the family and two domestic servants enhance one theme that is frequently central in Joaquin's writing – intergenerational conflict – but also add another that is often more peripheral – class. Such widening of interest, however, did not result in renewed popularity for Filipino theatre in English. As Doreen Fernandez notes, audience responses to performances of *Tatarin* in 1978 indicated that they would have preferred a Filipino translation, and indeed Joaquin's two other plays of the 1970s, *Fathers and Sons* and *The Beatas*, were only staged in the Philippines after being translated into Filipino (1996: 124).

Malaysia

English-language theatre in Malaysia has always been closely connected to that of Singapore, and as noted in Chapter 4, the early texts performed at the University of Malaya in the 1950s belong as much to a history of Malaysian theatre as they do to Singapore theatre. Connections continued in the 1960s: Singaporean Goh Poh Seng's *Room with Paper Flowers* was one of the first plays performed in the University of Malaya's Experimental Theatre in Kuala Lumpur. The years immediately after Singapore's separation from Malaysia in 1965 saw a blossoming of English-language theatre. Edward Dorall's *Arise O Youth!*, staged at the Dewan Bahasa dan Pustaka hall in 1966, has been described as 'the first Malaysian play in English to be given a public performance' (Fernando 1972a: ix). In his later plays, such as *A Tiger is Loose in Our Community*, Dorall shows a strong commitment to the use of varieties of Malaysian English including Manglish. Contemporary commentators like Lloyd Fernando, who published the plays in the two *New Drama* collections, were uncomfortable with this, preferring Patrick Yeoh's use of a more standard English that still preserved traces of the syntax of Malaysian English in plays such as *The Clay Model*, which was first performed in 1968 (Fernando 1972a: xii). Other prominent – and prolific – playwrights in English were Lee Joo For, Syed Alwi and K. Das: Das's *Lela Mayang* (1968, published 1972) drew on traditional Malay culture in both its plot and performance, incorporating the work of artists and musicians, and his *All the Perfumes* (1968) used props based on the traditional shadow theatre, or *wayang kulit*.

Founded in 1956, the *Dewan Bahasa dan Pustaka* (Institute for Language and Literature) is a Malaysian government institute responsible for the development of the Malay language and its literature. The institute has been responsible for initiatives such as the standardization of spelling in Malaysia and the region, and in the adoption of standard terms for scientific and technological concepts brought into Malay from other languages. It has also played an important role in the development of school textbooks, and the promulgation of Malay literature through publishing activities. In recent years, the *Dewan Bahasa dan Pustaka* has been critiqued for establishing a canon of Malay literature, promoting a normalized view of Malay identity and prioritizing literature produced solely in Malay as a national literature, thus marginalizing literary production in other languages.

The events of 13 May 1969 and the subsequent declaration of a national state of emergency led to a sharp decline in English-language theatre. Some writers such as Syed Alwi moved from English to Malay, and indeed much of the most interesting experimental drama in the 1970s was in the Malay language. Others, like Lee Joo For, emigrated or fell silent. English-language theatre did not vanish entirely – Ghulam-Sarwar Yousof's *Halfway Road, Penang*, a bleak account of the social pressures preventing interracial relationships, was performed in 1971 in Penang, despite difficulties with police permits, and later in Hawaii while he was studying for his doctorate (2001: 146; 2002: [ii])–but drama in English certainly lost public prominence, so much so that when it did re-emerge in the 1980s many commentators felt that it was an entirely new phenomenon.

The most influential figure in the re-emergence of Malaysian drama in English was Krishen Jit. After a career in student drama which saw him co-found the influential Literary and Dramatic Arts Society (LIDRA) at the University of Malaya, Jit seemed set for an academic career. Working in the history department at the university, however, he was drawn into both the study and practice of Southeast Asian performing arts, and in particular indigenous traditions that might provide the possibility of revising or transforming what he saw as the predominantly Western theatrical heritage and practice in modern drama in Malaysia, an experience that had marked his own initial theatrical apprenticeship as a student at the University of Malaya. After 1969 Jit, like many others, moved into Malay-language theatre, but by the late 1970s public controversy about a non-Malay taking such a prominent role in Malay-language culture caused him to reconsider his position, and indeed the position of drama within a Malaysian cultural landscape. As a Malaysian of Punjabi origin immersed in Southeast Asian cultures, Jit did not fit easily into the tightening categories of cultural affiliation under multiculturalism after 1969; after a break studying performance in the United States in the early 1980s, he returned to Malaysia to work on devised performances, and to co-found the Five Arts Centre in Kuala Lumpur.

Two plays directed by Jit in the middle of the 1980s marked a turning point in Malaysian drama in English. K. S. Maniam's *The Cord* was first performed in 1984, and provides an important representation of the lives and world views of Indian estate workers, whose experiences had been erased from both colonial and post-independence accounts of Malaysian cultural history. In *The Cord*, Maniam's characters engaged in a struggle over modernity, in which the bright attractions of the Yamaha motorcycle dreamed of by one of the characters, Ratnam, 'smooth, efficient and without feelings' (1994: 77), and the hard stick used by the administrator Muthiah to chastise his workers are opposed to the mutability of the *thundu*, a traditional towel-like piece of cloth that serves many purposes, ultimately as 'the simple cord of humanity, as we enter something bigger than our loneliness, bigger than our dignity, bigger than our power, bigger than all the machines we can build' (1994: 94). Maniam shows particular interest in women characters caught between the demands of modern wage-labour and traditional notions of propriety. In his second play, *The Sandpit*, he extends this concern further.

The Sandpit was first performed as a monodrama in 1988, in which Santha, a traditional wife whose husband maintains a polygamous relationship with a younger, more modern woman, describes both the abuse she has suffered and her husband's fear that motivates it. As in *The Cord*, Maniam uses a presiding motif, here Santha's weaving of the border of a sari, to frame the play, indicating her independence and patience. Two years later, Maniam fleshed out the play so that both women appeared on stage, each describing her own experiences and relationship with the husband, yet not talking directly to each other.

Perhaps the most overtly political English-language play staged in Malaysia in the 1980s was Kee Thuan Chye's *1984 Here and Now*, which was first performed in 1985 at the University of Malaya's Experimental Theatre, and directed by Krishen Jit. As its title suggests, Kee's play adapts George

Orwell's novel to Malaysia under the New Economic Policy, with the journalist Wiran replacing Orwell's Winston Smith in his futile attempt to contradict an oppressive social order. Like Orwell, Kee uses a transgressive private relationship, with the 'Prole' Yone substituting for Orwell's Julia, to personalize the more abstract politics of the text. Kee certainly hoped that his production would raise the consciousness of its viewers. In the intermission, actors passed out leaflets to audience members telling them they could 'make the end of this play the beginning' of their own actions in pursuit of social change (1987: 51), and Wiran's concluding speech was spoken directly to those gathered in the auditorium, asking them to 'stand up for … freedom, for racial equality and integration, for humanity and justice, for truth' (1987: 88). The play at times is successful in its critique of state-sponsored multiracialism – for instance in its use of the motif of a 'tiger dance', using a national symbol, instead of the traditional Chinese lion dance, to indicate the possibilities of the construction of hybrid cultural forms. Yet frequently the deployment of the categories of Party members and Proles from Orwell's novel fails to gain precise purchase on the more complex taxonomy of Malaysian multiracialism marked by *ketuanan Melayu* or Malay privilege, in which both class and race play roles. The fact that *1984 Here and Now* received a police permit and was performed, however, ensures it an important place in Malaysian theatre history, and its model of political allegory was influential on a later generation of Malaysian playwrights, notably Huzir Sulaiman.

Malaysian theatre in English continued its development in the late 1980s, aided also by a number of connections with Singapore: both of Maniam's plays were performed there, and productions frequently travelled from Kuala Lumpur to Singapore or in the opposite direction. Language policies limited the audience of such drama, but it did provide a space for political and social discussion and cultural memory that had relative autonomy from the state. In the late 1980s, Five Arts Centre was joined by other theatrical organizations which worked in English, or in English and other Malaysian languages, such as the satirical Instant Café Theatre and the Actors Studio.

Singapore

English-language theatre in Singapore, like fiction and poetry, developed later than its counterpart in the Philippines, but, as in Malaysia, it showed increasing vitality by the 1980s. As in the Philippines and Malaysia, the development of English-language drama took place in an environment of theatrical performance in other languages, and for a long time it had marginal status. In the 1960s, for example, Chinese drama, often with a radical social message, could attract full houses at the 900-seat Victoria Theatre, and its golden age only came to an end with government action against theatre practitioners in the 1970s.

English-language drama initially struggled to find an audience. Goh Poh Seng, who returned to Malaya after studying medicine in Dublin, built on the pioneering work of dramatists such as Lloyd Fernando and Lim Chor Pee, and wrote and staged three original plays. The first of these, *The Moon is Less Bright* (1964), is set in Singapore before and during the Japanese occupation of 1942–45, and illustrates a parallel difficulty concerning language use to that expressed by Lumbera. Goh's characters are members of a farming community, and their use of standard and sometimes wooden English seems forced. Goh himself was aware of this difficulty, and in his second play, *When Smiles Are Done*, he attempted, perhaps for the first time on the Singapore stage, to use a distinctively local form of English. Like Lim before him, Goh was also involved in setting up a theatre company, Centre 65, and indeed held performances in areas such as Queenstown, one of Singapore's new Housing Development Board (HDB) estates for working-class Singaporeans. Goh's third play, *The Elder Brother*, was performed in 1966, but it was clear that the audience for English-language theatre was limited: Goh was to recall later that at one performance in Queenstown the only members of the audience who were not associated with the theatre group were the minister of culture and his wife (Personal Interview).

From the late 1960s to the early 1980s, original plays in English continued to be written by Singaporeans, but only occasionally performed, the most substantial work being two plays by Robert Yeo, later published retrospectively as part of *The Singapore Trilogy* (2001). The first, *Are You There, Singapore?*, was written in 1969 but not staged until 1974. Yeo's play is set in London in the late 1960s, and its characters are Singaporeans studying abroad, caught up in political and subcultural movements that threaten the certainties that they have brought from their homeland. The play also highlights the tension between English and Chinese-educated Singaporean-Chinese, and its characters engage in vigorous political debate regarding the absence of a political opposition in the city-state. Yeo followed *Are You There, Singapore?* with a second play, *One Year Back Home*, in which Ang Siew Hua, the central character of Yeo's first drama, returns home as a single mother accompanied by her five-year-old daughter. The dramatic centre of the text, however, soon shifts elsewhere, to the conflict between Hua's brother, Siew Chye, and her friend Reggie Fernandez, who stand in a parliamentary by-election as government and opposition candidates respectively, and to Fernandez's arrest by the authorities. Yeo's integration of the personal and the political in the play is at times awkward, with characters shifting suddenly from casual banter to overly formal discussions of current affairs. Yet *One Year Back Home* is important in Singapore theatre history because Yeo persisted, despite opposition from civil servants, in getting a licence to perform the play in 1980, and agreed to make revisions which blunted, but did not destroy, the play's liberal politics. The difficulty Yeo encountered in the staging of *One Year Back Home* perhaps demonstrates, in hindsight, that theatre in English was beginning to move out of its marginal role and become potentially influential enough to attract the attention of the state: censorship, whether direct, indirect (through public criticism or the withdrawing of funding) or self-imposed, would be a recurrent feature of the theatre scene in Singapore from the 1980s onwards.

The 1980s saw a gradual development of Singapore drama in English. Director Max Le Blond's adaptation of the British playwright Peter Nichols' *National Health* as *Nurse Angamuthu's Romance* (1981) is often celebrated as the first time Singapore English was used on stage in a naturalistic and unselfconscious manner, and theatre groups such as the Third Stage, TheatreWorks, The Necessary Stage and Practice Theatre Ensemble were founded. A breakthrough came in 1985 with the first Singapore performances of two monodramas, Stella Kon's *Emily of Emerald Hill* and Kuo Pao Kun's *The Coffin is Too Big for the Hole* (collected in Kuo 2000a): though they differ substantially, each text has become canonical in any history of Singapore drama, and both have been restaged on several occasions.

Kon had been writing and publishing plays in the 1970s, but had difficulty getting them performed: *Emily*, indeed, was first staged in Malaysia and only belatedly performed during the 1985 Singapore Arts Festival. The play centres on the reminiscences of Emily Gan, a Straits Chinese matriarch, who recalls how she married into a rich family and came eventually to preside over the household and family home, but at great personal cost: the alienation of her husband and the suicide of her beloved son. Kon's monodrama concludes with Emily spotlighted on a darkening stage, her house now deserted by her children and surrounded by 'tall apartment blocks', desperately articulating memories of the past (Kon 1989: 60).

> The Straits Chinese are a hybrid cultural community living primarily in what was historically the British Crown Colony of the Straits Settlements (modern day Singapore and the Malaysian states of Malacca [Melaka] and Penang [Pinang]). Straits Chinese cooking and costume showed influence from Malay culture, and many Straits Chinese spoke in a Malay patois; the community, however, either practised traditional Chinese religions or Christianity. The Straits Chinese formed a comprador community under colonialism, many receiving an English education and serving as middle-men between the colonial rulers and a larger Asian population of colonial subjects.

A variety of elements of the play enabled it to resonate with audiences. First, Emily confidently and plausibly uses different registers of Singapore English as she changes, chameleon-like, to fit various social contexts. Second, the play speaks to the contradictory demands made of women to both embody tradition and to be modern in the context of Singapore's rapid development. Emily's experience is of an older generation, forced to gain power through becoming 'the very devil of a wife and mother', playing gender roles to the hilt (Kon 1989: 51). Yet the graduate mother controversy of 1983, in which then prime minister Lee Kuan Yew castigated educated Singaporean women for failing to do their reproductive duty, indicated that the contradictions faced by a previous generation of women had been rephrased, rather than having vanished. Third, in depicting hybrid, elite Anglophone Straits Chinese culture, Kon documented a cultural space where English had been historically important in Singapore. *Emily* is not simply a national allegory, despite some efforts to read it as such, but its representation of a Singaporean context in which English is central reflected not only a past elite culture, but also the experience of the new generation of Singaporeans for whom English constituted a national lingua franca. Through plays like *Emily*, English began to emerge as a powerful medium of Singaporean cultural expression, transgressing the function of the language as simply a medium for trade, science and technology to which state-sponsored multiracialism had assigned it.

The writer of *The Coffin is Too Big for the Hole*, Kuo Pao Kun, had travelled a very different route from Kon's in staging his first English-language play. Kuo had come as an immigrant to Singapore from China and come into contact with leftist intellectuals and cultural activists in Chinese-medium high school, gaining exposure to both modern Chinese and Western theatrical traditions. In 1959, he went to Australia to work as a Chinese translator and announcer at Radio Australia: later he studied at the recently founded National Institute of Dramatic Art in Sydney, returning in 1965 to a Singapore living through the trauma of separation from Malaysia. From 1965 onwards, Kuo threw himself into the vibrant Chinese-language theatre scene, founding the Singapore Performing Arts School and writing and directing plays that were critical of the compromises the post-independence government had made with multinational capitalism. In the early 1970s, several of Kuo's productions were banned, and he was detained without trial under the colonial-era Internal Security Act in 1976. Released from detention in 1980, he initially resumed work in Chinese theatre: *Coffin*, which was staged in separate performances in English and Mandarin – a practice that Kuo would continue with many of his later plays – was his first English-language play.

Coffin consists of a monologue by a young Chinese Singaporean concerning attempts to bury his grandfather's large traditional coffin in a small regulation-sized plot in a public cemetery, and his encounter with a bureaucracy that insists there is 'no room for exceptions' (Kuo 2000a: 66). His persistence finally results in a compromise being made, in which the coffin is allowed to occupy two plots: the official who previously proved so inflexible is now celebrated by the media for his flexibility, and awarded the title of 'Most Humane Personality of the Year' (2000a: 70). On one level Kuo's play is a simple allegory of a citizen's helplessness against the efficient but overwhelming intrusive bureaucracy that characterized the Singapore state after 1965. Like Kuo's second monodrama, *No Parking On Odd Days*, which describes a motorist's futile fight against an unjustly awarded parking fine, *Coffin* plays on similar experiences by members of the audience. The rationales given by elements of the state apparatus for their inflexibility are readily recognizable parodies of those contained in governmental speeches and official documents, as is the denial of agency of the protagonist of *Coffin* by the presentation of the policy exception as simply the result of official benevolence: *Coffin* is a very funny play in performance. Yet Kuo's allegory also displays a more serious side. In the play the coffin is eventually buried, but the monodrama begins and ends with the protagonist recounting dreams of it returning to haunt him, just as its physical presence dwarfs the actor in most performances of the play. At the end of *Coffin* the protagonist peels back another layer to his dream: he is anxious that if all the graves are the 'same size and the same shape, would my sons and daughters, and my grandsons and granddaughters after them, be able to find me out and recognize me?' (2000a: 71). Anxiety here is not directed simply towards bureaucracy, but to the erasure of cultural memory in a rapidly modernizing society which submits to the rationality of social engineering that selectively remembers and erases elements of cultural pasts.

Kuo's concern with loss of cultural depth was extended in *Mama Looking For Her Cat* (1988), which marked a further milestone in the development of Singapore theatre. *Mama*, in contrast to Kuo's earlier plays, is a multilingual drama, mixing English, Malay, Mandarin and Tamil, as well as the Chinese 'dialects' of Hokkien, Cantonese and Teochew, as it follows the eponymous mother's search for her missing pet. In the play's most famous scene, Mama discusses cats with an Indian man: lacking a shared language, the characters communicate through gestures and onomatopoeia rather than linguistic comprehension. This in itself was startlingly new, escaping the linguistic boundaries into which the state had attempted to shepherd artistic expression through multiracialism. Yet *Mama*, as several commentators have noted, does not simply provide a transparent representation of or, still less, a celebration of Singapore's polylingual environment: rather, it carefully excavates layers of historical sedimentation in language use, unearthing incomprehension and miscommunication as much as it reveals the possibilities of understanding. English and to a lesser extent Mandarin, after the introduction of the Speak Mandarin Campaign and strong governmental pressure against the public use of dialects, are languages of power, often used by a younger generation of Singaporeans without an awareness of how such language use is invested with privilege. In a haunting scene towards the end of *Mama*, developed by Kuo from workshopping, Mama dictates letters to her son who is studying abroad: she speaks in Hokkien and the words are written down by the children in

English. The children are impatient, and their translations are both shortened and stripped of affective elements, transforming a rich series of cultural references into strings of lifeless clichés (Kuo 2000a: 134).

While Kuo emerged as Singapore's most influential theatre practitioner, drama in Singapore developed further towards the end of the 1980s. Market differentiation emerged, with popular performances such as Michael Chiang's *Army Daze* (1987), about a group of young men in National Service and the nostalgic musical *Beauty World* (1987) achieving box office success. A variety of avant-garde or socially committed groups emerged, and some encountered new difficulties with the state in mounting performances. Members of the Third Stage were arrested, again using the colonial era Internal Security Act, when a 'Marxist conspiracy' against the government was unearthed in 1987; in 1988 the then Ministry of Community Development withdrew support for a TheatreWorks double bill on AIDS and safe sex, and the plays were refused performance permission because of their sympathetic portrayal of homosexual figures. The two plays involved, both written by writers who would become more prominent in the 1990s – Eleanor Wong's *Jackson on a Jaunt* (published in Wong 2006) and Chay Yew's *Ten Little Indians* – were, however, rewritten, resubmitted and staged only in the following year, Yew's play now retitled *As If He Hears*. Yew, concerned with the restrictions placed on him, would leave a Singapore to which he had only briefly returned, for a successful international career. Despite the loss of such talent, however, Singapore drama in English by the end of the 1980s had reached a level of engagement and sophistication unimaginable even a decade previously.

Hong Kong

In Hong Kong, English-language drama remained marginal during the period under study. As Mike Ingham has noted, drama in English up to the 1980s remained dominated by expatriate groups such as the Garrison Players and the Hong Kong Stage Club (2005: 3). An exception was the Wah Yah Dramatic Society, through which Terence Sheridan performed adaptations based on traditional Cantonese opera in English (Mimi Chan 1994). Published texts such as Val Lorenz's *Hong Kong Bridges* (1980) reflect such an ethos. Chan Wan Wah's *The Rebirth of an Ex-communist through Gestalt Therapy* (1977),a four-act play whose protagonists are refugees from mainland China, is more engaged with contemporary politics, and centres on a recent refugee from the mainland, Fan, who must unlearn Maoist modes of thought. Its dialogue, however, is wooden, and it is unlikely that the play was performed professionally. Initiatives such as the drama laboratory at the University of Hong Kong, founded by Jack Lowcock and Vicki Ooi, and the bilingual Chung Ying Theatre Company – established in early 1980s, commencing as an educational theatre group originally under the auspices of the Arts Council and developing into an independent theatre company in 1982 – indicated a growth of professional English-language drama that would continue in the 1990s: there are, however, few surviving play scripts.

Conclusion

- State-imposed language and cultural policies, as well as the aspirations of dramatists themselves, impacted English-language theatre throughout Southeast Asia from 1965–1990.
- English-language drama in the Philippines declined, and original productions were few.
- After a hiatus during the 1970s, English-language drama in Malaysia showed increased vitality in the 1980s, engaging with postcolonial politics and forgotten histories, suggesting alternative ways of being Malaysian, and imagining alternative futures.
- Singapore drama in English expanded in the 1980s: writers foregrounded gender and the erasure of cultural memory, and negotiated a space of critique despite state regulation.
- In Hong Kong, English-language drama remained marginal during the period, although theatrical activity in English had begun to move outside amateur expatriate circles by the late 1980s.

9 Expatriate, diasporic and minoritarian writing

Overview

This chapter recognizes the contribution made to writing in English by three types of writer: expatriate, diasporic and minoritarian (that is, those using English in countries where English is not one of the main languages). Expatriate writing is the cultural outcome of European control over various regions in which authors born outside Southeast Asia worked and lived for part of their lives. Diasporic writing shows insiders looking back on memories of life in a former homeland from the perspective of the distance they have put between themselves and their originary culture. Minoritarian writing shows individuals using English as part of their own bicultural identity even when the choice of language exchanges the likelihood of an audience at home for more dispersed audiences overseas.

Each type of writing faces specific problems not easy to overcome. Expatriate writing begs the question of how much is really understood of life in the region by writers whose attitudes to life and society bear the conditioning of their parental cultures, writers whose attitude to their new environments might be limited by their experience or prone to stereotypes. Diasporic writing tends to remain fixated on the pull of memory, which prevents homes left behind from remaining out of mind for long. Oscar V. Campomanes notes that 'Motifs of departure, nostalgia, incompletion, rootlessness, leave taking, and dispossession recur with force in most writing produced by Filipinos in the Unites States and by Filipino Americans' (1992: 51). Guilt, nostalgia or self-reflexivity about a way of life that has been left behind proves the defining (and also the limiting) condition of diasporic writing: the past retains its priority over the present; the audience implied by the writing hovers ambiguously between where the author lives and where the materials are drawn from. A book like *Burning Heart: A Portrait of the Philippines* (1999), in which the Filipino-American writer Jessica Hagedorn supplies the poems and Marissa Roth the photographs, is difficult to imagine as being conceived by anyone but a diasporic writer. Its evocations of the Philippines gravitate towards a mood of exasperated affection, as if in response to a parent whose controlling presence had been distanced but not outgrown.

Expatriate and diasporic writing from British Malaya

The attention merited by expatriate writing in a survey devoted primarily to the literary productions of people born and residing in the region is bound to be secondary, but awareness of its achievement proves relevant in establishing a relation between expatriate and local writing in English. Travel writing by Victorian itinerants such as Isabella Bird's *The Golden Chersonese and the Way Thither* (1883) was met with acerbic local responses, epitomized by Emily Innes's *The Chersonese with the Gilding Off* (1885). The best-known fiction set in the region was written by Joseph Conrad, based on his experience as a seaman, master and, later, ship's captain, commencing with *Almayer's Folly* (1895), which is set in Borneo. Conrad's other works set in Southeast Asia include *Falk: A Reminiscence* (1903), set in Bangkok, and *The Secret Sharer* (1910), set in 'The Cambogee' (Cambodia). Equally productive if less prominent was Hugh Clifford, a colonial administrator whose short stories and novels, beginning with the publication of *East Coast Etchings* (1896), reveal a much greater knowledge of Malay culture than Conrad's, but lack his literary flair. As Conrad acerbically commented, one could 'not expect to be, at the same time, a ruler of men and an irreproachable player on the flute' (1920: 9). A later generation of fictional works included Somerset Maugham's withering excavations of private colonial hypocrisy in short story collections such as *The Casuarina Tree* (1926), Henri Fauconnier's lyrically exoticizing account of the life of a rubber planter in *La Malaisie* (1930), translated as *The Soul of Malaya* (in 1931), and George Orwell's *Burmese Days* (1934).

Expatriate writing dealing with British Malaya during or after the Second World War produced several works of interest in the genres of fiction and autobiography. Signs of resistance to the outsider writing knowingly about Malaya and disseminating stereotypes and clichés to unknowing Anglophone readers was a complaint heard quite early in Malaya: 'Maugham is one of the chief writers responsible for this false impression of Malaya' (Ferroa 1936: 25). The memoirs of the English-born Canadian writer Patrick Anderson, who taught in Singapore during the early 1950s, *Snake Wine* (1955), reveal a sympathetic interest in Malayan society and culture, and a discerning eye for the abilities of his students. Other Malay expatriate fiction of note for the period from 1945 to 1965 includes the autobiographical *Figures of Speech* (1961) by D. J. Enright, a trilogy by Anthony Burgess, *The Long Day Wanes* (1956–59), Han Suyin's *And the Rain My Drink* (1956) and four novels by Katherine Sim: *Malacca Boy* (1957), *The Moon at my Feet* (1959), *Black Rice* (1960) and *The Jungle Ends Here* (1961). Other expatriate novels based on personal experiences in war-time Malaya include James Clavell's *King Rat* (1962), whose second novel, *Tai-pan* (1966), is set in 1840s Hong Kong and traces the rise to power of the British entrepreneur Jardine-Matheson.

The style, perspective and narrative skill brought to expatriate narratives set in British Malaya differs from author to author, but they all share some traits: fluency in the handling of the language and the genre; reliance on personal experiences; a tendency to represent local and colonial characters through well-worn stereotypes; an inclination to exoticize, demonize or caricature indigenous races; and the habit of working out a personal assessment of the failures and successes of colonial policy and its administrative results in Europe's colonies. Each is mindful of the good and bad perpetrated in rulers and the ruled by the encounter between hypostatized entities such as the East and the West; each gives intimations of how such oppositions might be slipped.

Burgess, for example, is lively and readable, wide-ranging in observed detail and topical reference, tragic-comic in vision, acutely aware of the decline of the British Empire in Malaya, and mindful, as remarked by Douglas Kerr, that 'the various disciplines imposed by the British ... from the educational system to the police force – were never very efficient or convincing in the first place' (2008: 195). Han Suyin, on the other hand, is lyrical but tough, sensitive to the complex realities of partisan politics; while Katherine Sim (who went to Malaya in 1938 with her husband) is the most open in her declaration of partisan loyalties. Joan Armstrong – a character in Sim's *The Jungle Ends Here* (1961) – finds that even a murder and assorted instances of violence among the people she had been associated with does not discourage her from saying, 'I love it all too well ...!' (1961: 283). Part of what she cherishes about Malaya, we are told, is the 'little men of the *ulu* – Malaya's great jungle hinterland ... for centuries chivvied and even enslaved by the Malays, driven by marauding attackers further and further into the *ulu* – up river into the depths of the jungle' (1961: 40).

Other novelists who set part of their story in Malaya include Nevil Shute, whose popular novel *A Town like Alice* (1950, titled *The Legacy* in the American edition) was made into a movie and a television series. It involves a female protagonist who narrates her experience of a long and harrowing march through the Malayan jungle during the Japanese Occupation of 1942–45. Ironically, the plausibility of the evocation is based on the real-life experiences of a Dutch woman who had to suffer a forced march over a thousand miles in two and a half years, along with a party of about fifty other Dutch civilian prisoners, but in Sumatra, not Malaya. Shute's evocations of the jungle, plausible thought they might seem, have something of the generic about them.

Turning from expatriate to diasporic writing from the Malayan region, we note that several women writers took up poetry before some of them turned to fiction. Wong May, Shirley Geok-lin Lim, Hilary Tham and Siew-Yue Killingley began with modest but promising work during the 1960s, then migrated Westwards (either in pursuit of a career, or through marriage).

Neither Lim nor Tham ever left their homeland behind in the sense that their writing has drawn upon memories of Malaysia throughout their careers. Lim has combined the career of academic with that of poet and fictional writer. She has been a consistently insightful critic of poetry from the region, while also taking on the role of spokesperson for diasporic writing in America. Her first volume, *Crossing the Peninsula* (1980), sketches in a lonely childhood, an acute sensitivity to the cultural circumstances of her youth in Malaysia, a dawning sense of how imagination and memory serve as bridges between external and internal realities, a sense of vocation developed from being drawn to the English language, the possibilities of emancipation opened up by Western culture, a sharp capacity to evoke individuals and places with economy of detail, and periodic twinges of remorse about the growing impulse to make a life away from the land of her birth. 'Dedicated to Confucius Plaza' ends with the implicitly tongue-in-cheek dramatization of an immigrant who declares bemusedly, 'It is not hard to be / An Asian-American Chinese' (1980: 49). The penultimate section of the volume collects a series of poems which give the first intimation of a sharply critical awareness of gender roles and the politics that subsidizes them. The volume won the Commonwealth Poetry Prize, the first time such an honour had been conferred on a poet from Southeast Asia.

Lim's next volume, *No Man's Grove* (1985), returns to several motifs from the first volume, among them the significance of family and former homeland in her changed circumstances in the United States. It also reveals a new confidence with formal experiments, which include several villanelles and 'Pantoun For Chinese Women', a moving and powerful poem on a feminist theme that is as deeply felt as it is artfully constructed. The poem dramatizes the predicament of a young mother who stands by helplessly while her husband helps dispose of their first-born child during the times in China when adherence to the one-family-one-child policy led many families to sacrifice female children in the hope of filling their allotment of one child with a son rather than a daughter. The poem ends on a note of sombre pathos: 'Milk soaks our bedding, I cannot bear the waste. / They say a child with two mouths is no good' (1985: 63–4).

Lim's *Modern Secrets* (1989) adds to the earlier body of work in terms of revisiting a theme taken up by Ee Tiang Hong's 'Song of a Young Malayan'. The title poem of the section titled 'Song of an Old Malayan' asks in tones of reproach, 'Will you sell me, also, down the river /of nationalism, my sometime brother' (1989b: 97). An obsessive return to Malayan motifs also characterizes a large part of *What the Fortune Teller Didn't Say* (1998), where father, mother, sister and other tokens of rootedness and uprooting appear and reappear, making Lim's entire *oeuvre* circle around what it meant to have left Malacca in a peculiar combination of choice and necessity, and how the leaving was never left behind in the poet's psyche, although the final section of the volume does make space for what is needed most in the diasporic condition, the viability of 'Learning to Love America'.

Hilary Tham left Malaysia for the United States with her Jewish-American husband. The steady output she sustained from there found ample room for Malayan memories of places and people in the first section of *Paper Boats* (1987), the poems of *Tigerbone Wine* (1992), and the verse and prose of *Lane With No Name: Memoirs of a Malaysian-Chinese Girlhood* (1997), whose affectionate memories anticipate the autobiographical mode (though not the cooking recipes) of Chin Woon Ping's more recent *Hakka Soul* (2008). The most charming part of Tham's poetry is the fictive persona of Mrs Wei: sixty-five, arthritic, irrepressibly direct, engaged and engaging. She appears in *Paper Boats* (1987), *Bad Names for Women* (1989) and *Men and Other Strange Myths* (1994). The 1989 volume stands out for the way in which it applies a very personal kind of gender awareness, dry and humorous, to the poet's two communal affiliations, the Chinese culture of her family upbringing in Malaysia, and the Jewish connection established through marriage and life in the United States. 'Mrs Wei in America' compares lifestyles in a wry tone that is at once laconic and feisty: 'Malaysian Government is like the American / price system: take it or leave it' (1989: 23). A second persona appears more briefly towards the end of the volume: Mama Washington, a black American counterpart to Mrs Wei. The dramatization of this character shows Tham to be a good mimic of local speech habits from her new environment: 'Girl, when you fry fish, you keep your eyes sharp set / and your stick handy for them alley cats' (1989: 64). Writers like Hilary Tham, Shirley Lim, and Chin Woon Ping show how Chinese-Malay cultural memories are preserved and transmitted in a bicultural symbiosis mediated through English.

Expatriate writing from Hong Kong

The foundation of Hong Kong as a British colony was a direct consequence of the aggressive British promotion of the opium trade, which was opposed by the Qing dynasty, and led to two wars (1840–42 and 1857–58), both won by the British, each followed by a firmer grip on the opium trade and territorial gains (Hong Kong island from the first victory, Kowloon from the second; to which the mainland New Territories were added in 1898, as a 99-year lease).

English and educational policies in Hong Kong

The 1860s saw a variety of colonial schools in operation, but it was only after the consolidation of British control in 1898 and the subsequent increase in the size of the expatriate community that English acquired a more distinct role in the colony. By 1960, about 9.7 per cent of the population claimed to know some English, a figure that rose to

31.6 per cent by 1991, and to 43 per cent by 2001. A very small percentage of the population regard it as their primary language (approximately 3 per cent), whereas Cantonese is the primary language for over 90 per cent of the population. The dominance of Cantonese has been reinforced by the pattern of immigration from the neighbouring provinces of mainland China. By the end of the Second World War, the population was approximately 600,000. It grew to 3.1 million by 1961, and 6.7 million by 2001 (Bolton 2002: 1). While a large part of the daily life of Hong Kong takes place in Cantonese, English remains what it was since the 1860s, the language of administration, law, business and expatriates. While it is the main language of higher education, its teaching was a matter of frequent anxiety before 1997, and since the hand-over to China, English is no longer taught extensively at school level. As a consequence, the use of English in ordinary use by the general population did not develop to the extent it has in Singapore, the Philippines or Malaysia.

In early 1938, the English writers W. H. Auden and Christopher Isherwood travelled together to China to report first-hand on the Sino-Japanese War. They kept a travel diary and Auden began writing the poems that would appear in *Journey to a War* (1939). Their journey took them through Port Said, Cairo, Djibouti, Colombo and Hong Kong, and in the last of these places Auden wrote two memorable sonnets, 'Macao', and 'Hong Kong', which capture a sense of the urgent anxiety and excitement that the two authors brought to their writing of the late 1930s. Macao, the haven of gamblers, is described as 'A weed from Catholic Europe', a 'city of indulgence' where 'nothing serious can happen'; whereas Hong Kong is perceived as 'a modern city' whose leaders may be 'wise and witty', and whose bankers may have erected in the East 'A worthy temple to the Comic Muse', but whose proximity to the war that thuds 'off-stage', 'like the slamming of a door', makes us wonder if we have only ourselves to blame – so Auden would have us believe, rather portentously – for 'what we are' (Auden 1977: 235). Another writer from the West who sojourned in Hong Kong during the 1930s was Robert Simpson, Professor of English at the University of Hong Kong.

Literary writing in English remained for Hong Kong a matter of expatriate interest for a long time after the Second World War. Given the tiny percentage of the population who used English with any kind of proficiency in the hectic commercial life of the city and the constant flow of immigrants, it is no surprise that writers either born in Hong Kong or writers who made Hong Kong their home in a more or less permanent way would not turn to English until the end of the twentieth century. As far as drama was concerned, Mike Ingham notes that 'what expatriate amateur theatre in Hong Kong ... as in other outposts of Empire excelled in was presenting light entertainment to while away the dull routine of military and administrative duty' (2005: 2). The expatriate contribution by way of poetry for the two decades following the Second World War rests primarily with the English poet Edmund Blunden.

Blunden was a veteran of the First World War, and worked as a Professor of English at Hong Kong University from 1953 to 1963. His charming personality and effectiveness as a teacher of English literature made a lasting impact on a generation of Hong Kong students. True to his origins in Edwardian and Georgian England, Blunden's poetry drew sustenance from the pastoral tradition, and as noted by Douglas Kerr, the poems written in Hong Kong show him 'time and again, seeking out images and landscapes of peace and quiet', a form of involuntary habit or indulgence which is saved, Kerr adds, 'from blandness and predictability' by 'a certain edge' (2001: 102). Kerr attributes both the search for peace and the edginess of that search to Blunden's traumatic experiences in the trenches during the First World War.

George Orwell in Burma and Anthony Burgess in Malaya were in the region primarily as employees of the colonial administration, but William Empson in Peking and Japan, Ronald Bottrall and Patrick Anderson in Singapore, James Kirkup in Japan and Malaysia, D. J. Enright in Japan, Thailand and Singapore, and Edmund Blunden in Japan and Hong Kong, like many other Englishmen who came to the East out of curiosity as well as the need for employment, made a very significant contribution in instilling in their Asian students a fuller appreciation for the English literary canon and the desire to emulate it.

In the genre of fiction, perhaps the most well-known contribution during this period was Richard Mason's novel *The World of Suzie Wong* (1957). A former student of W. H. Auden, Mason set the plot of his novel amidst the life of bars and 'yum-yum girls'. Michael Ingham explains, 'Yum, or yam ... means drink, and the term signified the practice of buying girls, who frequented the bar, a drink at an extremely inflated price, as a prelude to sex' (2007: 58). Mason's novel provided a vivid and largely sympathetic picture of this side of Hong Kong life, even though the romance between his protagonist and the prostitute Suzie is given a somewhat improbable happy ending, and the novel had to suffer the ambiguous fate of being made into a fairly successful Hollywood film.

The marginal genre of autobiographical prose deserves mention here, even if Hong Kong-Eurasians suffered from what Vicky Lee describes as a sense of 'fateful marginality' (2004: 7). Such narratives were published many years after the events they narrate, but retain interest for how they capture the mood and atmosphere of the period during and after the Second World War. Such narratives include Jean Gittins's *I Was At Stanley* (1946) and *Eastern Window–Western Skies* (1969), Irene Chong's *Clara Ho Tung: A Hong Kong Lady, Her Family and her Times* (1976), and *Looking at the Stars: Memoirs of Catherine Joyce Symons* (1996). The experiences of Eurasians in Hong Kong get diverse refractions in these narratives. A more immediately published and popular expatriate contribution to the prose narrative genre came from Austin Coates, a civil servant and traveller, whose novels, *City of Broken Promises* (1967) and *Myself a Mandarin* (1968), became international bestsellers.

James Clavell's *Tai-pan* (1966) remains memorable for its fictionalized treatment of the archetypal Hong Kong entrepreneur William Jardine. Another, very different kind of expatriate contribution from within Asia deserves special mention: Han Suyin's second novel, *A Many-Splendoured Thing* (1952), set partly in Hong Kong and partly in China. Based on personal experiences, this is one of the most moving and well-written books in English from an Asian during the 1950s. The subsequent writing from and about Hong Kong hardly provides an example more vivid than her representation of Hong Kong as a city of transients juxtaposed with the looming presence of the vast mainland to which it has so long served as conduit: 'squatters' colony, fun fair, bazaar and boom town ... And China just beyond the hills' (Han Suyin 1952: 35–36).

Diasporic writers from the Philippines

Migration from the Philippines to overseas destinations has been a long-established option for Filipinos seeking to overcome unpromising prospects at home through employment overseas, whether as manual labourers, domestic servants, qualified nurses or doctors. American colonialism produced the first wave of Philippine migration to the United States, largely to California and Hawaii. For two decades after the Second World War, Filipino war veterans and their families found homes in the United States, followed by waves of immigration facilitated by the provisions of the American Immigration and National Act of 1965, and later by the oppressive measures of the Marcos regime.

Carlos Bulosan arrived in the United States in 1930 at the age of eighteen as a migrant labourer. Jose Garcia Villa, on the other hand, treated himself haughtily as a self-exile who combined a determination never to return to the Philippines with the desire to 'make it good' among his American peers. Subsequent writers became part of the Filipino diasporic community through different routes and tackled questions discussed previously in Chapter 6. N. V. M. Gonzalez, for instance, studied creative writing at Stanford University in 1950, and spent long periods teaching in several American universities in a career as busy in the Philippines as in the United States. Bienvenido Santos spent the early 1940s in the United States, and taught there during the 1970s and early 1980s. Though almost all his writing was published from the Philippines, it was bicultural in orientation, and sensitive to the experience of travel and migration. A different pattern is exemplified in the career of Carlos A. Angeles, who worked in the United States throughout the period 1950–80, settled, gave up writing for long periods, and saw his writing split between the better-known poems set in the Philippines and the later ones based on his American life.

While most contemporary Americans are unmindful of their role as a colonial power in the Philippines, assimilation of American cultural norms led to the desire among many Filipinos to produce work that would gain recognition from audiences more paying, and also perceived as more prestigious, than those in the Philippines. Philippine writers, publishers and readers often behave as if there were only two audiences, one American and the other Filipino, with little interest in the literary cultures of the Anglophone world outside the United States. Vince Gotero diagnoses the fixation as a predicament 'where the solution to every problem is America: if we could only get to the US, if we could only be American' (2002: 69).

Diasporic writing has a double-edged quality. It attempts to exorcize a past that will not go away, while struggling with a sense of identity compounded of a double displacement (from the home left behind and from the place that is not yet home). In this predicament, belongingness is trapped on the bipolar plank of minority-versus-majority, reinforcing the entrapment from which it seeks escape. A number of anthologies reinforce this identity-politics even as they try to foreground the writing which, they argue, white America should not keep displacing into marginal vision: Luis H. Francia's *Brown River, White Ocean* (1993), Nick Carbó's *Returning a Borrowed Tongue* (1995), Luis H. Francia and Eric Gamalinda's *Flippin' Filipinos on America* (1996), Shirley Geok-lin Lim and Chua Cheng Lok's *Tilting the Continent: Southeast Asian American Writing* (2000), Luisa A. Igloria's *Not Home, But Here* (2003), and many similar anthologies promote resistance to marginalization while forcing themselves into the corner of marginalized protesters.

Jessica Hagedorn, in the introduction to her anthology of Asian-American fiction, *Charlie Chan Is Dead, An Anthology of Contemporary Asian American Fiction* (1993), declares: 'I read Asian American literature as a literature of protest and exile, a literature about place and displacement, a literature concerned with psychic and physical "home"' (1993: ix). With all the sympathy in the world for the diasporic search for a home that will suffice, it is still worth noting that 'exile' and 'displacement' are hardly apt when the migration is voluntary. When driven by motives of gain (whether economic or virtual), to invoke the moral indignation of 'protest' is less than apt, especially since what it objects to is not injustice but the inertia and insularity of a white majority readership whose liberal minority is being solicited for sympathetic attention. The motives for migration (as distinguished from the helplessness of true exile) offer much that is of general interest on the spectrum of honest self-analysis. For example, Carlos Bulosan's poem 'All the Living Fear' protects the desire that led to migration like a flame that must not be doused by the suffering it entails: 'Yes, it is worth all these – and the loneliness at night. / The bitterness of prejudice, the sharp fang of hunger, / The terror of rootlessness' (Francia and Gamalinda 1996: 219).

A more circumspect and ironic realization of the double-act required from the migrant who hopes to survive can be found in Luis H. Francia's 'A Snail's Progress', which develops a charming fantasy that snails worship a god called Speed, in whose spirit, at night, they shed their shells and whirl about like dervishes, the envy of every hare, only for them to assume again the monkish, slow mien we know them for in the day. The point of the poem comes up obliquely, mid-way, when the poet declares, in analogy, how immigrant selves cope with having to live in a white man's world by daytime, 'Brown thoughts concealed in the morning', 'Conspirators by night / Martyrs by light' (Francia and Gamalinda 1996: 242). Such writing defends migration, whereas the migrant-writer whose motives are suspect can become the deserving target for derision, as in 'Pinoy Septych', by (Butch) Jose Y. Dalisay, Jr., a poem which scorns 'fatting fictionists / Craving phoney exiles in the States' (Abad 1999: 308).

Regardless of motives, the Philippine-American writer, like other minority-group writers, tends to be placed in a cultural ghetto by the narrow appeal to a specific type of readership. Many Philippine writers have given voice to their awareness of this danger, speaking with bitterness of how postcolonial aspiration is always tarnished by its own obsequious self-effacement in a land too large and blinkered to notice the minority voices clamouring for 'white' attention, never more pungently than in Alfrredo Navarro Salanga's sardonic 'They Don't Think Much About Us in America': 'It's here, back home, / where the curdling / begins' (Francia and Gamalinda 1996: 251–252). The troubled feelings with which the migrant-poet acknowledges the mix of unease-amidst-desire is given voice by Fatima Lim-Wilson in many of her poems, as in 'Potluck': 'Take us into your heated homes / Where we shall sit in the shade of an indoor plant / Or on the wall, nailed through the heart' (1991a: 24). The stereotypes and prejudices that have to be contended with are also neatly dramatized in 'An Asian American's Found Pantoum' by Vince Gotero: 'Do you ever want to go back? / Math comes so easy to your kind', and 'You people are taking all our jobs' (2004: 27).

Minoritarian writing

In the context of Southeast Asia, 'minoritarian' refers to individuals using English in countries where it is a marginal literary language, as in the case of Brunei, Cambodia, East Timor (Timor Leste), Indonesia, Laos, Burma (Myanmar), Thailand and Vietnam. Much, though not all, minoritarian writing is by expatriates who came initially from Europe, either as employees in the colonial administrative apparatus or as travellers and adventurers driven by curiosity and the attraction of exploration. A large proportion of this writing is travel writing, mixed with autobiographical or historical materials, and including comments on local religions, politics, history, culture and colonial governance. A small portion of this body of writing is fictional in nature, and enacts, either directly or by implication, a range of variations on the East–West encounter.

Refractions of such encounters began in the nineteenth century and interested readers will find a very useful introduction to the material, especially the non-fictional writing, in the *Traveller's Literary Companion to South-East Asia* (1994), edited by Alastair Dingwall. Our focus in this narrative is less concerned with the non-fictional material than with the fictional, and the first thing to be noted about novels set in Burma or Thailand before the Second World War is that a good part of the personal experience of the author is adapted or transformed to the needs of the plot. For Burma, adventure and romance provide the stuff of Victorian and colonial yarns such as G. A. Henty's *On the Irrawaddy* (1896), H. Fielding-Hall's *Thibaw's Queen* (1899) and Sir George Scott's *The Repentance of Destiny* (1913), the last written under the pen-name Shwe Dinga. Romance set in exotic contexts dominates works like F. Tennyson Jesse's *The Lacquer Lady* (1929), along with much observed cultural detail. Maurice Collis's *She was a Queen* (1937) provides one of the most perceptive works set in Burma. Other fictional texts, popular in their time, include Edward Thompson's *Burmese Silver* (1937) and Nevil Shute's *The Chequer Board* (1947). More substantial novels include two from H. E. Bates, *The Purple Plain* (1947) and *The Jacaranda Tree* (1949), and Ethel Mannin's *The Living Lotus* (1956). More contemporary material can be found in Patrick Crutwell's *A Kind of Fighting* (1959) and Michael Pereira's *Stranger in the Land* (1967), while Paul Theroux puts in one of his inimitable travelogues in *The Great Railway Bazaar* (1975), whose journey brings him all the way through India to Burma and beyond. Locally born writers who put English to good use in their novels include MiMi Khaing (*Burmese Family*, 1946), Maung Thiha (*The Chindits and the Stars*, 1956) and Wendy Law-Yone (*The Coffin Tree*, 1983).

Regardless of the fact that Thailand was the only country in Southeast Asia not to have undergone direct colonial rule, Bangkok and the region surrounding it has proved enormously popular as a setting for writing that mixes the interest of travel to exotic places with personal experiences. The most well-known of the early texts to combine this appeal in English was Anna Leonowen's *The English Governess at the Siamese Court* (1870). The story as adapted and modified by Margaret Landon's *Anna and the King of Siam* (1944) served as the basis for a very popular Hollywood film, and led to a sequel in R. J. Minney's *Fanny and the Regent of Siam* (1962). Meanwhile, Somerset Maugham's *The Gentleman in the Parlour* (1935) remains one of the best examples of travel writing which mixes fascinating anecdotal narrative with a shrewd account of society and culture. The more recent fictional work using Thailand as a setting is geared towards various popular genres that mix adventure, crime and the exotic in varying proportions, as in J. C. Shaw's *The Seal of Taminarati* (1985), Jack Reynolds's *A Woman of Bangkok* (1985), Axel Aylwen's *The Falcon of Siam* (1989), Jason Schoonover's *Thai Gold* (1989), William Diehl's *Thai Horse* (1989), Anthony Grey's *Bangkok Secret* (1990) and a whole series of novels by the Canadian-born Bangkok-based Christopher Moore, such as *A Killing Smile* (1991), *A Bewitching Smile* (1992), and at least nine crime fiction books featuring the detective Vincent Calvino, from *Spirit House* (1992) to *The Risk of Infidelity Index* (2008)

While all these make interesting reading, there is more poignant and pertinent matter in the protest writing that the ongoing political situation in Thailand gives rise to, as in Naowarat Pongpaiboon's 'The Day That Killed the Dove', from the collective anthology *Mere Movement* (1984), written in reaction to the suppression of the demonstration of 6 October 1976 at Bangkok's Thammasat University, which notes: 'See helmets, machine guns that gleam. / See a quick saffron glint, a shaved head' (Dingwall 1994: 90). Though Thailand was the only ASEAN country not to have become a European colony, it has several outstanding writers in English with global reputations. Montri Umavijani wrote poetry mostly in English, bringing a Haiku-like economy and precision to his twenty-seven slim volumes, from *The Intermittent Image* (1968) and *A Long, Old Roman Road* (1989) to *Poems from Thailand, 1988–1991* (1991), meditating with Buddhist calm on the pursuit of knowledge through historical time.

Another Thai author of note is Pira Sudham, who studied in New Zealand, and now divides his time between England and Thailand's north-east region of Esarn. He was nominated for the Nobel Prize in Literature for 1990, largely on the basis of his passionate plea for justice and understanding for the rural peasantry of his part of Thailand. He is the author of *Siamese Drama or Tales of Thailand* (1983), *People of Esarn* (short stories and essays [1987]), *Monsoon Country* (1988) and *The Force of Karma* (2002). The latter two were revised and combined as *Shadowed Country* (2004). *Monsoon Country* is effective in chronicling the life of poverty, hardship and rapid change (sometimes violent and oppressive) undergone by the villagers from the north-east. The passion that drives his direct and simple narrative opposes the disparities of the two worlds he shuttles between, in one of which 'a watch, a bottle of wine, or a dinner in a restaurant, or a pair of shoes costs more than a pair of water buffaloes or what a peasant in Napo could earn in a year' (1988: 220). *The Force of Karma* makes surreal use of the belief in reincarnation to link events in England with lives and events in Esarn. The advertisement for his second book declares, 'I don't want people in our villages, so far removed from other peoples because of distance and poverty, to be born, suffer and to die in vain'; and that for the third reminds his readers, 'Liberty is a foreign word, found on a coin a foreigner dropped in the palm of my hand, but it has taken me years to fully understand its meaning'.

A very different kind of Thai fiction is authored by the England-educated S. P. Somtow (Somtow Sucharitkul), who is a prolific composer of classical music and operas (which draw upon Asian fable, myth and epic for music sung in English), and a prolific writer of Gothic fiction. Werewolves, vampires and zombies populate his fertile imagination with a deftness that can match the best writing in those sub-genres anywhere in the world. His peculiarly charming Bildungsroman, *Jasmine Nights* (1995), provides a comic variation on the growing-up novel. Its semi-autobiographical materials are refracted through ingenious fantasy, farce and sexual comedy, all set in 1960s Thailand, and latent with resistance to the stereotypes that are the staple of the blander varieties of multiculturalism. The funny and edgy side of a cosmopolitanism that recognizes the massive cracks and gaps between Thai and Western cultural habits and assumptions is neatly dramatized in *Dragon's Fin Soup: Eight Modern Siamese Fables* (2000). Somtow remains one of the most unusually rewarding authors to use English in Southeast Asia.

A large majority of the books in English about the largely non-English-speaking countries of Southeast Asia tend to be confined to translations of vernacular classics, books catering to tourism, travel, business, local religions, history, contemporary culture and society. Literary writing set in these parts of Southeast Asia include some remarkable expatriate and indigenous writing in English. In the early 1970s, in self-conscious emulation of Auden's commitment to the idea that a writer has a duty to remain alert to the political crises of his times, the English poet James Fenton travelled to the civil wars in Vietnam and Cambodia as a freelance reporter. The experience led to some of the most striking political poetry of the 1970s, which appeared in *The Memory of War* (1983), and was followed by a collaborative trip with Redmond O'Hanlon, which produced *Into the Heart of Borneo* (1984). Graham Greene's very topical and thoughtful novel *The Quiet American* (1979) is based in Vietnam, and Margaret Drabble's *The Radiant Way* (1987), *A Natural Curiosity* (1989) and *The Gates of Ivory* (1992) in 1980s Cambodia.

Indonesia has provided inspiration for a number of books in English, from Violet Clifton's *Islands of Indonesia* (1927) and Hickman Powell's *The Last Paradise* (1930) to G. E. P. Collins's *Twin Flower* (1934) and *Makassar Sailing* (1937). Later fiction set in post-independence Indonesia includes Eric Ambler's *The Night-corners* (1956), Laurens van der Post's *The Seed and the Sower* (1963) and *The Night of the New Moon* (1970), Derwent May's *The Laughter in Jakarta* (1965) and Christopher J. Koch's *The Year of Living Dangerously* (1978), which achieved wider circulation when it was made into a feature film. Equally interesting and powerful material can be found in Blanche d'Alpuget's *Monkeys in the Dark* (1980). More recent work of minoritarian interest comes from the bilingual Indonesian writer Laksmi Pamuntjak, columnist, pianist, and the author of a volume of short stories based on paintings, *The Diary of R. S.: Musings on Art* (2006), and two volumes of poetry: *Ellipsis* (2005) and *The Anagram* (2007) which experiment with free verse and the prose poem.

Works which set their narratives in Burma include Amitav Ghosh's *The Glass Palace* (2000) and Daniel Mason's *The Piano Tuner* (2002). Indigenous examples include the Burmese Harry Oo's *A Boy Soldier* (2007), which is set in the time of the 1970s war in the state adjoining the Chinese border. The English-language books of the Burmese-born Chinese-descent Minfong Ho are more consistent in their representations of life in Thailand and Burma, most notably in *Sing to the Dawn* (1975), *Rice without Rain* (1986) and *The Clay Marble* (1991). In the 1980s, Ho lived for a time in Singapore, and moved to the United States in 1990, turning her hand to children's writing. Asian-Americans add a new transnational dimension to the regional picture with a steady and ever-increasing output that engages with complex transnational realities, as in the Vietnamese-born Lan Cao's *Monkey Bridge* (1997) and Quang X. Pham's *A Sense of Duty: My Father, My American Journey* (2005).

Conclusion

- Writing by authors indigenous to Southeast Asia can be placed in a broader context by recognizing the contribution in English by expatriate and diasporic writing.
- The work in English from countries where the language is widely spoken and read needs to be complemented by recognition of the accomplishments of literary writing in English from regions where the language is not widely spoken or read, such as Thailand, Vietnam, Indonesia and Burma.
- Expatriate writing belongs largely to the colonial period, and engages with themes, settings and evocations of experiences centred on the encounter between European and Southeast Asian peoples.
- Diasporic writing is preoccupied with two major themes, of which the first concerns memories of the homes left behind.
- The second theme found in diasporic writing addresses the challenges and opportunities of resettlement and assimilation into new environments.

10 Contemporary fiction 1990–2008

Overview

Literary fiction in English in Southeast Asia since 1990 is marked by a paradox. The number of novels by migrants from Malaysia, Singapore or the Philippines published by North American, British and Australian houses has increased greatly. This has not, however, been matched by a similar increase in locally published work. In the Philippines, literary novels and short story collections continue to be published in small print runs by university presses; in Singapore, the hopes of the early 1990s, when the most significant Singapore novels for a generation were published, have mostly been disappointed; in Malaysia, a new generation of writers resident in the country has produced some novels, but the best of their writing has been in the form of short stories. While the volume of literary production in Hong Kong has increased, the absence of a local reading public in English has resulted in literature published there responding to generic trends elsewhere rather than developing an autonomous tradition. The rapid development of new media and creative industries in Southeast Asia has often meant that writers are no longer in the university, but rather work in a variety of genres and media, moving back and forth between journalism, essays, short fiction, blogging and indeed film.

The Philippines

The early 1990s in the Philippines shows continuities with the period immediately after the fall of Marcos. Writers of an older generation continued to be active. F. Sionil Jose, for example, published several novels: *Viajero* (1993) has perhaps the largest scope, reaching back to the precolonial Philippines and forward to describe the situation of Filipino labourers and domestic workers in the Middle East and East Asia. Linda Ty Casper's *Dream Eden* (1996) returns to the events surrounding the end of the Marcos regime and continued political instabilities under Aquino. Cristina Pantoja Hidalgo, better known for her travel writing and short fiction, also wrote two novels in the period, retrieving a counter-history of women's voices. *Recuerdo* (1996) is presented in an entirely epistolary form as a series of emails written by a mother, Amanda, to her daughter, Marisa. Amanda is in Bangkok, and her daughter, having spent many years abroad, is now back in the Philippines, attempting to reintegrate after an expatriate childhood. Through the medium of the letters, Amanda hopes to retell to her daughter stories received from her own mother, to 'pass the stories on to you now, Risa. Before I forget them' (1996: 6).

Recuerdo's theme of a retrieval of other voices is particularly relevant to the 1990s, which saw the emergence of previously marginalized communities in fiction. Danton Remoto and Neil Garcia edited the two volumes of *Ladlad*, the first anthology of gay literature, containing poetry and short fiction, and Garcia went on to pioneer queer literary studies at the University of the Philippines. In a different vein, Charlson Ong, following the earlier writing of Paul Stephen Lim, wrote fiction concerned with Chinese-Filipino identity and community. Ong's early short stories, such as his first collection, *Men of the East* (1990), dramatize the conflicts between an older generation of immigrants from Fujian province in China and their younger descendants who feel themselves to be fully Filipino. His first novel, *An Embarrassment of Riches* (2000), is set in the imaginary country of the Victorianas, west of the Philippines, in which many of the social and political conflicts in Philippine society are enacted in an exaggerated manner. *An Embarrassment of Riches* has an ethnic Chinese narrator, but mingles this with a creative reworking of elements of plot of Jose Rizal's two novels, *Noli me tangere* and *Il filibusterismo*, as it explores the problematics of Chinoy (Chinese-Filipino) belonging in the nation. Ong's second novel, *Banyaga* (2006), follows a century of Chinese-Filipino history, illustrating shifting identities as its characters negotiate communal identifications. 'Banyaga' means stranger in Filipino, and Ong's novel does not simply describe a unidirectional process of assimilation: rather, through its characters' shifting subject positions, it estranges a reader from a narrative of national history so that familiar landmarks are seen from a different point of view.

A parallel development in English-language writing looked not within the nation, but transnationally. The international success of Hagedorn's *Dogeaters* led to an explosion of activity in Filipino-American or Fil-Am writing, the majority of which lies outside the scope of this chapter. However, writers such as Ninotchka Rosa and Eric Gamalinda, resident in the United States, maintained a close contact with the Philippines and were influential there. Rosca's second novel, *Twice Blessed* (1992), again makes coded reference to the end of the Marcos years, also expressing, through its allegorical account of the aftermath of a fictional election, disappointment with the legacy of the Aquino years.

Gamalinda's first novel, *The Empire of Memory* (1992), is a novel which makes reference to real historical events, such as the visit of the Beatles to Manila in July 1966, and Imelda Marcos's hosting of the First Manila

International Film Festival in 1982, when pressure to finish the construction of the Film Center on time allegedly led to the entombing of workers when work hastily resumed after a concrete floor collapsed. The text centres on its protagonist, Alfonso, who becomes involved in rewriting history for Marcos's projected encyclopedia for the New Society. Al's research leads him to the fictional island of San Miguel, representing the Philippines in miniature. It is divided by a mountain range; on one side is the old Villa del Fuego, inhabited by members of the old elite with close family connections to the military; on the other is the huge United States naval base ironically named La Paz (i.e. 'peace'), and the town of Akeldama that provides it with cheap labour. In San Miguel, Al becomes fascinated by two stories: the history of the Zabarte family, who inhabit the Villa del Fuego, and the life story of the rise of Sal X, a young rock singer whose father was an American serving at the base. Sal participates in a ritual crucifixion held each year, and inspires messianic devotion in Akeldama: 'not just pop guru and honky tonk superstar: no, not an icon: a saint' (1992: 75). As it progresses, Gamalinda's novel becomes elaborately metafictional, ostensibly made up of notes and sections of documents retrieved by Al and a companion, and calling the processes of public memorialization and private remembrance into question. Gamalinda would continue to be influential, and indeed would win first prize in the prestigious Centennial Literary Contest organized in the first year of the Estrada administration for his novel *My Sad Republic* (2000), although he would also be critiqued from some quarters for his use of postmodern but ahistorical fictive strategies.

Gamalinda's work is representative of a turn to non-realist strategies in contemporary literary fiction in the Philippines. Alfred Yuson continued his use of exuberantly self-reflexive narratives first demonstrated in *Great Philippine Jungle Energy Café*. His second novel, *Voyeurs & Savages* (1998), begins with a description of how Filipinos came to be chosen as 'primitives' for exhibition in the St Louis World Exposition of 1904, and then goes on to explore the exploitative and complex relationship that evolved through American colonialism and then neocolonialism. Yuson's novel reaches back to the time of the revolutionary war, and forward into the present: in one scene, the son of a Filipino family which made its fortune running a brothel for American servicemen at Angeles City makes love to the descendant of one of the Americans responsible for procuring 'exhibits' for the Exposition in a college now built on the old Exposition site in St Louis. The story is told from many perspectives, Filipino and American, and, in an even more radically fragmentary narrative strategy than Gamalinda's, recycles documents such as a catalogue of the Exposition, letters sent home by an American soldier in the revolutionary war and email messages. The book ends with a series of stories told by a grandfather to his grandchild in the narrative present which seem fantastic but which culminate in historical reality, with Aguinaldo's unveiling of the Filipino flag, a moment 'of fairness, of beauty, of honor. And of great love for the land, the river, the sky ... And all the brave, beloved people who wanted only to share their many wonderful stories' (2003: 220).

Metafictional concerns are also present in Erwin E. Castillo's *The Fire-walkers* (1992), a short novel containing a series of interwoven narratives set in Cavite during the aftermath of the Philippine-American War, when 'pacification' activities are still ongoing. Sergeant of police Gabriel Diego investigates the mysterious deaths of children savaged by some unknown animal, while a storyline around him moves beyond the conventions of realism and then back again into apparently stable realist narrative. Gabriel has surrendered in the revolutionary war, and worked for the Americans: he has acted, and continues to act, as an interpreter, caught between nationalism and colonialism. At the conclusion of the narrative he walks through a fire to escape from American troops, reclaiming spiritual powers that derive from precolonial belief systems. Yet any celebratory nativism is undercut by the concluding line of the novel, in which a travelling showman indicates that such a spectacle is a wonderful money-making opportunity.

More recent fiction in English in the Philippines defies easy categorization, but two broad trends can perhaps be noted. First, there has been a proliferation of genres, with many writers crossing over from literary fiction to write in more popular or subcultural genres, such as chick lit and speculative fiction (see Chapter 13). Second, literary fiction itself has continued to make use of stylistic features that transgress the boundaries of realism, and might be identified as exhibiting postmodern or magical realist traits. While these developments do reflect international trends – postmodernism from North American fiction, magical realism from Latin America – they also draw on literary traditions in the Philippines. Several stories in Jose Garcia Villa's first collection of short stories, *Footnote to Youth* (1933), engage in elaborately metafictional narrative strategies, while N. V. M. Gonzalez arguably pioneered Filipino magical realism in his first novel, *The Winds of April* (1941).

Much recent fiction moves away from the direct political engagement of the writing of the late 1980s and early 1990s, and younger writers have often used regional settings, often in explicit contrast to middle-class life in Manila. Rosario Cruz Lucero's *Feast and Famine: Stories of Negros* (2003) grows out of the author's experience of a childhood in Negros, an island south of Manila famed for its sugar production. A representative story such as 'Doreen's Story' features a frame narrative in which the narrator meets the real-life food writer and scholar Doreen Fernandez. The bulk of the story consists of a narrative that Doreen tells about Anabella of Silay, an heiress living in a small town. This narrative is in turn intercut with discussions with another real-life figure, academic 'Jonathan' – apparently Jonathan Chua, editor of the study *The Critical Villa* – about the veracity of the story that Doreen tells. Vicente Groyon's *The Sky Over Dimas* (2004) is also substantially set in Negros. Its protagonist, Rafael, the son of a landowning family, now lives in Manila. He is self-absorbed, and has only reluctantly participated in the political activism during Marcos's last years, finding rallies and meetings 'tiresome and redundant' (2004: 132): during the people power rallies at EDSA (Epifanio de los Santos Avenue) in 1986 he has preferred to retreat to his room and read pornography. Rafael's life is disturbed, however, by rumours that his father, still living on the family hacienda, has gone mad, and he is ultimately forced to return to Negros to solve a family crisis. The return to Negros exposes Rafael to both oral and written versions of family histories dating back to his great-grandfather's time which overlap, but which are often irreconcilable: as one character remarks, 'it was ridiculously easy to create a history for oneself in those days, and it's surprising people didn't do it more often' (2004: 37). The novel concludes in Manila, Rafael keeping his rediscovered story linking past and present to himself, 'guarding it jealously, taking comfort in the desperate faint hope that it had to fit, had to belong to a larger narrative' (2004: 258).

Dean Francis Alfar's *Salamanca* (2006) reverses Groyon's plot, its protagonist Gaudencio Rivera abandoning Manila for a small town in Palawan, where he comes into contact with the legendary Jacinta Cordova, her beauty so radiant that it transforms the walls of the house in which she lives into 'a material that resembled the finest glass' (2006: 5). Gaudencio's and Jacinta's love is thwarted through his desertion, but they are later reunited in Manila. Alfar's narrative is clearly influenced by Latin American magical realists such as Gabriel García Márquez, and yet lacks the direct political concerns of earlier deployments of magical realist technique such as Rosca's *State of War*. Events such as Benigno Aquino's assassination and the protests concerning the execution of the domestic worker Flor Contemplacion in Singapore in 1995 are present as historical markers, yet, as in much contemporary Philippine fiction, they seem peripheral to the text.

Malaysia

The early 1990s in Malaysia, as in the Philippines, also saw publication of significant prose fiction by an older generation of novelists. Lloyd Fernando's *Green is the Colour* (1993) is set in a dystopian world after the calamity of the 1969 riots, its multiracial protagonists again searching to maintain cross-community connections in an increasingly chaotic social order. Fernando's poor health in the 1990s was to rob Malaysian literature in English of a significant voice: K. S. Maniam, in contrast, has prospered. Maniam's second novel, *In a Far Country* (1993), represents a stylistic departure from the largely realist Bildungsroman of *The Return* to a more complex, modernist narrative that moves beyond the confines of an Indo-Malaysian community. Maniam's third novel, *Between Lives* (2003), is narrated by a young Indo-Malaysian woman civil servant, Sumitra, who is asked to persuade an older Indian woman, Sellamma, to leave land that she has occupied for many years and which is now marked for development. Yet as she visits repeatedly and listens to the older women's memories, Sumitra is forced to confront her own affiliation with a past from which she has become alienated. In his novels and also in many short stories, most recently in the collection *Faced Out* (2004), Maniam interrogates contemporary Malaysian multiracialism, excavating minority and intercultural pasts that are excluded from official multiracial discourses. 'In Tandem' thus celebrates a homosocial relationship between two young boys, one Malay, one Indian, while in 'The Kling-Kling Woman' a young girl is inspired by stories of an Indian community past that is located in Malaya to confront social oppression in the present.

Maniam's productivity has been matched by Shirley Lim, now living in the United States but maintaining connection with Southeast Asia through periods of residence in Singapore, Malaysia and Hong Kong. In addition to two short story collections mixing older and more recent work (*Life's Mysteries* [1995] and *Two Dreams* [1997]), Lim has also published an influential volume of memoirs, *Among the White Moonfaces* (1996), two novels, *Joss & Gold* (2001) and *Sister Swing* (2006), and a novella for young adults, *Princess Shawl* (2008). *Joss & Gold*, in particular, exemplifies the concern of contemporary Singaporean and Malaysian literary texts with issues of diaspora. Its action spans Malaysia, the United States and finally Singapore, and the novel retains Lim's commitment to exploring the tensions experienced by women in rapidly modernizing Southeast Asian societies. Lim rewrites the script of Puccini's *Madame Butterfly:* her female protagonist, Li An, refuses to play Butterfly to the Pinkerton of Chester Brookfield, an American Peace Corps worker who makes her pregnant. When Chester returns to a transformed Singapore in the 1980s, he finds an assertive Li An bringing up their child as a single mother, without need of any help from him.

While new novelists such as Chuah Guat Eng, Marie Gerrina Louis and Ooi Yang-May have emerged, and there have been interesting hybrid narratives such as Rehman Rashid's autobiographical travelogue-cum-history *A Malaysian Journey* (1993), the most significant voices of a younger, urban generation in the 1990s were expressed through the medium of the short story. Karim Raslan's stories in the collection *Heroes* (1996) dramatize conflicts in middle-class metropolitan Malay families that question Malaysian culturalist and national narratives. Most reveal an unexpected secret or scandal hidden beneath an apparently respectable surface. A retired civil servant who celebrates his loyal service to the nation during the aftermath of the 1969 riots is revealed to be a coward; a charming young male representative of the new *bumiputera* middle class, 'ramrod straight, smooth shaven, golf-tanned and smiling' (1996: 121), has a transgendered lover, for all his apparent embodiment of heteronormativity. Raslan's social critique is sharpened by the fact that the stories, frequently narrated or focalized by women characters, celebrate women's desire. Yet the stories at times seem perhaps too attached to scandal, as if peeling back the surface of respectability is enough, rather than engaging more deeply with what lies beneath.

Dina Zaman's short story collection *Night and Day* (1997) also deals with urban life, but its characters are more solitary and inward-looking, and the effect is much darker. Zaman looks beyond middle-class life to those excluded from or marginalized by Malaysia's economic growth and social policies: foreign domestic workers, homeless people and sex workers. If sexuality in Karim Raslan is often scandalous, in Zaman's writing it is powerfully disturbing. In the title story of the collection a young middle-class woman picks up an impoverished male prostitute: violent sex is transformed disorientatingly into tenderness. The short story has continued to be an important form in Malaysia after 2000, published in literary journals such as *SARE*, magazines such as *Off the Edge* and in the annual short fiction collections published by Silverfish Books.

As in the Philippines, some recent English-language writing in Malaysia has been regional in emphasis: Che Husna Azhari's short story collection *Melor in Perspective* (1993), for instance, is set in Kelantan, on the east coast of peninsular Malaysia. However, the majority of writers are based in Kuala Lumpur, and, like their Philippine counterparts, move between different traditional and non-traditional media. Dina Zaman, Salleh ben Joned and Farish A. Noor, for instance, have all published essay collections that originally appeared in newspaper articles or in blogs: Amir Muhammad moves between blogging, newspaper columns and films. New generations of diasporic novelists are now publishing outside the country, from Beth Yahp's *The Crocodile Fury* (1993) through to Rani Manicka's *The Rice Mother* (2002) and *Touching Earth* (2004), both of which explore the history of characters of Sri Lankan Tamil origin in Malaysia. Two recent novels that have achieved prominence in Britain are Tash Aw's *The Harmony Silk Factory* (2005), a multilayered narrative set in the Kinta Valley, north of Kuala Lumpur, largely in the years immediately preceding the Second World War, and Tan Twan Eng's *The Gift of Rain* (2007), a more conventionally structured historical novel that commences in Penang before the beginning of the Pacific War: the latter was long-listed for the Man Booker Prize.

Singapore

In Singapore, the 1990s commenced with the publication of three significant novels. Gopal Baratham's *A Candle or the Sun* (1991) describes the activities of an evangelical sect, the Children of the Sun, and their subsequent detention by the state security apparatus. It has been widely read as referring to the 'Marxist conspiracy' of 1987, although the initial manuscript was apparently completed in 1987, and its author could claim with some justification that the detainees had 'stolen my plot' (in Ban Kah Choon 2000, 26). Baratham's novel, published by the London press Serpent's Tail, has perhaps a more important place in Singapore's literary history than its literary qualities merit: the narrative's characterization now seems stereotypical, and Baratham's cannibalization of previously written short stories, now presented as creations of one of the text's characters, seems more indicative of a lack of invention than metafictional sophistication. The two other novels, however, remain centrally important to any account of Singapore literature in English.

Suchen Christine Lim's *Fistful of Colours* (1993) rewrites androcentric pioneer narratives that constitute a dominant discourse in Singaporean autobiography and fiction. The novel, set in the middle of the 1980s but reaching back two generations into the recesses of family history, is cyclical rather than linear in structure, reflecting its retelling of suppressed elements of historical experience by marginal figures who are mostly women. Narrative structure is complemented by metafictional elements. Characters in the frame narrative of the late 1980s comment upon the manner in which historical remembrance takes place, and sometimes tell competing stories of the same incident from different points of view. The novel celebrates the complex hybridity of Singaporean social life, addressing a very specific discursive context: Asian Values discourse and its associated governmentality in late 1980s Singapore, and in particular the construction of an essential Chinese identity through vehicles such as the Speak Mandarin Campaign: to this it opposes Chinese and Singaporean identities lived in 'dialects' such as Cantonese, and also in English (1993). Philip Jeyaretnam's *Abraham's Promise* (1994) also reaches back in time through the consciousness of its protagonist, retired schoolteacher Abraham Isaac, who finds both his love of literature and his idealism eroded by the stress on pragmatism in Singapore's post-independence development. Like Lim's novel, *Abraham's Promise* rewrites the masculinist national narrative of the developmental state, here excavating an alternative story as Abraham comes to realize his past intolerance and indeed abuse of his wife, and comes to accept his son's homosexuality.

While Jeyaretnam would largely abandon writing for a successful career in law, Suchen Lim would continue, publishing the historical novel *A Bit of Earth* in 2001 and a collection of short stories, *The Lies that Build a Marriage*, in 2007; Baratham would also later publish a collection of short stories. Another established writer, Catherine Lim, has also been prolific, publishing a number of novels, such as *The Bondmaid* (1995), *The Teardrop Story Woman* (1998) and *Following the Wrong God Home* (2001). Lim has proved astute at supporting herself through her writing and marketing her work internationally as part of an upsurge of interest in the writings of the Chinese diaspora: hers is now the largest *oeuvre* of any Singaporean writer in English. Yet the 1990s also saw the emergence of a series of new voices. While the construction of state-sponsored multiracialism meant that ethnically Chinese writers in English often contested state narratives, rather than, as in the Philippines, attempting to write themselves into the national narrative, other community voices, just like in the Philippines, did attempt to be heard. Rex Shelley, a retired civil servant, wrote a series of novels tracing the history of the Eurasian community, exploring the complex realities that lay underneath its frequent presentation as an elite comprador community under colonialism. *The Shrimp People* (1991) traces, through a woman protagonist, the world of the Eurasian community in peninsular Malaya at a time of nationalist struggle, while *People of the Pear Tree* (1993) presents a revisionist account of the Eurasian agricultural community set up in Bahau, Negeri Sembilan, during the Japanese occupation of Malaya in the Second World War. As in the Philippines, the 1990s also saw the emergence of gay fiction in Singapore, marked by the publication of Johann S. Lee's *Peculiar Chris* (1992) and Andrew Koh's *Glass Cathedral* (1995). The tradition would be continued by Edmund Wee's *The Narcissist* (2004) and Lee's second novel, *To Know Where I'm Coming From* (2007).

Three important short story writers also emerged during this period, sharing similar themes against a background of slow but perceptible political liberalization during Goh Chok Tong's tenure as prime minister from 1990–2004. The first to be published, Claire Tham, would publish three short story collections, *Fascist Rock* (1990), *Saving the Rainforest* (1993) and *The Gunpowder Trail* (2003). Tham's earlier stories represented the changed perspective of Singaporeans born after 1965 who had no memories of ties with Malaysia: in many of the stories, characters struggle against social alienation or the arbitrary imposition of authority by figures who deem them to be subordinates. 'A Question of Song' casts a sardonic eye on the hierarchies of hall of residence life at the National University of Singapore, while in 'Homecoming' a young man returns to Singapore after his father's death, only to realize that he no longer feels any sense of belonging.

Simon Tay's *Stand Alone* (1991) explores and gently critiques middle-class values in contemporary Singapore society. Alfian Sa'at's collection *Corridor* (1999) probes more deeply into alienation and barely suppressed social conflicts than Tay's or Tham's work does. As the title of the collection, with its reference to the common corridors of older Housing Development Board (HDB) flats, suggests, most of Alfian's stories are set in Singapore's residential 'heartland' that, in a spatial paradox, surrounds the city centre. They are peopled by characters who attempt to renegotiate the social scripts that define their lives: transvestites, gay men and lesbians, and young men and women who resist the impositions of school and work, and the accompanying cultural norms that define Malay or Chinese identity. Alfian is particularly acute in raising class awareness. In the short story 'Umbrella', a young Malay boy living in an HDB flat is awed by the worldliness of his middle-class tutor, yet the incommensurability in their lives is never bridged.

Corridor also features the adept use of images as presiding motifs. In 'Winners', for instance, the life of a woman in an emotionally empty marriage is symbolized by a plastic clip in the shape of a koala bear bought on a holiday in Australia, holding anything that is pushed towards it in an 'empty embrace' (1999: 74).

The 1990s also saw a further development in Singaporean literature that paralleled that in the Philippines: the growth of writing by migrants who had either left Singapore permanently, or had spent a large proportion of their lives abroad. Fiona Cheong, a United States resident, published *The Scent of the Gods* (1991) early in the decade. The novel is told through the perspective of a young girl, Esha, who grows up in Singapore in the 1960s, her entry into adulthood paralleling, but also clashing with, the developmental narrative of the emergence of the new nation-state. *The Scent of the Gods* is particularly interesting in its illustration of Esha's investment in the affective power of older ways of knowing that are dismissed as 'superstition' by a modern rationality embodied in her elder brother Li Shin. Ming Cher's *Spider Boys* (1995) is set in the urban *kampong* (or 'squatter camp') of Bukit Ho Swee just before the fire of 1961 which cleared the way for redevelopment. Its author received only a few years of primary school education, and then left Singapore in the 1960s to travel the world as a merchant seaman, finally settling in New Zealand, where the book was published. The novel thus has two distinct features. First, it is written in a non-standard English that to an extent mimes the syntactic structure of Chinese 'dialects' the characters speak in the fictional world of the narrative: this approach is more radical than that of other writers, who will use 'Singlish' simply in characters' speech, but not in framing narration. Second, the fact that Ming Cher had lived outside Singapore for three decades before the publication means that the novel's representation of the past is not mediated by nationalist historiography: politicians and secret society members, for instance, are both seen by the characters as gangsters. While, as commentators have noted, attempts to market *Spider Boys* as an authentic fictional representation of Singapore's past are clearly problematic, it is equally clear that Ming Cher's is a unique voice in Singapore fiction.

Another author with transnational credentials is Tan Hwee Hwee, now resident in Singapore, but who has lived in the Netherlands, the United Kingdom and the United States. Tan's two novels, *Foreign Bodies* (1997) and *Mammon Inc* (2001), reflect Singapore's position as a node in increasingly globalized economic and cultural flows after the end of the Cold War. Tan's novels feature both Singaporean and non-Singaporean characters, performative identities, and a heady mixture of popular culture, myth and evangelical Christianity. *Mammon Inc*'s protagonist, Chiah Deng Gan, is a Singaporean student at the University of Oxford who struggles in a choice between a life of spiritual contemplation represented by Professor Ad-oy (a palindrome of the *Star Wars* character Yoda) and the temptations of the nakedly materialist Draco Sidious of the organization Mammon Corps.

Sidious wants Chiah Deng to work for him as an 'Adapter', a cultural mediator who will assist members of a mobile 'modern international professional elite' (2002: 2) to 'gain social acceptance' in the countries to which they are posted. In order to be employed by Sidious, Chiah Deng must pass a series of tests, and the last two are designed to demonstrate her talent in adapting: she is required to make her sister, Chiah Chen, a caricature of a materialist Singaporean, fit unobtrusively into a gathering of the British intellectual elite at Oxford, and then to make her very English flatmate Steve sit unobtrusively through a Singaporean family dinner. The novel climaxes with Chiah Deng, after agonized indecision, rejecting Ad-oy for Sidious, and surveying the 'kingdom' from the latter's headquarters in New York, the Big Apple now transformed into 'the apple in Eve's eye' (2002: 278).

The late 1990s and early years of the twenty-first century saw, in contrast to the Philippines, a decline in new writers of prose fiction in English. Tham, Suchen Lim and Catherine Lim continued to publish, and were joined by newer, but less consistently successful, voices. Daren Shiau's novel *Heartland* (1999) was a promising beginning, intercutting present-day Singapore with elements drawn from its colonial past, and exploring issues of social class in a manner that few other recent Singaporean texts have done. Yet prose fiction published in Singapore did not initially show the vibrancy of other genres, such as poetry, drama or the new media in the new millennium. Many novels have been published. Historical novels have included Ralph Modder's *Lions and Tigers* (1993) and *Souls the Gods Had Forsaken* (2003), and Walter Woon's *The Advocate's Devil* (2002) and *The Devil to Pay* (2005). A newly emergent genre has explored the experiences of Singaporeans abroad: Tan Teck Howe's *The Secret Goldfish and Other Follies* (2004) is an account of expatriate study at Oxford, while Claire Tham's *Skimming* (1999) follows a relationship that commences during the protagonists' study in Britain. Two later texts have matched the engagement or sophistication of the writing of the 1990s: Wena Poon's *Lions in Winter* (2007), an uneven but sporadically brilliant collection of short stories that explores the lives of Singaporeans outside Singapore, and Simon Tay's *City of Small Blessings* (2008), featuring a protagonist who migrates to Canada and then returns to Singapore.

In the meantime, writing published outside Singapore has increased in both quantity and quality. Australians Hsu-Ming Teo (*Love and Vertigo* [2000]; *Behind the Moon* [2005]) and Lau Siew Mei (*Playing Madame Mao* [2000]) have written, in very different manners, migrant narrative connecting Singapore and Australia. Canadian Lydia Kwa's *This Place Called Absence* (2002) weaves the life of a Singaporean-born psychotherapist in contemporary Vancouver with her reconstruction, through historical research, of the same-sex love affair between two sex workers in Singapore in the early twentieth century. Of American-based writers, Fiona Cheong has produced a second novel, *Shadow Theatre* (2002), while Vyvyanne Loh's novel *Breaking the Tongue* (2004), set in Singapore before and during the

Japanese occupation, is experimental in writing substantial sections of the end of the narrative in Chinese. Loh's novel, written by a Malaysian now resident in the United States, also raises the questions of the boundaries of Singapore literature: in a world marked by migrating subjects and audiences, this is becoming ever more difficult to answer.

Hong Kong

Hong Kong's retrocession to China in 1997 had three effects on writing in English in the territory. Tensions before the handover, and the rise of China as an economic and political power in the decade afterwards made Hong Kong a continued favoured location for popular novels of espionage and geopolitical intrigue by British and American writers, producing a local response through thrillers such as Margaret Siu's *Her Majesty the Comrade* (1997). Second, a growing emphasis on Mandarin, yoked to the relative ethnic homogeneity of Hong Kong's population, ensured that the status of English remained marginal when used to describe the everyday reality of most Hong Kong people. Yet the end of British colonialism had a third, unlooked-for effect: the problematization of the category expatriate, and the blurring of the boundaries between transnational and local. Many English-language writers in Hong Kong such as Xu Xi, Nury Vittachi, Roseanne Thong and Richard Tong have complex backgrounds that involve residence in other parts of Asia and the region. Cantonese-speaking Hong Kong writers in English who are literate in Chinese are also now likely to have spent significant amounts of time in Canada, the United States or Britain.

The New Territories in Hong Kong is the extension to the colony leased by China to the United Kingdom in 1888 for a period of 99 years. Historically it consisted of the area north of Boundary Street on the Kowloon peninsula, and all islands apart from Hong Kong Island itself, although in contemporary usage the northern section of Kowloon (New Kowloon) is now not considered part of the New Territories.

The most successful evocation of place in a recent Hong Kong novel in English is the account in Poh Wah Lam's *The Locust Hunter* (2004) of a child's experience of life in the rural New Territories in the 1970s. The novel, published abroad, celebrates a world that has now vanished. Most other novels produced in Hong Kong have been much less firmly rooted, and follow generic conventions. Nury Vittachi's *The Feng Shui Detective* (2000), for instance, regionalizes the detective story. Its protagonist, C. F. Wong, solves mysteries not through reason but through his skills as a geomancer, with the young British-Australian woman Joyce McQuinnie serving as his Watson.

Wong is based in Singapore, and roams to Malaysia and further afield to solve cases. The text targets a non-Singaporean or Malaysian reader, making use of occasional Cantonese (justified by the fact that Wong is originally from Guangdong province) and misspelled Malay. Yet Vittachi's inattention to questions of authenticity perhaps indicates his texts' audience: cosmopolitan expatriates of varied cultural heritages and affiliations who move within the region.

Xu Xi's novels, while more consciously literary than Vittachi's, exhibit similar characteristics. A novel such as *The Unwalled City* (2001) develops the twin heritage of a Joan Collins-style thriller and romance in a new direction: the expatriate man is no longer the centre of the narrative, which is now peopled largely with upper-middle-class Hong Kong-based professionals. The novel, set in the last few years immediately preceding Hong Kong's retrocession in 1997, charts a series of interlocking relationships among members of a transnational elite whose reach extends to Shanghai, Vancouver, Singapore and beyond. Cantonese and phrasebook Mandarin are scattered through the text like decorative confetti, while a breathless narrative proceeds through a series of climaxes, sexual and otherwise. In other novels such as *Chinese Walls* (1994) and *Hong Kong Rose* (1997), Xu Xi engages more explicitly with fictionalizations of her own complex history of migration, growing up in Hong Kong as a child of Indonesian-Chinese parents, and then spending many years in the United States. A parallel experience is documented in the thinly fictionalized novels of Richard Tong, *The Durian Effect* (2003) and *Me and My Potato* (2005), describing the migration to Hong Kong of an Australian of mixed Anglo-Celtic and Chinese heritage, and his subsequent marriage into a Hong Kong Chinese family.

As in Malaysia, some of the most vibrant writing in Hong Kong in English has been short fiction. Civil servant David T. K. Wong's pioneering collections *Lost River* (1990), *Hong Kong Stories* (1996) and *Connections* (2001) have been followed since 2000 by a number of stories by new writers. In part, the development of the Hong Kong short story in English has been enabled by the founding of literary magazines in the new millennium: the University of Hong Kong's *Yuan Yang*, Chameleon Books's *Dimsum* and the online journal *Cha*. Several collections of short stories show promise for the future. Dania Shawwa's edited collection *Hong Kong ID* (2005), for example, contains a variety of short stories by different contributors, many of whose experiences challenge the local/expatriate binary. Mani Rao is a migrant from India to Hong Kong who publishes poetry with accompanying Chinese translation; Roseanne Thong was born in the United States but later moved to Asia, spending fifteen years living in a variety of locations. Story content, too, shows Hong Kong at the intersection of transnational movements of people and culture: Karen Chaulam Cheng's 'No Suspicious Circumstances' features an older woman who has lost contact with a son who has migrated to Vancouver, Canada, while Yvonee Lee Wing Chi's short story 'The 2 of Them' centres on ICQ chat between two Hong Kong students who are fans of the Britpop rock band Suede. Xu Xi's essay 'Finding My English: One Hong Kong Writer's Evolution', which concludes the collection, offers interesting pointers regarding the location of such stories. Its author notes that she writes in a 'World English' informed by consciousness of 'a global culture that happens to find its voice in English' (2005: 184). Thus, the next generation of Hong Kong writers 'will likely be those who write bi-lingually or tri-lingually, who embody a bi- or tri-cultural sensibility that is Chinese Hong Kong' in which 'Chinese Hong Kong' is a political fact rather than an ethnic descriptor (2005: 184).

Indeed, such concerns with the global may well intersect with the concerns of writings in Chinese from and about Hong Kong. The Chinese University of Hong Kong journal *Renditions* has done much work over the years to bring Hong Kong writing in Chinese to an English-speaking readership, with regular special issues or sections on Hong Kong writing. From Eileen Chang to P. K. Leung, writers of Chinese fiction of Hong Kong have seen the territory's experience of modernity as fragmentary, continually renegotiated as it is caught in cultural flows that extend to China, the region and the world beyond.

Conclusion

* In the Philippines, Malaysia and Singapore, prose fiction has moved increasingly outside the confines of the university.
* While older generations of writers are still active, younger generations have introduced new forms and themes, often drawn from the experiences of urban living, globalization and popular culture.
* The Philippines retains a vibrant tradition of literary publication, but in Singapore and Malaysia, many newer voices are of migrants living or publishing outside Southeast Asia: it remains to be seen whether this is a passing phase, or a significant shift.
* Hong Kong seems exceptional in the cosmopolitan nature of its English-language fiction, yet may offer a glimpse of a future in which such writing circulates outside the boundaries of national traditions.

11 Contemporary poetry 1990–2008

Overview

The contemporary poets of Southeast Asia bring to writing a cosmopolitan awareness of allusion and reference that aligns their best work with what is currently being accomplished by practitioners in English at the international level. Their role models are drawn not simply from their respective national pasts but from the virtual museum of world poetry. Most contemporary poets treat urban life as a mixed blessing. They evince little enthusiasm for the theme of nation building or the urge towards collective identity that preoccupied their predecessors. They are more interested in the consequences and implications of living in a world that is globalized and postmodern. The relation of writing to history might interest some, but many more are interested in the spatial dimension of their environments, and how that is transformed by migratory displacements and relocations. Very little of their writing is directly political in its commitment, although much of it is ethically self-aware, and many profess admiration for poets and writing practices derived from regions where the responsibility of bearing witness to trauma and violence in the public sphere has been of paramount concern, as in East Europe, South America and the Middle East.

In terms of the number of writers active in the genre, poetry probably takes second place to fiction in Malaysia, Hong Kong and the Philippines; whereas in Singapore, it has retained a primary appeal for young writers, who turn to the genre in greater numbers than are drawn to fiction. Without counting publications from overseas-based Southeast Asians, a period of less than two decades, from 1990 to 2008, has seen the publication of over a hundred volumes of poetry in English from the Philippines, approximately the same number from Malaysia and Singapore combined, and the beginning of a much smaller but quite distinct new tradition of poetry in English from Hong Kong (and Macao). The issue is not one of mere quantity, but of interest and confidence in poetry as a vocation, and in English as the medium for that vocation, although for some it remains one among several viable linguistic options.

A quiet and casual tone is preferred; irony is much in evidence, also understatement. A gift for metaphor is prized: the capacity to spring a discovery – through any combination of image and idea – is rendered synonymous with the capacity to give pleasure or insight. Much of the writing is personal in tone: though the typical poem might not be literal or autobiographical in reference, it tends to be vocalized from the perspective of a singular subjectivity. The long poem is rarely attempted; a short verse line is preferred. Poets work hard at crafting the movement of syntax across line breaks where once their predecessors pored as much over the tension between surprise and expectation in the practice of rhyme and metre.

The Philippines

The last quarter-century has seen a lot of exciting new poetry from the Philippines, some of it by poets who began their careers in previous decades, and some from poets who published first volumes in the 1990s. The flourishing of poetry in the late 1980s and throughout the 1990s reflects the liberating effect on culture of the end of the period of martial law under Marcos. The university presses in Metro Manila have remained the primary patrons of poetry, supplemented by commercial publishers, of whom Anvil is the largest. Poets whose publications of the 1990s built upon past achievements and developed in new directions include Manuel Viray, Eric T. Gamalinda, Emmanuel Torres, Luis Cabalquinto, Ricardo M. de Ungria, Cirilio Bautista, Edith Tiempo, Alfred Yuson, Simeon Dumdum, Ramon C. Sunico, Marne L. Kilates, Marjorie M. Evasco and Ophelia Alcantara Dimalanta, to mention only the most prominent. While each of these poets produced work of significance and interest, a handful of volumes are worth singling out for styles and idioms whose self-reflexive ironies are distinctly postmodern in flavour.

Key Philippine poetry volumes of the 1990s:
Eric Gamalinda, *Lyrics from a Dead Language* (1990),
Zero Gravity (1999);
Emmanuel Torres, *The Smile on Smokey Mountain* (1991);
Ricardo de Ungria, *Decimal Places* (1991);
Alfred Yuson, *Trading in Mermaids* (1993);
Ramon Sunico, *Bruise: A2-Tongue Job* (1995);
Marne Kilates, *Poems en Route* (1998).

In contrast to the distinctly postmodern flavour of these volumes, Evasco's bilingual *Ochre Tones* (1999) shows the best that has been accomplished in the vein of what Simeon Dumdum describes in the 'Introduction' as a search for the spiritual in the physical and the physical in the spiritual, as in the poem 'Is It The Kingfisher', which affirms the feeling that 'the blueness embrace us', including 'The distance between us and the Self / We have longed to be' (Evasco 1999: 57). We find her gaining confidence in the role of a secular priestess who practises a poetics in which art celebrates its many unions with nature, while she also comes back to her mother tongue, Cebuano, through the practice of self-translation.

A different kind of magic is invoked, far less solemnly, in a Borges-like poem, 'Uqbaresque', by Eric Gamalinda, who invites his readers to imagine an invented world like our own, in which 'history must be implanted in those who populate it' (1999: 26). This move serves as the pretext for rethinking what beginnings can be like when they are imagined in all the mysteriousness, uncertainty and tentativeness that must precede any form of actualization. The motif of conventional love poetry is given a Marvellian twist in the persuasive reminder that 'There is only what if I touched you here', 'before we remember how to be born', when our hunger is 'as hard as a pearl' (1999: 27). The capacity to give voice to this new tone of surreal incipience represents a big leap forward for poetry from Southeast Asia. Gamalinda's title poem, 'Zero Gravity', is a tour de force in fleshing out a frame of mind that is described, self-reflexively, as 'Reckless / in our need for the possible' (1999: 47). It is not the fantastical that is pursued as if it were a chimera, but the chimerical that is focused on. 'Chosen' drives home an analogous point, that what it means to feel chosen ought to be not the hyperinflation of the impossible but 'the intrusion of the ordinary' (1999: 61).

Turning from the veterans to the newcomers who published a first volume in the 1990s, we can divide them into two groups: those born up to the 1950s and those born in or after the 1960s.

Philippine poets born up to the 1950s:

Myrna Peña-Reyes, Cesar Ruiz Aquino, Merlie M. Alunan, Elsa Martinez Coscolluela, Jaime An Lim, Arnold Molina Azurin, Francis C. Macansantos, Victorio N. Sugbo, Rowena Tiempo Torrevillas, Rofel G. Brion, Victor Jose Peñaranda, Babeth Lolarga, Constantino C. Tejero, Merlinda C. Bobis and Juaniyo Y. Arcellana.

Book-length publications have been supplemented by work published in periodicals and journals (such as *Caracoa, Flame, Folio, Chimera, Sands and Coral*), and the representation given to young writers in anthologies, of which the most noteworthy are the series of Likhaan volumes from the University of the Philippines Institute of Creative Writing, and the selections based on the Don Carlos Palanca Memorial Awards for Literature. In addition, poets have found representation in numerous online publications (such as *High Chair*, *Our Own Voice*, etc.). Several poets also maintain personal blogs and websites (e.g. Marne Kilates, Luisa Igloria and Eileen R. Tabios), which keeps their work accessible independent of print publication.

Philippine poets born in or after the 1960s:
Eileen Tabios, Fatima V. Lim-Wilson, Luisa B. Aguilar (Cariño), Isabelita Orlina Reyes, Danton Remoto, Nick Carbô, Jose P. Wendell Capili, Jim Pascual Agustin, J. Neil Garcia, Ruel S. de Vera, Ramil Digal Gulle, Paolo Manalo, Mabi David, Jose Beduya, Alex Gregorio, Lourd Ernest de Veyra, Conchitina R. Cruz, Dina Roma, Kristine Domingo and Marc Gaba.

Among the many anthologies published since the 1990s, two deserve special mention: *Ladlad: An Anthology of Philippine Gay Writing* (1994) and *Ladlad 2* (1996), edited by J. Neil C. Garcia and Danton Remoto. In the Philippine context 'ladlad' means 'to flaunt, expose, lay bare or bring out into the open' (Isabela Banzon: personal communication). Garcia points out that the anthologies have made it easier for gay writing to be assimilated into the academic curriculum, while serving 'as the catalysts for the formation of a broad-based gay and possibly lesbian coalition' in the Philippines (Garcia and Remoto 1996: xiv). Garcia is a prolific poet, critic and anthologist, and Remoto chairs the LGBT (lesbian-gay-bisexual-transsexual) lobby in Manila, and is active in politics. Each has a following among young and radical readers. Their collective enterprise is significant in the context of the struggle of the *bakla*, a term that 'conflates the categories of effeminacy, transvestism, and homosexuality' (Garcia and Remoto 1994: 197) to gain self-respect and acceptance in society. As with any embattled minority which has suffered the consequences of repression, guilt, prejudice and conditioning, the need to give voice to a sense of difference in identity and of community in difference becomes the overwhelming motive and justification for such writing, at once the source and the limit-condition of its appeal.

The two *Ladlad* anthologies represent poets speaking the difference of an identity based on sexual orientation. A lot of the writing is inevitably about gay sex, and the results confirm the recognition that to write interestingly about sexuality is never easy, regardless of the nature of the writer's sexual preferences. In speaking gay sexuality, what comes across more powerfully than either the tenderness or exuberance of desire is the sense of isolation that discrimination has bred into the fabric of gay experience, as when Jaime An Lim writes 'I am haunted by the sadness of men' (1994: 151), or when Remoto writes of 'lips and fingers touching, / groping for each other's loneliness' (1994: 176), or in 'Room', of 'the cruelty of dreams, // the sadness of this room, / of life' (1996: 135); or in 'Images of John (1967–1992)', of 'How hard it is / to find somebody / who will open windows and doors / to let you in' (Carbó 1995: 178–179).

Moving from poems centred around a complex but single topic to the more general task of surveying notable achievements among the newcomers, we propose to touch briefly upon the salient features of the writing of four poets (fully aware that there are several others of equal significance). One was born in the 1950s: Ricardo de Ungria; two were born in the 1960s: Fatima V. Lim-Wilson and Luisa Igloria (who began her career under the name Maria Luisa B. Aguilar Cariño); and one was born in the 1970s: Conchitina R. Cruz. This small sampling, which includes two who have settled in the United States (Lim-Wilson and Igloria), enables us to trace the outlines of developments that stretch across more than a quarter-century of writing, while illustrating some of the best that has been achieved by contemporary poets born in the Philippines.

Ricardo de Ungria is the author of seven volumes, from *R+A+D+I+O* (1986), *Voideville* (1991), *Decimal Places* (1991), *Nudes* (1994), *Body English* (1996) and *Waking Ice* (2000) to *Pidgin Levitations* (2004). He began publishing in the 1970s, obtained an MFA from Washington University (St Louis) in 1990, and has worked in numerous academic positions in the Philippines. His poems are sure-footed in their movement across the line breaks of free verse, and their negotiation between the grammar of sense and the syntax of the musical phrase. He is adept at sustaining a balance between apparent simplicity of means and complex, often fairly intellectualized, ends. For instance, in 'Angel Radio', from *Decimal Places* (1991), the artist as the young man finally abroad for the first time in America (the land of his dreams), is droll in his personal stock-taking, the adult treating the child as the father of the man, remembering himself 'dressed by mother for the world' (1991: 115). A half-guilty, half-exhilarated brooding over the land to which Filipino heroes came, never to return (Villa in his Greenwich apartment, Bulosan in Bakersfield), measures 'how far we can get / away from the mind of God' (1991: 116). The poem concludes with the dramatization of a mock-ironic self-introduction as from 'Pepe' (the Philippine nickname for Jose, as in Jose Rizal, the national hero), and the tone of the writing seems to parody (as Isabela Banzon points out in a personal communication) a primer on English introduced by America into their Philippine colony, as well as Kipling's notorious description of the natives who must be civilized as part of the role passed on in 'The White Man's Burden' (1899) from British to American colonialism: 'Hello Sirs! My name is Pepe. / I have a cow. / A cow is an animal / with four corners' (1991: 117). The naïve tone is deliberate, so is the mock-optimism: 'The sky is blue and so are you'; and yet there is sheer desperation in what drives the poem towards jumping off at the deep end: 'God loves you so and so you take / no prisoners. Off the bridge we go' (1991: 117).

Ricardo de Ungria's poems enjoy the kind of complexity in which concrete and sensory elements relate in unexpected ways to abstract and conceptual elements. The figurative means deployed for some thematic end complicate any possible response to the theme, turning it inside out, as with the ending of the third variation from 'Blue (Variations on a fragment from Sappho)', from *Nudes*:

> Yet as a flower sharpens
> Her longing on shafts of the sun,
> Pleased to be held as she opens,
> So will silence stain your hand.
> (1994: 28)

Ordinarily, we might suppose that the synaesthesia of silence staining a hand might be purely negative in connotation. Yet here the idea is preceded by an image used as analogy in which heliotropism is a figure for desire and pleasure: as in the case of a flower that is held, and happy to be held, as she opens to the phallic and penetrative gaze and touch of the sun's rays. In what sense could the lover's silence (and the reproach Sappho's voice administers to the apparently reluctant auditor of the poem) be similar to what the flower enjoys and suffers at the hands or eyes of the sun? Light=Pleasure is used as an analogy for Silence=Stain, turning the idea of pleasure and pain inside out: the one laden with the other; neither left uncomplicated by the traversal through analogy. Such effects are typical of de Ungria at his best, giving his work the savour of metaphysical wit and sensuous intellection.

Fatima V. Lim-Wilson and Maria Luisa B. Aguilar-Cariño began writing while students in the Philippines, and published several volumes of distinction before migrating to the United States. Their later poems may have been written from their new homes overseas, but their writing continues to draw upon Philippine memories, themes and motifs, and therefore we address their work here rather than in Chapter 9. Lim-Wilson is the author of *Wandering Roots, 1978–1988 / From the Hothouse, 1989–1990* (1991), published from the Philippines, and *Crossing the Snow Bridge* (1995), published from the United States, where she now teaches. Some of her later poems deal with the experience of living overseas, but the bulk of her writing is based on Philippine experiences. Her gift is unusual in nature, because it has less to do with originality of language than with a capacity for unexpected modes of perception that lead to disquieting realizations. Unrepressed aspects of experience merge fear, fantasy, desire and memory, becoming the locus for the simultaneous coexistence of the magical, the startling, the felicitous and the painfully pleasing.

Thus for example, 'From the Forbidden Tree' imagines what it might have been like to have been Eve 'bored with the man / Of the missing rib' (Lim-Wilson 1991a: 70); 'Devil' imagines being visited by his presence, 'Reeking with lust, thin-flanked and hairy', before whom the speaking voice of the poem declares, 'See, I unclasp myself before you' (1991a: 72). Several other poems, such as 'Casting Call' and 'The Resident Alien as Acrobat', from her American volume, represent a merger of the feminist and the diasporic impulses, united in their resistance to masculine colonization. A mirror poem, 'Mirror, Mirror', first hopes the mirror might hide her, then declares that that won't happen, for 'I am much too small and frightening' (1991a: 77). 'A Poem For This Night' ends with the prayer 'make me blind' (1991a: 79). 'Window Poem' speaks as glass that watches over the adult become a child again, guided to a time when the glass can shatter. 'Empty Room Poem' ends with the room whirling, 'vacuum-filled with ghosts' (1991a: 89).

Lim-Wilson's world dissolves the distinction sometimes made between imagination and fancy. Often a single line is sufficient for the newness of what is at work, as in 'The sun pants scaling noon' (1991b: 9), or 'To the left of my eye, / A star swells' (1991b: 21). Childhood recollected is a series of troubled memories, a time of life 'When I thought it best to leave / Some things misunderstood' (1991a: 4). The image of the father recurs: 'your children cannot ask you In what tongue you speak in your sleep' (1991a: 3). In 'Homing' the speaking voice of the poem speaks of stumbling into 'the darkened room / Where I fumble with the buttons / Of my childhood' (1991b: 1), and ends with the image of the face of the dead father in his casket, burning. Another Father poem speaks of 'the drink / Brewed from the root / Twisted into a man' (1991a: 5). The casualness or apparent inconsequentiality with which the oddest things are said is a key part of the effectiveness of such poems. From overseas, a letter to the mother is matter-of-fact about the business of keeping in touch from a distance, 'Each promising to see through the other's deceit' (1991a: 7). Everything meant is said; nothing is left unsaid simply to save us or her the disquiet that accompanies the saying. When asked to give an account of where she comes from, the poet provides a tangy self-representation of the Philippines:

> 7,000 and more islands scattered over the pacific
> Like the brown-green clusters of carabao turd.
> [...]
> Natives with Chinese eyes and Malayan skin,
> Castillian airs and made in U.S.A. minds,
> We cross ourselves in the pit before the cockfight.
> (1991a: 16)

The Plath-like starkness of Lim-Wilson's gift is best illustrated by the poem 'The Medium', in which the form of the dramatic monologue allows the speaking voice of the poem to evoke a process of miraculous possibility all the more startling for the calm manner in which the allegorical nature of self-discovery is dramatized:

> I sit, a Madonna in middle age.
> The child
> Leaps exultant,

In the tabernacle
Of my womb.

(1991a: 63)

The uncanny and the miraculous find ready room in Lim-Wilson's poems. 'Miracle of Roses' imagines a young girl accompanied everywhere by a scent of roses. The poem ends with an oddly disturbing image: 'The young woman, in giving thanks, / Unclasps her hands. / Blood-tipped buds peek / Between the teeth of sleeping children' (1991b: 20). After a visit to an Egyptian sarcophagus in the Ashmolean Museum at Oxford, when a lover puts a hand in her hand, she shudders 'Remembering the ancestor / Left behind', his 'Heart floating / in a smaller, / Stone-sealed vessel' (1991b: 24). In 'Angel', having been made love to by an angel, 'When we came / Apart, I shimmered for days, shot through / With aureole light' (1991b: 34). In 'The Legend of Lanzones', when after a feast of fruit two make love, 'We explore each other, / Our fingers sticky with sin' (1991b: 48). In 'Offspring', while a mother breast-feeds her baby, feeling like a cow with swollen udders, the poet leans over the crib to check on 'my manuscript, my dear child / feeding on black blood' (1991b: 44). 'Mother Tongue' ends:

Mother, when did I unlearn to speak?
I can no longer hear you, not even in sleep.
Scanning mirrors, I catch shadows.
I can only smile at myself now,
Biting back my forked tongue.

(1991b: 28)

Crossing the Snow Bridge (1995) reveals a new self-awareness about language as an expressive medium. The Filipina making accommodations to her American home cannot shed the sense of growing into 'a hunchback, trailing my master, / Unctious and anxious' (1995: 3). No path to diasporic salvation but through an exorcism of self-loathing.

Lim-Wilson's most productive period seems to have been the first two decades of writing. In contrast, her compatriot Luisa A. Igloria, who left the Philippines to study at the University of Chicago in 1992, has kept up a steady output, publishing volumes from the Philippines as well as the United States, where she now lives and teaches creative writing. Her first four volumes of poetry were published under the name Maria Luisa B. Aguilar-Cariño: *Cartography* (1992), *Encanto* (1994), *In the Garden of the Three Islands* (1995) and *Blood Sacrifice* (1997). Her latest volumes are *Trill & Mordent* (2005) and *Juan Luna's Revolver* (2009). Igloria could be said to be the most accomplished contemporary poet writing in English to have been born in the Philippines. Her writing is supple and well centred, both in terms of each poem having a sense of where it wants to go, and also in the sense that means are deployed towards ends with a balanced felicity which produces poems deeply satisfying not for this or that image or metaphor but for how a powerful and intelligent feeling grows to a moment of thoughtful self-realization. This is readily shareable with the reader because the poem has worked its way to its moment of cognitive realization by means that appear in retrospect both natural and spontaneous, regardless of the craft and labour the semblance of naturalness might entail.

The poet describes the evolution of her early themes in terms of her dissertation thesis: 'the articulation of what it means to be a Filipino/Filipina: … an interrogation of the concepts of *home, imagination, location*, and *dislocation*'. This reads apt for its academic purpose, but even more to the point, the poet tells us that her work 'celebrates the formative influences and enchantment found in everyday life experiences, in folk culture and mythic belief, in memory and personal history as the sources of strength and voice' (Abad 1999: 615). All this the poems from *Encanto* (1994) bear out amply, intent on what is entailed in the urge to 'walk / without once looking back', as declared in 'Journey to Luna' (Igloria 1994: 36–37). The poet is nothing if not articulate about the journey she must undertake. 'Familiar' evokes memories of a Baguio childhood companioned by a clear recollection of how, through all the accompaniment of sing-song voices 'bordering the road' of childhood there was the magical incantation of words to cherish as word-hoard:

> [...] *bizarre, irrevocable,*
> *reproach, syllable, steerage, ballast,*
> *gesture* – taking them with me to sleep
> like furry animals, hiding them
> in my mouth like pebbles
> newly dug up from the moonlit
> garden – taste of earth,
> crushed bones, verbena, flared
> nasturtiums.
>
> (1994: 15)

'Postcard from Persephone' uses the Greek myth to indicate what this child of the Philippine Demeter thinks of her troth to the seven pomegranate seeds of the United States: 'Where I am going the cold / barely touches me' (Igloria 1994: 53). 'Manchachawak' admits that 'the edges / of this body soften like bruised / fruit', and feels 'The terror of a collapsed / universe', but is fixed on the recognition that 'New York lies / far beyond these islands' (1994: 63).

Poem after poem impresses with the sense of rightness it fosters for the reader, even when (or especially when) what is being worked out is a nuanced disengagement from engagement, a shedding of loved old skins for needed new ones, which 'Ransom' describes as 'things I have undone' (Abad 1999: 427 [not in 1997: 103]). 'For the Lover' enacts a quiet and steady valediction of love. The act of love-making – 'we devour each other' – is placed within the context of something 'beckoning / to a fate beyond the dark / outline of your head'. The growing awareness kept the poet intent on a purpose whose attendant guilt when acknowledged, as here, still leaves room for 'the clear / notes of a waltz, / delivering me / at last / to this / knowledge', which, presumably, is not a knowledge of guilt, but of that which guilt could neither stop nor deflect, a new self-realization (Carbó 1995: 17–20).

The note prefacing *In the Garden of the Three Islands* (1995) underlines the connection teased out by the poet in all her work between memory, consciousness and 'the landscapes which the self inhabits and traverses' (Igloria 1995: 2). The poems are rich in synergies of metaphor and tactile synaesthesia: light fractured into 'a likeness of repose' (1995: 5), 'fibrous bark' scraped into a lover's tea (8), branches with 'difficult / sap' heavy in their veins (14), snow thick as 'unparsed speech' (23), an aunt sidling up with 'the bones of an old story' (53), a book 'fragrant with words' (56), 'the bone of memory / Scorched clean again' (111). The power of her gift for out-of-the-way but apt-when-encountered imagery is displayed to advantage in 'Gabi', where townswomen at their routine tasks by a river's bank advise against bathing by moonlight, but the poet slips into a reverie in which old folk beliefs mutate:

> Trailing a spasm
> of fish, moth wings
> and beggar's ticks,
> the river god breaks through the wet
> underworld of dreams.
>
> (1995: 10)

'The Other Annunciation', from *Blood Sacrifice* (1997), is not overawed at likening the poet's choices to those of Christ the carpenter: just as 'A seam on the burnished wood / now barely noticeable' might be 'a remnant of a casual / encounter with lightning'; likewise, the presentiments of change in the poet, though 'hardly yet breath', are declared 'already married to the coming / days of this life' (Igloria 1997: 87). Likewise, 'Reading Botticelli' ventures a daring speculation about the Florentine painter's 'The Annunciation' (in The Uffizi, Florence). The Madonna as represented could be imagined weak at the knees, about to fall; the archangel might then carry her to a couch, and 'chafe her pulse-points' to bring her back to consciousness before departing, 'But not before / registering the knowledge / through his tunic, of her / nipples lifted / in ecstasy': because the moment of falling unconscious was the moment of her access to the knowledge of 'To whom she truly / belongs' (Abad 1999: 431–432). The poem thus merges the phenomenal and the noumenal in an ecstasy of knowing that could be said to symbolize the nature of perception, when focused on ultimate issues, as quintessentially poetic, the fancy becoming imagination.

Among the younger poets practising from the Philippines, Conchitina Cruz is of particular interest. She is the author of *Dark Hours* (2005) and *elsewhere held and lingered* (2008). Her poems are distinguished by their introspective absorption, combining economy of articulation with a disembodied self-reflexivity which separates the self that writes from the self whose experiences, thoughts and feelings are written about. *Dark Hours* is remarkable for its handling of the prose poem, which provides surreal representations of the experience of individuals as part of the life of a specific (though unnamed) city. The prose poem, as used by Cruz, has a movement that is unlike most free verse; it is characterized by a rhythm that is incremental and cumulative, partaking more of the musical form of variations on a theme than of linear progression. The prose poem piles up phrases, sentences, images and metonymies in series whose momentum merges the personal and the solitary with the impressionistically urban. It moves towards conclusions that have the capacity to surprise as well as please, as when 'Smile' ends with the lines 'the room is flooded with the radiance of the moment, a man and a woman in the middle of a sweet misunderstanding' (Cruz 2005: 11), or when the poem 'I must say this about the city' ends with 'I am all alone the room is bare and // like a god grown weary the tree outside the window lays its shadow on the floor beside me' (2005: 12).

The eight-page sequence 'Geography Lesson' is a laconic tour de force (as if at a tangent to the book of blank pages envisioned by Mallarmé): where the reader might expect a text, the book gives blank pages, except that each page has a numbered footnote which provides a set of dry comments suitable for a Borgesian tourist guide. Each note participates in the overall visual experience of reading a book by inverting the conventional relation between text and footnote: the blankness of the space above each note implies an open-ended self-effacement by a text that absents itself in deference to a note, allowing the author to reduce her role to that of an enigmatic annotator, and forcing the reader to conjecture a text of his or her own that would fit the supplied footnote. The relations of primary to secondary sense, of author to reader, and of *ergon* (the main body) to *parergon* (its supplement or addendum) are turned inside out. The poet places the reader where Bishop Berkeley placed God, for 'Such is the curse of this place: if you close your eyes, it disappears' (2005: 24).

A more recent poem, 'This Hand', from *elsewhere held and lingered* (2008), plays a different variant on this technique: it gives the reader both main text and footnoted subtext, but places them in a relation that is oblique. The poem continues the urban theme of *Dark Hours*: 'Ensconced in a napkin on the table, the city becomes an image of delight' (Cruz 2008: 40), to which the footnote adds, 'The dresser mirror again, to which the poet's cherished vocabulary adds: *eternal delight*'. The poem is thus able to have its cake of assertion and yet complicate the claim through the device of an undercutting commentator. Cruz shows herself to be the poet of an analytically feminine selfhood intent on linking personal memories and experiences to an inescapable sense of living in a city. Her poems are imbued with a sense of dreams as well as dilapidation, a desire for relationship as well as solitariness, of a history both personal and communal that the contemporary poem can neither quite wholly comprehend nor affirm without qualification. They exemplify a degree of quiet sophistication not only in the deployment of technique in service of the materials out of which poems are being made, but also to the ways in which formal means enable fresh and varied insights into experiences and ideas that remain personal, but with applications that are more general in scope.

The current scene of writing in the Philippines is lively and alert, as evident from an anthology such as J. Neil Garcia's *At Home in Unhomeliness* (2007), from which several young poets stand out for their talent, among them Paolo Manalo, author of the experimental freewheeling *Jolography* (2003), Marc Gaba, whose chapbook *How Sound Becomes A Name* (2007) was published by *High Chair* (whose web journal is distinguished for the quality of the poems, criticism and interviews it publishes), followed by a new American volume from Tupelo Press, and Angelo V. Suárez, whose third book in particular, *Dissonant Umbrellas* (2007), is poised and striking, with a rhythmic quality and directness of access that are charming. Other poets associated with *High Chair*, who share common concerns about poetry, and hone their craft with regular attendance at various writing workshops, include Allan Popa (who writes bilingual poetry), Mabi David, Kristine Domingo and Alex Gregorio.

Also of note is Jose Perez Beduya, whose *Seem* (2007) is characterized by a faintly surreal minimalism, as in 'An insomniac taking his cloud / of thoughts indoors to arrange them // on a page' (2007: 8). Another poem, 'Switch', meditates on the paradox of 'the dark / returning the act // of reading to the realm / of the physical' (2007: 3), and puns neatly on the possibilities latent to the notions of sight and vision (2007: 3–4). A more complex conceit is unveiled in the second part of the poem 'No Place In Nature', where it is said that the blank veil of faith needs to be held up, 'Because one must / be rendered // to be remembered, / suffered by another // body' (2007: 7). The word 'render' thus becomes laden with a double meaning, as does the idea of being suffered by another body. The minimalism works by placing ordinary words at pressure points in the system of articulation used to make meaning out of faith even as faith is made up of working new meanings into place in the poem.

Likewise, Marc Gaba's *How Sound Becomes A Name* (2007) represents a bold step forward in terms of formal experiments in how syntax and typography can be broken down and re-assembled in new configurations which become an integral part of a reconfigured mode of poetic signification. 'Study of Copernicus, 1514', for example, gives a new role to syntactic dislocations in poetic cohesion. A different but equally fascinating experiment is conducted in the poem 'Logic Diptych', in which the two facing pages of the printed text are placed in a visually antithetical relation across the split introduced by the inside-spine of the book. The first set of lines separates and pairs these two lines: 'the second glorious mystery of the lord Thus printed' | 'a fourth glorious mystery the assumption of the blessed' (2007: 4–5), and the rest of the diptych proceeds along similar lines of disjunction-cohesion. The combined roles of antithesis, apposition and conventional punctuation marks are re-worked around the pause represented by the diacritical mark for a caesura in several poems, such as 'Swift':

> then off | with you
> Idea | meaning: no afterlife | then nothing
> [...]

(2007: 9)

Such poems show a willingness to take language for a walk past the familiar markers that grammar and convention subsist on, in order to see how meanings can be crystallized around an unusual process of fragmentation and collage. The lessons of the more experimental forms of contemporary American poetic idioms are thus assimilated into writing that opens up new possibilities for expression and communication in Southeast Asia.

Other young Philippine poets of note include Joel Toledo (who is part of the Bayaw Poetry Collective, which organizes 'Happy Mondays' poetry readings at the café Mag: Net Katipunan), Naya S. Valdellon (author of *Reluctant Firewalker* [2005]), John Labella (currently studying in the United States), Mark Cayanan (whose writing is drawn towards confessional modes while problematizing the lyric 'I') and Adam David (who is among the most avant-garde and experimental writers of his generation). While a lot of the poetic energies developed in the Philippines are centred round Metro Manila, there is a lot of writing being practised in various other regions and cities such as Baguio, Dumaguete, Cebu, Iligan and Davao. In general, the younger Philippine poets show themselves responsive to the more open-ended approaches to the relation between language, experience and the idea of art that characterize contemporary postmodern poetry, in which, as remarked by Frederic Jameson, what might once have been characterized as schizophrenia now appears to hover with some complaisance between 'joyous intensities' and 'euphoria' (1991: 29).

Malaysia

Given the lack of enthusiasm for English in Malaysian government policy over the decades since the 1960s, it is no surprise that poetry in English has been slow to prosper in contemporary Malaysia, although there have been small signs of a revival of interest in using the language for creative purposes during the last decade, as in recent publications from Silverfish Books, and privately printed works such as Bernice Chauly's semi-autobiographical *going there and coming back* (1997) and *The Book of Sins: Poetry and Prose* (2008), even if commitment and sincerity are more clearly in evidence than literary accomplishment. Far more lively material, largely of a satirical nature, comes from an older poet, Salleh Ben Joned, whose *Adam's Dream* (2007) mixes linguistic ventriloquism with parody to hilarious, if sometimes coarse, effect. He also shows himself robust at adapting English to the Malay verse form of the 'pantun' (an oral form based on quatrains comprising two end-stopped couplets rhyming *abab*, in which the two couplets relate to one another in complementary or antithetical fashion, with the poem varying in length from four to twelve lines). Here are two stanzas from 'Pantuns for Perverts':

> What makes the parrot a very queer bird?
> Its talent to mimic and its hooked bill.
> What makes the shrill patriot a cringing turd?
> Because he has the brain of a mandrill.
> [...]
> Why do the gullible value snake vomit?
> Because old superstition taught them to.
> Our Anwar as seditious sodomite?
> Those Front buggers swear to it; it must be true.
>
> (2007: 105)

For those familiar with the events surrounding the imprisonment in 1999 of Anwar Ibrahim, deputy prime minister of Malaysia, on charges of alleged corruption and homosexuality, the topicality of the poem and its polemics is self-evident and outspoken. Speaking aloud on public issues has not been easy or productive for writers using English in Malaysia. The more common pattern for writers drawn to the cultural capital promised by the English language is to migrate to the West, and exceptions such as Salleh, who has lived for a time in Australia, or Wong Phui Nam, who chose to stay put, are rare. Therefore, when one speaks of someone such as Chin Woon Ping or Shirley Lim making contributions to Malaysian poetry in English, it must be understood that they write of, and keep returning to, Malaysian themes from settled positions outside Malaysia.

Chin's *The Naturalization of Camellia Song* was published from Singapore in 1993 and followed, again from Singapore, by *In My Mother's Dream* (1999). The first book includes work dating as far back as 1971, and the multilingual play 'Details Cannot Body Wants', which was first performed in Singapore (where the poet taught for a time) in 1992 and subsequently publicized as 'the first Singapore play to receive a Restricted (R) rating'. Although put together as a volume from the United States, the first book focuses largely on the author's childhood and development, a formation in which awareness of selfhood is shaped by a sense of place, family, gender, the body and the community of experience created by empathizing with women in various gender roles within Southeast Asian societies. The second book reproduces several poems from the first. In general, the best poems have the peculiar effect of making one feel that being literate, observant, articulate and gender-conscious (all virtues in themselves that the poet displays convincingly) does not somehow suffice to close the gap between what we *see* the poems trying to do and what we ought to be able to *feel* they do. In effect, they read like very good translations from some lost language, rendered into fluent English, but with some of the nuances flattened out, as in the poem 'Someone Else's Dream', which wonders 'why I often feel / Trapped in someone else's dream' (Chin 1999: 69).

Singapore

Singaporean poets who began their careers in previous decades and continued producing new work of considerable interest include Edwin Thumboo, Goh Sin Tub, Robert Yeo, Lee Tzu Pheng, Kirpal Singh and Leong Liew Geok. Leong's *Love Is Not Enough* (1991), like her pioneering anthology *More Than Half the Sky: Creative Writings by Thirty Singaporean Women* (1998), gives careful and precise articulation to a new sense of empowerment acquired through dramatizing the way 'A Chauvinist Pig Speaks', as when he assumes that wives exist merely to clean up the mess left by husbands (1991: 70).

Among younger poets, Boey Kim Cheng followed up the promise of *Somewhere-Bound* (1989) with *Another Place* (1992) and *Days of No Name* (1996), while *After the Fire* (2006) combines new poems with a selection from the previous work. Boey is currently settled in Australia, a relocation which contributes to the irony that the more firmly he seems to want to get Singapore out of his system, the more he gets involved in its haunting presences and absences. Even though he can be regarded as a diasporic writer, a large part of his *oeuvre* depends on references to Singapore for its orientation, and we therefore find it useful to survey his work here. For Boey, writing has always been an exorcism of memory even as it expresses the longing to find fulfilment in the practice of a vocation whose call must be answered in a world where it can at best overlap only partially with a profession or a career. He brings to all his work a fascination with the role of poet that is at once both a strength and part of the reason why he can sometimes appear to take himself a little too seriously. On the one hand, his sense of vocation is drawn towards 'making words a ritual / appeasing as wafer to the tongue' (1996: 59); on the other hand, the poetic function resonates always to 'an inner music / of irresolution' (1996: 51) which, despite many felicities of expression, cannot quite shed the impression of being a trifle too earnest in its self-absorption.

The early verse is tense with metaphor and symbol, and peopled by elementary presences like darkness, forest, sky, hill and house, with a Cross suspended above them all. 'Prayer' broods on 'a dark day longing / for the font the stars / draw such pure fire from' (Boey 1989: 14). Not everything is archetypal. The poet gives signs of finding Singapore an environment in which the composure of 'our nice, ordinary, selves' (1989: 24) is paid for in several ways that the second volume elaborates on, in part the cost paid by Singaporeans (mostly quite willingly) for what the poet complains is 'the country's damaging interest / in everybody's welfare' (1992: 42), and in part the poet's grappling with an innate restlessness that worries over a routine life in which 'The smog hangs over the city, / like a swarm of locusts. / I am encased all day / in a barrel of lard' (1992: 36). The title of the first volume, *Somwhere-Bound*, gives intimation of a need for more by way of experience than seems possible within the organized and claustrophobic world of Singapore. 'Dreamwashed' finds a striking image to express both urgency and unease: 'We sit on the pier / of sleep, afraid to launch / into dreams / there is no coming back from' (1988: 46). The poet is intent on a search for a more apt fulfilment of the poetic calling, while also worrying if he has it in him, like Rimbaud, to give up poetry at some point in his life. 'Everyman' speaks of having met 'Rimbaud on a dark road / leaving a luminescent set of prints / as he walked away from poetry' (1988: 70).

Boey's second volume wills the poet out of Singapore. His journey takes him to Europe, but not before he has immersed himself in India, home to squalor as well as spiritualist alternatives to Singapore or the West, and 'a land where God has left many things / undone' (1992: 13), where 'The hands of this poem are useless stumps', which 'cannot even begin to turn the page', because the poet comes 'from a race that has no word for despair' (1992: 11). He is thus 'driven by mixed impulses / to lose and to find' (1992: 23), and the trip helps counter self-estrangement with the strangeness of cultural difference, making India a means towards the end of 'the quest for whatever grinds / to a halt, and wakes / the mind to its loss' (1992: 23). The poet is fully aware that he is 'In Transit', and uses travel as 'a floating spar that may bear him somewhere' (1992: 26). Back home, the poems of the second volume measure the increasing gap between the pasts Singapore leaves behind and the futures it keeps unfolding eagerly as 'the nation's high-rise dreams' (1992: 51). 'The Old-Timers' voices sympathy for those becalmed in the waters of Singapore's past ('the dense waters of their dreams'), underdogs to the myth of modernity who remain helpless as 'progress / eats into their lives' (1992: 51). The poet is fed up with 'perpetual unrest' in the routine life of Singapore housing estates: 'the endless knockings, / the stampeding feet, the hurricanes of bad temper, / the eternal television, the thrashing bodies' (1992: 49). Leaving Singapore, he hopes, might bring him close to 'the realm of reality still available outside' (1992: 58): leaving readers uncertain if the restlessness he imputes to society as a malaise might also be a precondition to a selfhood from which there could be long-term relief only by changing one's country. But changing one's country has become inevitable, once it is seen, unblinkingly that

> The country wears perfect rows
> of shining teeth.
> Anaesthesia, amnesia, hypnosis.
> They have the means.
> They have it all so it will not hurt,
> so history is new again.
> The piling will not stop.
>
>   (1992: 63)

The third volume shows Boey more relaxed and in America, where he is among fellow poets and undergoes experiences that include fascinated friendship turning to love. The book as a whole reads even more like a verse chronicle of his current life than the preceding volumes. The anecdotal aspect of this method makes for a less tense atmosphere, and the verse lines too are more laid-back than in the preceding work, less prone to the lugubrious.

The new poems from *After the Fire* (2006) are a valediction of mourning for a past that includes his recently deceased father and the island of his birth, both now left behind, with reflections on what they have meant and what the poet will carry with him of that commingled past. The title poem is a sober elegy, in which evocations of his father merge seamlessly with images of kelong and sea:

> The nets are reeled in, like a retiarus
> ceiling, and there is a heaven of fish
> heaving, thrashing scales, and mouths
> agape in hosannas of death, all winched
> and dropped on the floodlit deck.
>
>   (2006: 20)

The grandmother (wife to an educated man in colonial days, and after his death, third or fourth concubine to a shipping magnate who went bust) is evoked through a five-year-old boy's memory of calloused hands, symbolizing a hard but obdurate life in 'her kitchen, her apothecary / of herbal and verbal cures' (Boey 2006: 22). Familial presences are like place names and events buried in memory, tokens of an attachment that the poet clarifies for himself in welcoming awareness of how parenting makes the past relate to a future differently. Self-reflexivity has some relief in watching a child grow, especially when it is one's own, for in that continuity lies the hope that 'my daughter can recover / what is lost in translation' (2006: 33), of names, pasts and the memories that make vital links of them. Meanwhile, the idea of home has a chance, in Australia, to become 'a country intuited, landfall / not verified but a rumour / tilting the compass point / in the direction / beyond the map's reach' (2006: 59), and India is returned to in several poems, including his longest, 'Bodhgaya', as part of the business of renouncing 'our renunciations of the spirit trade' (a rare sign of wry humour in the poet). Boey remains consistent in his steadfast unwillingness to stop looking for something that he never quite seems to find, whose search keeps him always on the edge of an incipient finding that can be shared with his readers.

A generation of young Singaporean poets born in the late 1960s and 1970s have done much to liven up the local literary scene, chief among them Yong Shu Hoong, Alvin Pang, Felix Cheong, Aaron Lee, Alfian Sa'at, Cyril Wong, Ng Yi-Sheng and several others. Alvin Pang is the author of *Testing the Silence* (1997), and *City of Rain* (2003). He has also co-edited an anthology of urban poetry from Singapore, a collection of love poems from Singapore and the Philippines, and a collection of poems from Australia and Singapore: in other words, he is very active in the promotion of poetry, locally and internationally. His poems are characterized by care with diction and phrasing: what is left out and left unsaid becomes as expressive as what is said. He is also able to encompass a wide range within the understated end of the tonal spectrum, from meditation to unsentimental love poems to writing that is satirical. Wry and shrewd, the poems promote intelligence and sensitivity even as they show what can be accomplished if pleasure in using language is balanced with a sharp eye for what can, and does not, please. Brief extracts from two of his more recent online poems (2007) show how these qualities work well together. Here is part of a dramatized conversation from 'why i write: albany remix':

> He tells you about his latest business venture, his MBA, his posting to Shanghai.
>
> You tell him you're a poet.
>
> The poor chap blinks. Maybe he hasn't heard you quite right. It does not compute.
>
> You look so normal.
>
> (Pang 2007: online)

And here is a contemporary take on Cavafy (and Coetzee), which finds the world today not really all that different in certain essential aspects from how they saw it in their time, the new flavour no less refreshing for being served from an old bottle in 'when the barbarians arrive':

> lay out the dead, but do not mourn them overmuch.
> a mild sentimentality is proper. nostalgia will be expected on demand.

cremate: conserve land, regret no secrets. prepare ashes for those with cameras.

hide your best furniture. tear down monuments. first to go are statues with arms outstretched in victory, and then anything with lions.

(Pang 2007: online)

Aaron Lee, who studied law, is the author of the quietly attractive *Visitation of Sunlight* (1997) and *Five Right Angles* (2007). He has also co-edited two anthologies with Alvin Pang. At his best, Lee can access a form of carefully qualified syntax applied to the ethics of motive and agency in interpersonal behaviour. Desire and regret, reproach and blame, guilt and guiltlessness are clarified in a style that has what Ezra Pound once asked of modern poetry, the virtues of good prose. In 'Pilate's Perspective', for example, a lawyer-like skill is applied (tongue-in-cheek) to a logic hovering somewhere between sober and sombre: 'Everyone / has free will afterall, / so don't go grabbing at straws.' '/(A man in your position / neither knows nor can tell / between hay and straw, though / there may be a future / for you in cultivation / someday)' (Lee 2007: 24). The ability to hold zany glimpses of humanity up to a light that is at once witty, sad and compassionate is neatly illustrated in 'The Life Of The Party Tells All': 'Afterwards / I kissed the head nurse and took out the trash, / along with all the shards of diminished hope / they had surrendered', and the poem ends with: 'I am the shape / of everything into which I have been poured. / The room behind me empties / and I am filled to the brim with, where I go' (2007: 35). One is left wondering how the life of the party might be distinguished from the biggest party-pooper ever.

Yong Shu Hoong published his first volume in the same year as Alvin Pang and Aaron Lee. He has worked at developing and managing websites, and is the author of *Isaac* (1997), *Isaac Revisited* (2001), *dowhile* (2002) and *Frottage* (2005). He writes in a relaxed style, adapting American influences more smoothly into his personal idiom than many of his contemporaries, assimilating his poetic style to the habits and energies of an everyday speech rhythm made alert by an understated precision of observation. Dry wit comes naturally: 'all I can remember of the army' includes 'the virgin kiss of a cigarette but / the beginning of beer's aftertaste' (1997: 40). The tension slackens a little in the intermediate volumes, but the Singapore Literature Prize-winning *Frottage* shows poems that combine the unexpected and the apt with ease, as in 'Seashell Flowers':

From their milky-white opacity
you'd think they're made of calcite
(or something else rigid) but
the waves unfurl upon the shore
like blossoms impatient for ruin.

(2005: 21)

Felix Cheong is the author of three books of poetry, *Temptation and Other Poems* (1998), *Watch the Stars Go Out* (1999) and *Broken by the Rain* (2003), along with an edited book of interviews and a book of children's fiction. The most recent poems are interesting in how they adopt a formula recommended in *The Complete Book of Puppetry*: observation, imitation, identification, selection and invention. The result is a series of dramatic monologues in several of which the identity of the dramatized voice is signalled by the title: suicide, detective, serial killer, wife-beater, prostitute and stripper. In other poems, the speaking voice works its way through sharp insights into personal preoccupations towards a suggestive evocation of sharply individualized sensibilities. Both kinds of poem reveal a broad empathy for the differences and diversity that constitute society, displacing the solipsism inherent to lyric poetry with an imaginative identification with other selves that makes for a salutary reading experience. Cheong's volume could be said to illustrate the more extreme end of a spectrum rich in human diversity and complexity, of which a more specifically Singaporean version is given voice with skill and dramatic flair in Roger Vaughan Jenkins's *From the Belly of the Carp* (1995).

Alfian Sa'at illustrates the role of poet as rebel in safe and over-protected Singapore. Of mixed Indonesian and Hakka descent, he writes bilingually in English and Malay (one of the very few writers in Singapore, along with the poet-dramatist Elangovan, to be creatively multilingual). He gave up his studies in medicine to write full-time, in several genres including theatre, and has published two volumes of poetry in English, *One Fierce Hour* (1998) and *A History of Amnesia* (2001). In Chinese-dominated Singapore, Alfian has had to face the danger of being typecast as a Malay Muslim, a corner he first painted himself into then tried to move out of, with only partial success in his second volume. His career illustrates the limited scope for, and the cost of, being provocative about what he describes in an interview as 'a lot of top imposed stories, policies and even propaganda', in a largely complacent, repressed society, where writers and readers alike are prone to a type of conformity described by fellow-poet Yong Shu Hoong, in an interview, as 'a mix of paranoia, contentment and cautious hope' (Tay 2002: online). Alfian's poems, as distinguished from the attention he gets in the press (generally for the wrong reasons), are fairly direct in the attitudes they take and the feelings with which they take them. His most well-known poem, 'Singapore You Are Not My Country' (1998), exemplifies an energetic attempt to assert a notion of nation that bypasses and challenges, because it is thwarted by, the idea of nation disseminated by the state:

Singapore I am on trial.
These are the whites of my eyes and the reds of my wrists.
These are the deranged stars of my schizophrenia.
This is the milk latex gummy moon of my sedated smile.

> I have lost a country to images, it is as simple as that.
> Singapore you have a name on a map but no maps to your name.
> (1998: 41)

The rhetoric is pungent even when exaggerated; the self-dramatization effective in polarizing resistance to what most Singaporeans are likely to take far more mildly as the price paid in terms of constraints and conditioning for the security and efficiency of the life granted them by the Leviathan of the state. Alfian could be said to inhabit the position, or struggling to free himself from the fate, of the rebel in a civil society based on rational Enlightenment principles that equate progress with a balance between security and prosperity. This fate heads inexorably towards romantic nostalgia and a bitterness that is repelled by what it does not like, but the interesting challenge and opportunity before Alfian is in how his future work will come up with viable alternatives that can strengthen his evident gift for words against the solicitations of mere anger and bitterness.

Cyril Wong is the most prolific of contemporary poets in Singapore, with at least seven volumes of poetry in as many years:from *squatting quietly* (2000) to *tilting our plates to catch the light* (2007). Wong has many styles, all of them limber, which combine the anecdotal and the confessional with the intuitive and the empathetic. Like several of his contemporaries, he suffers from over-exposure within a small society fairly repressive about its gay minority, and the tendency to repetitive glibness which sits cheek by jowl with a desire to share more of his personal life with readers than the latter might want or stand to profit from. But the good poems show what several contemporaries can boast: a gift for metaphor and a fluency in the use of English, a Singaporean idiom merging seamlessly with the global contemporary. At his best, he can be memorable, as in the beginning of 'seventh month':

> August: time of death, a path opens
> to the past like a wind through grass,
> the way lit by sparks, flaming paper.
> (2006: 20)

All the contemporary poets mentioned so far, like many others that could be cited if there were more space (for example, Heng Siok Tian, Paul Tan, Eddie Tay, Aaron Maniam, and the photo-poem collection *light is like water* (2007) by Jennifer Koh, amateur photographer, and Jasmine Cheah, inventive poet), write in styles that can be termed casual-colloquial. But several other young poets take further steps to arrive at various kinds of cool-quirky, while also revisiting the familiar modernist motif of 'épater les bourgeois', *ad hoc* and sometimes *ad nauseum*. This mode is illustrated by Yeow Kai Chai's *Secret Mantra* (2001) and the densely knowing *pretend*

I'm not here (2006); another, more accessible instance is provided by Ng Yi-Sheng, the author of *last boy* (2006) which won the Singapore Literature Prize in 2008. Ng maintains a lively blog site and an active profile in performance poetry as well as gay writing. His poems are, for the most part, fantastical, witty, disconcerting and delightful. 'Leda Revisited', for instance, might have startled Yeats with its description of Zeus trying 'to steal / a truant kiss with a bony beak', while Leda remarks of the rape, drily:

> Once I plucked a skin like that,
> seated in the kitchen, before the feast.
> I have cracked this gooselike neck before
> and heard no songs.
> I could fill this god with breadcrumbs.
> Yet I stand here, open as a cage,
> he, too, is searching for a god inside me.
>
> (2006: 19)

Perhaps, in such writing, the desire to startle and amuse produces a surplus that entertains more than it enlightens or enriches. Roy Campbell, a South African poet, once protested that he knew too many writers who used the snaffle and curb well but lacked a horse. In neat and clean Singapore, the younger poets continue to show signs of a dishevelled energy that seems to thrive in inverse portion to how much their society is sanitized by a paternal nation-state.

Hong Kong

Until 1997, the use of English for creative purposes in Hong Kong remained largely an expatriate activity in what Ackbar Abbas noted has always been 'a city of transients ... not so much a place as a space of transit' (1992: 4). After the Edmund Blunden years, there were a succession of writers from overseas living in Hong Kong for varying lengths of time, who published poems that remain marginal to the life of Hong Kong but distinctive for the interactions they represent between individual sensibilities and the unique living spaces of Hong Kong.

Representative volumes of poetry by expatriates resident in Hong Kong:
Martin Booth, *Paper Pennies* (1967), *Teller* (1973);
Clive Simpson, *Sirens* (1974);
Andrew Parkin (ed.) *Tolo Lights: A Collection of Chinese and English Poems* (1995), *From the Bluest Part of the Harbour: Poems from*

Hong Kong (1995), *Hong Kong Poems* with Lawrence Wong Kwok-pun (1997);
Alan Jefferies, *Blood Angels: Poems 1976–1997* (1998),
Timothy Kaiser, *Food Court* (2003);
Gillian Bickley, *Moving House and Other Poems* (2006), *Sightings* (2007).

Timothy Kaiser, for example, is able to capture the flavour of local speech habits neatly in a ventriloquist poem like 'Lunch Hour Detention with Little Ming': 'Again I go to China, Ming. business. / you go to school. / lots of food in freezer' (2003: 43).

The early part of the largely expatriate legacy can be sampled in an anthology such as Joyce Hsia and T. C. Lai's *Hong Kong: Images on Shifting Waters* (1977), and more recent developments are represented in Florence Lam's *First Hong Kong Poetry Festival A Collection of Poems* (1998) and Xu Xi and Mike Ingham's *City Voices: Hong Kong Writing in English, 1945 to the Present* (2003). Although Hong Kong locals such as Joyce Hsia, Ho Hon Leung, Jim Wong-Chu and a few others had published poems in the period from the 1970s to the 1990s, poetry in English had to wait until Louise Ho's *Local Habitation* (1994) before it had achieved memorable substance. Since then, Ho has published *New Ends, Old Beginnings* (1997), and younger poets to join the ranks include Agnes Lam, author of *Woman to Woman* (1997) and *Water Wood Pure Splendour* (2001), the Indian-born Hong Kong-settled Mani Rao, who has authored several volumes of poetry, from *Wingspan* (1987) to *100 Poems 1985–2005* (2006), and Jennifer Wong, the author of *Summer Cicadas* (2006). Special mention must be made of the enduring achievement of Leung Ping-Kwan, who writes in Chinese and helps in the translation of his own poems, which have the best claim of being representative of Hong Kong as a city, culture and society: *City at the End of Time* (1992) and *Travelling with a Bitter Melon: Selected Poems, 1973–1998* (2002).

Among poets writing in English, Louise Ho writes the most spare and sprightly lines, which can take on big subjects and their attendant complexities with relative ease. Her second volume shows a marked improvement over her earlier work. The uniqueness of post-1997 Hong Kong is anticipated neatly in 'Island': 'We shall be / A city with a country / An international city becoming national' (Ho 1997: 60). Similar observations had been made in 1992 by Ackbar Abbas when he had remarked of what the post-1997 period might represent for Hong Kong as a unique form of postcoloniality, because it would be the only one where the postcolonial condition would have preceded decolonization (1992: 6). Ho represents a similar view of Hong Kong's relation to mainland China in a neat encapsulation at the end of 'Living on the edge of Mai Po Nature Reserve':

> The horizon closes in like two long arms.
> We are surrounded,
> China holds us in an immense embrace.
> Merely the lie of the land.
>
> (1997: 18)

The 1989 suppression of the democracy movement in Hong Kong evinces a sober recognition in 'Remembering 4th June, 1989': 'But think, my friend, think: China never / Promised a tea party, or cakes / For the Masses' (Ho 1997: 23). That is why an old beginning becomes a new ending for Hong Kong, and 'As we near the end of an era / We have at last / Become ourselves' (1997: 24), which happens 'By understanding // Each in his own way / The tautness of the rope / Underfoot' (1997: 25). When the Hong Kong born poet tries out Australia as an alternative home, the reaction, in 'Migratory', is direct and unsparing: 'Tender is the meat, tasty is the fruit / It is the loss, the loss / That grips like a vice' (1997: 32), and what she means by the notion of loss is her own incapacity to live for long in 'The shock of the void' (1997: 32).

Agnes Lam practises a form of quiet minimalism in which description combines with feelings suggested and evoked with restraint. Mani Rao, too, writes in a conversational-contemporary idiom. She has the ability to bring the movement of her poems to sudden sharp moments of surreal concentration, as in 'Don't / the stars want to hug? // Language can at best mortify thought' (2006: 98). But her poems do not often cohere as wholes, remaining less than the sum of their parts because individual perceptions and images jostle or follow one another without becoming integrated into an experience that the reader might regard as unified.

Shirley Lim, while Professor at the University of Hong Kong in the late 1990s, helped foster a renewed interest in writing from school-children and college students. Some of the results that ensued from her initiative include the setting up of the ongoing journal *Yuan Yang: A Journal of Hong Kong and International Writing* (1999), and several anthologies, such as Shirley Lim and Page Richards's *Moving Poetry: Hong Kong Children's Poems* (2001), the collectively edited *Outloud: an anthology of the Outloud Readings Hong Kong* (2002) and *Poetry Live! An anthology of Hong Kong poetry, specially selected for use in schools* (2005), Tammy Ho's *Hong Kong U Writing: An Anthology* (2006) and the Hong Kong Writers' Circle's *Sweat & the City: stories and poems from the Hong Kong Workplace* (2006). Other compilations such as *Turning Pages* (2008) confirm the interest in writing in English as a trend that promises to last in an ever-changing Hong Kong.

Macao, adjacent to Hong Kong, has also had a recent burgeoning of interest in poetry, both from expatriates and locals. Apart from a series of parallel-text translations under the series editorship of the Macao-resident Australian poet Christopher (Kit) Kelen, published by the Association of Stories in Macao (ASM), there is evidence of new work in *Souvenir of an Australian-Macao Poetry Evening* (2007), which features the local poet-translators Hilda Tam, Yao Feng, Amy Wong Kuok, Elisa Lai Kin Teng and Agnes Vong Lai Leng. Kelen is also the author of *New Territories* (2003), which features poems juxtaposed against digital images processed by him and Carol Archer.

A good deal of what is published in the anthologies and collections from Macao and Hong Kong might not have the relative weight and authority that poets now writing in English can draw upon in the Philippines, Singapore, or even Malaysia, where local traditions have grown over several generations. However, poets from Hong Kong and Macao draw nourishment from the bilingualism activated through translation that poets in Singapore have largely given up on, which poets in Malaysia and the Philippines continue to draw upon, even if marginally. In that sense, Hong Kong and Macao contribute their own unique quality to the distinctive mix that is poetry in English from Southeast Asia.

Conclusion

- The genre of poetry has flourished in all parts of English-speaking Southeast Asia, producing work of great variety and range which uses English comfortably, with few of the tensions that marked the work of earlier poets mindful of writing in English from recently decolonized societies.
- Philippine poetry in English continues to develop in ways that grow out of its tutelage under American influences, supplemented by a culture of poetic workshops and mentorship, and characterized by preoccupations that are urban, regional or diasporic.
- Malaysian poetry in English has languished from the consequences of state policies, and most of the poets born in the country who professed a sense of vocation tied to English found themselves preferring migration.
- Singaporean poetry in English remains the dominant literary genre among younger writers, who are increasingly open to modes and styles very different from those of their predecessors.
- Hong Kong and Macao have shown a new interest in using English, both in terms of local talent and the contribution of expatriate writers.

12 Contemporary drama 1990–2008

Overview

A survey of English-language drama in Southeast Asia from 1990 raises a number of methodological questions. As with earlier drama, only a small proportion of performances result in published texts, and a focus on such texts is likely both to privilege drama with identifiable authors above devised performances, and to focus on more conventional plays over more experimental works that mix media, such as performance art, and which are often documented using video technology rather than through scripts. Interlinguistic and intercultural performances have problematized the notions of English language and Southeast Asian drama, while the availability of new electronic media and distribution systems have meant that the function of published play scripts has been transformed. This chapter again makes a strategic choice to focus on dramatic texts that are available in print form, despite the limitations such a perspective imposes: to counter such limitations, it does contain suggestions regarding where one might look for more comprehensive performance histories of English-language theatre. In the four major sites of English language cultural production in Southeast Asia, indeed, differences in language and education policies, as well as the politics of writers' choices regarding language medium, have resulted in radically diverging experiences in the evolution of English-language drama.

The Philippines

From 1990 onwards, bilingualism among the middle classes has meant that theatre in English in the Philippines has remained marginal compared to poetry and prose. The major English-language theatre company, Repertory Philippines, has mostly focused on performing canonical British and American plays. The Carlos Palanca Awards continue to be given for English-language plays, but very few of the winners have been performed professionally, and indeed for several years in the 1990s and early 2000s no plays were deemed worthy of the top category of award. When classics of

Philippine English-language literature such as F. Sionil Jose's novels have been adapted for performance, they have been translated into Filipino. A production of Jose's *The Pretenders* in 2007 outdid its original in verisimilitude: its characters spoke English, Tagalog or Ilokano according to the social context of their conversations, while taking into account the fact that Ilokano would be incomprehensible to many members of the audience. The result was, inevitably, a production largely in Filipino/Tagalog.

The Carlos Palanca Memorial Awards for Literature were established in 1950, and have become the most prestigious literary awards in the Philippines. The prizes are awarded annually to specific literary works in a number of different genres and in three linguistic categories: Filipino, English and Regional Languages.

An example of the continued possibilities of drama in English is Chris Millado's *scenes from an unfinished country* (1995), emerging from the playwright's collaborative work with Pintig, a Filipino-American theatre company. The play has a complex structure that meditates on an identity forged in resistance. In its framing narrative, members of a contemporary Filipino-American theatre company rehearse a modern revival of one of the anti-colonial 'seditious' plays performed in the early years of American colonization. Such scenes are intercut with a second narrative, in which a group of Filipinos in 1905 rehearse and perform the same play, and are later hunted down and tortured by the colonial authorities. On one level, the play is about the struggle to claim a Filipino-American identity based on a recognition of difference, of 'liberty and justice for all' (2000: 240): such praxis is paralleled to both ongoing resistance to American intervention in Central America, and continuing civil rights struggles focused on race and sexuality in the United States. Through the 1905 narrative, the play shatters myths of benevolent colonialism by revealing the devastation caused by American military intervention. Yet it also explores the problematics of heroic national narratives of resistance that refuse to acknowledge different levels of individual and collective complicity. If the characters of the 1905 narrative can be easily mapped onto the stereotypical characters of the seditious play as traitors, heroes and enemies, the characters in the 1995 narrative all embody a complex series of affiliations to both the United States and the Philippines. In the present, the play suggests, agency and the possibilities of resistance are less simple, yet they are still necessary. Both the Philippines and the United States, Millado suggests, are unfinished countries, with neither nation yet embodying the hopes for social equality on which it was founded.

Malaysia

English-language theatre in Malaysia from 1990 has evolved in a manner almost directly opposite to that of the Philippines. Despite educational policies that until recently stressed BM (Bahasa Malaysia), and indeed under current revisions still only envision English as a language of trade, science and technology, English-medium theatre has come to occupy an important space of social critique, evading the burden of embodying a national culture placed on Malay-language productions, particularly those through the *Istana Budaya* (Cultural Palace). In the 1980s, as we have seen, groups such as the multicultural Five Arts Theatre Company, through the influence of Krishen Jit, pioneered a politically engaged and reflective theatre. Five Arts continued to work with members of an older generation, staging K. S. Maniam's *The Sandpit* in 1991 and a Maniam retrospective season in 1994. An adaptation of Lloyd Fernando's *Scorpion Orchid* was performed in Singapore and Malaysia in 1994 and 1995, and a new play by Kee Thuan Chye in 1994. The company also began working with new generations of playwrights, and the Kuala Lumpur theatre scene expanded in response to new audiences resulting from Malaysia's economic boom. Instant Café Theatre, founded in 1989, produced two important new playwrights, Huzir Sulaiman and Jit Murad, both members of the elite, whose own multiracial backgrounds and education abroad had given them critical distance from nationalist cultural discourses. The same year saw the formation of The Actors Studio Theatre by Joe Hasham and Faridah Merican, providing an important venue in central Kuala Lumpur, and in the 1990s additional companies such as DramaLab and Kuali Works were established. Kuali Works was Malaysia's first all-female arts company, and in 1998 it staged Shahimah Idris's *From Table Mountain to Teluk Intan,* a monodrama that recounted a woman's migration from Cape Town to Australia then to Malaysia (Lo 2004: 169). Political theatre gained a new urgency in the turbulence of the *reformasi* (political reform) movement that followed the sacking by Mahathir bin Mohamad of his deputy Anwar Ibrahim in 1998; while political engagement faded away in the early years of the new millennium, a new generation of writers and performers drawn into theatre began producing new work. It is too early to know how renewed political engagement in the wake of strong opposition gains in the 2008 general election will influence theatrical practice.

The vibrancy of Malaysian theatre in English after 1990 can be represented by three published plays. Kee Thuan Chye's *We Could **** You Mr Birch* (published 1995) is a continuation of work by a generation of playwrights active in the 1980s. Like Kee's earlier *The Big Purge* (1988), the play uses metatheatrical techniques to question received histories. The story the play deals with is well known to Malaysians: the killing of the British Resident of Perak, James Birch, in 1875 by a local Malay ruler, Maharaja Lela. This incident led to British intervention in the Malay States and eventually to British rule throughout the Malayan peninsula through the 'forward movement' of the late nineteenth century. Maharaja Lela's defiance is now seen in nationalist historiography as the heroic anticolonial resistance of a patriot almost a century before the nation was founded. Kee maintains a postcolonial critique of British imperialism in the play, Birch's hypocrisy shown by the fact that he outlaws slavery, but keeps women slaves as concubines. Yet the Malay rulers and Chinese capitalists with whom the British resident comes into contact are not presented heroically – they also jostle for position, personal wealth and the patronage of the colonizer.

Throughout Kee's play, actors taking the parts of Birch, Maharaja Lela and others emerge from character and question the manner in which the story is told, drawing parallels with the politics of patronage and rent-seeking by elites in contemporary Malaysia. The play integrates these two convergent narratives much more successfully than Kee's early *1984 Here and Now*, since there is none of the metaphorical strain that marks the earlier drama's efforts to bring its two chronotopes together. The play concludes with Maharaja Lela being tried by the British, now deserted by his erstwhile allies. As one actor reads out an excerpt from authorized history, in which the British, after Birch's death, finally abolish slavery, he is interrupted by modern Malaysians talking intently to their stockbrokers on mobile phones, their chorus of 'Buy! Buy!' 'Sell! Sell!' drowning out the climax of a historical narrative. Kee has remained active in the arts scene in Malaysia, and a new play, *The Swordfish, then the Concubine*, was staged in Singapore in 2008.

One of the most important plays by a newly emergent generation of playwrights was Leow Puay Tin's *Family*. Like many practitioners involved in the Kuala Lumpur theatre scene, Leow has maintained close connections with Singapore, and *Family* emerged from the TheatreWorks Writers' Laboratory in the city-state. The play was first staged as *The Yang Family* in a site-specific performance in a shop house in Amoy Street, Singapore, in 1996, and later staged in Kuala Lumpur in 1998, with revisions that made it less Chinese and more focused on the intercommunal politics of multiculturalism. In the published version, however, the play narrates the story of a century of history of a Chinese-Singaporean family. Like *Emily of Emerald Hill*, in which Leow had previously acted the title role, *Family* focuses on the figure of an ethnic Chinese matriarch, Mrs Yang, who holds the family together after the death of her husband and then of her sons. Yet Leow's text is in many ways more ambitious than *Emily*. In contrast to Kon's smooth control of flashbacks through the manipulation of one voice, *Family* consists of a series of fragments taken from different periods of Mrs Yang's life, presented as monologues, dialogues, chants and choruses. Leow herself commented that the play script might be performed in many ways, serving as a series of 'building blocks or modules' (1996: 162) for a director and cast. In a further contrast to *Emily*, *Family* focuses on immigrant southern

Chinese culture rather than the Straits Chinese elite; while *Emily* explores the struggles of one woman for agency, *Family* shows how different generations of women used different tactics in similar struggles.

The episodic and fragmentary nature of Leow's drama also enables her to move outside the chronotope of developmental national narratives in both Singapore and Malaysia, narratives which at one level the growing economic prosperity of the Yang family seems to reflect. The last four scenes of the play thus occur after the death of Mrs Yang, and draw on syncretic Chinese beliefs and ritual practices concerning the afterlife. In one of these scenes, Mrs Yang urges her sons out to battle in a reprise of the heroic sacrifice for one's country that is a staple of traditional Chinese legends such as that of the Southern Song dynasty general Yue Fei. As they depart she slips from public observance of convention to a private emotional resistance: despite realizing they can no longer hear or see her, she now begs them not to leave her. In a concluding scene, Mrs Yang is exposed to a vision of hell, and can finally express the suffering that she has had to endure in her life as a woman forced to perform a series of social roles. Yet despite this suffering, she cannot escape desire for life and thus gain release from the cycle of birth and death: she chooses to be reborn. Women's struggles with and attempts to find empowerment through social scripts not of their own devising have been central elements in Leow's other plays, notably in her monodrama *Ang Tau Mui*, in which a cleaner negotiates her identity as a 'modern woman' through the consumption of goods and of images such as those of the Hong Kong movie star Ling Dai.

Huzir Sulaiman's play *Atomic Jaya*, which premiered in 1998 and was published in the 2002 collection *Eight Plays*, is similar to Leow's in that it also has a female protagonist, but it is radically different in tone and content. The action centres on Mary Yuen, a scientist who has returned from a doctorate in the United States to a mundane job researching the effect of radiation on food at a government institute in Malaysia. Mary is approached by an official from the Malaysian ministry of defence and invited to participate in a project to produce the nation's first atomic bomb. Having accepted, she is placed in charge of a racially representative but technologically incompetent team of scientists. The play develops into a hilarious and withering satire of the Malaysian developmental state; its title, indeed, recalls the grandiose projects commenced in the 1990s under the leadership of Prime Minister Mahathir, including the creation of a new administrative centre at Putrajaya and the development of the 'intelligent city' of Cyberjaya as part of the projected Multimedia Super corridor, designed to propel Malaysia into the digital age. Ministerial announcements denying the secret programme show linguistic incompetence and political scapegoating that are exaggerated but only too recognizable, a government spokesperson confusing 'uranium' with 'Iranian' while launching diversionary attacks on a 'Western Financial Jewish Conspiracy' threatening the country (2002: 19). Very few sacred cows are left unslaughtered. The play foregrounds racial stereotypes that many Malaysians hold and express privately, but do not articulate in public discourse: the cricket-mad and loquacious Indian, the unscrupulous Chinese businessman, the incompetent Malay civil servant, or the oversexed and culturally inept foreigner – here represented by the eastern European uranium smuggler Otto. *Atomic Jaya* is tightly plotted, with satirical scenes involving interaction between characters interwoven with others in which Mary, in monologue, summarizes key narrative elements. Mary's own voice is central to the play's humour: she mediates between the domestic and the political, participating in complex family politics concerning the legacy of her dying grandmother, and worrying about being single at thirty-five, all the time expressing a naïve and yet ultimately idealistic detachment from the events of the plot.

Huzir's plays perhaps probe less deeply than Leow's, Kee's or indeed Maniam's. Yet the playwright's theatrical practice has not remained static, and indeed the distinction between the social engagement of Five Arts and the satire of Murad and Huzir has to an extent been eroded. As the website http://kakiseni.com bears witness, theatre in Kuala Lumpur has now become part of a larger discussion, largely English-medium, concerning the place of the arts in Malaysian society, attracting participation not only from theatre practitioners, but also those involved in fiction, essay writing, journalism and film. A further feature of the Kuala Lumpur theatre scene is its close connection with Singapore, with artists and productions moving back and forth: this contrasts with the growing separation between Malaysian and Singaporean fiction and poetry.

Singapore

As in Malaysia, but on a larger scale, English-language theatre in Singapore grew and diversified in the 1990s and the first decade of the new millennium. Expansion was the result of a number of factors: the growth of English as a lingua franca, increasing audiences through greater economic affluence, government policies stressing investment in creative industries, and a partial relaxation of overt censorship mechanisms. Each of these factors might inhibit as much as it enabled. Governmental approaches to the arts as an industry, for instance, privileged infrastructural projects and what Bertolt Brecht called 'culinary theatre', designed for apolitical entertainment and the display of cultural capital over the concerns of smaller, more socially engaged or avant-garde groups. While censorship regimes were loosened, it might be argued that the state has become more effective in encouraging self-censorship and self-regulation by artists. Yet collectively the changes provided a space of opportunity for writers and theatre practitioners.

Writing in 2004, Tan Chong Kee attempted to classify Singapore theatre, now predominately but not exclusively English-language, into three different categories. The first was an increasingly active 'socially engaged theatre', marked for Tan by companies such as the Theatre Practice, Necessary Stage, the Indian community-based Agni Kootthu, Toy Factory and the more recently formed Wild R!ce. A second group was more commercially orientated, aiming for 'profitable entertainment or prestigious spectacle' (2004: xi), and exemplified in the musicals or popular plays of Action Theatre and Singapore Repertory Theatre, as well as the more consciously high-cultural productions of Singapore's most internationally prominent theatre company, Ong Ken Seng's TheatreWorks. In a third, smaller category, Tan placed a number of organizations that he characterized as practising 'art for art's sake', notably Theatre Ox, and Spell#7. While one might quibble at the neatness of Tan's taxonomy – Wild R!ce have at times been unabashedly populist, while Spell#7's Paul Rae's *National Language Class* (2007, restaged 2008) was a profound, if indirect, exploration of the politics of language policy – the schema does give a sense of the complexity and variety of dramatic productions in Singapore since the 1990s, and indeed illustrates the difficulty of attempting a comprehensive account. As in the account of contemporary Malaysian drama above, the discussion here therefore eschews an overview by concentrating on a small number of important dramatists whose work has been influential in Singapore in the last two decades, narrowing in each case further to a single specific text, and attempting to use these works as prisms through which to view larger developments. Significant playwrights excluded from discussion thus include Alfian Sa'at, Jeff Chen, Michael Chiang, Chong Tze Chien, Elangovan, Goh Boon Teck, Russell Heng, Desmond Sim, Tan Tarn How and Ovidia Yu. The fact that much contemporary theatre in Singapore is collaboratively devised also means that the ensuing discussion, while giving an important overview, is perhaps not entirely reflective of current trends.

The first and most influential of the figures under consideration is Kuo Pao Kun. Until his untimely death in 2002, Kuo was perhaps the most important artistic figure in Singapore, founding the Substation in Armenian Street in 1990 as an alternative home for the arts, and working, through the Practice Theatre Ensemble, to devise a theatre training programme that might draw young practitioners from the region. At the time of writing, several of Kuo's plays from the 1990s have not yet been published in English: the multilingual *Sunset Rise* (performed 1999), for instance, or his last work, the collaboratively written *One Hundred Years in Waiting* (performed 2001) which, through its use of the persona of Chen Cui Fen, Chinese revolutionary Sun Yatsen's lover and comrade-in-arms, questioned the memorialization and remembrance of national heroes. His most significant work from the period is *Descendants of the Eunuch Admiral*, first performed in both English and Mandarin versions in 1995, and published in 2003.

Kuo's play features the figure of Zheng He, the admiral sent by the Chinese Ming Dynasty on expeditions to Southeast Asia and beyond, to whom temples still exist in the region today. Like Kee's *Birch*, the play draws a parallel between a historical figure and contemporary society, yet the text is more open than Kee's. The play's diffuse but suggestive allegorizing of

Zheng He's experiences makes audiences seek for correspondence between the life of the admiral and their own lives: Singaporeans are, impossibly, all descendants of the eunuch admiral. On occasion, Kuo's allegory has a very direct target: in a passage late in the play, he refers to an enlightened ruler who 'voluntarily stepped down and forbade his children and relatives from succeeding him', a transparent rebuke to Lee Kwan Yew, whose son Lee Hsien Loong was at that time deputy prime minister (2003: 62). Yet for the most part it causes the audience to look inwards and reflect on the manner in which Zheng He's own experience, caught on an early wave of globalization at the beginning of Southeast Asian modernity, mirrors their own conditions of existence in a Singapore now caught in late modern flows of people and capital.

In many ways, the parallels between Zheng He's experience and those of the modern Singaporean subject are disturbing. Zheng He submits to the Emperor's wishes, agreeing to forgo an autonomous life. The play focuses repeatedly on techniques of castration that evolve gradually from the violent and painful to the pleasurable: the last technique described involves massage, so that 'nothing is cut off, all the parts are preserved' and the experience of castration 'is received by the subject as comforting, enjoyable and even desirable' (2003: 65). Such a description resonates with Kuo's own remarks on the emptiness and loss of vital life-forces in Singaporean modernity, an absence achieved as much by persuasion and the pleasures of consumption as by overt repression.

Yet *Descendants* is more than simply a critique of the People's Action Party's vision and realization of developmental modernity in Singapore as inauthentic or ersatz. The play also explores other concerns of Kuo's – the position, for instance, of Singaporeans as 'cultural orphans', dispossessed by migration and the cultural dislocations of colonialism. Zheng He and the modern Singaporeans who dream of him exist in a liminal space in terms of home, gender, culture and history that may be disconcerting, but also offers the possibilities for new affiliations and growth. In a final scene, Kuo's admiral continues searching, noting that '[e]very land and sky and water is home' (2003: 60): embracing identities based on movement, flux and change. A scene towards the end of the play paints a picture of a precolonial marketplace of cultural plenitude and interaction in an atmosphere of equality, and the play concludes with the words 'the Market is calling me' (2003: 67). Singapore's position as a marketplace, Kuo suggests, is its condition of possibility. The market may be made use of by both colonial plural society and the post-independence developmental state to produce docile subjects, but it also contains the possibility of other futures, of the development of the culture of 'play' that Kuo felt was lacking in Singapore (2000: 215).

Kuo's politics, expressed through allegory, find a parallel in the very different theatrical practice of The Necessary Stage. Artistic director Alvin Tan has stressed a model of community theatre as social interaction that moves beyond a simple pedagogy. Drama practitioners, Tan stresses, 'need to learn or be exposed to the community. We need them as much as they need us', and indeed various communities and practitioners are never easily separated – art is not a 'one-way "gift"' (1997: 256). Like Kuo, the company's resident playwright, Haresh Sharma, has made extensive use of an open approach in which director and playwright perform research, and the playwright then writes a draft, which is then discussed with the cast and director and rewritten substantially, then fine-tuned in rehearsal (1997: 260).

While Sharma is best known in Singapore for the play *Off Centre*, which dramatizes conflicts and the joys of friendship in the lives of two characters struggling with mental illness, his work may be best represented by the monodrama *Rosnah*, which follows the experiences of a young Malay woman studying in the United Kingdom. The play, as with most of Sharmas's work, evolved from a process of collaboration, in this case with Alvin Tan and Malay actor Alin Mosbit. *Rosnah* was performed in different productions for different audiences, first in the Housing Development Board 'heartland' setting of Tampines Regional Library, then at the alternative arts venue of the Substation, and was later produced in Melbourne in 1997, becoming more fragmented and self-referential as it was rewritten. The published script in the collection *This Chord and Others* is from the Melbourne performance, and depicts Rosnah caught 'in transit' between cultural contexts and lives. She struggles to negotiate her own identity in a relationship with a liberal English boyfriend who speaks of the fascination of exotic 'intercultural relationships' (1999: 183), yet she cannot see him fitting into her world in Singapore, nor can she define her own sense of self with reference to the various communities she is part of. Sharma's script is highly intertextual, making references to popular culture, the Malay myth of the woman warrior Siti Zubaidah and the feminist writer Virginia Woolf. The play is also self-referential, with the actor who plays Siti moving in and out of character, and interacting with the audience. As with much contemporary Singapore theatre, it also expresses confidence in representing a linguistic continuum that reflects the everyday use of language in Singapore: Rosnah code-switches from formal Singapore English, to Singlish, and in and out of Malay.

The commitment of The Necessary Stage to work with communities at times involved pushing against political boundaries. *Off Centre*, for instance, had its funding withdrawn by the Ministry of Health because of alleged misrepresentation of the mentally ill. In 1993, the company staged two examples of forum theatre – *MCP* and *Mixed Blessings*, dealing with spouse abuse and an interracial love affair respectively – which were explicitly designed to demand audience intervention. Each play was performed once, and then, after a discussion, performed again, with any member of the audience able to intervene. Thus the spectators became the 'spect-actor[s]' (Krishnan 1997: 201) and took on roles within the play, and in the process moved from 'passive consumers to active producers of meaning' (1997: 206).

Press coverage of the Marxist roots of such theatrical practice led to public criticism of Tan and Sharma, and to a withdrawal of National Arts Council funding for such productions. In recent years, The Necessary Stage has continued its social engagement, with productions such as *Mardi Gras* aimed at the gay community; Sharma remains resident playwright, but has been joined by a younger generation of writers. While the unpolished nature of productions has sometimes been criticized, the company has also been defended as producing works with a necessary 'element of rawness, of being works-in-progress' (Wong Wai Yen 1997: 199).

The controversy over Forum Theatre is symptomatic of an ongoing negotiation between the state and theatre practitioners regarding the politics of drama in Singapore. After the end of the Cold War, Marxism has receded as a concern for the state, but it has been replaced by other sites of political contestation. A performance by Shannon Tham and Josef Ng in late 1993 that involved the cutting of pubic hair was sensationalized by the media and then condemned by the National Arts Council as 'acts vulgar and distasteful' deserving 'public condemnation' (Devan 1997: 241): what was forgotten in subsequent discussion was the performance's significance as a protest against the entrapment of gay men by the police. The state's desire to control and curtail discussion and criticism of religious practices resulted in perhaps the most famous case of censorship, concerning *Talaq*, a play produced in 1999 by the Indian-community based theatre company, Agni Kootthu, depicting marital rape and violence directed towards Indian Muslim women. While censorship regimes have relaxed, with a ratings system introduced in the 1990s, and the transfer of responsibility of issuing licences to perform from the police to the Film and Publications Unit of the Ministry of Information, Communications and the Arts in 2002, some commentators have noted that the system now encourages greater self-censorship, with a perceived liberalization masking more sophisticated forms of control (Chong 2004).

One area in which drama in Singapore has realized possibilities as a space of 'free and fair play' (Kuo 2000b: 215) and social exploration has been in its depiction of sexuality: from the 1990s onwards, Singapore theatre has been actively engaged with gay, lesbian, transgender and bisexual communities, even as section 377A of the city-state's criminal code continues to outlaw acts of 'gross indecency' between men. A consistent and evolving exploration of queer issues is found in the work of Eleanor Wong, and in particular the *Invitation to Treat* trilogy of plays written and performed between 1993 and 2003, which follow the life of lesbian lawyer Ellen Toh. In the first play, *Mergers and Accusations,* Ellen attempts to defy both the 'bloody macho posturing' (2005: 12) of the corporate world and heteronormative expectations of gender roles by entering an open marriage with her colleague, Jon Chin: she climbs the corporate ladder, while he stays at home to care for their child. The relationship collapses because of Jon's frustration at a stalled career, and Ellen's discovery of a life partner in the British lawyer

Lesley Ryan. *Wills and Successions* adds a further dimension regarding the manner in which queerness becomes socially embedded and contested in Singapore: family, here represented by Ellen's evangelical Christian sister, Grace. The play dramatizes Grace's struggle to accept Ellen's sexuality, and also Ellen's attempts to rediscover Singapore as home after years spent in London with Lesley. It is only after Lesley's death that Grace can publicly acknowledge her sister's companion as family, noting that Lesley has passed on, 'leaving behind her family. Her father and mother, her two brothers, her spouse Ellen and myself' (2005: 170). The third play in the trilogy, *Jointly and Severably,* is set later in Ellen's life when her daughter Samantha is now a young woman, and the conflicts regarding power and intergenerational love it dramatizes are marked by a much greater sense of queer community solidarity.

It would be wrong to see Wong as a dramatist solely concerned with queer issues, and indeed other plays, such as *The Campaign to Confer the Public Star on JBJ* (first performed in 2006), explore concerns to do with civil service bureaucracy and emergent civil society voices. The realist mode of her drama, indeed, contrasts with the more elaborately parodic and intertextual nature of recent queer theatre in Singapore, such as Alfian Sa'at's *Asian Boys* trilogy, the last play of which rewrites Singapore's first gay novel, Johan S. Lee's *Peculiar Chris*. As the diversity of Singapore theatre grows, indeed, it becomes more difficult to generalize about possible developments and futures. One central strand, however, given the nature of Singapore as a multicultural society and its strategic place in Asian and global markets, has been the question of intercultural theatre. Intercultural theatre has been most visible as a grand project expressed in such performances as TheatreWorks's *Lear* and *Desdemona* and later projects, bringing together and juxtaposing the work of performing artists from across Asia. Yet it has also, arguably, informed the movements across languages and the regional connections made by many Singaporean theatre practitioners. As a supplement to interculturalism, The Necessary Stage's Alvin Tan has explored the notion of intracultural performance that concentrates on process, not product, and refuses to reify cultural difference (1997: 270).

As with fiction and poetry, the boundaries of Singapore drama are becoming more porous. To writers such as Huzir Sulaiman, a Malaysian citizen now resident in Singapore, we might add the more complex case of Chay Yew. Yew left Singapore for the United States with his family in the 1970s, later completing an MFA at Boston University; his brief return to the city-state was marked with difficulties over the censorship of the performance of the play *As If He Hears* in 1988. Yew's initial success came with *Porcelain* (1992), a play first written in the United Sates but adapted to a London setting when the author was a resident playwright for the Mu-Lan Theatre Company. The play centres on a series of interviews that the English psychologist John Worthing conducts in prison with a young British-Asian man, John Lee, who has murdered his working-class lover.

John's recollections dramatize the racism and homophobia of the society in which he lives, and indeed of his interlocutor: caught in a series of mirrors of exoticizing representation, the young man finds no community that he can call home. Much of the drama of *Porcelain*, indeed, results from John's conscious manipulation of a series of intertexts (Puccini, Bizet, Wilde) and a storytelling technique that questions Worthing's desire for narrative closure. Yew next returned to the United States, producing plays that speak more affirmatively of the possibilities of intercultural relationships and alliances (*A Language of Their Own*) or range more widely historically (*Red*, set in China during the Cultural Revolution). Although Yew now works in the United States and identifies as Asian-American, his plays have continued to have an importance in Singapore's theatre history: *Red* had its Asian premiere at the 2001 Singapore Arts Festival, while *Porcelain* was performed by Toy Factory Theatre in 2005.

Hong Kong

In Hong Kong, English-language theatre in the 1990s moved decisively away from an expatriate ethos to engagement with the experience of all those who lived and worked in the territory. The number of bilingual and multilingual productions has increased, and Hong Kong's arts festivals have also resulted in English-language productions from other parts of Asia being staged in the city. Mike Ingham identifies the founding of the Fringe Club in Central in the early 1990s as a catalyst in the development of a cosmopolitan English-language or multilingual theatre in Hong Kong, and he also notes that dance and multimedia or performance art-based productions have enabled artists who exist in one linguistic world to cross to another. However, more detailed consideration of drama in Hong Kong is foreclosed by the lack of written texts, a fact that makes Ingham and Xu Xi's anthology *City Stage* (2005) even more significant.

The anthology does not attempt to give a chronological history of the development of English-language drama in Singapore, but is rather arranged thematically. Many of the plays collected in the volume attempt to excavate pasts now occluded in Hong Kong's present. Veronica Needa's 'Face' explores a Eurasian woman's negotiation with Chineseness in both Hong Kong and Britain, her own sense of self frequently contradicted by the way in which others categorize her. Mok Chiu-Yu and Evans Chan's 'The Life and Times of Ng Chung Yin' demonstrates the complex politics of location in contemporary theatrical texts. It addresses the possibilities of political activism in the present by recounting the life of a campaigner for human rights of a previous generation; in exploring Ng's life, however, it emphasizes both his location in Hong Kong and his frequent travels, his struggles against both British colonial power and Chinese political repression. The past revisited here is thus hybrid and cosmopolitan, and one that cannot be easily contained by a narrative that celebrates without question the retrocession of 1997. Given the status of English in Hong Kong it is unlikely that English-language drama will assume the prominence it has gained in Malaysia or Singapore; it represents, however, a marginal space that offers the possibility of defamiliarizing critique.

Conclusion

- Recent drama in English serves as a reminder that language policies and the way in which national, social and theatrical communities are imagined can produce very different outcomes.
- English-language drama in the Philippines has largely ceased to exist outside the university; Hong Kong English-language theatre occupies a cosmopolitan but marginal place.
- English-language drama in Malaysia has grown to become a counter-discursive, if elite, space.
- In Singapore, English has come to constitute the medium of the majority of theatrical productions: these range from commercially mainstream musicals to consciously political or avant-garde productions.
- In each area, drama practitioners, individually and collectively, have sought to respond to and creatively make use of the social and cultural space available to them.

13 From the contemporary to the future

Overview

A concluding chapter needs to look both backwards and forwards: to trace the route that a literary history has travelled, and also to look speculatively towards the future. In the course of our narrative, we have frequently encountered notions of technological modernization, social modernity, and modernist literary or artistic movements. Our literary history began with an account of how work in English by writers from Southeast Asia had its origin in British and American colonialism, which presented itself rhetorically as a modern form of government, bringing the fruits of the Enlightenment to subject peoples: those struggling against colonialism, in turn, did so by claiming modernity as their own. We conclude first with a retrospective account of the extent to which notions of the 'modern', in its many refractions (modernity, modernization, modernism, postmodernity and postmodernism) have a bearing on Anglophone literary developments in Southeast Asia, and especially to how those notions blend with, and at times challenge, contemporary ideas about cosmopolitanism and intercultural hybridity. We then move to an examination of how such concepts intermesh with changing technologies of reception and production, and how digital technologies in particular have challenged both linguistic boundaries and divisions between elite and mass culture.

From decolonization through modernity to cosmopolitanism

Given the complicated relation of the word 'modern' to its derivatives, it might be useful to recognize that neither modernity nor modernism are monolithic or homogeneous, and that the former, in all its diverse manifestations, can be said to refer to a societal project, whereas the latter can be treated as a hold-all term referring to a loose set of aesthetic ideas, practices and strategies that were at odds with, or ran against the grain of, the former. Some accounts treat both the societal project of modernity and the aesthetic tendencies and practices loosely grouped under the notion of modernism as having spread from Europe and the United States to their respective colonies in Southeast Asia (and elsewhere), in a slow and uneven process that followed belatedly and overlapped partially with the colonial and postcolonial experiences of subject cultures. Other accounts resist the idea that modernity and modernism diffused outwards as the social and cultural consequences of Empire, and argue that various forms of social and cultural self-modernization were already latent, incipient or under way even as colonialism gave them expression in English, at least as far as the verbal arts were concerned (as distinguished from the pictorial, plastic and performance arts).

While a large part of the impetus behind aesthetic or literary modernism could be regarded as part of a historical past, modernization (i.e. the post-industrial or technological transformation of societies under specific notions of progress) continues to affect Southeast Asia in the context of the politics of nationalism and the rapid technologization and urbanization of societies. Some commentators claim bluntly that the logic that drove societal modernity in the former colonies of Europe and the United States was, and remains, the problem of catching up.

> When the colonial system in its classical form, wealth-collecting metropoles carrying off products from wealth-yielding possessions, began to break down during and after the Second World War, the relation between countries in which industrialism, science, and the like had settled … and those in which they had not, had to be phrased in a more forward-looking way. And for that, the modernization idea seemed especially well made, convenient at once to ex-masters and ex-subjects anxious to restate their inequalities in a hopeful idiom. There were advanced (developed, dynamic, rich, innovative, dominant) societies that had been modernized, and there were backward (underdeveloped, static, poor, hidebound, dominated) ones that had not, or not yet, and the challenge … was seen as turning the second into the first. The whole pattern of global connections was reformulated in these terms – as an effort to 'close the gap', bring the world up to speed.
>
> Clifford Geertz (1995: 137)

According to such views, bringing the nation-states of Southeast Asia 'up to speed' remains a project indefinitely under way in the Philippines, Malaysia, Singapore and indeed all over Southeast Asia. The applicability of the notion also includes Hong Kong after 1997, since the complex renegotiation of its relation to mainland China entails a preview of China's own future in development along lines already well marked out in Hong Kong from its days as a commercially successful British colony. However, in sceptical or cautionary resistance to the drift of such arguments, others argue that these claims constitute a rhetoric of dependency that gives only part of a more complex picture, in which dependency and derivativeness are countered in the former European and American colonies by notions of seeking one's own modernity through a reworking of traditions: indigenous cultural tendencies actively and sometimes resistantly interactive with derivative tendencies.

Regardless of which interpretive narrative we find more persuasive, the processes of decolonization were associated with the project of nationalism in most parts of Southeast Asia (as with former colonies elsewhere), while Hong Kong remains an anomalous case to this day. As regimes of varying stamina, competence and commitment re-formalized the former European colonies of Southeast Asia into modern nation-states, literary cultures struggled to define and evolve an incipient sense of local traditions. This incipience remained uncertain about whether to be co-opted into the agenda of nation building or to resist it in the spirit of romantic alienation or modernist autonomy. Some commentators argue that ideas of the modern nation-state and ideas of aesthetic autonomy are both European in provenance. These ideas, they further argue, are either dissembled as – or mistaken for – universals of societal motivation. In this perspective, part of the problem for new nation-states has been the need to distinguish between ideas that are needed for their situation, regardless of provenance, and ideas that are likely to abet various forms of neocolonial dependency. The anxiety boils down to the question of how to undertake modernization while resisting the likelihood of cultural Westernization (and the neocolonial aspects of all the transformations that are sometimes referred to, rather euphemistically, as globalization).

Any attempt to think of Southeast Asia as emerging from decolonization into globalization through nationalism ends up having to recognize that cultural developments such as modernism and postmodernism affected artists and writers in the former colonies as part of two complexly interwoven processes: a tendency to look Westward for ideas about the aesthetic vanguard, which was partially counteracted and counterbalanced by intimations and intuitions of how artists and writers might draw sustenance from indigenous or non-European elements of societal and aesthetic modernity. Under these complex circumstances, literary modernism developed rather slowly and intermittently in the work of authors and artists whose commitment to nation did not preclude adaptability and combinative skill in reconciling the indigenous and the derivative elements of creative inspiration. Thus, Philippine writing continued to be shaped by American models long after the country was given its independence by the United States, and remains ambivalently attached to that connection to this day, although Philippine writers have also shown a remarkable capacity to adapt, modify and indigenize what they admire to suit the uniqueness of their specific cultural circumstances.

The earliest writer from Southeast Asia to manifest awareness of what was at stake in the break from tradition signalled by modernist thinking was Jose Garcia Villa (1908–97), whose creative years stretched from the late 1920s to the early 1950s. From his position in alienated space – neither based in the Philippines after his early years, nor quite part of the New York avant-garde that praised him in the 1940s – Villa's adoption and adaptation of modernist ideas was reflected in the acute self-reflexivity he brought to language, and the extreme compression, elision and eccentric pressure to which grammar, syntax and style were subjected in his poems. His determination to problematize the relation of writing to representation and self-expression constitute the most significant part of his contribution to the community of authors born in Southeast Asia. He assumed the right to make severe demands of his readers: hardly any other writer from the region dared go as far. Villa's version of modernism was based on the rejection of realist and bourgeois modes of representation in favour of an idea of the artistic vocation that adopted a posture of uncompromising aestheticism which was passionate, eclectically derivative and not without an element of affectation. While he had his imitators in the Philippines, his example provoked more than it guided, and his self-exile in New York ensured that the impact of his example on subsequent developments in Southeast Asia was indirect.

Of the small group of experimentally inclined writers from Malaysia-Singapore who refracted the influence of literary modernism, which included Wang Gungwu, Wong Phui Nam and Lee Kok Liang, the most sustained in his radicalism was from a poet and artist from a later generation, Arthur Yap (1943–2006). His work embodied forms of modernist and postmodernist awareness whose implications have yet to be followed up in subsequent writing from the region. In Yap, an acute form of self-reflexivity about the use of English in the context of Singaporean society and its mores controlled the tone and the syntax: irony became the principal cognitive instrument; satire and subversive humour the chief antidotes to every aspect of urban experience that was perceived as inert, passive, complacent or disingenuous. The compression or elimination of connectives, the telescoping of syntax and thought processes, an obsessive interest in jokes, mimicry, parody and subversion are some of the main elements of Yap's postmodernism of the 1960s, 70s and early 80s. Very little of the radical element in either Villa or Yap survived in subsequent writing from their respective societies until the generation of Alfred Yuson, Eric Gamalinda and Simeon Dumdum Jr. in the Philippines and Ng Yi-Sheng in Singapore. What then did modernism and postmodernism amount to for Southeast Asian writing in English? And what did societal modernity amount to for Southeast Asia? The two questions are inseparable. Consider first a contemporary view of how the idea of modernity got applied to a postcolonial nation. The Singaporean academic Wee Wan-Ling summarizes the history of state policy in Singapore after 1965 in terms of a three-part hypothesis: the postcolonial state fostered a notion of collective identity derived from Western models, which was used first to de-territorialize constituent communities from their ethnic roots, and then to re-territorialize them 'to create a society ready for the jump to export-oriented industrialization' (2008: 8). The drive to modernize was inseparable from the need to de-individuate civil society from old cultural loyalties at one level while also trying hard, at another level, to cultivate a sense of the local, the regional and the uniquely communal-national. In Southeast Asian contexts, modernity had a problematic application because it risked 'contaminating' alleged Asian values with the 'corruptibility' associated with Western culture, even while the model of development pursued by the state was derived from the West. Likewise – it could be said – modernism was difficult to cultivate or assimilate (except with moderate or limited success) in Southeast Asia because the struggle to become modern and the struggle to become modernist *at once* or concurrently threatened to split artistic commitment between an idealized nation and an idealized view of aesthetic autonomy. Villa's modernism represses the idea of a Philippine community or nation, subsuming it in a subjective sense of elective affinity to Art with a capital A; Yap's modernism struggles resistantly against the state-sponsored ethos of social modernity, lamenting from the margins of his island-nation that 'there is no future in nostalgia' (Yap 2000: 59), yet unable to hold back the enormous weight of nostalgia from his poems.

Later Philippine writers, such as Yuson, Gamalinda and Dumdum, adopted styles that are more aptly regarded under the constellation of an Asian version of postmodernism than of modernism, given the period in which they became active as writers, and the extremely ironic self-reflexivity of their work, which is analogous, in some ways, to the magical realisms of Márquez and Rushdie, in subjecting realist and naturalist modes of fictive and poetic narration and representation to the subversive pressures of parody and fantasy, while adopting surreal and Dadaist modes of resistance to bourgeois habits of literary practice and cultural conventionality.

In the meantime, a different strand of continuity can be discerned as having developed a capacity for sustainable growth in Southeast Asia over the last half-century. It could be described as a form of syncretism which goes under several related names, such as multiracial coexistence and cultural hybridity. A form of social and cultural cosmopolitanism has become a pervasive feature of contemporary cultures in Southeast Asia, regardless of the many differences between nation-states, and regardless of internal differences of the kind produced by class, ethnicity, gender, religion and politics. Other distinctions, such as rural and urban, apply in the case of Malaysia and the Philippines, while Singapore and Hong Kong remain urban spaces with tenuous or attenuated links to their geographical and cultural hinterlands. Ethnic affiliations are far more sensitive in Malaysia than in Hong Kong, and less so in Singapore; whereas issues of class make a greater difference in the Philippines. Regardless, in Malaysia as well as the Philippines, the power of metropolitan culture (from Kuala Lumpur and Metro Manila respectively) tends to marginalize cultural practices from the provinces in ways that are symptomatic of how the manifestations of late (and belated) capitalism in Southeast Asia present themselves as increasingly urban in orientation.

The Southeast Asian varieties of cosmopolitanism entail the coexistence in crowded spaces of multilingual and multi-ethnic communities whose internal differences have had to accommodate to a combination of state policies and the imperatives of belated modernization. In British Malaya, an intellectual such as Wang Gungwu tried to articulate a notion of cosmopolitanism as early as the 1950s, well before political independence had become a reality. The idea was then tied to a rather uncertain ideal of a Malayan consciousness which he (and others like him) hoped would evolve separately from the cultural roots of the various ethnic groups that contributed to that mix (Chinese, Indian and Malay). The hope was that this new literary culture would succeed in defining a local consciousness while adapting literary models assimilated through the British colonial educational system: 'This synthetic product would then be infused with the stuff of European poetry and bound firmly in the English language' (Wang 1958: 7). During the 1950s, the attempt to create a national consciousness through cosmopolitan literariness may have had no better outcome than the brief-lived amalgam called *Engmalchin*, but the logic of that attempt did transform the polity after independence.

In contemporary Southeast Asia, the rapid transformation of societies by technology and the digital media, and the massively increased permeability between cultural and social barriers that has been produced by globalized media, has seen to it that the centre of gravity has shifted, when it comes to cultural and literary matters, from productions based on the older technologies of paper and printed book towards the digital, and towards the performance arts.

Throughout Southeast Asia, several presentiments of the future are more evident in the performance arts than in literary writing. Increasingly, theatrical productions have moved away from the printed text towards various forms of hybrid performance. In the case of Singapore, this has happened most noticeably with the directors Kuo Pao Kun and Ong Keng Sen (the latter with reference to the Shakespeare productions he has directed: *Lear*, 1997, 1999; *Desdemona*, 2000; *Search: Hamlet*, 2002). The decentring of textuality in performance is an over-determined feature in most Southeast Asian societies. It gives freedom to improvise; in specific cases, it might help gain quicker approval by local censor boards; and it also helps to defuse part of the problem endemic to Southeast Asian speech-act situations, in which varieties of local English speech rhythms are not as suited to 'serious' plays as to comedy, satire and melodrama.

Whatever the reasons for the decentring of language in the arts, the multilingual and multicultural dimensions of Southeast Asian cultural systems combine in performance without necessarily being synthesized into anything that could be described as unified entities. Ong makes the point explicitly in the 1999 Programme Note for *Lear*: 'I wanted these cultures to exist together as one but not in an amalgam which would reduce their difference' (1999: 6). The case exemplifies a larger pattern of change, in which issues of identity, community and affiliation are delinked, in cultural practice, from narrowly exclusive notions of ethnicity, nation and notions of monolithic cultural systems.

The incomplete, the fragmentary, the partially verbalized, all become a more prominent component of what is purveyed as opportunity for aesthetic experience. James Clifford, for instance, notes that the term 'cosmopolitan', when it is 'separated from its (European) universalist moorings, quickly becomes a travelling signifier, a term always in danger of breaking up into partial equivalences: exile, immigration, migrancy, diaspora, border crossing, pilgrimage, tourism' (1998: 363). For better and worse, contemporary literary writing in Southeast Asia is increasingly obliged to accommodate itself to the intercultural dimension of a fluid identity politics.

Literary cultures in the era of digital technologies

Such recognition also returns us to a physical manifestation of the modern-izing process: the emergence of new technologies. In the last decade of the twentieth century, a series of technological and social changes in Southeast Asia have forced a revaluation of what we have called Southeast Asian writing in English in this volume. New forms of writing have emerged, many bridging the literary and the popular and finding new means of distribution through electronic and digital media; in some of these forms, the notion of writing itself is pushed to its limits. Many of these forms challenge the concept of an English-medium text: they may use heavily localized varieties of English or they may often – through, for example, the use of subtitles written in a number of languages in short film – mimetically represent a multilingual environment.

On one level, these changes have been enabled by technology. From the early 1990s the internet has opened up a variety of possibilities for writers. Email groups such as the arts community in Singapore have enabled new networks to come into existence, a function now supplemented through the use of website forums, collective blogs (weblogs), and more recently, social networking sites. Such connections have given writers unprecedented opportunities to make contact with other writers on a local, national, regional or international scale. The internet provides a means of distribution that has fewer barriers than print publication, and this has been exploited by writers working in traditional genres. Poetry websites, for instance, have proliferated in Singapore, Malaysia, Hong Kong and the Philippines, while government agencies, libraries and other groups have founded online repositories for significant writing that is now out of print or difficult to obtain.

Literary journals, whether academic or more popular in scope, have also found that the web offers the possibility of reaching larger audiences at substantially reduced costs, and several now exist solely in web-based forms. Yet new technologies have in turn influenced generic conventions, and have often resulted in their transformation. In Malaysia, blogging has arguably led to the rediscovery and further development of the political essay. Changes in camera editing and storage technology have also made the making of short films much easier, and created new distribution networks (Khoo 2007). While this study has consciously chosen not to engage with film, the convergence of media technologies and the movements across genres by individual artists has now made the distinction between filmic and more traditional literary texts less tenable, and future literary histories of the region may need to account for this.

Technologies are always closely intertwined with social change. While the precise contours of change vary in specific locations, it is possible to make some broad generalizations. In Singapore, Malaysia and Hong Kong, writing has moved outside of the university in a decisive manner. Until the early 1980s, the majority of writers of the Singapore and Malaysian literary canons in English were associated with the university: this is no longer so. The university may still play a facilitative role, particularly in the teaching of creative writing: the University of the Philippines, Diliman, for instance, and Ateneo de Manila University have vibrant creative writing programmes, while the University of Hong Kong and the National University of Singapore have given increased attention to creative writing in English in recent years. However, the growing professionalization of English academia has meant that the number of scholar poets or novelists has declined. In their place, in the world outside the university, each society has seen the growth of what are sometimes termed the 'creative industries': the arts, media, advertising and associated areas. Older generation writers who did exist outside the university might have a single stable profession such as law, medicine or teaching: younger writers are likely to move from one to another, producing work in several media, and using the income from more commercial work in advertising, copy-writing, journalism and editing to cross-subsidize less popular or more specialist forms. For many younger writers in the urban centres of Southeast Asia, portfolio careers have replaced single professions, and the interpenetration of media has resulted in a mingling of previously distinct popular and high-cultural literary forms.

Technological and social changes have resulted in two further effects on literature. The first is a growing transnationalism. Web-based networks and journals offer access to any internet user, even if they have a national or regional focus. Yet such transnational audiences are not necessarily homogenizing: they have, if anything, enabled the formation of 'glocal' networks, linking Southeast Asian expatriates to countries of origin, or forging new regional imaginaries. The second effect is renewed complexity in literature's engagement with politics. In Singapore and Malaysia in particular, the state's hegemonic dominance of traditional media has made the internet a ready site for alternative journalism, and for satire that has often taken literary or paraliterary forms.

The Philippines

The Philippines give ample evidence of new textual genres in English that bridge popular and elite literary culture. Philippine writers have a long tradition of involvement in journalism, and this continues to this day; many writers, however, have moved beyond the editorials or discursive journalistic essay form pioneered by Nick Joaquin into new directions. Tara Sering, for instance, worked as a journalist and editor both within the region for *Elle* (a women's magazine in Singapore) and for *Mabuhay* (a Philippine Airlines' in-flight magazine). Her knowledge of these popular audiences has seen her become the leading writer of the budding genre of Philippine chick lit in English. Sering and other chick lit authors are published by companies such as Summit in initial print runs of 10,000: many of their novels go through at least one reprinting, thus gaining audiences twenty times larger than that of literary fiction. While Sering and her fellow authors have been criticized for acceptance of a shallow consumer culture, they have defended themselves by arguing that they describe a reality for young professional women, which is both conforming and transgressive. A novel such as Sering's *Almost Married* (2003) represents a localization of the chick lit genre in a Philippine context: its protagonist, Karen, negotiates the growing intensity of commitments in her relationship with her boyfriend, Bert Reyno, in a manner reminiscent of Bridget Jones. What is different in Sering's novel from British or American chick lit, however, is its focus on family relationships: Karen worries about her relationship to her 'very-soon-to-be in-laws' (2003: 38), or her father's reaction to Bert. Dialogue mixes English, Taglish and Tagalog, while breathless second-person narration maintains an ironic distance. Tellingly, attempts to infuse such popular genres with great social engagement have largely failed: Anvil Books' Rosa series, which attempted to weave a consciousness of social inequality into the romance format, was a commercial flop.

The internet has been important in enabling less commercially focused groups of writers to come together and produce work that challenges traditional generic categories. Dean Francis Alfar's novel *Salamanca* has been discussed in an earlier chapter, but perhaps more significant has been his position as editor of (as of early 2008) three short story collections of *Philippine Speculative Fiction*. Alfar's blog *Notes from the Peanut Gallery* forms a node in a network of contacts among young writers: the genre of 'speculative fiction' makes creative use of Robert Heinlein's term to incorporate science fiction, fantasy and forms of allegory. Alfar's collections are more consciously literary and less popular than Sering's novels, but they also break the mould in Philippine writing, reaching an audience of young professionals that overlaps with, but is different from, that of literary fiction. While not dismissing academic discussion, Alfar has stressed the need, above all, to write, and to write regularly and frequently, to build up a common body of work before prematurely theorizing. In his introduction to the second volume of *Philippine Speculative Fiction*, the writer also notes that speculative fiction deals with social issues as much as realism does, but 'offers the experience through a different lens' (2006a: x). The specifically Filipino element of such fiction is still evolving and indeed needs to be negotiated with, Alfar suggests, recognizing both 'the importance of our cultural identity, black marks and all, but also ... the value of being freed from the shackles of guilt, of being able to tell stories of the fantastic in non-nationalistic terms' (2006a: x).

An example of the possibilities offered by such fiction is Joshua L. Lim So's 'Feasting'. Set in a seaside village, the story opens with accounts of legends of the taste of meat exchanged by members of a fishing community who have never eaten food that is not drawn from the sea. A young married man, Makaon, mysteriously leaves the community after being promised work at the end of the ocean. Four times a year, he sends his family a package containing a pound of meat: his family subsists on it and prospers. Eventually there comes a time when the package does not arrive. Its place is taken by a wooden crate that, when opened, reveals a skeleton stripped of all flesh save that on the two hands, along with a note indicating that Makaon's services are 'no longer required' (2006: 99). The story's conclusion thus allegorizes the rural face of transnational migrant labour, and – through the relationships between Makaon's mother, wife and son – the disruption of community and family life it brings even as it offers the prospect of wealth to the migrant labourer's family. 'Feasting' thus exemplifies Alfar's point regarding the possibilities offered by speculative fiction: it is no less socially engaged than social realist fiction in a Philippine tradition that stretched back to the 1930s, yet it offers the possibility of rephrasing such social engagement through allegory rather than a simple claim of referentiality.

Alfar's work, including his own collection of short stories *The Kite of Stars* (2007) straddles the popular and the literary. A collection such as *Pinoy Amazing Adventures* (2006), edited by Emil Flores, is, in contrast, more clearly targeted at a popular science fiction audience, while Karl de Mesa's short story collection *Damaged People* (2006) draws on another popular genre, horror, to produce 'gothic-punk' stories that reference Catholic ritual, indigenous mythology and contemporary popular culture and media: the Gothic sublime of earlier Filipino writers such as Joaquin is here replaced with a firm anchorage in the mundane. In all these collections, the incorporation of irony and popular cultural motifs into fiction that still maintains social awareness challenges two dominant paradigms of creative writing in the Philippines: the concern with social realism, and a stress on formalism that grew out of the influence of American New Criticism. It is arguable that science fiction, the gothic and chick lit collectively provide an equally radical challenge to the boundaries of the literary, and indeed offer more exciting points of departure, than the more conventionally literary fashions for postmodern storytelling and magical realism that have become established as features of canonical writing from the 1990s onwards.

Generic innovation, however, is only part of the story, with the internet providing scope for the reinvention of the traditional literary or poetry journal. A journal such as *Literatura*, for instance, bridges print and digital media by publishing winners of the annual Carlos Palanca Awards. *High Chair* operates as a web-based journal for poetry, but also as a publisher of poetry chapbooks, consciously eschewing a popular audience in favour of a concentration on the development of a community of poetry readers. The literary internet in the Philippines is richer than that in Singapore or Malaysia, but also more chaotic: many journals or informational sites are started up by individuals or groups, but are then discontinued, or run into problems with hosting. The gateway site http://panitikan.com.ph, established in 2005 by the National Commission for Culture and the Arts and the University of the Philippines Likhaan Institute of Creative Writing, perhaps offers the best entry-point into this ever-changing landscape.

Malaysia, Singapore and Hong Kong

In both Malaysia and Singapore, the presence of new media technologies has had mixed effects on more traditional literary forms. The essay and poetry have perhaps been revitalized by new media in Malaysia and Singapore respectively. The novel in English has, as we saw in earlier chapters, effectively been outsourced, with significant new texts largely written and published by writers in the diaspora: the short and the indie film have perhaps taken on the role of the novel in serving as a national allegory, or in contesting the historical representation of the imagined community of the nation.

Superficially at least, the situation in Malaysia resembles that in Singapore. Kuala Lumpur's transformation into a major international city in the last decade of the twentieth century resulted in the formation of a class of people working in a largely Anglophone creative industry sphere that had greater cultural and political autonomy and greater scope for international and transnational connections than the public sphere in the national language, Bahasa Malaysia. In this sense, Kuala Lumpur and Singapore show many parallels, with the Malaysian government, albeit with less efficiency and less efficacy, encouraging developments in information technology and with a subsidiary interest in the creative industries. Key differences between Malaysia and Singapore, however, are the relative strength in the former country of civil society and the authority and influence of public intellectuals, and this has led to the intersection between new technologies and social change developing on different lines.

Malaysia has not developed an online literary journal of the longevity and comprehensiveness of Singapore journals like *QLRS* or *Softblow*, although there have been gestures in this direction, for instance the online journal *Asiatic* published by the English-medium Islamic University of Malaysia. However, the new technologies have enabled the growth of two forms of writing associated with the literary. The first is the formation of a critical community of writers and discussants on the arts through the website http://kakiseni.com, first established in 2001. Kakiseni posts not only listings of arts events and reviews, but also publishes critical essays by arts practitioners and public intellectuals that are preserved in a free-access archive: the site has a greater comprehensiveness and presence than its Singaporean equivalents, the arts community Yahoo! Group or the online *Substation Magazine*, which is more narrowly concerned with the visual and the performing arts. The second is the mutual influence of blogging on print media, and resulting developments in the essay form.

An example of the latter might be the work of Farish Noor, and in particular the collection of essays *The Other Malaysia* (2002). These essays were originally written by the author over several years and published on the alternative news and commentary website http://www.malaysiakini.com, an important space for "'contentious" journalism' on the internet (George 2006: 158–175). The essays frequently adopt the rhetorical tactic of retrieving historical incidents and figures which are then tied to an incident in the present, thus disrupting the 'common sense' interpretation given in the media through a hegemonic account of Malaysian history that radically simplifies Islam and sees conflicts occurring between rather than within communities. What is particularly interesting is the use of the essay form. The essays are much shorter than academic papers, and are written with rhetorical sensitivity and flair, and yet the book itself, through its many small fragments, does similar intellectual work to a more formally structured academic study, while at the same time reaching a wider audience: it went into a second printing in 2005. The interpenetration of digital and print technologies is illustrated by the fact that Farish Noor's work has been republished as part of a new website called *The Other Malaysia* set up by 'a number of Malaysian scholar-activists ... interested in unearthing aspects of Malaysian history, politics and culture that have thus far been sidelined, marginalised or erased in the official historiography of the post-colonial state' (Online: 'Welcome ...', para 1).

In Singapore, to a greater degree than Malaysia, the growth of creative industries has been enabled, if not entirely controlled, by the state. The late 1980s and 1990s saw a growth in new educational institutions for the arts and the expansion of older ones: Ngee Ann Polytechnic opened its School of Film and Media Studies in 1989, while what is now the La Salle College of the Arts grew exponentially in the 1990s. Singapore's National Arts Council was set up in 1991, and the then minister for the arts George Yeo articulated aspirations in 1995 to become a 'global city for the arts' (Kwok and Low 2002: 152). Singapore was also conceived as becoming a media hub: Channel News Asia, a regional rival to CNN, was set up in 1999, while initiatives such as the SingaporeONE ADSL high-speed network ensured that the city was wired to support the latest in digital media. In 2002, a *Creative Industries Development Strategy* referenced the American academic Richard Florida's *Rise of the Creative Class* (2002), and envisioned media, design, the arts and culture doubling their share of Singapore's GDP from 2000 to 2012 (Leo and Lee 2004: 214). If many of the new initiatives have been top-down and concerned with infrastructure, cultural capital and indeed, in many accounts, a hegemonic containment of creativity as a commoditized industry, they have provided opportunities for Singaporeans to explore new quasi-literary forms and to reinvent old ones.

Such reinvention of older literary forms on the internet in Singapore is represented by *QLRS* (*Quarterly Literary Review Singapore*), edited by the poet Toh Hsien Min. The web-based journal has taken over the function promised by *Singa* or *Tumasek* to previous generations: a regularly published literary magazine, incorporating both new creative and critical work. In addition to publishing new writers, *QLRS* has also provided scope for more established ones such as Robert Yeo and Daren Shiau to publish work in progress, and has also done important historical documentation work, bringing to light, for example, an unpublished poem by Singapore's premier poet, Arthur Yap. More specialized in terms of subject-matter and indeed literary approach is Cyril Wong's poetry webzine *Softblow*. While very different in editorial style, both publications are transnational in terms of contributors and, presumably, audiences, with a centre of gravity in Southeast Asia in general and Singapore in particular. Changes similar to those described above are also under way in Hong Kong. While many of the tendencies towards portfolio careers and the increased visibility of the creative industries are present in the territory, cultural production is largely in Chinese. The most popular web-based literary magazine in English is *Cha,* publishing fiction, poetry and artwork.

Our narrative of writing in English from the diverse literary cultures of Southeast Asia ends with the recognition that just as English exists in Southeast Asia amidst a huge variety of other languages, literary language is increasingly subject to permeability between the hieratic and demotic aspects of language as speech, between cultures once monolingual but now irrevocably (though always only partially) polyglot. Yet another dual recognition is also worth articulating at the end of such a narrative: the future history of literary English in Southeast Asia will have to reckon more and more with a two-way permeability alongside literatures in the other languages of the region, just as it will have to reckon with literary language making itself more and more porous to much else in the world of creativity that is not tied to the orthodox history of print cultures.

Conclusion

- The writing of the twenty-first century appears well placed to combine the legacies of regional experiments with the assimilation and adaptation of modernist and postmodernist tenets and practices, even though modernity in its social applications and modernism and postmodernism in their literary applications have encountered specific challenges in Southeast Asia. The new technologies and associated mediums of expression developed at the end of the twentieth and the beginning of the twenty-first century offer both opportunities and challenges to writing in English in Southeast Asia, as the role and place of the printed literary text gets realigned in its form and function within regional and international cultural systems

- The difficult tasks of conventional publication and distribution are now often simplified through widespread and relatively easy access to digital media and the internet.

- Digital media do not simply replace the print text; the growth in creative industries and connections forged through new channels of communication has led to increased generic experimentation and larger audiences for printed books.

- A combination of technological and social factors has led the repositioning of traditional genres and the creation of new sub-genres.

Works cited

The following list is confined to works cited from or discussed in the book.

Abad Gemino H. (1973) *Fugitive Emphasis*, Quezon City: University of the Philippines Press.

—— (1976) *In Another Light: Poems and Essays*, Quezon City: University of the Philippines Press.

Abad, Gemino H. and E. Z. Manlapaz (1988) *Index to Filipino Poetry in English, 1905–1950*, Manila: National Bookstore.

—— (ed.) (1989) *Man of Earth: an Anthology of Filipino Poetry and Verse from English, 1905 to the Mid 1950s*, Quezon City: Ateneo de Manila University Press.

—— (ed.) (1993) *A Native Clearing: Filipino Poetry and Verse from English Since the 1950s to the Present: From Edith L. Tiempo to Cirilo F. Bautista*, Quezon City: University of the Philippines Press.

—— (ed.) (1999) *A Habit of Shores: Filipino Poetry and Verse from English, '60s to the '90s*, Quezon City: University of the Philippines Press.

—— (2004) *In Ordinary Time: Poems, Parables, Poetics 1973–2003*, Quezon City: University of the Philippines Press.

Abad, Gemino H., Cirilo F. Bautista, Alfrredo Navarro Slanga, Ricardo M. de Ungria, Alfred A. Yuson (1983) *In Memoriam, Benigno S. Aquino, Jr., 1932–1983. A Poetic Tribute by Five Filipino Poets*, Philippine Literary Arts Council (PLAC).

Abbas, Ackbar (1992) 'The Last Emporium: Verse and Cultural Space', Introduction to *City at the End of Time*, poems by Leung Ping-kwan, trans. Gordon T. Osing and the author, Hong Kong: Twilight Books Company, 3–19.

Aguilar-Carino, Maria Luisa B. [see Igloria, Luisa A.]

Alatas, Syed Hussein (1971) *Thomas Stamford Raffles, 1781–1826, Schemer or Reformer?*, Singapore: Angus and Robertson.

Alfar, Dean Francis (2006) *Salamanca*, Quezon City: Ateneo de Manila Press.

—— (ed.) (2006) *Philippine Speculative Fiction*, Vol. 2, Pasig City: Kestrel.

—— (2007) *The Kite of Stars and Other Stories*, Quezon City: Anvil Publishing.

—— *Notes from the Peanut Gallery*. Online. HTTP available: http://deanalfar. blogspot.com (accessed 14 May 2008).

Alfian bin Sa'at (1998) *One Fierce Hour*, Singapore: Landmark Books.

—— (1999a) *Corridor*, Singapore: Raffles.

Alfon, Estrella D. (1960) *Magnificence*, Manila: Regal.

—— (1938) 'One Day and the Next', in Leopoldo Y. Yabes (ed.), *Philippine Short Stories 1925–1940* (1975), 383–92.

Allot, Anna, Patricia Herbert and John Okell (1989) 'Burma', in Patricia Herbert and Andrew Milner (eds), *South-East Asia Languages and Literatures: A Select Guide*, 1–22.

Alunan, Merlie M. (2004) *Selected Poems*, Quezon City: University of the Philippines Press.

Alvero, A. S. (1950) *Moon Shadows on the Waters* [1934], 2nd edn, Manila: Far Eastern Publishing Company.

An Lim, Jaime L. (1998) *Trios*, Diliman, Quezon City: University of the Philippines Press.

Andaya, Leonard Y. (1992) 'Interactions with the Outside World and Adaptation in Southeast Asian Society, 1500–1800', in Nicholas Tarling (ed.), *The Cambridge History of Southeast Asia*, Vol. 1, 345–401.

Angeles, Carlos A. (1963) *a stun of jewels*, Manila: Alberto S. Florentino.

—— (1993) *A Bruise of Ashes: Collected Poems 1940–1992*, Quezon City: Ateneo de Manila University Press.

'Anonymous student' (1949) 'Ode to an Amoeba', *The Cauldron*, Vol. 3, no. 3 (June), 28.

Anuar, Hedwig [Aroozoo, Hedwig] (1999) *Under the Apple Tree: Political Parodies of the 1950s*, Singapore: Landmark Books.

Arcellana, Francisco (1962) *Selected Stories*, Manila: Alberto S. Florentino.

—— (1973) *15 Stories*, Manila: Alberto S. Florentino.

Arguilla, Manuel E. (1940) *How My Brother Leon Brought Home a Wife and Other Stories*, Manila: Philippine Book Guild.

Auden, W. H. (1977) *The English Auden*, ed. Edward Mendelson, London: Faber.

Aw, Tash (2005) *The Harmony Silk Factory*, London: Penguin.

Baratham, Gopal (1991) *A Candle or the Sun*, London: Serpent's Tail.

Ban Kah Choon (2000) *Of Memory and Desire: The Stories of Gopal Baratham*, Singapore: Times Books International.

Banzon, Isabela (1987) *Paper Cage*, Manila: The Mabolo Group.

—— (2003) 'Challenging Traditions: Prosody and Rhapsody in the Poetry of Angela Manalang Gloria', National Commission for Culture and the Arts. Online. Available HTTP: http://www.ncca.gov.ph/about_cultarts/articles.php?artcl_Id=23 (accessed 9 December 2006).

—— (2009) *Lola Coqueta*, Quezon City: University of the Philippines Press.

Bautista, Cirilo F. (1970) *The Archipelago*, Manila: San Beda Review.

—— (2006) *Believe and Betray: New and Collected Poems*, Manila: De La Salle University Press.

Bautista, Maria Lourdes S. and Andrew B. Gonzalez (2006) 'Southeast Asian Englishes', in Braj B. Kachru, Yamuna Kachru and Cecil L. Nelson (eds), *The Handbook of World Englishes*, Malden, Oxford, Carlton: Blackwell, 130–44.

Beduya, Jose Perez (2007) *Seem*, Quezon City: High Chair.

Bellwood, Peter (1992) 'Southeast Asia before History', in Nicholas Tarling (ed.), *The Cambridge History of Southeast Asia*, Vol. 1, 51–136.

Benjamin, Walter (1999) *Selected Writings, Volume 2, 1927-1934*, ed. Michael W. Jennings, Howard Eiland and Gary Smith, trans. Rodney Livingstone, Cambridge, Mass.: The Belknap Press of Harvard University Press, 464 [459–465].

Benson, Eugene and L. W. Conolly (eds) (1994) *Encyclopedia of Post-Colonial Literatures in English*, London and New York: Routledge, 2 vols.

Bernad, Miguel A. (1961) *Bamboo and the Greenwood Tree: Essays on Philippine Literature in English*, Manila: Bookmark.

Birch, David (1997) 'Singapore English Drama: A Historical Overview 1958–1985', in Sanjay Krishnan (ed.), *9 Lives: 10 Years of Singapore Theatre*, Singapore: The Necessary Stage, 22–52.

Boey Kim Cheng (1989) *Somewhere-bound*, Singapore: Times Books International.

—— (1992) *Another Place*, Singapore: Times Books International.

—— (1996) *Days of No Name*, Singapore: EPB Publishers.

—— (2006) *After the Fire: New and Selected Poems*, Singapore: First Fruits.

Bolton, Kingsley (2002) 'Hong Kong English: Autonomy and Creativity', in Kingsley Bolton (ed.), *Hong Kong English: Autonomy and Creativity*, Hong Kong: Hong Kong University Press, 1–25.

—— (2003) *Chinese Englishes: A Sociolinguistic History*, Cambridge: Cambridge University Press.

Brillantes, Gregorio C. (2000) *The Distance to Andromeda and Other Stories* [1960], Quezon City: University of the Philippines Press.

Brooks, Cleanth (1939) *Modern Poetry and the Tradition*, Chapel Hill: University of North Carolina Press.

Bulosan, Carlos (ed.) (1942) *Chorus for America: Six Filipino Poets*, Los Angeles: Wagon and Star.

—— (1943) *The Voice of Bataan*, New York: Coward-McCann.

—— (1944) *The Laughter of My Father*, New York: Harcourt Brace.

—— (1946) *America is in the Heart*, New York: Harcourt Brace.

Burning Heart: A Portrait of the Philippines, photographs by Marissa Roth; text by Jessica Hagedorn, New York: Rizzoli, 1999.

Campomanes, Oscar V. (1992) 'Filipinos in the United States and Their Literature of Exile', in Shirley Geok-lin Lim and Amy Ling (eds), *Reading the Literatures of Asian America*, Philadelphia: Temple University Press, 49–78.

Carbó, Nick (ed.) (1995) *Returning a Borrowed Tongue*, Minneapolis: Coffee House Press.

Carunungan, Celso Al (1960) *Like a Big Brave Man*, New York: Farrar, Straus and Cudahy.

Casper, Leonard (1964) *The Wounded Diamond: Studies in Modern Philippine Literature*, Manila: Bookmark.

—— (ed.) (1966) *New Writing from the Philippines*, New York: Syracuse University Press.

—— (1991) *In Burning Ambush: Essays 1985–1991*, Quezon City: New Day Publishers.

—— (1995) *The Opposing Thumb: Decoding Literature of the Marcos Regime*, Quezon City: Giraffe.

Castillo, Erwin E. (2003) *The Firewalkers* [1992], Quezon City: University of the Philippines Press.

Chan, Lily (1986) *Struggle of a Hong Kong Girl*, ed. Anne Wong, New York: Vantage.

Chan, Mimi (1994) 'Drama (Hong Kong)', in Eugene Benson and L. W. Conolly (eds), *Routledge Encyclopedia of Post-Colonial Literatures in English*, 382–83.

Chan, Mimi and Roy Harris (eds) (1991) *Asian Voices in English*, Hong Kong: Hong Kong University Press.

Chan Wan Wah (1977) *The Rebirth of an Ex-communist through Gestalt Therapy*, Hong Kong: Yue Man.

Che Husna Azhari (1993) *Melor in Perspective*, Bangi: Furada Publishing House.

Cheong, Colin (1989) *The Stolen Child: A First Novel*, Singapore: Times Books International.

Cheong, Fiona (1991) *The Scent of the Gods*, New York: Norton.

—— (2002) *Shadow Theatre*, New York: Soho.

Cher, Ming (1995) *Spider Boys*, Auckland: Penguin.

Chin, Woon Ping [Holaday] (1983) 'Singing in a Second Tongue: Recent Malaysian and Singaporean Poetry in English', *Journal of Commonwealth Literature*, 18.11: 27–41.

—— (1999) *In My Mother's Dream*, Singapore: Landmark Books.

Chong, Terence (2004) 'Mediating the Liberalisation of Singapore Theatre: Towards a Bourdieusian Analysis', in Tan Chong Kee and Tisa Ng (eds.) *Ask Not: The Necessary Stage in Singapore Theatre*, 223–47.

Clavell, James (1966) *Tai-pan*, New York: Atheneum.

—— (1981) *Noble House*, New York: Dell.

Clifford, James (1998) 'Mixed Feelings', in Pheng Cheah and Bruce Robbins (eds), *Cosmopolitics: Thinking and Feeling Beyond the Nation*, Minneapolis and London: University of Minnesota Press, 362–70.

Comber, Leon (1991) 'Publishing Asian Writers in English', in Mimi Chan and Roy Harris (eds), *Asian Voices in English*, 79–86.

Conrad, Joseph (1920) *An Observer in Malay: Hugh Clifford's 'Studies in Brown Humanity'*, London: Richard Clay.

Cordell, Alexander (1965) *The Sinews of Love*, London: Gollancz.

Cruz, Andres Cristobal (1960) *Estero Poems*, Manila: Filipino Signatures.

Cruz, Conchitina (2005) *Dark Hours*, Quezon City: University of the Philippines Press.

—— (2008) *elsewhere held and lingered*, Quezon City: High Chair.

Dalisay, Jose Y, Jr. (1985) 'Sarcophagus', *Philippine Studies* 33: 288–94.

Dato, Rodolfo (ed.) (1924) *Filipino Poetry*, Manila: J. S. Agustin.

Davis, John Gordon (1974) *The Years of the Hungry Tiger*, London: Michael Joseph.

Demetillo, Ricaredo (1959) *La Via: A Spiritual Journey*, Quezon City: University of the Philippines.

—— (1961) *Barter in Panay*, Quezon City: University of the Philippines Office of Research Coordination.

de Casparis, J. G. and I. W. Mabbett (1992) 'Religion and Popular Beliefs of Southeast Asia before c.1500', in Nicholas Tarling (ed.), *The Cambridge History of Southeast Asia*, Vol. 1, 276–340.

de Mesa, Karl R. (2006) *Damaged People: Tales of the Gothic-Punk*, Quezon City: University of the Philippines Press.

de Ungria, Ricardo M. (1991) *Decimal Places*, Pasig City: Anvil Publishing.

—— (1994) *Nudes: Poems*, Pasig City: Anvil Publishing.

—— (ed.) (1995) *A Passionate Patience: Ten Filipino Poets on the Writing of their Poems*, Pasig City: Anvil Publishing.

—— (2000) *Waking Ice*, Manila: Anvil Publishing.

Devan, Janadas (1997) 'Notes on Proscriptions and Manners', in Sanjay Krishnan (ed.), *Nine Lives: 10 Years of Singapore Theatre, 1987–1997*, 238–46.

Dingwall, Alastair (ed.) (1994) *Traveller's Literary Companion to South-East Asia*, Brighton: In Print Publishing.

Dina Zaman (1997) *Night and Day*, Petaling Jaya: Rhino Press.

Dixon, Chris (1991) *Southeast Asia in the World Economy*, Cambridge: Cambridge University Press.

Dizon, D. Paulo (1990) *Twilight of a Poet* [1962], Quezon City: New Day.

Dumdum, Jr., Simeon (1999) *Poems: Selected and New (1982–1997)*, Quezon City: Ateneo de Manila University.

—— (1982)*The Gift of Sleep*, Quezon City: New Day Publishers.

—— (1987) *Third World Opera*, Rpt. Detroit: Cellar Book Shop, 1988.

Dumdum, Jr., Simeon, Timothy Mo and Resil Mojares (2004) 'In Conversation: Cebuano Writers on Philippine Literature and English', *World Englishes*, 23.1: 191–8.

Ee Tiang Hong (1960) *I of the Many Faces*, Malacca: Wah Seong Press.

—— (1973) *Lines Written in Hawaii*, Honolulu: East-West Culture Learning Institute.

—— (1976) *Myths for a Wilderness*, Singapore: Heinemann Asia.

—— (1982) 'Creative Alternatives in Malaysia: Cecil Rajendra and Muhammad Haji Salleh', in Bruce Bennett, Ee Tiang Hong and Ron Shepherd (eds), *The Writer's Sense of the Contemporary: Papers in Southeast Asian and Australian Literature*, Nedlands: Centre for Studies in Australian Literature, 41–5.

—— (1985) *Tranquerah*, Singapore: National University of Singapore.

—— (1987) 'History as Myth in Malaysian Poetry in English', in Kirpal Singh (ed.) *The Writer's Sense of the Past*, Singapore, Singapore University Press, 10–16.

—— (1994) *Nearing a Horizon*, Singapore: UniPress.

—— (1997) *Responsibility and Commitment: The Poetry of Edwin Thumboo*, ed. Leong Liew Geok, Singapore: Singapore University Press.

Elegant, Robert S. (1977) *Dynasty*. New York: McGraw-Hill.

Elliott, Lorraine (2004) 'Environmental Challenges, Policy Failure and Regional Dynamics in Southeast Asia', in Mark Beeson (ed.), *Contemporary Southeast Asia: Regional Dynamics, National Differences*, New York: Palgrave Macmillan, 178–97.

Elson, Robert E. (1992) 'International Commerce, the State and Society: Economic and Social Change', in Nicholas Tarling (ed.), *The Cambridge History of Southeast Asia*, Vol. 2, 127–96.

Enright, D. J. (1959–60) 'The Flowers that Bloom in Spring – A Letter from Singapore', *Magazine of the University of Malaya Student's Union*, 12–15.

—— (1962) 'Reflections on the Malayan Writers' Conference', *Focus*, 2.1: 19–21.

Enriquez, Amigdio Alvarez (1959) *The Devil Flower*, New York: Hill and Wang.

Espino, Federico Licsi, Jr. (1976) *Opus 27: Poems*, Manila: Pioneer Press.

Evasco, Marjorie (1987) *Dreamweavers: Selected Poems, 1976–1986*, Manila: Editorial and Media Resources Corp.

—— (1999) *Ochre Tones: Poems in English & Cebuano*, Marikina City, Philippines: Salimbayan Books.

Farish A. Noor (2002) *The Other Malaysia: Writings on Malaysia's Subaltern History*, Kuala Lumpur: Silverfish.

Fernandez, Doreen G. (1996) *Palabas: Essays on Philippine Theater History*, Quezon City: Ateneo de Manila University Press.

Fernando, Lloyd (1957) 'Theatre', *Write*, 1 (December): 8.

—— (ed.) (1972a) *New Drama One*, Kuala Lumpur: Oxford University Press.

—— (ed.) (1972b) *New Drama Two*, Kuala Lumpur: Oxford University Press.

—— (1976) *Scorpion Orchid*, Kuala Lumpur: Heinemann Asia.

—— (1986) *Cultures in Conflict: Essays on Literature and the English Language in Southeast Asia*, Singapore: Graham Brash.

—— (1993) *Green is the Colour*, Singapore: Landmark Books.

Ferroa, E. (1936) 'Malaya and the Novelist', *Raffles College Magazine*, 6.1: 25–7.

Flores, Emil (ed.) (2006) *Pinoy Amazing Adventures*, Quezon City: PSICOM.

Francia, Luis H. and Eric Gamalinda (eds) (1996) *Flippin' Filipinos on America*, New York: The Asian American Writers' Workshop.

Galang, Zoilo M. (1921) *A Child of Sorrow*, Manila: Zoilo M. Galang.

—— (1923) *Tales of the Philippines*. Manila: Fajardo Press.

—— (1924) *The Box of Ashes and Other Stories*, Manila: Zoilo M. Galang.

Galdon, Joseph A. (ed.) (1979) *Essays on the Philippine Novel in English*, Quezon City: Ateneo de Manila University Press.

Gamalinda, Eric (1992) *The Empire of Memory*, Manila: Anvil Publishing.

—— (1991) *Lyrics from a Dead Language*, Manila: Anvil Publishing.

—— (1999) *Zero Gravity*, Farmington, Maine: Alice James Books.

—— (2000) *My Sad Republic*, Quezon City: University of the Philippines Press.

Garcia, J. Neil C. (ed.) (2007) *At Home In Unhomeliness: An Anthology of Philippine Postcolonial Poetry in English*, Manila: UST Publishing House.

Garcia, J. Neil C. and Danton Remoto (eds) (1994) *Ladlad: An Anthology of Philippine Gay Writing*, Pasig City: Anvil Publishing.

—— (eds) (1996) *Ladlad 2: An Anthology of Philippine Gay Writing*, Pasig City: Anvil Publishing.

Geertz, Clifford (1995) *After the Fact: Two Countries, Four Decades, One Anthropologist*, Cambridge, MA: Harvard University Press.

George, Cherian (2006) *Contentious Journalism and the Internet: Towards Democratic Discourse in Malaysia and Singapore*, Singapore: Singapore University Press.

Goh Kiat Seng (1958) 'Towards a Malayan Culture', *Write*, 5: 10–11.

Goh Poh Seng (1964–6) *The Moon is Less Bright*; *When the Smiles are Done*; *The Elder Brother*, bound typescript, Singapore: National University of Singapore Central Library.

—— (1972) *If We Dream Too Long*, Singapore: Island Press.

—— (1977) *The Immolation*, Singapore: Heinemann Asia.

—— (2005) Personal Interview with Philip Holden, Vancouver, Canada, 25 July.

Goh Sin Tub (1987) *The Ghost Lover of Emerald Hill and Other Stories*, Singapore: Heinemann Asia.

Gonzalez, Andrew B. (1980) *Language and Nationalism: The Philippine Experience Thus Far*, Quezon City: Ateneo de Manila University Press.

—— (ed.) (1988) *The Role of English and its Maintenance in the Philippines*, Manila: Solidaridad.

Gonzalez, N. V. M. (1947) *Seven Hills Away*, Denver: Alan Swallow.

—— (1953) 'Imaginative Writing in the Philippines', in T. D. Agcaoili (ed.), *Philippine Writing: An Anthology*, Westport, CT: Greenwood Press, 321–8.

—— (1954) *Children of the Ash-Covered Loam and Other Stories*, Manila: Benipayo.

—— (1956) *A Season of Grace*, Manila: Bookmark.

—— (1957) *The Bamboo Dancers*, Manila: Benipayo.

—— (1963) *Look, Stranger, on This Island Now*, Manila: Benipayo.

—— (1964) *Selected Stories*, Denver: Alan Swallow.

—— (1998) *The Winds of April* [1941], Quezon City: University of the Philippines Press.

Gopinathan, S. (1998) 'Language Policy Changes 1979–1997: Politics and Pedagogy', in S. Gopinathan, Anne Pakir, Ho Wah Kam and Vanithamani Saravanan (eds), *Language, Society and Education in Singapore: Issues and Trends* [1994], Singapore: Times Academic Press, 19–44.

Gotero, Vince (2002) 'Brave New Archipelago: Recent Filipino American Writing', *North American Review*, 287.3–4: 69–72.

—— (2004) 'Moments in the Wilderness: Becoming a Filipino American Writer', *Melus*, Filipino American Literature, 29.1: 19–40.

Grijns, C. D. *et al.* (1989) 'Indonesia', in Patricia Herbert and Andrew Milner (eds), *South-East Asia Languages and Literatures: A Select Guide*, 123–52.

Groyon, Vicente G. (2004) *The Sky Over Dimas*, Manila: University of Santo Tomas Press.

Guerrero, Wilfrido Ma. (1962) *7 More Plays*, Quezon City: Bookmark.

—— (1976) *My Favorite 11 Plays*, Quezon City: New Day.

Hagedorn, Jessica (ed.) (1993) *Charlie Chan is Dead: An Anthology of Contemporary Asian American Fiction*, New York: Penguin.

—— (2001) *Dogeaters* [1990], New York: Penguin.

Han Suyin [Elizabeth Chou] (1952) *A Many-Splendoured Thing*, London: Jonathan Cape.

—— (1980) *My House Has Two Doors*, London: Jonathan Cape.

—— (1991) 'Plenary Lecture', in Mimi Chan and Roy Harris (eds), *Asian Voices in English*, 17–22.

Harrex, Syd (1994) 'Lee Kok Liang', in Eugene Benson and L. W. Conolly (eds), *Encyclopedia of Post-Colonial Literatures in English*, Vol. 1, 833–4.

Herbert, Patricia and Andrew Milner (eds) (1989) *South-East Asia Languages and Literatures: A Select Guide*, Honolulu: University of Hawaii Press.

Heryanto, Ariel and Sumit K. Mandal (2003) 'Challenges to Authoritarianism in Indonesia and Malaysia', *Challenging Authoritarianism in Southeast Asia: Comparing Indonesia and Malaysia*, London: Routledge Curzon, 1–23.

Hickey, Raymond (2004) 'South-East Asian Languages', *Legacies of Colonial English: Studies in Transported Dialects*, Cambridge: Cambridge University Press, 559–85.

High Chair Online. HTTP available: http://www.highchair.com.ph/ (accessed 14 May 2008).

Ho, Louise (1997) *New Ends Old Beginnings*, Hong Kong: Asia 2000.

Ho Minfong (1984) *Sing to the Dawn*, Singapore: Eastern Universities Press.

Hosilos, Lucila V. (1976) *Philippine-American Literary Relations, 1898–1941* [1969], New York: Oriole.

Hufana, Alejandrino G. (1961) *Poro Point: An Anthology of Lives*, Quezon City: University of the Philippines.

—— (1964) *Curtain-Raisers: First Five Plays*, Quezon City: University of the Philippines-Social Science Research Council.

Huzir Sulaiman (2002) *Eight Plays*, Kuala Lumpur: Silverfish.

Igloria, Luisa A. [Maria Luisa B. Aguilar-Carino] (1994) *Encanto*, Manila: Anvil Publishing Press.

—— (1995) *In the Garden of the Three Islands*, Wakefield, Rhode Island and London: Asphodel Press/Moyer Bell.

—— (1997) *Blood Sacrifice*, Manila: University of the Philippines Press.

—— (2005) *Trill & Mordent*, Cincinnati: WordTech Editions.

—— (2009) *Juan Luna's Revolver*, Notre Dame, IN: University of Notre Dame Press.

Ilio, Dominador I. (1955) *The Diplomat and Other Poems*, Quezon City: Guinhalinan Press.

Ingham, Michael (2007) *Hong Kong: A Cultural History*, Oxford and New York: Oxford University Press.

Ingham, Mike and Xu Xi (eds) (2005) *City Stage: Hong Kong Playwriting in English*, Hong Kong: Hong Kong University Press.

Jameson, Fredric (1991), *Postmodernism, or, The Cultural Logic of Late Capitalism*, London and New York: Verso.

Javellana, Stevan (1976) *Without Seeing the Dawn* [1947], Quezon City: Phoenix.

Jeyaretnam, Philip (1987) *First Loves*, Singapore: Times Books International.

—— (1988) *Raffles Place Ragtime*, Singapore: Times Books International.

—— (1994) *Abraham's Promise*, Singapore: Times Books International.

Jit, Krishen (1989) 'Modern Theatre in Singapore: A Preliminary Survey', *Tenggara*, 23: 211–26.

—— (2003) *An Uncommon Position: Selected Writings*, Singapore: Contemporary Arts Centre.

Joaquin, Nick (1952) *Prose and Poems*, Manila: Graphic House.

—— (1966) *A Portrait of the Artist as Filipino: An Elegy in Three Scenes* [1952], Manila: A. S. Florentino.

—— (1972) *The Woman Who Had Two Navels* [1961], Manila: Solidaridad.

—— (1977) *A Question of Heroes*, Manila: National Book Store.

—— (1979) *Tropical Baroque: Four Manileño Theatricals*, Quezon City: National Bookstore.

—— (1983) *The Aquinos of Tarlac: An Essay of the History of Three Generations*, Manila: Cacho Hermanos.

—— (1987) *Collected Verse*, Quezon City: Ateneo de Manila University Press.

—— (2003) *Cave and Shadows* [1983], Pasig City: Anvil Publishing.

Jones, R. A. *et al.* (1989) 'Malaysia', in Patricia Herbert and Andrew Milner (eds), *South-East Asia Languages and Literatures: A Select Guide*, 99–122.

Jose, F. Sionil (1962) *The Pretenders*, Manila: Solidaridad.

—— (1978) *Tree*, Manila: Solidaridad.

—— (1979) *Mass: A Novel*, Manila: Solidaridad.

—— (1979) *My Brother, My Executioner*, Quezon City: New Day Publishers.

—— (1984) *Po-on*, Manila: Solidaridad.

—— (1993) *Viajero*, Manila: Solidaridad.

—— (1999) *Don Vicente*, New York: Modern Library.

Jurilla, Patricia May B. (2008) *Tagalog Bestsellers of the Twentieth Century: A History of the Book in the Philippines*, Quezon City: Ateneo de Manila University Press.

Kahn, Joel S. (ed.) (1998) *Southeast Asian Identities: Culture and the Politics of Representation in Indonesia, Malaysia, Singapore, and Thailand*, New York: St Martin's Press; Singapore: Institute of Southeast Asian Studies.

Kaiser, Timothy (2003) *Food Court*, Hong Kong: Chameleon Press.

Kakiseni.com. Online. HTTP available: http://www.kakiseni.com.my/ (accessed 14 May 2008).

Kalaw, Maximo Manguiat (1964) *The Filipino Rebel: A Romance of American Occupation in the Philippines* [1930], Manila: Filipiana Book Guild.

Karim Raslan (1996) *Heroes and Other Stories*, Singapore: Times Editions.

Kathigasu, Sybil (1954) *No Dram of Mercy* London: Spearman, 1954; rpt. Singapore: Oxford University Press, 1983.

Kee Thuan Chye (1987) *1984 Here and Now*, Petaling Jaya: K. Das Ink.

—— (1995) *We Could **** You Mr Birch*, rev. edn, Penang: Kee Thuan Chye.

Kerr, Douglas (2001) 'Introduction to *A Hong Kong House*', *Edmund Blunden: A Hong Kong House, Poems 1951–1961* [1962], Hong Kong: Hong Kong University Press, 99–106.

—— (2008) *Eastern Figures: Orient and Empire in British Writing*, Hong Kong: Hong Kong University Press.

Khoo Gaik Cheng (2007) 'Just-Do-It-(Yourself): Independent Filmmaking in Malaysia', *Inter-Asia Cultural Studies* 8.2: 227–47.

Kilates, Marne L. (1988) *Children of the Snarl and Other Poems*, Manila: Aklat Peskador.

Koh, Andrew (1995) *Glass Cathedral*, Singapore: EPB Publishers.

Koh Tai Ann (ed.) (2008) *Singapore Literature in English: An Annotated Bibliography*, Singapore: National Library Board and Nanyang Technological University.

Kon, Stella (1989) *Emily of Emerald Hill: A Monodrama*, London: Macmillan.

Krishnan, Sanjay (1997) 'What Art Makes Possible: Remembering Forum Theatre', in Sanjay Krishnan (ed.), *Nine Lives: 10 Years of Singapore Theatre, 1987–1997*, Singapore: The Necessary Stage, 200–11.

Kuo Pao Kun (2000a) *Images at the Margins: A Collection of Kuo Pao Kun's Plays*, Singapore: Times Books International.

—— (2000b) 'Knowledge Structure and Play – A Side View of Civil Society in Singapore', in Gillian Koh and Ooi Giok Ling (eds), *State-Society Relations in Singapore*, Singapore: IPS and Oxford University Press, 210–18.

—— (2003) *Two Plays by Kuo Pao Kun: 'Descendants of the Eunuch Admiral' and 'The Spirits Play'*, ed. C. J. W.-L. Wee and Lee Chee Keng, Singapore: SNP.

Kwa, Lydia (2002) *This Place Called Absence*, Rutherford, NJ: Kensington.

Kwan-Terry, John (1984) 'Narration and the Structure of Experience: The Fiction of Lee Kok Liang', in Colin E. Nicholson and Ranjit Chatterjee (eds), *Tropic Crucible: Self and Theory in Language and Literature*, Singapore: Singapore University Press, 143–62.

—— (1991) 'Ulysses Circling the Merlion: The Invention of Identity in Singapore Poetry in English and Chinese', in Edwin Thumboo (ed.) *Perceiving Other Worlds*, Singapore, Times Academic Press for UniPress, 115–38.

Kwok Kian-Woon and Kee-Hong Low (2002) 'Cultural Policy and the City-State: Singapore and the "New Asian Renaissance"', in Diana Crane, Nobuko Kawashima and Ken'ichi Kawasaki (eds), *Global Culture: Media, Arts, Policy and Globalization*, London: Routledge, 149–68.

Lam, Agnes (1997) *Woman to Woman*, Hong Kong: Asia 2000.
—— (2001) *Water Wood Pure Splendour*, Hong Kong: Asia 2000.
Laslo, Pablo (ed.) (1934) *English-German Anthology of Filipino Poets*, Manila: Libreria Manila Filatelica.
Latorena, Paz (1975) 'Desire' [1928], in Leopold Y. Yabes (ed.), *Philippine Short Stories 1925–1940*, 73–9.
Lau Siew Mei (2000) *Playing Madame Mao*, Rose Bay: Brandl and Schlesinger.
Laya, Juan Cabreros (1950) *This Barangay*, Manila: Inang Wika.
—— (1972) *His Native Soil* [1941], Quezon City: Kayumanggi.
le Carré, John (1977) *The Honourable Schoolboy*, London: Hodder & Stoughton.
Lee, Aaron (2007) *Five Right Angles*, Singapore: Ethos Books.
Lee, C. Y. (1964) *The Virgin Market*, New York: Farrar, Straus & Cudahy.
Lee Ding Fai (1980) *Running Dog*, Hong Kong: Heinemann Asia.
Lee, Johann S. (1992) *Peculiar Chris*, Singapore: Cannon International.
—— (2007) *To Know Where I'm Coming From*, Singapore: Cannon International.
Lee Kok Liang (1963) *The Mutes in the Sun and Other Stories*, Kuala Lumpur: Rayirath (Raybooks) Publications.
—— (1981) *Flowers in the Sky*, Kuala Lumpur: Heinemann Asia.
—— (2003) *London Does Not Belong to Me*, ed. Syd Harrex and Bernard Wilson, Petaling Jaya: Maya Press.
Lee, Vicky (2004) *Being Eurasian: Memories Across Racial Divides*, Hong Kong: Hong Kong University Press.
Lee, Tzu Pheng (1980) *Prospect of a Drowning*, Singapore: Heinemann.
—— (1988) *Against the Next Wave*, Singapore: Times Books International.
—— (1991) *The Brink of an Amen*, Singapore: Times Books International.
Leo, Petrina and Terence Lee (2004) 'The "New" Singapore: Mediating Culture and Creativity', *Continuum* 18.2: 205–218.
Leong Liew Geok (1991) *Love Is Not Enough*, Singapore: Times Books International.
Leong, Margaret (1958) *Rivers to Senang*, Singapore: Eastern Universities Press.
Leow Puay Tin (1996) 'Family', in Chin Woon Ping (ed.), *Playful Phoenix: Women Write for the Singapore Stage*, Singapore: Theatreworks: 159–269
Leung Ping-Kwan (1992) *City at the End of Time*, Hong Kong: Asia 2000 Limited.
—— (2002) *Travelling with a Bitter Melon: Selected Poems, 1973——1998*, Hong Kong: Asia 2000 Limited.
Licad, Abigail (2006) Review of *Pinoy Poetics*, ed. Nick Carbo, *Galatea Resurrects #1 (A Poetry Review)*. Online. HTTP available: http://galatearesurrection. blogspot.com/ (accessed 5 May 2008).
Lim, Beda (1950) 'Talking of Verses by Malayan Students', *Magazine of the University of Malaya Students' Union* (1949–1950), 1–4.
Lim Boon Keng (1927) *Tragedies of Eastern Life: An Introduction to the Problems of Social Psychology*, Shanghai, Commercial Press.
Lim, Catherine (1978) *Little Ironies: Stories of Singapore*, Singapore: Heinemann Asia.
—— (1980) *Or Else, The Lightning God and Other Stories*, Singapore: Heinemann Asia.
—— (1982) *The Serpent's Tooth*, Singapore: Times Books International.
—— (1995) *The Bondmaid*, Singapore: Catherine Lim.
—— (1998) *The Teardrop Story Woman*, London: Orion.

—— (2001) *Following the Wrong God Home*, London: Orion.

Lim Choon Yeoh and Lionel Wee (2001) 'Reduplication in Colloquial Singapore English', in Vincent B. Y. Ooi (ed.), *Evolving Identities: The English Language in Singapore and Malaysia*, Singapore: Times Academic Press, 89–101.

Lim Chor Pee (196?) *Mimi Fan*, photocopied typescript, National University of Singapore Library.

—— (196?) *A White Rose at Midnight*, photocopied typescript, National University of Singapore Library.

Lim, E. H. (1946) 'On the Road to Arab Street', *Raffles College Union Magazine*, 1: 28–9.

Lim, Janet (1958) *Sold for Silver: An Autobiography*, London: Collins.

Lim, Shirley Geok-lin (1980) *Crossing the Peninsula & Other Poems*, Kuala Lumpur: Heinemann Asia.

—— (1982) *Another Country and Other Stories*, Singapore: Times Book International.

—— (1985) *No Man's Grove*, Singapore: Department of English Language and Literature, National University of Singapore.

—— (1989a) 'Finding a Native Voice – Singapore Literature in English', *Journal of Commonwealth Literature*, 24: 30–47.

—— (1989b) *Modern Secrets*, Mundelstrup, Denmark and Sydney: Dangaroo Press.

—— (1993) *Nationalism and Literature: English Language Writing from the Philippines and Singapore*. Quezon City, New Day Publications.

—— (1994) *Writing S.E./Asia in English: Against the Grain, Focus on Asian English-language Literature*, London: Skoob Books.

—— (1995) *Life's Mysteries: The Best of Shirley Lim*, Singapore: Times Books International.

—— (1996) *Among the White Moonfaces: Memoirs of a Nonya Feminist*, Singapore: Times Books International.

—— (1997) *Two Dreams: New and Selected Stories*, New York: Feminist Press.

—— (1998) *What the Fortune Teller Didn't Say*, Alburquerque, NM: West End Press.

—— (2001) *Joss & Gold*, Singapore: Times Books International.

—— (2006) *Sister Swing*, Singapore: Marshall Cavendish.

—— (2008) *Princess Shawl*, Petaling Jaya: Maya Press.

Lim, Suchen Christine (1984) *Rice Bowl*, Singapore: Times Books International.

—— (1990) *Gift from the Gods*, Singapore: Graham Brash.

—— (2001) *A Bit of Earth*, Singapore: Times Books International.

—— (2003) *Fistful of Colours* [1993], Singapore: EPB.

—— (2007) *The Lies that Build a Marriage: Stories of the Unsung, Unsaid and Uncelebrated in Singapore*, Singapore: Monsoon Books.

Lim Thean Soo (1951) *Selected Verses*, Singapore: privately printed.

—— (1953) *Poems (1951–1953)*, Singapore: S. Sim at the University of Malaya.

—— (1978) *Ricky Star*, Singapore: Pan Pacific.

Lim-Wilson, Fatima (1991a) *Wandering Roots 1978–1988*, Pasig City: Anvil Publishing.

—— (1991b) *From the Hothouse 1989–1990*, Pasig City: Anvil Publishing.

—— (1995) *Crossing the Snow Bridge*, Columbus, OH: Ohio State University Press; Manila: De La Salle University Press.

Lin Tai-yi (1964) *Kampoon Street*, Cleveland: World Publishing Company.

Lin Yu-tang (1965) *The Flight of the Innocents*, Hong Kong: Dragonfly Books.

Literature and Society: A Symposium on the Relation of Literature to Social Change (1964), Manila: Alberto S. Florentino.

Literatura. Online. HTTP available: http://www.geocities.com/phil_literatura/main. html (accessed 14 May 2008).

Litmus One (Selected University Verse: 1949–57) (1958), Singapore: University of Singapore, Raffles Society.

Lo, Jacqueline (2004) *Staging Nation: English Language Theatre in Malaysia and Singapore*, Hong Kong: Hong Kong University Press.

Loh, Vyvyane (2004) *Breaking the Tongue*, New York: Norton.

Lopez, Salvador P. (1940) *Literature and Society: Essays on Life and Letters*, Manila: University Book Supply.

Lorenz, Val (1980) *Hong Kong Bridges*, Delhi: Services Press.

Low Ee Ling and Adam Brown (2003) *An Introduction to Singapore English*, Singapore: McGraw-Hill Education (Asia).

Lucero, Rosario Cruz (2003) *Feast and Famine: Stories of Negros*, Quezon City: University of the Philippines Press.

Lumban, M. (1932) 'Tell Malaya', *Raffles College Magazine*, Vol. 2, no. 3 (Michaelmas Term 1931), 6–10.

Lumbera, Bienvenido (1984) 'The Dramatic Impulse and the Filipino', *Revaluation: Essays on Philippine Literature, Cinema, and Popular Culture*, Manila: Index Press, 161–79.

McArthur, Tom (ed.) (1992) *The Oxford Companion to the English Language*. Oxford, New York: Oxford University Press.

Macaulay, Thomas Babington (1952) *Macaulay: Prose and Poetry*, ed. G. M. Young, London: Rupert Hart-Davis.

Malaysiakini. Online. HTTP available: http://www.malaysiakini.com/ (accessed 14 May 2008).

Manalang Gloria, Angela (1993) *The Complete Poems of Angela Manalang Gloria*, ed. Edna Zapanta-Manlapaz, Quezon City: Ateneo de Manila University Press.

Maniam, K. S. (1981) *The Return*, Kuala Lumpur: Heinemann Asia.

—— (1989) *Plot, The Aborting, Parablames and Other Stories*, Kuala Lumpur: AMK Interaksi.

—— (1993) *In a Far Country*, London: Skoob Books.

—— (1994) *Sensuous Horizons: The Stories and the Plays*, London: Skoob Books.

—— (2003) *Between Lives*, Petaling Jaya: Maya Press.

—— (2004) *Faced Out*, Petaling Jaya: Maya Press.

Manicka, Rani (2002) *The Rice Mother*, London, Sceptre

—— (2004) *Touching Earth*, London: Sceptre.

Marino, Pilar E. (ed.) (1989) *Philippine Short Stories in Spanish: 1900–1941*, Quezon City: Office of Research Coordination, University of the Philippines.

Marquez-Benitez, Paz (1975) 'Dead Stars' [1925], in Leopoldo Y. Yabes (ed.), *Philippine Short Stories: 1925–1940*, 1–19.

Millado, Chris (2000) 'Scenes from an Unfinished Country', in *The Likhaan Book of Philippine Drama 1991–1996*, Quezon City: University of the Philippines Press, 180–243.

Mo, Timothy (1978) *The Monkey King*, London: André Deutsch.

—— (1982) *Sour Sweet*, London: André Deutsch.

—— (1986) *An Insular Possession*, London: Chatto and Windus.

Modder, R. (1993) *Lions and Tigers*, Singapore: Roseapple.

—— (2003) *Souls the Gods Had Forsaken*, Singapore: Horizon.

Mojares, Resil B. (1983) *Origins and Rise of the Filipino Novel*, Quezon City: University of the Philippines Press.

National Library Board, Singapore, *NORA: NLB Online Repository of Artistic Works*. Online. HTTP available: http://www.nlb.gov.sg (accessed 14 May 2008).

New, Christopher (1979) *Goodbye Chairman Mao*, New York: Coward, McCann & Geoghan.

Ng, Francis P. (1935) *F. M. S. R.: A Poem*, London: Arthur H. Stockwell.

Ng Yi-Sheng (2006) *last boy*, Singapore: Firstfruits Publications.

Ngiam Tong Dow (1958), 'Correspondence', *Write*, no. 2 (January), 2.

Nguyen The Anh (1989) 'Vietnam', in Patricia Herbert and Andrew Milner (eds), *South-East Asia Languages and Literatures: A Select Guide*, 77–98.

Nor Faridah Abdul Manaf and Mohammad A. Quayum (2001) *Colonial to Global: Malaysian Women's Writing in English 1940s-1990s*, Kuala Lumpur: International Islamic University Malaysia.

Ong, Aihwa (1987) *Spirits of Resistance and Capitalist Discipline: Factory Women in Malaysia*, Albany: State University of New York Press.

Ong, Charlson (1990) *Men of the East and Other Stories*, Quezon City: University of the Philippines Press.

—— (2000) *An Embarrassment of Riches*, Quezon City: University of the Philippines Press.

—— (2006) *Banyaga: A Song of War*, Manila: Anvil Publishing.

Ong Keng Sen (1999) *LEAR*, Singapore Programme.

Ong, Richard (1949) 'Asian Peasant', *Raffles College Union Magazine*, Vol. 3 (1948–1949), 22–23.

Ooi Yang-May (1998) *The Flame Tree*, London: Hodder and Stoughton.

—— (2000) *Mindgame*, London: Coronet.

Owen, Norman G. (1992) 'Economic and Social Change', in Nicholas Tarling (ed.), *The Cambridge History of Southeast Asia*, Vol. 2, 467–528.

—— (ed.) (2005) *The Emergence of Modern Southeast Asia: A New History*, Singapore: Singapore University Press.

Pang, Alvin (2007a) 'Verbosity', 'why i write: albany remix' (30.09.2007). Online. HTTP available: http://www.verbosity.net/creative/read.asp?id=141 (accessed 15 June 2008).

—— (2007b) 'Verbosity', 'when the barbarians arrive' (26.09.2007). Online. HTTP available: http://www.verbosity.net/creative/read.asp?id=139 (accessed 15 June 2008).

—— (ed.) *Poetry Billboard*. Online. HTTP available: http://www.poetrybillboard.com/ (accessed 14 May 2008).

Panganiban, Jose Villa (1927) *Stealer of Hearts*, Manila: University of Santo Tomas.

Panitikan.com.ph. Online. HTTP available: http://panitikan.com.ph/ (accessed 14 May 2008).

Pantoja Hidalgo, Cristina (1996) *Recuerdo*, Quezon City: University of the Philippines Press.

Pennycook, Alastair (1994) *The Cultural Politics of English as an International Language*, Harlow, Essex and New York: Longman.

—— (1998) *English and the Discourses of Colonialism*, London and New York: Routledge.

Platt, John and Heidi Weber (1980) *English in Singapore and Malaysia – Status: Features: Functions*, Kuala Lumpur: Oxford University Press.

Platt, John, Heidi Weber and Mian Lian Ho (1983) *Varieties of English around the World: Singapore and Malaysia*, Amsterdam and Philadelphia: John Benjamins.

—— (1984) *The New Englishes*, London and Boston: Routledge.

Poh Wah Lam (2004) *The Locust Hunter*, London: Black Amber Books.

Polotan, Kerima (1962) *The Hand of the Enemy*, Manila: Regal.

Poon, Wena (2007) *Lions in Winter*, Petaling Jaya: MPH Publications.

[Puthucheary] J. J. (1951) 'Malayan Literature as Seen through the Eyes of J. J.', *The New Cauldron* (Michaelmas and Hilary terms 1950–1951), 18–20.

Price, Anthony (1974) 'This Crippled but Colourful Dialect: The Language of Malayan Plays', *Journal of Commonwealth Literature*, 9.1: 3–10.

Puru Shotam, Nirmala (1989) 'Language and Linguistic Policies', in Kernial Singh Sandhu and Paul Wheatley (eds), *Management of Success: The Moulding of Modern Singapore*, Singapore: Institute of Southeast Asian Studies, 503–22.

Quah Sy Ren (2006) 'Performing Multilingualism in Singapore', in Jennifer Lindsay (ed.), *Between Tongues: Translation and/of/in Performance in Asia*, Singapore: NUS Press, 88–103.

Quayum, Mohammad A. (2003) 'Malaysian Literature in English: A Bibliography of Primary Works', *The Journal of Commonwealth Literature*, 38.2: 146–52.

Rajaratnam, S. (1987) 'Malayan Culture: A Reply to the Sceptics' [1959], *The Prophetic and the Political: Selected Speeches and Writings of S. Rajaratnam*, ed. Chan Heng Chee and Obaid ul Haq, Singapore: Graham Brash, 111–15.

Rao, Mani (2006) *100 Poems 1985–2005*, Hong Kong: Chameleon Press.

Rehman Rashid (1993) *A Malaysian Journey*, Petaling Jaya: Rehman Rashid.

Reid, Anthony (1988) *Southeast Asia in the Age of Commerce, 1450–1680. Volume One: The Lands Below the Winds*, New Haven: Yale University Press.

—— (1992) 'Economic and Social Change, c.1400–1800', in Nicholas Tarling (ed.), *The Cambridge History of Southeast Asia*, Vol. 1, 460–507.

—— (1999) *Charting the Shape of Early Modern Southeast Asia*, Chiang Mai: Silkworm.

Rivera, Aida L. (1957) *Now and at the Hour*, Manila: Benipayo Press.

Roces, Alejandrino R. (1959) *Of Cocks and Kites and Other Short Stories*, Manila: Regal.

Rosca, Ninotchka (1992) *Twice Blessed*, New York: Norton.

—— (2005) *State of War* [1988], Pasig City: Anvil Publishing.

Roseburg, Arturo G. (1959) 'Introduction' to Alejandro. R. Roces *Of Cocks and Kites and Other Short Stories*, iii–v.

Rotor, A. B. (1937a) 'The Filipino Short Story: Ten Years of Experiment', *Philippine Magazine*, 34 (January):19–20, 41–2.

—— (1937b) *The Wound and the Scar: Selected Stories*, Manila: Philippine Book Guild.

—— (1975a) 'Flower Shop' [1934], in Leopold Y. Yabes (ed.), *Philippine Short Stories, 1925–1940*, 51–61.

—— (1975b) 'Zita' [1930], in Leopold Y. Yabes (ed.), *Philippine Short Stories, 1925–1940*, 108–119.

Salanga, Alfrredo Navarro (1984) *The Birthing of Hannibal Valdez*, Quezon City: New Day.

—— (1998) *Buena Vista Ventures: Poetry and Prose*, ed. Danton Remoto, Manila: Office of Research and Publications, Ateneo de Manila University Press.

Salleh Ben Joned (2007) *Adam's Dream*, Kuala Lumpur: Silverfish Books.

Santillan-Castrence, P. (1967) 'The Period of Apprenticeship', in Antonio G. Manuud (ed.), *Brown Heritage: Essays on Philippine Cultural Tradition and Literature*, Quezon City: Ateneo de Manila University Press, 546–74.

Santos, Bienvenido (1955) *You Lovely People*, Manila: Benipayo Press.

—— (1956) *The Wounded Stag: Fifty Poems*, Manila: Capitol.

—— (1982) *The Praying Man*, Quezon City: New Day.

—— (1983) *Distances: In Time, Selected Poems*, Quezon City: Ateneo de Manila University Press.

—— (1986a) *Villa Magdalena* [1965], Quezon City: New Day.

—— (1986b) *The Volcano* [1965], Quezon City: New Day.

—— (1991) *Brother, My Brother: A Collection of Stories* [1960], Manila: Bookmark.

Sarkissian, Margaret (2000) *D'Albuquerque's Children: Performing Tradition in Malaysia's Portuguese Settlement*, Chicago: University of Chicago Press.

Satha-Anand, Chaiwat (2006) 'Fostering "Authoritarian Democracy": The Effect of Violent Solutions in Southern Thailand', in Vedi R. Hadiz (ed.), *Empire and Neoliberalism in Asia*, London: Routledge, 169–87.

Schneider, Edgar W. (2007) *Postcolonial English: Varieties around the World*, Cambridge: Cambridge University Press.

Sering, Tara F. T. (2003) *Almost Married*, Quezon City: Summit.

Sharma, Haresh (1999) *This Chord and Others: A Collection of Plays*, London: Minerva.

—— (2000) *Off Centre*, Singapore: Ethos.

Shawwa, Dania (ed.) (2005) *Hong Kong ID: Short Stories from the City's Hidden Writers*, Hong Kong: Haven Books.

Shelley, Rex (1991) *The Shrimp People*, Singapore: Times Books International.

—— (1993) *People of the Pear Tree*, Singapore: Times Books International.

Shiau, Daren (1999) *Heartland*, Singapore: SNP Editions.

Sim, Katherine (1961) *The Jungle Ends Here*, London: Hodder & Stoughton.

Singh, Kirpal (1978) 'Singaporean and Malaysian Literature in English', in Chris Tiffin (ed.), *South Pacific Images*, Brisbane: University of Queensland, 68–80.

—— (1986) *Palm Readings*, Singapore: Graham Brash.

Siu, Margaret (1997) *Her Majesty the Comrade: A Novel of Hong Kong 1997*, Hong Kong: Marsell.

So, Joshua L. Lim (2006) 'Feasting', in Dean Francis Alfar (ed.), *Philippine Speculative Fiction*, Vol. 2, Pasig City: Kestrel, 93–99

Soh, Michael (1973) *Son of a Mother*, Singapore: Oriental University Press.

Solomon, J. S. (1988) *The Development of Bilingual Education in Malaysia*, Kuala Lumpur: Pelanduk Publications.

Stockwell, A. J. (1992) 'Southeast Asia in War and Peace: The End of European Colonial Empires', in Nicholas Tarling (ed.), *The Cambridge History of Southeast Asia*, Vol. 2, 329–86.

'Straits Chinese Volunteer' (1901) 'The Belicose Mongolians', *Straits Chinese Magazine*, 5.2 (Dec): 135–6.

Sudham, Pira (1988) *Monsoon Country*, Bangkok: Shire Books.

'Talaq Documents' (2001) *Focas: Forum on Contemporary Art and Society*, 1: 181–210.

Tan, Adrian (1988) *The Teenage Textbook, or, the Melting of the Ice Cream Girl*, Singapore: Hotspot Books.

Tan, Alvin (1997) 'A Necessary Practice', in Sanjay Krishnan (ed.), *Nine Lives: 10 Years of Singapore Theatre, 1987–1997*, 251–72.

Tan Chong Kee (2004) 'Introduction', in Tan Chong Kee and Tisa Ng (eds.) *Ask Not: The Necessary Stage in Singapore Theatre*, ix-xvi.

Tan Chong Kee and Tisa Ng (eds.) (2004) *Ask Not: The Necessary Stage in Singapore Theatre*, Singapore: Marshall Cavendish.

Tan, Gene (ed.) (1994) *Celebrations: Singapore Creative Writing in English, A Bibliography*, Singapore: National Library.

Tan Han Hoe (ed.) (1958) *30 Poems (University of Malaya Poems 1957–1958)*, Singapore: Raffles Society, University of Malaya.

Tan Hwee Hwee (1997) *Foreign Bodies*, London: Penguin.

—— (2002) *Mammon Inc* [2001], London: Penguin.

Tan Teck Howe (2004) *The Secret Goldfish and Other Follies*, Singapore: Firstfruits.

Tan Twan Eng (2007) *The Gift of Rain*, Newcastle: Myrmidon.

Tarling, Nicholas (ed.) (1992) *The Cambridge History of Southeast Asia: Volume 1: From Early Times to c.1800*, Cambridge: Cambridge University Press.

—— (ed.) (1992) *The Cambridge History of Southeast Asia: Volume 2: The Nineteenth and Twentieth Centuries*, Cambridge: Cambridge University Press.

Tay, Eddie (2002) 'On Writing Poetry in Singapore', *Quarterly Literary Review Singapore*, Vol. 1 No. 3 (April). Online. HTTP available: http://www.qlrs.com/issues/apr2002/interviews/apysh.html (accessed 15 June 2008).

Tay, Simon (1991) *Stand Alone*, Singapore: Landmark.

—— (2008) *City of Small Blessings*, Singapore: Landmark.

Taylor, Keith W. (1992) 'The Early Kingdoms', in Nicholas Tarling (ed.), *The Cambridge History of Southeast Asia*, Vol. 1, 137–82.

Teo, Hsu-Ming (2000) *Love and Vertigo*, St Leonards, NSW: Allen & Unwin.

—— (2005) *Behind the Moon*, Crows Nest, NSW: Allen & Unwin.

Tham, Claire (1990) *Fascist Rock: Stories of Rebellion*, Singapore: Times Books International.

—— (1993) *Saving the Rainforest and Other Stories*, Singapore: Times Books International.

—— (1999) *Skimming*, Singapore: Times Books International.

—— (2003) *The Gunpowder Trail and Other Short Stories*, Singapore: Times Books International.

Tham, Hilary (1989) *Bad Names For Women*, Washington, D.C.: Word Works Capital Collection.

The Other Malaysia. Online. HTTP available: http://www.othermalaysia.org/ (accessed 14 May 2008).

Theroux, Paul (1976) *Saint Jack* [1973], London: Penguin.

Thompson, Roger M. (2003) *Filipino English and Taglish: Language Switching from Multiple Perspectives*, Amsterdam and Philadelphia: John Benjamins.

Thumboo, Edwin (1956) *Rib of Earth*, Singapore: Lloyd Fernando.

—— (ed.) (1973) *Seven Poets: Singapore and Malaysia*. Singapore: Singapore University Press.

—— (ed.) (1985) *Anthologies of ASEAN Literatures: The Poetry of Singapore*, Singapore: ASEAN Committee on Culture and Information.

—— (1988) 'History, Language, Paradigms, Lacunae', in Edwin Thumboo (ed.), *Literature and Liberation: Five Essays from Southeast Asia*, Manila: Solidaridad Publishing House, 123–53.

—— (1990) 'New Literatures in English: Imperatives for a Comparative Approach', in Wolfgang Zach (ed.), *English Literature(s): New Perspectives*, Frankfurt: Peter Lang, 17–29.

—— (1993) *The Third Map: New and Selected Poems*, Singapore: Unipress, The Centre for the Arts.

—— (2008) *Still Travelling*, Singapore: Ethos Books.

Tiempo, Edilberto (1953) *Watch in the Night*, Manila: Archipelago.

Tiempo, Edith (1966) *The Tracks of Babylon and Other Poems*, Rpt, Quezon City: Giraffe Books, 1998.

—— (1978) *A Blade of Fern*, Hong Kong: Heinemann Asia.

—— (1993a) *The Charmer's Box: Poetry*, Manila: De La Salle University Press.

—— (1993b) *Extensions, Beyond*, Manila: La Diane, 1993.

—— (1999) *An Edith Tiempo Reader*, ed. Gemino H. Abad, Isagani R. Cruz, Cristina Pantoja Hidalgo, Alfred Yuson and Edna Zapanta-Manlapaz, Manila: University of the Philippines Press.

Toh Hsien Min (ed.) *QLRS: Quarterly Literary Review Singapore*. Online. HTTP available: http://www.qlrs.com/ (accessed 14 May 2008).

Tong, Richard (2003) *The Durian Effect: A Transethnite in Beijing's Backyard*, Hong Kong: Blue Melon.

—— (2005) *Me and My Potato*, Hong Kong: Blue Melon.

Tsai, Jung-Fang (1993) *Hong Kong in Chinese History; Community and Social Unrest in the British Colony, 1842–1913*, New York: Columbia University Press.

Tsang, Steve (2004) *A Modern History of Hong Kong*, Hong Kong: Hong Kong University Press.

Tu Weiming (1991) 'Cultural China: The Periphery as the Center', *Daedalus*, 120.2: 1–32.

Ty Casper, Linda (1963) *The Transparent Sun and Other Stories*, Manila: Alberto S. Florentino.

—— (1964) *The Peninsulars*, Manila: Bookmark.

—— (1980) *Dread Empire*, Hong Kong: Heinemann Asia.

—— (1996) *Dream Eden*: Quezon City, Ateneo de Manila University Press.

Villa, Jose Garcia (1933) *Footnote to Youth: Tales of the Philippines and Others*, New York: Scribner's.

—— (1942) *Have Come, Am Here*, New York: Viking.

—— (1993) *Selected Poems and New* [1958], Makati: Bookmark.

—— (2002) *The Critical Villa: Essays in Literary Criticism by Jose Garcia Villa*, ed. Jonathan Chua, Quezon City: Ateneo de Manila University Press.

Vittachi, Nury (2000) *The Feng Shui Detective*, Hong Kong: Chameleon.

Wang Gungwu (1950) *Pulse*, Singapore: B. Lim.

—— (1958) 'Trial and Error in Malayan Poetry', *Malayan Undergrad* (July): 6–7.

Watson Andaya, Barbara (1992) 'Political Development between the Sixteenth and Eighteenth Centuries', in Nicholas Tarling (ed.), *The Cambridge History of Southeast Asia*, Vol. 1, 402–507.

Wee, C. J. W[an]-L[ing] (2008) *The Asian Modern: Culture, Capitalist Development, Singapore*, Hong Kong: Hong Kong University Press.

Wee, Edmund (2004) *The Narcissist*, Singapore: Times Books International.

Wickberg, Edgar (2006) 'Hokkien-Philippines Familial Transnationalism, 1949–1975', in Maria N. Ng and Philip Holden (eds), *Reading Chinese Transnationalisms: Society, Literature, Film*, Hong Kong, Hong Kong University Press, 17–36.

Wignesan, T. (ed.) (1964) *Bunga Emas: An Anthology of Contemporary Malaysian Literature, 1930–1963*, Kuala Lumpur: Anthony Blond with Rayirath.

Wong, Cyril (2006) *like a seed with a singular purpose*, Singapore: Firstfruits Publications.

—— (ed.) *Softblow*. Online. HTTP available: http://www.softblow.com (accessed 14 May 2008).

Wong, David T. K. (1990) *Lost River and Other Stories*, Hong Kong: Asia 2000.

—— (1996) *Hong Kong Stories*, Hong Kong: CDN.

—— (2001) *Connections: Stories of East Asia*, Hong Kong: Asia 2000.

Wong, Eleanor (2005) *Invitation to Treat: The Eleanor Wong Trilogy*, Singapore: Firstfruits.

—— (2006) *Earlier*, Singapore: Firstfruits.

Wong, Francis Hoy Kee and Ee Tiang Hong (1975) *Education in Malaysia*, Kuala Lumpur: Heinemann Asia.

Wong Phui Nam (1958) *Toccata on Ochre Sheaves*, Singapore: Raffles Society, University of Malaya.

—— (1968) *How the Hills are Distant*, Kuala Lumpur: *Tenggara*, Department of English, University of Malaya.

—— (1987) 'Statement', in Kirpal Singh (ed.), *The Writer's Sense of the Past*, Singapore: Singapore University Press, 215–17.

—— (1989) *Remembering Grandma and Other Rumours*, Singapore: Department of English Language and Literature, National University of Singapore.

—— (2006) *An Acre of Day's Glass: Collected Poems*, Petaling Jaya, Kuala Lumpur: Maya Press.

Wong Wai Yen, Audrey (1997) 'Collaboration and Social Commitment in The Necessary Stage', in Sanjay Krishnan (ed.), *9 Lives: 10 Years of Singapore Theatre*, 193–9.

Woon, Walter Cheong Ming (2002) *The Advocate's Devil*, Singapore: Times Books International.

—— (2005) *The Devil to Pay*, Singapore: Marshall Cavendish.

Wu Shu-chiung [Ruth Huang] (1924) *Yang Kuei-Fei: The Most Famous Beauty of China*, London: Brentano's.

—— (1931) *Hsi Shih … Beauty of Beauties: A Romance of Ancient China about 495–472 B.C.*, Shanghai: Kelly & Walsh.

—— (1934) *Chao Chün: Beauty in Exile*, Shanghai: Kelly & Walsh.

Xu Xi (1996) *Daughters of Hui*, Hong Kong: Asia 2000.

—— (1997) *Hong Kong Rose*, Hong Kong: Asia 2000.

—— (2001) *The Unwalled City*, Hong Kong: Chameleon.

—— (2005) "Finding My English", in Dania Shawwa (ed.), *Hong Kong ID: Stories from the City's Hidden Writers*, Hong Kong: Haven Books, 175–87.

Xu Xi and Mike Ingham (eds) (2003) *City Voices: Hong Kong Writing in English: 1945 to the Present*, Hong Kong: Hong Kong University Press.

Yabes, Leopoldo Y. (ed.) (1975) *Philippine Short Stories: 1925–40*, Quezon City: University of the Philippines Press.

Yahp, Beth (1993) *The Crocodile Fury*, Singapore: Heinemann Asia.

Yap, Arthur (2000) *the space of city trees: selected poems*, London: Skoob Books.

Yeo, Robert (1986) *The Adventures of Holden Heng*, Singapore: Heinemann Asia.

—— (1999) *Leaving Home, Mother: Selected Poems*, Singapore: Angsana Books.

—— (2001) *The Singapore Trilogy*, Singapore: Landmark.

Yew, Chay (1997) *'Porcelain' and 'A Language of Their Own': Two Plays*, New York: Grove.

Yong Mun Cheong (1992) 'The Political Structures of Independent States', in Nicholas Tarling (ed.), *The Cambridge History of Southeast Asia*, Vol. 2, 387–466.

Yong Shu Hoong (1997) *Isaac*, Singapore: Firstfruits Publications.

—— (2005) *Frottage*, Singapore: Firstfruits Publications.

Yousof, Ghulum-Sarwar (2001) 'An Interview', *Mirror of a Hundred Hues: A Miscellany*, Gelugor: The Asian Centre, 133–54.

—— (2002) *Halfway Road, Penang* [1982], Gelugor: The Asian Centre.

Yu, Ovidia (1989) *Miss Moorthy Investigates*, Singapore: Hotspot Books.

Yuson, Alfred A. (1980) *Sea Serpent: Poems*, [S.l.]: Monsoon Press.

—— (1993) *Trading in Mermaids*, Pasig City: Anvil Publishing.

—— (1996) *The Great Philippine Jungle Energy Café* [1988], Quezon City: University of the Philippines Press.

—— (2003) *Voyeurs & Savages* [1998], 2nd edn, Manila: Anvil Publishing.

Zapanta-Manlapaz, Edna (ed.) (1994) *Songs Of Ourselves: Writings by Filipino Women in English*, Pasig City: Anvil Publishing.

Zulueta da Costa, R. (1937) *First Leaves*, Manila: McCullough.

—— (1940) *Like the Molave and Other Poems*, Manila: McCullough.

Guide to further reading

Bibliographies

Journal of Commonwealth Literature, annual bibliographies (one issue every year is devoted to regional bibliographies for the Commonwealth nations, which include useful surveys of primary and secondary materials concerning Singapore and Malaysia).

Koh Tai Ann (ed.) (2008) *Singapore Literature in English: An Annotated Bibliography*, Singapore: National Library Board and Nanyang Technological University.
The most up-to-date bibliography of primary material in English from Singapore, arranged by genres and with helpful annotations.

Quayum, Mohammad A. (2003) 'Malaysian Literature in English: A Bibliography of Primary Works', *The Journal of Commonwealth Literature*, 38.2: 146–52.
A thorough list divided by genres that covers the primary material in English from Malaysia.

Tim Yap Fuan (ed.) (2000) *Singapore Literature: A Select Bibliography of Critical Writings*, Singapore: National University of Singapore Library.
A useful list of critical work on the writing in English from Singapore, arranged by genre.

Yabes, Leopoldo Y. (1958) *Philippine Literature in English, 1898–1957: A Bibliographical Survey*, Quezon City: University of the Philippines Press.
A pioneering bibliographical survey that is now in need of updating.

Primary materials

Anthologies

Anthology of ASEAN Literatures (vols. 1, 1a, 1b, 2a, 2b, 3a, 3b), (1983–200) Singapore: ASEAN Committee on Culture and Information.
This set is invaluable for its inclusiveness and representation of English-language writing within the context of all the other languages in the ASEAN region, but it is primarily an anthology, and the critical material is limited to short introductions; also, curiously enough, it is circulated privately, and not as a commercial item that can be ordered from a publisher or a bookseller.

Abad, Gemino H. (ed.) (1998), *The Likhaan Anthology of Philippine Literature in English from 1900 to the Present*, Quezon City: University of the Philippines Press.

A very handy compilation which represents canonical work in poetry, drama, fiction and criticism within the covers of a single volume.

Francia, Luis H. (ed.) (1993) *Brown River, White Ocean: An Anthology of Twentieth-century Philippine Literature in English*, New Brunswick, N.J.: Rutgers University Press.

The most internationally accessible anthology of Philippine writing English.

Garcia, J. Neil C. and Danton Remoto (eds) (1994) *Ladlad: An Anthology of Philippine Gay Writing*, Pasig City: Anvil Publishing.

A first anthology of gay writing from the Philippines that has attracted a lot of attention locally and internationally, and was followed up with a second anthology of similar scope.

Poon, Angelia, Philip Holden and Shirley Geok-lin Lim (eds) (2009) *Writing Singapore: A Historical Anthology of Singapore Literature in English*, Singapore: NUS Press (forthcoming).

A projected historical anthology of literature in Singapore which covers work from the 1890s to the present.

Quayum, Mohammad A. (ed.) (2003) *Petals of Hibiscus: A Representative Anthology of Malaysian Literature in English*, Kuala Lumpur: Pearson Education.

Useful selection of Malaysian Literature in English over three generations.

Xu, Xi and Mike Ingham (eds) (2003) *City Voices: Hong Kong Writing in English: 1945 to the Present*, Hong Kong: Hong Kong University Press.

The best introduction to English writing from (and about) Hong Kong.

Yabes, Leopoldo Y. (ed.) (1975) *Philippine Short Stories: 1925–40*, Quezon City: University of the Philippines Press.

Important anthology of the best short stories from a period when the genre was central to Philippine literary production in English. Many of the stories were not published in book form.

Selected fiction: Philippines

Alfar, Dean Francis (2006) *Salamanca*, Quezon City: Ateneo de Manila University Press.

Magical realist novel by one of the most productive of a young generation of Filipino writers.

Alfon, Estrella D. (1960) *Magnificence*, Manila: Regal.

Short story collection that expresses a strong concern for the position of women against the background of a larger struggle for social equality.

Arguilla, Manuel E. (1940) *How My Brother Leon Brought Home a Wife and Other Stories*, Manila: Philippine Book Guild.

The most influential short story collection to emerge in the pre-war period, combining – and sometimes juxtaposing – accounts of rural and urban life.

Bulosan, Carlos (2006) *America is in the Heart* [1946], Pasig City: Anvil.

Personal history that includes testimony regarding the lives of Filipino migrant workers in America in the 1930s.

Brillantes, Gregorio C. (2000) *The Distance to Andromeda and Other Stories* [1960], Quezon City: University of the Philippines Press.
Short story collection set in provincial Tarlac, showing the ambivalent effects of modernization in the post-war period.

Dalisay, Jose Y., Jr. (2002) *Oldtimer and Other Stories* [1984], Quezon City: University of the Philippines Press.
Early short stories by an important contemporary prose writer and journalist.

—— (2005) *Selected Stories*, Quezon City: University of the Philippines Press.
A selection of the most significant stories written later in Dalisay's career.

Gamalinda, Eric (2000) *My Sad Republic*, Quezon City: University of the Philippines Press.
Winner of the English novel award in the Centennial Literary Prize in 1998, written by an influential author who now lives in the United States.

Gonzalez, N. V. M. (1998) *The Winds of April* [1941], Quezon City: University of the Philippines Press.
The most significant novel written in English in the Philippines before the outbreak of the Second Word War.

—— (1960) *Bamboo Dancers*, Manila: Benipayo.
Gonzalez's most influential novel, describing the expatriate experiences and then return of a Filipino from America in the post-war years.

Groyon, Vicente (2004) *The Sky Over Dimas*, Manila: University of Santo Tomas Press.
One of a growing number of novels by a new generation of writers that explores relationships between regional cultures and the metropolitan centre of Manila.

Joaquin, Nick (1972) *The Woman Who Had Two Navels* [1961], Manila: Solidaridad.
Possibly the most important Filipino novel of the twentieth century, with a complex and fragmentary plot set partly in Hong Kong.

—— (2003) *Cave and Shadows* [1983], Pasig City: Anvil.
Joaquin's second novel, which explores the disturbing presence of colonial and precolonial pasts in contemporary life.

Jose, F. Sionil (1999) *Don Vicente*, New York: Modern Library.
Contains the full text of *Tree* and *My Brother, My Executioner*, two central texts in Jose's epic Rosales series of five novels.

—— (1993) *Viajero*, Manila: Solidaridad.
The most important of Jose's novels after the completion of the Rosales saga.

Lucero, Rozario Cruz (2003) *Feast and Famine: Stories of Negros*, Quezon City: University of the Philippines Press.
Formally innovative short stories that express a strong sense of regional identity.

Ong, Charlson (2000) *Men of the East and Other Stories*, [1990] Quezon City: University of the Philippines Press.
Pioneering series of stories describing the experience of Chinese immigrants to the Philippines, contrasting their experiences with that of later-generation Chinoy [Chinese Filipino] characters who feel no attachment to China.

—— (2006) *Banyaga: A Song of War*, Manila: Anvil Publishing.
Epic narrative that plots the fluid identity of a Chinese Filipino family over a century of conflict and social change.

Rosca, Ninotchka (2005) *State of War* [1988], Pasig City: Anvil Publishing.
Important novel about the period of martial law, set on an island that symbolizes the Philippines in miniature .

Santos, Bienvenido (1980) *Villa Magdalena* [1965], Quezon City: New Day.
Exploring conflicts within an elite family, this is one of several significant novels by this important writer who eventually migrated to the United States.

Tiempo, Edith (1979) *A Blade of Fern*, Hong Kong: Heinemann.
One of a number of important novels by a writer who was also a formative force in teaching creative writing in the Philippines.

Yuson, Alfred A. (1996) *The Great Philippine Jungle Energy Café* [1988], Quezon City: University of the Philippines Press.
Exuberant postmodern novel that plays with two characters, the researcher and writer Roberto Aguinaldo in the present and the historical revolutionary León Kilat.

Selected fiction: Malaysia

Dina Zaman (1997) *Night and Day*, Petaling Jaya: Rhino Press.
Short story collection set in urban Kuala Lumpur in the 1990s, looking not only at the experience of the elite but also that of the marginalized.

Fernando, Lloyd (1976) *Scorpion Orchid*, Kuala Lumpur: Heinemann Asia.
Novel set in Singapore in the 1950s, exploring tensions across ethnicity and class in a society undergoing decolonization.

—— (1993) *Green Is the Colour*, Singapore: Landmark Books.
Novel set in a dystopic alternative future that emerges from the political tensions and civil disturbances in Kuala Lumpur following the federal election of 1969.

Karim Raslan (1996) *Heroes and Other Stories*, Singapore: Times Editions.
Short story collection that exposes the hypocrisies of the cultural elite in Kuala Lumpur during the Malaysian economic boom of the 1990s.

Lee Kok Liang (1963) *The Mutes in the Sun and Other Stories*, Kula Lumpur: Rayirath (Raybooks) Publications.
Sophisticated stories which range widely in setting and theme, and explore the fault-lines of a modernizing society.

—— (2003) *London Does Not Belong to Me*, ed. Syd Harrex and Bernard Wilson, Petaling Jaya: Maya Press.
Posthumously published novel that describes the experiences of a Malayan-Chinese student in London in the 1950s.

Lim, Shirley Geok-Lin (2001) *Joss and Gold*, Singapore: Times Editions.
Transnational novel centred on the lives of a young Chinese Malaysian woman and an American Peace Corps worker, with three sections set in Malaysia, America and Singapore respectively.

Maniam, K. S. (1981) *The Return*, Kuala Lumpur: Heinemann Asia.
Autobiographical novel that describes the struggles of a young Indian Malaysian who moves outside his family and community into a wider world, precipitating a personal struggle for cultural identity.

—— (2000) *Between Lives*, Petaling Jaya: Maya Books.
As with many of Maniam's works, this novel attempts to rediscover a historical past of the Indian presence in Malaysia.

Tan Twan Eng (2008) *The Gift of Rain,* Newcastle: Myrmidon.
Sprawling epic novel that describes interactions between British, Chinese, Eurasian and Japanese characters before and during the Japanese occupation of Penang in the Second World War, while also documenting the consequences of these events in the present.

Selected fiction: Singapore

Alfian bin Sa'at (1999) *Corridor,* Singapore: Raffles.
Short story collection exploring the lives of a new generation of Singaporeans who have grown up living in a developed, highly urbanized environment.
Baratham, Gopal (1991) *A Candle or the Sun,* London: Serpent's Tail.
Novel describing the persecution and detention of members of a religious group by the city-state's authorities.
Cher, Ming (1995) *Spider Boys,* Auckland: Penguin.
Novel set in an urban kampong (shanty town) in the 1960s; written in what the author describes as 'roadside English', producing a unique voice and perspective on a historically important time.
Goh Poh Seng (1972) *If We Dream Too Long,* Singapore: Island Press.
The first post-independence novel in Singapore in English; describes the experiences of a clerk who is disorientated by social and economic changes in a modernizing society.
Jeyaretnam, Philip (1994) *Abraham's Promise,* Singapore: Times Books International.
Elegiac novel narrated by an older man who is alienated by Singapore's rapid economic growth and utilitarian modernity.
Lim, Catherine (1978) *Little Ironies: Stories of Singapore,* Singapore: Heinemann Asia.
First collection of short stories by Singapore's most prolific novelist and short story writer in English.
Lim, Suchen Christine (2003) *Fistful of Colours* [1993], Singapore: EPB.
Most important novel by a prose writer whose deeply historical fiction has become central to the Singapore canon.
Lim, Thean Soo (1978) *Ricky Star,* Singapore: Pan Pacific.
Historically significant novel set in Singapore during the years of its transformation from a colonial entrepôt to an economically developed city-state.
Poon, Wena (2007) *Lions in Winter,* Petaling Jaya: MPH Publications.
Collection of short stories that explores the experiences of Singaporeans who migrate, live abroad or return, and the cultural negotiations they are forced to make.
Shelley, Rex (1991) *The Shrimp People,* Singapore: Times Books International.
The first of a series of novels by this author that disinter the forgotten history of the Eurasian community in Singapore
Tan Hwee Hwee (1997) *Foreign Bodies,* London: Penguin.
Powerful debut novel that mixes the experience of transnational migrants, religious devotion and a hidden history of sexual abuse.
Tay, Simon (1991) *Stand Alone,* Singapore: Landmark.
Collection of short stories (and three poems) that explores, and gently critiques, middle-class aspirations in an increasingly prosperous and developed Singapore.

Tham, Claire (1990) *Fascist Rock: Stories of Rebellion*, Singapore: Times Books International.

First of three short story collections by a writer who distills an increasing need for autonomy and personal choice felt by a new generation of Singaporeans in the early 1990s.

Selected poetry: Philippines

Angeles, Carlos A. (1993) *A Bruise of Ashes: Collected Poems 1940–1992*, Quezon City: Ateneo de Manila University Press.

Collects all the major work by a highly original poet, whose career ranges from poems written from wartime Manila to his later writing from the United States.

Bautista, Cirilio F. (2006) *Believe and Betray: New and Collected Poems*, Manila: De La Salle University Press.

A recent collection from the most prolific prize-winning poet from the Philippines.

Cruz, Conchitina (2005) *Dark Hours*, Quezon City: University of the Philippines Press.

A very promising and original volume of poems by one of the youngest poets from the Philippines.

De Ungria, Ricardo M. (1991) *Decimal Places*, Pasig City: Anvil Publishing.

A representative selection from an engaging, sophisticated and intellectually self-aware poet.

Dumdum, Jr., S. (1999) *Poems: Selected and New (1982–1997)*, Quezon City: Ateneo de Manila University.

This selection gives a good idea of what it means to be contemporary and postmodern from the Philippines: witty, satirical, thoughtful.

Evasco, Marjorie (1999) *Ochre Tones: Poems in English & Cebuano*, Marikina City: Salimbayan Books.

One of the finest contemporary women poets from the Philippines, with a range that covers the personal, the mythopoeic and the shamanic.

Gamalinda, Eric (1999) *Zero Gravity*, Farmington: Alice James Books.

Witty, surreal and wry poems with a unique mix of the serious and the ironic.

Igloria, Luisa A. [Aguilar-Carino, M. L. B.] (1994) *Encanto*, Manila: Anvil Publishing Press.

A representative volume by a major poetic voice who moved from the Philippines to the United States in the early 1990s: sensitive, ambitious, nuanced.

Joaquin, Nick (1987) *Collected Verse*, Quezon City: Ateneo de Manila University Press.

This collection brings together the verse of one of the most significant authors from Southeast Asia.

Lim-Wilson, Fatima (1991) *Wandering Roots 1978–1988*, Pasig City: Anvil Publishing.

Intense poems that evoke the poet's early life and imaginings: sensitive, gripping and disturbing.

Manalang Gloria, Angela (1993) *The Complete Poems of Angela Manalang Gloria*, ed. Edna Zapanta-Manlapaz, Quezon City: Ateneo de Manila University Press.

The first major woman poet from the Philippines, whose lapidary style makes for memorable reading.

Santos, Bienvenidos (1983) *Distances: In Time, Selected Poems*, Quezon City: Ateneo de Manila University Press.
  The selected poems of a variegated talent, who deploys a wide range of styles and voices.
Tiempo, Edith (1999) *An Edith Tiempo Reader*, ed. Gemino H. Abad *et al.*, Manila: University of the Philippines Press.
  A sampler that brings together selections from the verse, fiction and criticism of one of the most influential and respected of Philippine authors.
Villa, Jose Garcia (2008) *Doveglion: Collected Poems,* ed. John Edwin Cowen, New York: Penguin.
  A selection from the most provocative and rebellious Philippine author, who spent the major portion of his life in self-exile in New York.
Yuson, Alfred A. (1993) *Trading in Mermaids*, Pasig City: Anvil Publishing.
  Lively, humorous and perceptive poems from a major contemporary Philippine author.

Selected poetry: Malaysia

Ee Tiang Hong (1976) *Myths for a Wilderness*, Singapore: Heinemann Asia.
  A moving account in verse of the poet's Peranakan culture in Malacca and his increasing alienation from the cultural politics of nationalism.
—— (1985) *Tranquerah*, Singapore: National University of Singapore.
  An autobiographical collection that develops a poetics of cultural alienation and dislocation.
Lim, Shirley Geok-Lin (1980) *Crossing the Peninsula & Other Poems*, Kuala Lumpur: Heinemann Asia.
  This volume won the Commonwealth Poetry Prize: a sensitive poetic account of growing up in Malaysia in the 1960s and 1970s.
Salleh Ben Joned (2007) *Adam's Dream*, Kula Lumpur: Silverfish Books.
  Lively, satirical poems from a bilingual author who manages to keep a critical distance from many of the mores of his society.
Wong Phui Nam (2006) *An Acre of Day's Glass: Collected Poems*, Petaling Jaya: Maya Press.
  The collected poems of the one major poetic voice in English who chose to stay on in Malaysia when so many of his poetic colleagues chose migration or exile.

Selected poetry: Singapore

Alfian bin Sa'at (1998) *One Fierce Hour,* Singapore: Landmark Books.
  Passionate, rebellious, brooding poems from Singapore's 'angry young man' of poetry.
Anuar [Aroozoo], Hedwig. (1999) *Under the Apple Tree: Political Parodies of the 1950s*, Singapore: Landmark Books.
  Brilliant light verse from the 1950s, alert to the political realities of the period preceding and following decolonization in British Malaya.
Boey Kim Cheng (2006) *After the Fire: New and Selected Poems*, Singapore: First Fruits.
  A contemporary poet with a gift for metaphor who chose to leave Singapore for Australia during the 1990s.

Lee Tzu Pheng (1988) *Against the Next Wave*, Singapore: Times Books International.
   A representative volume from the best woman poet from Singapore: a thoughtful sensibility, quiet but intense.
—— (1991) *The Brink of an Amen*, Singapore: Times Books International.
The same poetic voice as above, expanded in scope and range.
—— (1997) *Lambada by Galilee and Other Surprises*, Singapore: Times Books International.
   A poet whose capacity for faith is matched by her capacity for sharp and discerning critical irony.
Ng Yi-Sheng (2006) *last boy*, Singapore: Firstfruits Publications.
   Something of an *enfant terrible* in contemporary Singapore, and winner of the Singapore Literature Prize in English for 2008.
Pang, Alvin (2003) *City of Rain*, Singapore: Ethos Books.
   A fine contemporary poet, alert, ironic, understated in style, intellectually limber.
Thumboo, Edwin (1993) *A Third Map: New and Selected Poems*, Singapore: Unipress.
   A selection from Singapore's prominent poet, covering more than four decades of writing.
Yap, Arthur (2000) *the space of city trees: selected poems*, London: Skoob Books.
   Witty, ironic, sharply quizzical: these are among the most original work in poetry from Southeast Asia.

Minoritarian writing

Han Suyin (1952) *A Many-Splendoured Thing*, London: Jonathan Cape.
   A personal story of love and self-discovery set in a turbulent time for modern China and Hong Kong.
Ho, Louise (1997) *New Ends Old Beginnings*, Hong Kong: Asia 2000.
   Poems that reflect on what it means to be living in a contemporary Hong Kong poised on the historical cusp between its status as the last British colony and a special administrative zone of the People's Republic of China.
Mo, Timothy (1982) *Sour Sweet*, London: Abacus.
   A novel which treats the lives of Hong Kong Chinese immigrants to Britain.
—— (1986) *An Insular Possession*, London: Chatto & Windus.
   A fascinating historical reconstruction of the period of the Opium Wars whose outcome gained Hong Kong for the British.
Somtow, S. P. (1994) *Jasmine Nights*, New York: St Martin's Press.
   A *bildungsroman* set in Thailand whose style, tone and overall effect have the charm, candour and memorable inventiveness of a novel such as J. D. Salinger's *Catcher in the Rye*.
Sudham, Pira (1988) *Monsoon Country*, Bangkok: Shire Books.
   A powerful and moving evocation of the hard life of the peasantry in Thailand.

Drama

Chin Woon Ping (ed.) (1996) *Playful Phoenix: Women Write for the Singapore Stage*, Singapore: TheatreWorks.
   Contains six plays by women, including important work by Eleanor Wong and Malaysian Leow Puay Tin.

Guerrero, Wilfrido Maria (1976) *My Favorite 11 Plays*, Quezon City: New Day.
    One of a number of selections of plays by the most significant dramatist in the
    early years of Philippine theatre in English.
Huzir Sulaiman (2002) *Eight Plays*, Kuala Lumpur: Silverfish.
    Witty, satirical and politically incisive plays by one of the most prolific playwrights
    to emerge from the theatre scene in Kuala Lumpur in the 1990s.
Ingham, Mike and Xu Xi (eds), *City Stage: Hong Kong Playwriting in English*,
    Hong Kong: Hong Kong University Press, 2005.
    The most comprehensive anthology of Hong Kong drama in English; most of the
    work published here appears in print for the first time.
Joaquin, Nick (1979) *Tropical Baroque: Four Manileño Theatricals*, Quezon City:
    National Bookstore.
    Contains four plays, including 'A Portrait of the Artist as Filipino', widely
    considered to be the central text in Filipino drama in English.
Juan, Anton (ed.) (2000) *The Likhaan Book of Philippine Drama, 1991–1996: From
    Page to Stage*, Quezon City: University of the Philippines Press.
    Contains plays from the 1990s in both Filipino and English, the latter including
    work by Chris Millado, Elsa Coscoluella and Floy Quintos.
Kee Thuan Chye (1995) *We Could **** You Mr Birch*, Penang: T. C. Kee.
    Kee's most successful play, questioning historical narratives by juxtaposing early
    British colonization with events in contemporary Malaysia.
Kon, Stella (1989) *Emily of Emerald Hill: A Monodrama*, London: Macmillan.
    Monodrama featuring a chameleon-like Straits Chinese matriarch; its use of
    Singapore Englishes of different registers made the play a significant milestone
    in the evolution of Singapore drama in English, and it is now regularly restaged.
Kuo Pao Kun (2000) *Images at the Margins: A Collection of Kuo Pao Kun's Plays*,
    Singapore: Times Books International.
    Includes early allegorical monodramas such as 'The Coffin is too Big for the Hole'
    and also the important multilingual play 'Mama Looking for Her Cat'.
—— (2003) *Two Plays: 'Descendants of the Eunuch Admiral' and 'The Spirits Play'*,
    Singapore: SNP Editions.
    Examples of Kuo's mature work; the breadth of reference of 'Descendants', which
    draws together the experiences of the Chinese Ming dynasty admiral Zheng He
    and of contemporary Singaporeans, makes it his most important play, and perhaps
    the most significant Singaporean play of the 1990s.
Maniam, K. S. (1994) *Sensuous Horizons: The Stories and the Plays*, London: Skoob
    Books.
    Contains two versions of both 'The Cord' and 'The Sandpit'.
Sharma, Haresh (1999) *This Cord and Others: A Collection of Plays*, London:
    Minerva.
    Contains a number of play scripts, including the transnational drama 'Rosnah'.
Yeo, Robert (2001) *The Singapore Trilogy*, Singapore: Landmark.
    Three interconnected plays by an important historical figure in the development
    of Singapore drama in English, published together for the first time.

Diasporic writing

Aw, Tash (2005) *The Harmony Silk Factory*, London: Penguin.
    Formally innovative novel that focuses on the experience of a group of Chinese,
    British and Japanese characters in the Kinta Valley, Malaysia, in the years
    immediately before the Second World War.

Cheong, Fiona (1991) *Scent of the Gods,* New York: Norton.
Lyrical novel seen through the perspective of a young child in a Straits Chinese family in the years immediately before and after Singapore's independence in 1965.

Francia, Luis H. and Eric Gamalinda (eds) (1996), *Flippin' Filipinos on America,* New York: The Asian American Writers' Workshop.
A very handy anthology that gives an excellent idea of the range of responses evoked in literary writing by Filipinos who have settled in the United States.

Hagedorn, Jessica (2001) *Dogeaters* [1990], New York: Penguin.
Postmodern novel set in Manila, framed by the voice of a young girl who will later migrate to the United States.

Kwa, Lydia (2003) *This Place Called Absence,* New York: Kensington Books.
Lyrically written novel that links together two lesbian relationships: one involving professional migrants in contemporary Vancouver, and the other Cantonese sex workers in Singapore in the early 1900s.

Lim, Shirley Geok-lin (1995) *Life's Mysteries: The Best of Shirley Lim,* Singapore: Times Books International.
Short stories written over two decades by a Malaysian writer who migrated to the United States; the later stories are set in the US, or explore intercultural conflict and negotiation.

Lim-Wilson, Fatima (1995) *Crossing the Snow Bridge,* Columbus: Ohio State University Press; Manila: De La Salle University Press.
Sharp rendition of the Asian-American side of the diasporic experience, along with a verse chronicle of what it means to keep remembering the Philippines, but from a distance.

Loh, Vyvyanne (2004) *Breaking the Tongue,* New York: Norton.
Novel set in Singapore during the Japanese occupation; features a Straits Chinese protagonist engaged in the recovery of an essential Chinese identity.

Tham, Hilary (1989) *Bad Names For Women,* Washington, D.C.: Word Works Capital Collection.
Shrewd, humorous poems by an expatriate writer who manages to represent the Malaysian-Chinese, Jewish and American sides of her experience with verve and intelligence.

Teo, Hsu-Ming (2000) *Love and Vertigo,* St Leonards, N.S.W.: Allen & Unwin.
Novel that features a young Australian protagonist who attempts to connect to a family history rooted in Singapore and Malaysia.

Yew, Chay (1997) *'Porcelain' and 'A Language of Their Own': Two Plays,* New York: Grove Press.
Features two of Yew's most important early plays that bring together queer and intercultural issues.

Secondary materials

General and comparative criticism

Bennett, Bruce, Ee Tiang Hong and Ron Shepherd (eds) (1982), *The Writer's Sense of the Contemporary,* Nedlands: Centre for Studies in Australian Literature.
Selected proceedings of a seminar. Essays deal with a variety of topics concerning writing in English in Australia, Papua New Guinea, Singapore and Malaysia, most concentrating on individual writers or works.

Bennett, Bruce (ed.) (1988) *A Sense of Exile*, Nedlands: Centre for Studies in Australian Literature.
Selected proceedings of a symposium. Essays deal with a variety of topics concerning writing from Australia, Indonesia, the Philippines, Singapore and Malaysia. Interesting individual readings.

Bennett, Bruce and Dennis Haskell (eds) (1992) *Myths, Heroes and Anti-heroes*, Nedlands: Centre for Studies in Australian Literature.
Edited collection of selected conference papers on individual colonial and postcolonial writers in Singapore and Malaysia.

Bennett, Bruce, Jeff Doyle, and Satendra Nandan (eds) (1996) *Crossing Cultures: Essays on Literature and Culture of the Asia-Pacific*, London: Skoob Books.
Edited collection of selected conference papers on individual writers or genres in Singapore and Malaysia.

Benson, Eugene and L. W. Conolly (eds) (2005) *Encyclopedia of Post-Colonial Literatures in English*, London and New York: Routledge. 2nd edn.
Second edition of a very useful reference work which includes entries of varying length on a wide range of Southeast Asian topics and regions of relevance to Anglophone literary traditions.

Chan, Mimi and Roy Harris (eds) (1991) *Asian Voices in English*, Hong Kong: Hong Kong University Press.
The collection comprises two essays on multi-ethnicity in Singapore writing and one on the social context of English-language drama in Malaysia.

Kintanar, Thelma B., Ungku Maimunah Mohd, Tahir, Koh Tai Ann and Toeti Heraty (eds) (1994) *Emergent Voices: Southeast Asian Women Novelists*, Quezon City: University of the Philippines Press.
Consists of five essays on women's writing in Indonesia, the Philippines, Singapore, Malaysia and Brunei. Several essays are limited in reference to language or genre; for instance, there is an essay on women novelists in modern Malay literature but none on writing by Malaysian women in other genres or languages.

Holden, Philip (2008) 'Colonialism's Goblins: Language, Gender and the Southeast Asian Novel in English at a Time of Nationalism', *Journal of Postcolonial Writing* 44: 159–70.
Compares the politics of the use of English in three novels of the 1970s and 1980s from the Philippines, Singapore and Malaysia.

Lim, Shirley Geok-lin (1993) *Nationalism and Literature*, Quezon City: New Day Publishers.
Insightful study focused on close analysis of four key writers from Singapore and the Philippines: Edwin Thumboo, Arthur Yap, Nick Joaquin and F. Sionil Jose.

—— (1994) *Writing S.E./Asia in English: Against the Grain*, London: Skoob Books.
Collection of previously published essays, of which several are on South Asian Literatures or Asian women's writing.

Patke, Rajeev S. (2006) *Postcolonial Poetry in English*, New York and Oxford: Oxford University Press.
Provides an overview of poetry in English from English-speaking postcolonial societies, drawing on Southeast Asian materials from Singapore, Hong Kong and Malaysia for some of its illustrations and case studies.

Roskies, David M. (ed.) (1993) *Text/Politics in Island Southeast Asia: Essays in Interpretation*, Athens, Ohio: Ohio University Center for International Studies.
Ten essays on writing (in all languages) from Indonesia and the Philippines.

Roxas-Tope, Lily Rose (1998) *(Un)Framing Southeast Asia*, Quezon City: University of the Philippines, Office of Research Coordination.
Exploratory attempt to bring together English-language literature from Singapore, the Philippines and Malaysia in a coherent narrative. After a short introduction, the book is organized into thematic sections which feature close readings of individual authors.

Sahlan Mohd. Saman (1984) *A Comparative Study of the Malaysian and the Philippines War Novels*, Bangi: Penerbit Universiti Kebangsaan Malaysia.
Surveys fiction concerning the experience of the Second World War in a comparative perspective.

Singh, Kirpal (ed.) (1987) *The Writer's Sense of the Past*, Singapore: Singapore University Press.
Selected proceedings of a seminar. Essays deal with a variety of topics concerning writing in English in Australia, America, India, Singapore and Malaysia, most concentrating on individual writers or works.

Suryadinata, Leo (ed.) (1993) *Chinese Adaptation and Diversity: Essays on Society and Literature in Indonesia, Malaysia and Singapore*, Singapore: Singapore University Press.
Scholarly and informative: useful more for its information content than its critical views, now partly superseded by subsequent research.

Talib, Ismail (2001) *The Language of Postcolonial Literatures: An Introduction*, London: Routledge.
This book places discussions of the use of English in literature from the multilingual societies of Singapore and Malaysia in the context of parallel developments in other societies and cultures.

Tham, Seong Chee (ed.) (1981) *Essays on Literature and Society in Southeast Asia*, Singapore: Singapore University Press.
First literary-academic compilation to use Southeast Asia as a regional unit of study: the essays contextualize English-language writing within all the other traditional languages of the region.

Thumboo, Edwin (ed.) (1988) *Literature and Liberation: Five Essays from Southeast Asia*, Manila: Solidaridad.
Essays on writing in several Southeast Asian countries; critical and autobiographical in nature, with personal accounts by Ee Tiang Hong and other writers.

—— (ed.) (1991) *Perceiving Other Worlds*, Singapore: Times Academic Press.
A large miscellany: cutting-edge criticism for its times.

—— (ed.) (2007) *Writing Asia: The Literatures in Englishes. Vol 1. From the Inside: Asia-Pacific Literatures in Englishes*, Singapore: Ethos.
The majority of the essays in this edited collection concern English-language literature from Singapore, Malaysia and the Philippines.

Wicks, Peter (1991) *Literary Perspectives on Southeast Asia: Collected Essays*, Toowoomba, Queensland: University of South Queensland Press.
A personal perspective from a sympathetic Australian academic.

World Literature Today 74.2 (Spring 2000): *English-language writing from Malaysia, Singapore, and the Philippines.*
The various articles in this special issue provide a good overview of the literary productions in English from Southeast Asia.

Select criticism: Hong Kong

Bolton, Kingsley (ed.) (2002) *Hong Kong English: Autonomy and Creativity*, Hong Kong: Hong Kong University Press.
  The collection of essays provides a diversity of viewpoints and information on the role of the English language in British Hong Kong. Literary uses of English are marginal to the focus, which is primarily socio-linguistic.

Select criticism: Malaysia

Brewster, Anne (1989) *Towards a Semiotic of Post-Colonial Discourse*, Singapore: Heinemann Asia for Centre for Advanced Studies.
  Useful text which concentrates on the early development of English-language poetry in Malaya.
Fadiliah Merican *et al.* (eds) (2004) *Voices of Many Worlds: Malaysian Literature in English*, Singapore: Times Books.
  A series of biographical chapters on major Malaysian writers in English with useful bibliographical material.
Fernando, Lloyd (1982) *Cultures in Conflict: Essays on Literature and the English Language in Southeast Asia*, Singapore: Graham Brash.
  Valuable as reflections by a prominent Malaysian writer and intellectual: the issues and topics addressed belong to the 1970s.
Nor Faridah Abdul Manaf and Mohammad A. Quayum (2001) *Colonial to Global: Malaysian Women's Writing in English 1940s–1990s*, Malaysia: International Islamic University Press.
  Comprehensive account of a tradition of women's writing in English in Malaysia. Includes reference to many writers who receive scant critical attention elsewhere.
Patke, Rajeev S. (2003) 'Nationalism, Diaspora, Exile: Poetry in English from Malaysia', *Journal of Commonwealth Literature* 38.3: 71–85.
  A discussion of the factors that have contributed to the diasporic displacement of many English-language poets from Malaysia.
Quayum, Mohammad A. (2007) *One Sky, Many Horizons: Studies in Malaysian Literature in English*, Kuala Lumpur: Marshall Cavendish.
  Collection of essays by the most productive Malaysian-based scholar of Malaysian literature in English.
Quayum, Mohammad A. and Peter Wicks (eds) (2001) *Malaysian Literature in English: A Critical Reader*, Kuala Lumpur: Longman/Pearson Education Malaysia.
  Edited collection of individual essays comprising some of the most significant criticism on Malaysian literature in English over the previous three decades.

Select criticism: Philippines

Abad, Gemino H. (2008) *Our Scene So Fair: Filipino Poetry in English, 1805 to 1955*, Quezon City: University of the Philippines Press.
  Useful and wide-ranging survey of Filipino poetry by its premier anthologist.
Bernad, Miguel A. (1961) *Bamboo and the Greenwood Tree: Essays on Filipino Literature in English*, Manila: Bookmark.
  Early critical account of Philippine Literature in English. New Critical in approach and hostile to popular culture.

Casper, Leonard (1964) *The Wounded Diamond: Studies in Modern Philippine Literature*, Manila: Bookmark.
Early attempt to survey literary production in English; influenced by contemporary paradigms of New Criticism.
Crogan, Richard V. (ed.) (1975) *The Development of Philippine Literature in English (Since 1900)*, Quezon City: Alemar-Phoenix.
An anthology, with a brief introductory historical and critical essay followed by a chronology. Does not deal with developments over the last thirty years.
Fernandez, Doreen G. (1996) *Parabas: Essays on Philippine Theater History*, Quezon City: Ateneo de Manila Press.
Most comprehensive history of drama in the Philippines, covering all periods from the precolonial to the present.
Galdon, Joseph A. (ed.) (1979) *Essays on the Philippine Novel in English*, Quezon City: Ateneo de Manila University Press (1st edn. 1972).
Series of essays based on lectures from the Ateneo de Manila Department of English. The introductory essay is an important attempt to give an overview of Philippine literature in English at the time of writing.
Garcia, J. Neil C. (2004) *Postcolonialism and Filipino Poetics: Essays and Critiques*, Quezon City: University of the Philippines Press.
Wide-ranging series of essays addressing issues such as postcoloniality and gender, and also engaging with and attempting to challenge critical frameworks devised by a previous generation of Filipino scholars.
Hau, Caroline S. (2000) *Necessary Fictions: Philippine Literature and the Nation, 1946–1980*, Quezon City: Ateneo de Manila University Press.
Covers the specified period under the notion of 'nation' as a 'necessary fiction'.
—— (2004) *On the Subject of the Nation: Filipino Writings from the Margins, 1981–2004*, Quezon City: Ateneo de Manila University Press.
Moves beyond literature in English to consider such topics as literature written in Chinese in the Philippines, and the role of popular biography.
Hidalgo, Cristina Pantoja (1998) *A Gentle Subversion: Essays on Philippine Fiction in English*, Quezon City: University of the Philippines Press.
Up-to-date survey of a single genre.
Lim, Jaime An (1993) *Literature and Politics: the Colonial Experience in Nine Philippine Novels*, Quezon City: New Day Publishers.
Confined, as specified, to nine novels written over a period of more than a century, but dealing with successive periods of Spanish, American and Japanese colonialism.
Lopez, Salvador P. (1940) *Literature and Society*, Manila: Philippine Book Guild.
Foundational text influenced by Marxist criticism, dismissing concerns with the aesthetic and urging the production of social realism.
Lumbera, Bienvenido L. (1984) *Revaluation: Essays on Philippine Literature, Cinema and Popular Culture*, Manila: Index Press.
A collection of essays by an important cultural critic, many influenced by a Marxist commitment to literature's social role.
Manuud, Antonio G. (ed.) (1967) *Brown Heritage: Essays on Philippine Cultural Tradition and Literature*, Quezon City: Ateneo de Manila University Press.
Important introductory essay attempts a periodization of Philippine Literature in English up to this point, and also seeks to define literary production in terms of recurrent themes.

Mojares, Resil B. (1998) *Origins and Rise of the Filipino Novel*, Quezon City: University of the Philippines Press.
First published in 1983, this updated study covers the novel form until 1940. The major emphasis is on texts written in indigenous languages, especially Tagalog.

Pison, Jordana Luna (2005) *Alternative Histories: Martial Law Novels as Counter-Memory*, Quezon City: University of the Philippines Press.
A Foucauldian reading of a number of the most important novels written concerning the martial law period under Marcos. Writers featured include Gamalinda, Rosca, Hagedorn, Joaquin, Ty Casper and Yuson.

Reyes, Soledad S. (2005) *A Dark Tinge to the World: Selected Essays (1987–2005)*, Quezon City: University of the Philippines Press.
Essays in both English and Filipino by a pioneer of cultural studies in the Philippines; many analyze processes such as canon formation or the social role of literature.

San Juan, Epifanio, Jr. (1984) *Toward a People's Literature: Essays in the Dialectics of Praxis and Contradiction in Philippine Writing*, Quezon City: University of the Philippines Press.
Politically committed and aware of theoretical developments in a global context, especially as seen from a Left perspective.

—— (1996) *Mediations from a Filipino Perspective*, Quezon City: Anvil.
Personal and politically self-aware perspective on writing and society in the Philippines.

Teodoro, Luis V. Jr. and Epifanio San Juan, Jr. (1981) *Two Perspectives on Philippine Literature and Society*, Honolulu: Philippine Studies Program, Center for Asian and Pacific Studies, University of Hawaii.
Lively and committed essays, now slightly dated, but with a significant political awareness of the role of literary writing in Philippines society.

Villa, Jose Garcia (2002) *The Critical Villa: Essays in Literary Criticism*, ed. Jonathan Chua, Quezon City: Ateneo de Manila University Press.
Jonathan Chua's superb retrospective collection of Villa's critical writing, much of which was originally published in magazines in the 1930s.

Select criticism: Singapore

Cheong, Felix (ed.) (2004) *Ideal to Ideal: 12 Singapore Poets on the Writing of their Poems*, Singapore: Firstfruits.
Interesting accounts by individual poets of the process of composition of a single poem. The chosen poets range from Goh Poh Seng to Cyril Wong.

Chua Beng Huat (ed.) (1999) *Singapore Studies II: Critical Surveys of the Humanities and Social Sciences*, Singapore: Singapore University Press for the Centre for Advanced Studies.
The bibliographies update those from the book edited in 1986 by Basant Kapur.

Holden, Philip (1998) 'Colonial Fiction, Hybrid Lives: Early Singaporean Fiction in *The Straits Chinese Magazine*', *Journal of Commonwealth Literature* 33.1: 85–98.
The first detailed study of writing in English in Singapore before the 1950s.

Hyland, Peter (ed.) (1986) *Discharging the Canon: Cross-cultural Readings in Literature*, Singapore: Singapore University Press.
Many lively critical essays: a collection notable for its diversity, but many of the essays assume a reasonable familiarity with regional issues and authors.

Kapur, Basant (ed.) (1986) *Singapore Studies: Critical Surveys of the Humanities and Social Sciences*, Singapore: Singapore University Press for the Centre for Advanced Studies.
The individual chapters on literary genres constitute the primary bibliographical tools for the period up to 1985. The essays accompanying the bibliographies are useful but dated.

Patke, Rajeev S. (2000) 'Singapore Poetry in English', *World Literature Today* 74: 2 (Spring): 293–99.
Provides a brief but comprehensive overview of poetry in English from Singapore.

Poon, Angelia (2005) 'Performing National Service in Singapore: (Re)imagining Nation in the Poetry and Short Stories of Alfian Sa'at', *Journal of Commonwealth Literature* 40.3: 118–138.
Explores the manner in which the writings of Singapore's most versatile playwright, poet and prose writer reconfigure national discourses.

Quayum, Mohammad A. and Peter Wicks (eds) (2002) *Singapore Literature in English: A Critical Reader*, Serdang: Universiti Putra Malaysia Press.
Edited collection of individual essays that exemplifies some of the most significant criticism on Singapore literature in English over the previous three decades.

Singh, Kirpal (ed.) (1998–2008) *Interlogue: Studies in Singapore Literature*. Vols. 1–7, Singapore: Ethos.
An ongoing series of collections comprising critical essays devoted to specific genres, interviews, as well as monographs on single authors such as Robert Yeo and Edwin Thumboo.

Wee Wan-Ling, C. J. (2004) 'Staging the Asian Modern: Cultural Fragments, the Singaporean Eunuch, and the Asian Lear', *Critical Inquiry* 30: 771–99.
The most perceptive account of the social and theatrical context of Kuo's most important work.

Glossary of terms

Bildungsroman A novel concerning a protagonist's growth from childhood to adulthood, often featuring a movement from the home out into the world, and the passage through a series of experiences that establish the protagonist's autonomy as an individual.

Chronotope A portmanteau word popularized by the Russian literary theorist Mikhail Bakhtin, the chronotope points to the close relationship between place and time in literary works. In Bakhtin's account, social conceptions of time from a particular historical period are often expressed in the form of narrative: thus the chronotope of the road in a narrative of a journey might express contemporary concepts of individual development or social change.

Code-mixing Code-mixing refers to the practice among bilingual speakers using one language to introduce occasional elements of another language into their utterance, such as words, phrases and idioms, as a way of facilitating the linguistic interaction. Code-mixing generally involves a movement from a more formal to a less formal register between the two linguistic codes, and it does not impede communication, provided the parties involved in the interaction have a reasonable degree of familiarity with the second language.

Code-switching Code-switching is a specific kind of code-mixing which involves a choice made by a bilingual speaker or writer to switch from a construction begun in one language to its completion in another language. Such switching can occur for a variety of reasons: the speaker or writer feels more comfortable in the second language (the one that is switched to), or recognizes the need to bring in a nuance in the second language that is unavailable in the first, or feels that using the two languages together will be conducive to the desired social interaction.

Cosmopolitanism A philosophical perspective which emphasizes the commonalities between human beings, rather than stressing national or cultural differences. From the 1990s onwards, cosmopolitanism has become a key item of vocabulary for scholars in the humanities and social sciences to describe artistic production and social practices that seek to interrogate, or escape, the frameworks of nation or cultural community.

Dialect   Dialect refers to a variety of language unique to a specific speech-community, often associated with a specific region, and bearing the relation of a sub-set to a larger language-family. A language may comprise several dialects, each distinct from the others in some respects, while they all retain common features that are the defining characteristic of the language-group of which they are part.

Diaspora   Diaspora refers to the displacement of peoples from a region or place that is identifiable as their homeland to another region to which they are impelled either by chance, opportunity or accident. Diaspora involves displacement and relocation, and in terms of agency and motivation, both displacement and relocation can partake variably of the willing and the involuntary.

Diglossia   The term refers to 'the use of two or more varieties of language for different purposes in society' (McArthur 1992: 312).

Globalization   A concept commonly used to explain transformations on a global scale after the end of the Cold War, in which capital, people, and cultural products and forms increasingly flow across national borders, their movement enabled by neo-liberal economic policies and developments in information technology. Globalization has been celebrated as enabling cultural interchange and also critiqued for its production of inequality and migrant populations of workers who do not enjoy the full rights of citizenship.

Hegemony   Hegemony refers to a process in which a dominant class maintains its position in society not simply through a threat of force but also by gaining consent of subordinated classes. Hegemony works through cultural elements in a society, such as the media and the education system, that encourage subordinated classes to see their position as natural; the concept has been used to explain the successful maintenance of social order by elites in both colonial and post-independence societies. The term was first used in this precise sense by Italian Marxist theorist Antonio Gramsci.

Heteroglossia   A term popularized by the Russian theorist Mikhail Bakhtin, heteroglossia refers to the presence of a variety of 'languages' within a single literary work. In Bakhtin's account, such languages are not necessarily different foreign languages, but rather modes of utterance and styles of writing that emerge from specific social locations. In a literary text, such languages undergo dialogism, in which they are brought together and overlap, but are never fully resolved into a single uniform language. Heteroglossia thus indicates the potential of a literary text to challenge social norms by bringing into dialogue a variety of voices, some dominant and some marginalized.

Historiographic metafiction   This term refers to literary texts that engage in metafictional strategies, making a reader aware of their artificiality and constructedness as literary texts, in order to call attention to the fact that official histories are also narratives that need to be questioned. A common move in historiographic metafiction is for an apparently genuine historical account that readers have accepted the reliability of to be suddenly revealed as a fake produced by an interested third party. The term was first used by Canadian scholar Linda Hutcheon.

Modernism   While 'modern' is often used to evoke vital elements of the contemporary in a loose and flexible manner, 'modernity' refers in a more specific sense to the Utopian desire to maximize human progress through the application of human reason to nature and humanity, societies and institutions, on the basis of ideas that had their historical origin in European Enlightenment thought of the eighteenth century; and in contrast, 'modernism' is a retrospective term which describes a set of tendencies in the arts and writing of the late nineteenth and early twentieth centuries which set itself in an antithetical or oppositional relation to the European project of modernity. Modernism articulates a sense of crisis within modernity, a rupture in the self-understanding which Immanuel Kant had identified as the key feature of the European Enlightenment.While modernity operates in the spheres of the social, the economic, the technological and the conceptual levels of thought and action, modernism represents an aesthetic revolution resulting from an acute degree of self-reflexivity about European traditions of representation in writing and the arts, which leads to a break from those traditions.

Multilingualism   The term refers to social and cultural conditions where more than one language is in common use. In individuals, multilingualism refers to the capacity to understand, speak and write more than one language; in state policy, multilingualism refers to state policies and planning governing the use of more than one language in education and general social usage. Societies become multilingual through sustained interactions between peoples with different linguistic backgrounds, and societies remain multilingual so long as there are interpersonal incentives to multilingual usage and no state policies legislating against a specific language and its use in education and in society.

Multiracialism   Multiracialism is the name given to a collection of government policies in Singapore and Malaysia that accord rights not simply to individuals, but also to cultural groupings. Multiracialism is similar to multiculturalism practised in other countries, but the decision to affiliate to a cultural group is not elective, as it might be in the United States or Canada. Rather, citizens are given a racial identity at birth, following the racial identity of their fathers, and such an identity will be inscribed on birth certificates, identity cards and passports. Racial identity in Singapore influences the second language one studies at school, the ethnic self-help group to which a contribution is paid monthly from one's salary, and other elements of life including area of residence in public housing. Multiracialism is defended by its proponents as reducing inter-ethnic conflict. It is critiqued by others as a legacy of colonialism which paradoxically increases the intercommunal divisions it claims to manage.

Nativism   This term refers to a variety of philosophies and movements that stress cultural indigeneity. In postcolonial terms, nativism has proved a powerful mode of reclaiming cultures that have been disavowed or discriminated against under colonialism. However, it frequently relies on an essentialized model of culture based on an idealized and imaginary traditional precolonial past, and cannot reconcile this with the demands of modern life and the presence of populations of more recent immigrants who now look on the new nation as their home.

Neocolonialism   Neocolonialism refers to a situation in many newly decolonized countries in Africa and Asia in the 1960s and afterwards. Although formal colonialism ended, the structure of colonial society remained, with a native elite replacing the colonizers, and acting as a front for continued economic exploitation of the country by transnational corporations with ties to the former colonial power. The term was popularized by the first president of Ghana, Kwame Nkrumah.

Orientalism   A term popularized by the Palestinian-American scholar Edward Said, Orientalism refers to a conceptual division of the world into a binary opposition between East and West, Orient and Occident. In Said's account, the identity of Europe or the West is produced through a binary opposition to Asia or the East. The Orient is thus disavowed, and becomes everything the Occident is not: Asia is associated with tradition, darkness and femininity, in contrast to the modernity, enlightenment and masculinity of the West. Said emphasizes that Orientalism operates discursively as social common sense, and that it is difficult to avoid falling back into Orientalist tropes unless a writer or commentator becomes actively conscious of their presence.

Postcolonial   In a literal sense postcolonial refers to the period that follows political decolonization; in more wide-ranging terms, postcolonial refers to all the ways in which dependency and resistance to colonial institutions, formations and practices are combined as mindsets and cultural predicaments, as well as more specific goal-oriented actions, among those who came under colonial rule.

Postmodernism   A term that has been in popular usage in the late 1980s and which refers to distinctive characteristics of artistic production in late capitalist societies. Postmodernist literary works are often fragmentary and elaborately self-referential. The distinction between modernism and postmodernism is much debated. Postmodernist writing tends to dissolve the distinction between high and low cultural forms, and is often playful; modernist texts take themselves more seriously, and are frequently positioned as high cultural works of art.

Racialization   While references to race often posit differences based on essential genetic or cultural differences between groups of people, such groups are often constructed by governmental regulation or discourses. Racialization thus refers to the manner in which political policies and larger social discourses encourage individuals to think of themselves as members of racial groups.

Subaltern   A concept found in the work of Italian Marxist Antonio Gramsci, and popularized by the Subaltern Studies group of Indian historians from the 1980s onwards. Subalterns are members of groups that are subordinated or marginalized by the narratives of power in both the colonial and post-independence periods. Much discussion of the status of subaltern discourse has explored the attempt to which historical writing might represent subaltern voices without incorporating them into new totalizing narratives.

Index

eBooks – at www.eBookstore.tandf.co.uk

A library at your fingertips!

eBooks are electronic versions of printed books. You can store them on your PC/laptop or browse them online.

They have advantages for anyone needing rapid access to a wide variety of published, copyright information.

eBooks can help your research by enabling you to bookmark chapters, annotate text and use instant searches to find specific words or phrases. Several eBook files would fit on even a small laptop or PDA.

NEW: Save money by eSubscribing: cheap, online access to any eBook for as long as you need it.

Annual subscription packages

We now offer special low-cost bulk subscriptions to packages of eBooks in certain subject areas. These are available to libraries or to individuals.

For more information please contact webmaster.ebooks@tandf.co.uk

We're continually developing the eBook concept, so keep up to date by visiting the website.

www.eBookstore.tandf.co.uk